Her Way

Also by Don Van Natta Jr.

First Off the Tee: Presidential Hackers,
Duffers, and Cheaters from Taft to Bush

Her Way

The Hopes and Ambitions
of Hillary Rodham Clinton

JEFF GERTH *and*
DON VAN NATTA JR.

LITTLE, BROWN AND COMPANY
New York   Boston   London

Little, Brown and Company
Hachette Book Group USA
237 Park Avenue, New York, NY 10017
Visit our Web site at www.HachetteBookGroupUSA.com

First Edition: June 2007

ISBN 0-316-01742-6 / 978-0-316-01742-8
LCCN 2007928427

10 9 8 7 6 5 4 3 2 1

RRD-VA

Printed in the United States of America

For Janice and Jessica, the two Js and so much more

—J.G.

For my mother, with love

—D.V.N.

Contents

PART THREE   First Woman

A Note from the Authors

We embarked on *Her Way* with the ambitious goal of writing a comprehensive and compelling portrait of Hillary Rodham Clinton, one of America's most famous and yet enigmatic public figures.

This is an unauthorized biography. Before we began, we contacted Senator Clinton's representatives to request her cooperation and the cooperation of her aides and most-loyal supporters. We then met with Senator Clinton's communications director, who told us that any cooperation from the senator and members of her office was unlikely. We were later told that Senator Clinton declined to be interviewed by us. Many of her friends, former aides, associates, and even fellow senators also declined to speak with us. Some, including at least one leading Democratic senator, refused our interview request after a member of Senator Clinton's office advised them not to cooperate with our project.

Despite these roadblocks, we conducted more than five hundred interviews, including some with the senator's closest friends, aides, former aides, and confidants. And we examined thousands of pages of previously undisclosed documents, some of which were unearthed from government archives through the Freedom of Information Act and from the Library of Congress.

Senator Clinton's voice is not missing from these pages. We examined more than a thousand of her speeches, public statements, and interviews given over the course of thirty-eight years. We quote a number of her recollections and observations from her autobiography, *Living History*, which was published in 2003. And we attended some of her Senate press conferences and campaign events.

Most of the information in this book is derived from named sources cited in the endnotes. However, dozens of people who spoke with us agreed to do so only if we promised not to quote them by name. Many of these people said they feared retribution from Senator Clinton or her staff if they were quoted by name in this book.

In *Living History*, Senator Clinton acknowledged, "I'm sure there are many other—even competing—views of the events and people I describe. That's someone else's story to describe."

What follows in these pages is certainly not the final word on Hillary Rodham Clinton. But we hope you will agree that our story is a fair and rigorously reported portrait of Senator Clinton's fascinating life and historic career.

—*Jeff Gerth and Don Van Natta Jr.*
May 2007

Her Way

In to Win

Rules for traveling with a candidate: Always be on time.
Do as little talking as humanly possible. Remember to lean
back in the parade car so everybody can see the President.
  — Eleanor Roosevelt, in 1936[1]

We'll have a woman president by 2010.
  — Hillary Rodham Clinton, in 1991[2]

"WHEN WILL A WOMAN become president of the United States?"

The tantalizing question was broadcast across America on a Tuesday evening in September 1934. To many, the idea of a female commander in chief was perhaps a bit preposterous, considering that women had won the right to vote only fourteen years earlier. But for a young lawyer and women's rights activist named Lillian D. Rock, the historic day when Americans would elect their first female president was not hard to imagine.[3]

Mrs. Rock posed her question to Eleanor Roosevelt during the First Lady's weekly radio program, broadcast from Rockefeller Center in Manhattan. On each show, Mrs. Roosevelt delivered a few comments about the news of the day before answering listeners' questions. Most of these inquiries were routine and even humdrum, but Lillian Rock's question — beamed across America on the NBC radio network — seemed to surprise the First Lady, who asked for a moment to think before replying. While the Beautyrest Orchestra (the show was sponsored by the Simmons mattress company) played "Smoke Gets in Your Eyes," Mrs. Roosevelt sat behind a silver microphone and puzzled over the best way to respond.

When the music ended, the program's host said, "Mrs. Roosevelt promised she would give her opinion of the question brought up by Lillian D. Rock—'When will a woman become president of the United States?'...Mrs. Roosevelt!"

"I do not think that it would be impossible to find a woman who could be president, but I hope it doesn't happen in the near future," said Mrs. Roosevelt,[4] speaking, as she always did, methodically, carefully choosing every word.

There are exceptional women just as there are exceptional men, and it takes an exceptional man to be a successful and useful president. Though women are doing more and more and are proving each year that they are capable of assuming responsibilities which were considered to be out of their province in the past, I do not think that we have yet reached the point where the majority of people would feel satisfied to follow the leadership and trust the judgment of a woman as president. And no woman could therefore succeed as president any more than could any man who did not have the trust and confidence of the majority of the nation, for this is a democracy and governed by majority rule.

People say no woman could stand the physical strain, but that I think is nonsense.... No man works harder in the fields than the farmer's wife in her home and on the farm. Women have carried the same jobs in factories, even in mines up to a few years ago. And besides their industrial jobs, they have almost always carried on the work of the home—sometimes badly, to be sure—but still that work has always been before them when the other work was done....

Women have not as yet had, however, as many years of background in public life; or as many years of experience in learning how to give and take in the world of affairs, and I personally would be sorry to see any woman take any position of responsibility which she was not well equipped to undertake and where she could not command the following, which she would need for success. Some day, a woman may be president, but I hope it will not be while we still speak of 'a woman's vote.' I hope it will only become a reality when she is elected as an individual because of her capacity and the trust which the majority of the people have in her integrity and ability as a person....

The future lies before us, however, and women have a big contribution to make. So let us hope that when a woman does assume

any important office, it will be because the services she can render
are apparent to all.

The audience applauded, and Mrs. Roosevelt smiled.

"I'M IN, AND I'M IN TO WIN."

With that supremely confident pronouncement, Hillary Rodham Clinton took the first bold step toward becoming America's
first female president. Her declaration came in an e-mail message
that landed in millions of Americans' in-boxes at 10:00 a.m. sharp
on Saturday, January 20, 2007.

On her Web site, Hillary posted a not-quite-two-minute-long
video announcing her intention to fulfill her heroine Eleanor Roosevelt's vision and make history. Sitting on an overstuffed couch
in the sunroom of her home in Washington, DC, her back leaning against a big flower-print cushion, Hillary, clad in a burgundy
blazer and glowing in perfect makeup, looked directly at the camera with a sure smile and began: "I announced today that I'm forming a presidential exploratory committee. I'm not just beginning a
campaign, though. I'm beginning a conversation...with you, with
America. We all need to be part of the discussion if we are all going
to be part of the solution. And all of us have to be part of the solution."[5]

With her right arm draped across the pillow, Hillary appeared
relaxed, confident, energized, and refreshed. Her message was one
of inclusion, but she pointedly made the announcement alone,
without her husband or their daughter. Their absence was conspicuous, but after all, this was Hillary's moment.

"You know, after six years of George Bush, it's time to renew
the promise of America," she went on, with a hint of a smile. "Our
basic bargain—that no matter who you are or where you live, if
you work hard and play by the rules, you can build a good life for
yourself and your family. I grew up in a middle-class family in the
middle of America, and we believed in that promise. I still do. I've
spent my entire life trying to make good on it—whether it was
fighting for women's basic rights or children's basic health care, protecting our Social Security or protecting our soldiers. It's a kind of
basic bargain, and we've got to keep up our end."

She spoke intimately, as she might to a friend, as if her
announcement were the most casual and proper thing to do. "Let's
talk, let's chat," she said brightly. "Let's start a dialogue about your

ideas and mine. Because the conversation in Washington has been just a little one-sided lately, don't you think? And we can all see how well that works. And while I can't visit everyone's living room, I can try."

During her Senate campaign in 1999 and 2000, a listening tour had helped Hillary overcome the image of a carpetbagger who had moved to New York to use it as a launching pad for the presidency. Since entering the Senate, in just six years, Hillary had transformed herself into a hardworking leader and a formidable politician with a very real chance of becoming the forty-fourth president of the United States. It was quite an accomplishment when one considered the way that Hillary had first introduced herself to America, fifteen years earlier—nearly to the day—than the initiation of her presidential campaign. Then, Hillary was appearing on national television, sitting on a couch in a suite at the Ritz-Carlton Hotel in Boston. Next to her was her husband, Bill Clinton, who was running for president. It was Super Bowl Sunday, and the Clintons were appearing together on CBS-TV's *60 Minutes* to discuss the allegation that Bill had carried on a twelve-year affair with a former television reporter and lounge singer named Gennifer Flowers.

"I have acknowledged wrongdoing," Bill said. "I have acknowledged causing pain in my marriage."[6]

With that, America began to get to know the woman sitting alongside him.

HILLARY WAS UNLIKE any political spouse that America had seen. A graduate of Wellesley College and Yale Law School, she was a corporate lawyer and a maverick who had fought for the rights of women and children. Now millions of Americans watched as she stood by her husband at a moment of crisis that endangered his campaign and, presumably, their union. Hillary sat poised, almost defiant. When she spoke, she told America that she believed her husband's explanation, and she made it clear that her faith in him should be good enough for everyone. She was not, she sharply declared, with a slight slip into the southern drawl she had picked up during her years in Arkansas, "some little woman standing by my man like Tammy Wynette." Elaborating, Hillary explained, "I'm sitting here because I love him, and I respect him, and I honor what he's been through and what we've been through together. And, you know, if that's not enough for people, then heck, don't vote for him."[7] Both comments struck some viewers as tart, clinical, and even arrogant.

Although Hillary's raw, standoffish performance might not have been the best way for Americans to get to know her, it helped her husband overcome the scandal and go on to become a two-term president — and that was the point. It had long been that way. From that couch in Boston to the one she sat on in Washington to launch her presidential bid, Hillary Rodham Clinton had traveled an extraordinary and uniquely American journey as a pioneering woman, as Bill's spouse and political partner, as a mother and a First Lady, as a lawyer, strategist, and policymaker, and finally as a United States senator. Through every tweak in her public image, through the dozens of physical and political makeovers, Hillary herself has been the meticulous architect of her persona. As a result, she is perhaps the most closely observed politician in America — and also the most enigmatic.

To some, she is a pioneer and hero. To others, the sum of all fears. Some of that affection and distaste has to do with policy, but much of it has to do with personality. Her high negative national ratings exist in large part because Hillary strikes some as inauthentic, as a politician who rarely allows anyone to get a glimpse of her vulnerabilities.[8] If Bill Clinton was partly defined by the sheepish mannerism of biting his lower lip when asking for forgiveness, his wife was defined by the opposite — a stiffness of upper lip and a reluctance to ask for help or seek relief. If her husband's blunders often were the product of impulse, some of Hillary's biggest mistakes began as rather inconsequential errors in judgment and exaggerations. When they were seized on by her critics, Hillary followed — and continues to follow — the same pattern: She dug in because she feared that admitting a mistake would arm her enemies and undermine her carefully cultivated image as an extremely bright person who yearns only to do good for her fellow citizens.

For example, in the heat of her husband's 1992 presidential campaign, Hillary realized that her legal work for a troubled savings and loan, Madison Guaranty, was problematic. Yet she refused to publicly acknowledge that she should not have done some of that work. That year, she also prevented disclosure of evidence that she had padded her legal bills, had frequent business and legal dealings with state regulators who worked for Bill when he was governor of Arkansas, and did not grasp the complexities of various legal and commercial concepts. The silence, campaign aides say, was intended both to help Bill's chances of winning and to preserve Hillary's reputation as one of America's top lawyers.[9]

In the end, of course, she succeeded. Only after the 1992 election did much of her legal work, as well as information about her lucrative and controversial commodity trades, become known. The Madison case eventually caught up with her when a lawyer working for independent counsel Kenneth W. Starr had Hillary named in a draft indictment.[10] She was never actually charged, but the searing, years-long experience with Starr and the ferocious anti-Clinton right-wing media left deep scars on her public image and wounds on her psyche. Any inclination to expose and disclose receded further.

A decade later, as a United States senator from New York, Hillary voted to give President George W. Bush the authority to go to war against Iraq. Like the president, Hillary significantly overstated the underlying intelligence to help justify her vote. Nine months after the war began, she called for "patience" in Iraq, saying "failure is not an option."[11] When, as some of her fellow Democrats had predicted, Iraq turned into a disaster, she refused to admit that her vote had been a mistake. Her reasons were simple: If she admitted an error regarding such a crucial matter of national security, it would not only undermine her image as the brainiest senator in Washington, but it would also call into question the viability of her becoming commander in chief. Senator John Kerry, the Vietnam War veteran who acknowledged he had made a "mistake" in voting for the war, had never been able to escape his tortured legacy on Iraq. Hillary, one of her advisers said, wanted to avoid Kerry's "flip-flop" image to ensure that nothing "undermines the thought that she is strong and believes in what she does," especially as a woman making a historic run for the White House.[12] So Hillary proceeded to shift the blame onto President Bush in an increasingly aggressive set of attacks that criticized him for ignoring diplomacy and mismanaging the war. In the process, she rewrote her own legislative record on the matter.

For years, Hillary has known that the standard for the first female president would be far higher than that for a man. A woman president would have to be super strong. She would have to be, or at least appear to be, infallible. Hillary's heroine Eleanor Roosevelt said in 1934, "It is certain that women do not want a woman for president, nor would they have the slightest confidence in her ability to fulfill the functions of that office. Every woman who fails in a public position confirms this, but every woman who succeeds creates confidence."[13]

Those words capture Hillary's burden and the hurdles she must now overcome. But they also represent a challenge to Hillary and her place in history.

More than three decades ago, in the earliest days of their romance, Bill and Hillary struck a plan, one that would become both the foundation and the engine of their relationship. They agreed to work together to revolutionize the Democratic Party and ultimately make the White House their home.[14] Once their "twenty-year project" was realized, with Bill's victory in 1992, their plan became even more ambitious: eight years as president for him, then eight years for her.[15] Their audacious pact has remained a secret until now.

While their plan was hatched together, Hillary had her own ideas about what it would take to achieve victory. She concluded that if she had any chance of winning the ultimate prize of her life, she would need to pursue it her way. That meant, among other things, carefully crafting a persona and a narrative to present to the American public that knew both so much and so little about her.

Of course, Hillary Clinton is far from the only politician to exaggerate her past accomplishments, to stuff the unpleasantness of the past into corners where few look, to make mistakes and then pretend not to have done so. She is not the only politician to have said one thing and done another, to have left former friends and allies on the side of the road as she's moved ahead. Nor is she the only politician in America with tremendous ambition and an affection for both power and money (especially money that can be donated to help fund a perpetual campaign). The truth is that she has these things in common with almost every player on the national stage. Yet if a candidate asks us to consider her the smartest and most qualified of the pack, then she should shine brighter than all the rest.

And Hillary Rodham Clinton is unique in that never before has such a high-profile candidate occupied the spotlight for so long without the public's learning the facts about so much that is crucial to finally understanding her. For decades, Hillary and Bill Clinton, along with a core group of friends and supporters, have told one story. Now it is time for another.

PART ONE

First Partner

It seems to be the fate of idealists to obtain what they have struggled for in a form which destroys their ideals.

—Bertrand Russell

CHAPTER 1

Chase and Run

IN THE STUDENT LOUNGE of Yale Law School, in September 1970, Hillary Rodham could not help noticing a tall, handsome young man with a reddish brown beard and an unruly mane of chestnut brown hair. He was talking energetically and expansively with a small circle of rapt students, and Hillary later observed that he looked more like a Viking holding court than a first-year law student trying to win over a few friends.

The first words that Hillary heard him say, in a syrupy southern drawl, were "...and not only that, we grow the biggest watermelons in the world!"[1]

"Who *is* that?" Hillary asked a friend.

"Oh, that's Bill Clinton," the friend replied. "He's from Arkansas, and that's all he ever talks about."[2]

Hillary did not meet Bill that day. In fact, nearly two semesters passed before they would finally be introduced. Through that fall and into the spring, however, the two spent a lot of time just staring at each other across the student lounge or the law library. One spring evening in the library, Hillary observed Bill in the hallway, talking to a student named Jeff Gleckel, who was attempting to persuade Bill to write for the *Yale Law Journal*. As he listened to Jeff's pitch, Bill once again found himself glancing over at Hillary.

Finally, Hillary decided that enough was enough. She stood up from behind her desk, walked over to her admirer, extended her hand for a shake, and said, "If you're going to keep looking at me, and I'm going to keep looking back, we might as well be introduced. I'm Hillary Rodham."[3]

Bill was flummoxed and flattered by this young woman's forwardness—her boldness nearly left him speechless, which in itself was quite a feat. But for Hillary, it was neither a surprising move nor an uncharacteristic one. As long as anyone could remember, Hillary Rodham had seized the initiative in a way that made people's heads spin.

"I WASN'T BORN A FIRST LADY OR A SENATOR," Hillary Rodham Clinton wrote in the opening paragraph of her 2003 autobiography, *Living History*. "I wasn't born a Democrat. I wasn't born a lawyer or an advocate for women's rights and human rights. I wasn't born a wife or mother. I was born an American in the middle of the twentieth century, a fortunate time and place."[4]

Hillary Diane Rodham was born in Chicago on October 26, 1947. Her childhood, spent primarily in the leafy suburb called Park Ridge, was a happy one, thanks to her parents, Hugh and Dorothy Rodham. Her father was a scrappy and hard-edged Welshman from Scranton, Pennsylvania, who had found work as a traveling salesman in the Midwest at the Columbia Lace Company.[5] It was there that he met Dorothy Howell, who was applying for a job as a typist. She was immediately attracted to his cocksure demeanor and disciplined work ethic; she even found charm in his acerbic sense of humor. In 1927, Dorothy's parents had divorced when she was only eight years old, a decision that embarrassed the family because divorce was not common in the 1920s. Her mother and father had then sent Dorothy and her brothers and sisters to live in California with their grandparents. Despite understandable reservations about matrimony, Dorothy married Hugh in early 1942, not long after the Japanese bombed Pearl Harbor, and the children quickly arrived—first Hillary, then Hugh Jr., and finally Tony.

The Rodhams worked to ensure that Hillary and her two brothers grew up with every advantage in a pleasant, secure environment. They lived in a well-kept two-story brick home on the corner lot of Elm and Wisner streets, a house bought by Hugh with cash. "We had two sundecks, a screened-in porch and a fenced-in backyard where the neighborhood kids would come to play or to sneak cherries from our tree," Hillary wrote in her autobiography. "The postwar population explosion was booming, and there were swarms of children everywhere. My mother once counted forty-seven kids living on our square block."[6]

Parked in their driveway was a shiny Cadillac, its presence a bit deceiving.[7] Hugh was one of the few tradesmen who lived on Elm Street. Most of the fathers of Hillary's young friends were lawyers, doctors, or accountants who commuted on the train every day to their offices high above the Loop. Hugh's fancy car was not so much a sign of well-being as a professional necessity: He needed it to make sales rounds for the drapery company named Rodrik Fabrics that he had founded a few years before the family moved to Park Ridge. Hugh worked fourteen hours a day at his fledgling business, which manufactured draperies for hotels and office buildings, single-handedly attending to every task—from taking orders by phone to sewing the draperies by hand to finally hanging them himself. Only years later, when his two sons were old enough to pitch in on the occasional Saturday, did he get help.[8]

Hugh was "a small businessman, who taught us by his example the values of hard work and responsibility," Hillary once said.[9] A Republican, he was proud that he had served as a chief petty officer in the navy, where he had prepared young recruits to fight in the Pacific theater. At home, Hugh suffered no fools gladly, demanding that his children be smart and tough and absorb life's many jabs without complaint. Hillary recalled that Hugh's strictness was reserved more for his sons than for her. But his lofty expectations that they excel in school and think on their feet were applied to Hillary as well.

Hillary's mother, Dorothy, was later described by her daughter as "a classic homemaker."[10] She woke up at 6:00 a.m. sharp, made the beds, cleaned the clothes, washed the dishes, and whipped up homemade lunches of chicken-noodle and tomato soup and grilled-cheese, peanut butter, and bologna sandwiches. From an early age, Dorothy noticed, Hillary seemed imbued with a sense that she was special. As a youngster, she spent hours dancing in the sunshine in her backyard with her arms stretched above her head, reaching for the maple trees and the sky. She imagined a platoon of "heavenly movie cameras watching my every move," Hillary later recalled.[11] And when interacting with other children or meeting adults, Hillary demonstrated a maturity far beyond her years.

Dorothy Rodham often said that it seemed as if her only daughter was born an adult.[12]

Though she might have carried a grace and strength that belied her age, Hillary still had to deal with the usual childhood battles. At the age of four, shortly after the family moved to Park Ridge, Hillary struggled to find a niche among the neighborhood's chaotic group of preschool children. She was given an especially hard time by a young girl named Suzy O'Callaghan, who was stronger and tougher than all the girls and most of the boys. Suzy often beat up the neighborhood kids, including Hillary, who ran home crying one day to tell her mother.

If she expected sympathy, her mother delivered none. "There's no room in this house for cowards," Dorothy told her daughter. "Go back out there, and if Suzy hits you, you have my permission to hit her back. You have to stand up for yourself."[13]

Sure enough, Hillary stomped outside and, with a circle of boys and girls watching (and Dorothy spying from behind the dining-room curtain), she returned one of Suzy's punches, knocking the bully to the ground. Hillary returned triumphantly to her house, telling her mother, "I can play with the boys now! And Suzy will be my friend!" "Boys responded well to Hillary," Dorothy later said with pride. "She took charge, and they let her."[14]

Indeed they did. Hillary emerged as one of the natural leaders in the children's marathon games of basketball, ice hockey, kickball, and softball. Yet she preferred imaginative contests, like a rather complicated one called "chase and run," which resembled hide-and-seek. When Hillary was ten or eleven years old, she began to join the grown-ups, playing pinochle with her father, her grandfather, her uncle Willard, and some of their odd pals, including two cranky old men named Old Pete and Hank, both terrible sore losers. ("Is that black-haired bastard home?" Old Pete would ask Hillary of her father as he marched up the front porch stairs, rattling his cane. "I want to play cards.")[15] More than once, Old Pete toppled a card table after a tough defeat.

Hillary learned lessons about work and sportsmanship from the men in the family, but it was her mother who provided the most direct and intimate evidence of the importance of scholarship for girls at a time when few opportunities were available to them. "My mother loved her home and her family, but she felt limited by the narrow choices of her life," Hillary wrote in her autobiography. "It is easy to forget now, when women's choices can seem overwhelming, how few there were for my mother's generation."[16] Hillary saw her mother's frustration with the limited number of personal and professional choices. She was also touched by her mother's lifelong zeal for learning. Dorothy took college courses, and though she never graduated, she managed to accumulate dozens of credits in a wide range of subjects. "My mother wanted us to learn about the world by reading books," Hillary recalled. And much of Hillary's childhood was spent doing exactly that. "She took me to the library every week, and I loved working my way through the books in the children's section."[17]

LONG BEFORE SHE ENTERED PUBLIC LIFE, Hillary struggled to reconcile often diametrically opposed values and viewpoints offered by her father and her mother. "I grew up between the push and tug of my parents' values, and my own political beliefs reflect both," Hillary wrote in her autobiography. "My mother was basically a Democrat, although she kept it quiet in Republican Park Ridge. My Dad was a rock-ribbed, up-by-your-bootstraps, conservative Republican and proud of it. He was also tightfisted with money."[18]

In *Living History,* Hillary connected her father's staunch Republican politics with a disciplined fiscal conservatism, and the link was hardly an accident. As he had shown with his Cadillac purchase, Hugh Rodham believed firmly in the axiom "Cash is king," and he ran his business on a "strict pay-as-you-go policy."[19] Like many who grew up during the Depression, he was driven to work hard by the fear of falling back into the quagmire of poverty. A by-product of his frugal ways was an intense dislike of wastefulness, even if the wasted amounted to no more than a few pennies. "If one of my brothers or I forgot to screw the cap back on the toothpaste tube, my father threw it out the bathroom window," Hillary recalled. "We would have to go outside, even in the snow, to search for it in the evergreen bushes in front of the house. That was his way of reminding us not to waste anything. To this day, I put uneaten olives back in the jar, wrap up the tiniest pieces of cheese and feel guilty when I throw anything away."[20]

Hugh Rodham was "highly opinionated, to put it mildly," Hillary said. "We all accommodated his pronouncements, mostly about Communists, shady businessmen or crooked politicians, the three lowest forms of life in his eyes."[21] Every night at the dinner table, he moderated raucous debates about politics or sports, and by the age of twelve, Hillary had learned to defend her positions on a wide array of issues, though she had also realized that it rarely made sense to directly confront her father. "I also learned," she wrote, "that a person was not necessarily bad just because you did not agree with him, and that if you believed in something, you had better be prepared to defend it."[22]

When she was attending Maine East junior high school, Hillary was influenced profoundly by her first history teacher, Paul Carlson.[23] Carlson, a burly, deeply conservative man, taught a course entitled History of Civilization, a class that came to life in particularly vivid fashion when the subject turned to World War II. The hero of most lessons was General Douglas MacArthur, whose face in a portrait stared down at the ninth-grade students from the front of the classroom.[24]

Carlson's zeal for history left an impression on Hillary, but he would also leave a lasting mark in a decidedly different way. In class one day, Carlson played an audiotape of MacArthur's famous farewell speech before both houses of Congress. After the old general's famous coda, "Old soldiers never die; they just fade away," Carlson told his students, "Better to be dead than Red!" A student named Ricky Ricketts, who was seated in alphabetical order directly in front of Hillary, began laughing, and Hillary joined in. Carlson asked them, "What do you think is so funny?"

"Gee, Mr. Carlson," Ricky replied, "I'm only fourteen years old and I'd rather be alive than anything." This reply just made Hillary and Ricky laugh harder, and Carlson became enraged by their disrespectful outburst. His face flushed, he shouted, "Quiet! This is serious business!" But Hillary and Ricky could not contain their laughter and were thrown out of the classroom. It would be the only time in Hillary's life that she was disciplined by one of her teachers.[25]

Although Hillary now insists that her brand of politics was influenced equally by the divergent leanings of her mother and her father, there is no doubt that Hugh Rodham shaped most of his daughter's early political beliefs. As a preteen, Hillary was a spirited and deeply conservative young Republican. In the fall of 1960, when she was in the eighth grade, her father supported Vice President Richard M. Nixon for the presidency, as did Hillary's eighth-grade social studies teacher, Mr. Kenvin.[26] And, of course, Hillary also wanted Nixon to win. The day after the election, Hillary's social studies teacher showed his students the bruises he said he had received when he challenged the Democratic Party's poll watchers at his voting precinct on Election Day. Hillary and her friend Betsy Johnson were infuriated. To Hillary, her teacher's ordeal dramatically supported her father's contention that Chicago mayor Richard J. Daley's "creative vote counting had won the election for President-Elect Kennedy." Hillary and Betsy were so upset about what had happened to Mr. Kenvin that they took a moment during their lunch period to use a pay phone outside the school cafeteria to call Mayor Daley's office to complain.[27]

On the Saturday morning after the election, the determined young women decided to help a Republican group check voter lists against addresses in an attempt to find voter fraud. Both girls participated without getting permission from their parents. Hillary was driven to a poor neighborhood on the South Side, where she went knocking on doors, an act that was "fearless and stupid," she recalled. "I woke up a lot of people who stumbled to the door or yelled at me to go away. And I walked into a bar where men were drinking to ask if certain people on my list actually lived there."[28] Hillary found clear evidence of voter fraud — a vacant lot that was listed as the address for a dozen alleged voters. She was thrilled with her detective work and could not wait to tell her father that she had discovered that Daley had indeed stolen the election for Kennedy. "Of course, when I returned home and told my father where I had been, he went nuts. It was bad enough to go downtown without an adult, but to go to the South Side alone sent him into a yelling fit," she recalled. "And besides, he said, Kennedy was going to be President whether we liked it or not."

A year after Kennedy's victory, in the fall of 1961, another change in administration would further challenge Hillary's beliefs. A twenty-six-year-old Methodist youth minister named Donald Jones arrived at First Methodist Church in Park Ridge, having completed four years of service in the navy and a degree from Drew University's Divinity School. Jones was a complete departure from three previous youth ministers at the church;[29] he was tall, had a blond crew cut, and drove a 1959 fire-engine red Impala convertible, a "controversial" choice of car, Jones recalled.[30] More than a few young girls had crushes on him. Most notably, every Sunday and Thursday evening, beginning that September, Reverend Jones taught his University of Life program, which included a heavy helping of radical politics, poetry, art history, and countercultural thought. His message was that a Christian life should embody "faith in action," which included trying to help people who were less fortunate. At thirteen, Hillary accompanied Jones's group on a visit to a community center on Chicago's South Side. There, Hillary and her fellow students spent a few hours with a group of inner-city children, analyzing the meaning of a painting that they had never seen before, Picasso's *Guernica*. Jones recalled that "the whole point was to get inner-city kids and suburban kids in a conversation around something that none of them knew anything about."[31] While the suburban kids were largely silent, a young black girl said that the painting made her wonder, "Why did my uncle have to get shot because he parked in the wrong parking place?"[32]

Hillary said that Reverend Jones helped her "reconcile my father's insistence on self-reliance and my mother's concerns about social justice."[33] But his views and teaching also put Jones in direct conflict with Paul Carlson in the fight for the youngsters' hearts and minds. (When Carlson heard about the trip, he was livid.) Hillary tried to remain on the fence, listening carefully to the diametrically opposed views but refusing to pick a side. She kept her kinship with Jones a secret from her father, though she shared it with her mother, "who quickly came to find in Don a kindred spirit," Hillary later recalled.[34]

Perhaps the greatest revelation Jones offered was that there were less fortunate people than Hillary and her friends in Park Ridge, and that America was experiencing the beginnings of a great disenchantment. "In the discussions we had sitting around church basements, I learned that, despite the obvious differences in our environments, these kids were more like me than I ever could have imagined," Hillary said. "They also knew more about what was happening in the civil rights movement in the South. I had only vaguely heard of Rosa Parks and Dr. Martin Luther King, but these discussions sparked my interest."[35]

When Hillary was seventeen, Jones announced that he was going to take the group to hear King speak at Chicago's Orchestra Hall. Hillary was thrilled, though some of her friends' parents refused permission for their children to listen to the "rabble-rouser." More than one thousand people were there, and Hillary was enchanted with King and his speech, which was entitled "Remaining Awake through a Revolution."[36] "The old order is passing away and a new one is coming in," King said that night. "We should all accept this order and learn to live together as brothers in a world society, or we will all perish together."[37] After the speech, Jones escorted Hillary and her friends to meet King.

Despite being exposed to what at the time was considered radical thinking, Hillary remained basically content to "parrot" the conventional and decidedly conservative beliefs that were deeply held in Park Ridge.[38] The political climate proved too much for Jones, and after enduring two years of bitter confrontations with Carlson, he left United Methodist and became a professor at Drew University, where he stayed for the rest of his career.

"I now see the conflict between Don Jones and Paul Carlson as an early indication of the cultural, political and religious fault lines that developed across America in the last forty years," Hillary recalled years later. "I liked them both personally and did not see their beliefs as diametrically opposed then or now."[39] Her willingness to play down this conflict reveals an ideological war within Hillary; sometimes she works as a facilitator to find common ground between antagonists, but other times she intensifies a conflict by going on the attack. Jones and Hillary remained close across all the years; he helped preside over the wedding of her brother Tony Rodham in the White House Rose Garden on May 28, 1994.[40]

THOUGH SHE WAS FAR from politically radicalized, hearing and meeting Martin Luther King Jr. fired something deep inside Hillary, a desire to try to change the world — or, for a start, her high school, Maine South. Hillary was viewed by some of her classmates as aloof, but a few friends attributed it to her poor eyesight. "She saw shapes, but she couldn't make out the person until they got very close," recalled Mike Andrews, a classmate. "And with all the kids passing in the hall, you might miss somebody. So I think a lot of people probably remember her as being aloof or something like that, but I never found that a problem."[41]

In 1964, Hillary decided to run for senior class president or, simply, "The Presidency," as she had called it in a letter to a friend. Although Hillary was already serving as the vice president of her junior class, this was a bold move. In Park Ridge, girls did not usually run for the top office.

She was running against two boys, one of whom told her that she was "really stupid if I thought a girl could be elected President," Hillary recalled years later.[42] His insult pretty much defined the tenor of the campaign, and the personal negativity directed at her by both boys deeply hurt her feelings. She delivered an address to an assembly of five thousand students, and her eloquence and poise impressed not only them but many teachers. As her mother had always remarked, she seemed mature beyond her years. But it was not enough to convince a sufficient number of students to vote for her. Hillary took her defeat (to a boy named John Kirchoff) hard. But as she would do many more times in her life, she did not wallow in self-pity. Instead, she picked herself up and sought new challenges, including heading the student government's Organizations Committee.[43]

By this point, Hillary was also focusing on college. Most of her friends were applying to schools in the Midwest to remain close to home. Hillary planned to do the same until two teachers at Maine South — a recent graduate of Smith College and a recent graduate of Wellesley College — urged her to apply to their alma maters. An all-women's-college education was special, they argued, with fewer "distractions." Hillary asked her parents' advice. Dorothy said she should go wherever she wanted, but Hugh was reluctant to see her enroll in an Eastern college, especially Radcliffe, which he had heard was "full of beatniks." Hillary never visited either campus, but she attended local alumnae-held events for both Wellesley and Smith, and was impressed with the energy of the students and both colleges' commitment to academic excellence. In the end, she chose Wellesley, "based on the photographs of the campus," she said.[44]

Hillary's high school government teacher, Gerald Baker, warned her that college would likely change her conservative politics. "You're going to go to Wellesley," he told her, "and you're going to become a liberal and a Democrat." Hillary blanched at that prediction.

"I'm smart," she replied. "I know where I stand on the issues. And that's not going to change."[45]

When her parents drove her from Park Ridge to Boston, the family got lost and ended up in Harvard Square. The beatnik atmosphere they found there merely confirmed Hugh's suspicions that Wellesley might be a bad idea. But once the Rodhams finally found the Wellesley campus outside Boston, with no bohemians in sight, "he seemed reassured," Hillary recalled.[46]

Years later, Hillary said her mother "cried the entire thousand-mile drive back from Massachusetts to Illinois."[47] Her tears were understandable. Theirs was a close, tight family, and with Hillary's departure, things would not be the same. Dorothy Rodham's only daughter was now on her own.

CHAPTER 2

The Art of Making Possible

"I ARRIVED AT WELLESLEY carrying my father's political beliefs and my mother's dreams and left with the beginnings of my own," Hillary wrote in her autobiography. "But on that first day, as my parents drove away, I felt lonely, overwhelmed and out of place."[1]

This mix of emotions was understandable. Wellesley College was a world apart from Park Ridge. In the mid-1960s, student activism, spurred by growing disenchantment with the war in Vietnam and racism at home, was beginning its quick ascent around the country. Wellesley was beginning to change too, though more tentatively than other campuses; the college still retained its reputation as a place where students were far more committed to finding a husband than forging a career. (A survey published in *McCall's* magazine early in Hillary's college career saluted Wellesley girls as "making good wives" and noted that seniors were expected to produce "a ring by spring.")[2] Hillary's class would accelerate the transformation of Wellesley from a genteel island to a campus with much more in common with the "beatnik" Harvard Square vibe.

When Hillary arrived in September 1965, Wellesley was ninety years old, and its Latin motto — *Non ministrari sed ministrare,* "Not to be ministered unto, but to minister" — was particularly attractive because it hewed so closely to many of the lessons she had learned in her Methodist youth group. She was not alone. The young women in the class of '69 viewed the motto not as a domestic mantra but as something of a grand call to arms: go out into the world, it commanded, and change the status quo through excellence and ambition in your chosen professions.[3] Seventeen-year-old Hillary Rodham knew how a male-dominated society's expectations had severely limited her mother's opportunities, so the promise offered by Wellesley's motto roared loudly in her ears.

But first Hillary had to conquer the campus itself, a sumptuous new home that was at once awesome and intimidating. Most young women in her class seemed sleek and sophisticated; many were already world travelers. Hillary spoke with the nasal honk of a native Chicagoan and had only left America once, for a visit to the Canadian side of Niagara Falls.[4] A number of the students spoke at least one foreign language, and some spoke three or four or even five; Hillary had been exposed to only two years of high school Latin. And many of Hillary's peers were intelligent daughters of privilege who had attended some of New England's most exclusive boarding schools; Hillary was the product of a public high school that no longer seemed as if it had adequately prepared her for the intellectual rigors of college. She was surprised to discover that her freshman math and geology courses proved to be so confounding, and she quickly abandoned any thought of becoming a doctor or a scientist. The traditional liberal arts were barely more welcoming. "Mademoiselle," Hillary's French teacher told her, "your talents lie elsewhere."[5] Hillary had to become accustomed to no longer being the undisputed academic star, as she had been back home.

There were other reasons to be glum. Everywhere Hillary looked, in her dorm, in her classrooms, in the library, she saw beautiful young women. In particular, she noticed the striking looks of two debutante freshmen; she was quick to label them a "Carnegie" and a "Shell Oil."[6] Hillary dismissed another freshman as "the swinger" — a girl who seemed interested only in attracting a bevy of good-looking suitors from Harvard Yard. Believing herself to be at a distinct competitive disadvantage, Hillary decided to consciously remain on the sidelines. She perpetually shielded her attractive face with large Coke-bottle glasses, and she wore her hair in a ponytail tied with a thick rubber band or pulled up in a no-nonsense bun. To Hillary and her friends, spending little or no time on their looks represented "a safe zone...to eschew appearances—in every sense of the word—Monday through Friday afternoon." Meanwhile, some of her more glamorous classmates dismissed Hillary as an aloof, shy bookworm who was something of a loner.[7]

Increasingly isolated and continuing to struggle with her academic confidence, Hillary phoned her parents that October to wave the white flag. She told them flatly that she was not smart enough to succeed at Wellesley. Her father's immediate reaction was not surprising—he told her to return home at once. But Dorothy Rodham would have none of it. She told Hillary that she had not raised a quitter and that dropping out of Wellesley would be a catastrophic mistake.[8] Hillary realized that given her mother's stance, she simply could not go home again. So she hung in there and tried to make the best of it.

"THE CREAM OF THE CREAM." From their first day on campus, the women at Wellesley were told repeatedly that they represented the best and the brightest; in everyone's favorite shorthand phrase, "the cream of the cream." Johanna Branson, a dancer and art history major from Lawrence, Kansas, who was a classmate of Hillary's, said twenty-five years later that the "cream of the cream" label "sounds really bratty and elitist now. But at the time, it was a wonderful thing to hear if you were a girl....You didn't have to take second seat to anybody."[9]

Not having to take a second seat to anyone (and in particular a young man) packed a powerful appeal for Hillary, who despite her initial misgivings about her academic aptitude had quickly understood that an all-female college extended an array of opportunities that would be unavailable at a coeducational school. An environment free of male competition encouraged the students to feel free to "take risks, make mistakes, and even fail in front of one another," Hillary noted in her autobiography. "It was a given that the President of the class, the editor of the paper and the top student in every field would be a woman. And it could be any of us."[10]

Emboldened by her mother's laying down the law, Hillary promptly placed herself on a fast track among the students vying for political leadership roles. As a freshman, she was elected president of the college's Young Republicans, an impressive achievement. But not long after winning election, she began harboring doubts about the Republican Party's policies on the Vietnam War and civil rights. Hillary's views were moved in part by the lectures of her liberal-minded political science professors. She also began reading the *New York Times*, a development that annoyed her father. Before the end of her freshman year, Hillary realized that she could no longer in good conscience remain the Young Republicans' president. So she resigned and, as she put it, "submerged myself in learning everything I could about Vietnam."[11] By the last months of Hillary's sophomore year, in early 1967, the war's tide was turning quickly, and the unrest related to the civil-rights struggle was growing. As Hillary later put it, "Current events provided more than enough material" for her to rethink the conservative positions that she adopted in Park Ridge.[12]

Hillary's self-education on Vietnam was to some degree effortless, as nearly everyone on campus was absorbed by the war. The issue deeply divided young people, including her friends at Wellesley, and sparked lengthy, spirited debates about the war's merits. At coed colleges, the debates could have an added personal element. Some "boys in ROTC programs" were anxious to go to Vietnam after they graduated, Hillary recalled in her autobiography, but others spoke openly about resisting the draft.[13] At times, she viewed the conflict as justified, but other times she believed it was wrong. "Even though as a woman I knew I couldn't be drafted," Hillary said, "I spent countless hours wrestling with my own contradictory feelings."[14]

DESPITE ITS COMPLICATIONS, Vietnam was a simple issue compared with the difficulty that Hillary had regarding her own self. The question that confronted her was fundamental: Who do I want to be, right now? She wrestled with the identity question primarily during her sophomore year, her struggle revealed in a series of letters to a high school classmate named John Peavoy. In the letters, Hillary estimated that she had undergone at least "three-and-a-half metamorphoses" in a short period of time. She laid out a series of options, choosing her own labels for whom she might want to become:

- "educational and social reformer,"
- "alienated academic,"
- "involved pseudo-hippie,"
- "compassionate misanthrope," or
- "political leader."[15]

Hillary is silent in her autobiography about this confused chapter of her college years. Of course, many people spend their college years trying on different hats. But Hillary's commitment to carefully selecting a persona that would suit her best is revealing partly because of the determined and calculating way that she went about it. She wanted to weigh every pro against every con, consider each possibility from every angle. Her letters to Peavoy show not an undergrad easing into a way of life but an almost scientific devotion to self-creation.

She tested the "educational and social reformer" persona in part by trying to befriend the few black students on campus. Before she entered college, the only African Americans Hillary knew worked for her father or in their home. "I had not had a black friend, neighbor or classmate until I went to college," she later wrote.[16] In her class of four hundred students, only six were African American. Hillary became friends with one of them, Karen Williamson, and the two went to a church service off campus together one Sunday morning. Hillary later admitted that she was "self-conscious about my motives and hyperaware that I was moving away from my past."[17]

After she attended the service with Karen Williamson, Hillary could not wait to call her family and a few friends in Park Ridge to deliver what she felt was exciting news. But they were not impressed, quickly criticizing her for bragging about an overt political act. Don Jones later recalled that her family and friends "thought she did this not out of goodwill but as a symbolic gesture to a lily-white church."[18] Hillary herself later acknowledged that as a freshman, if she had seen a white student accompanying a black student to church, her immediate reaction would have been, "Look how liberal that girl is trying to be — going to church with a Negro."[19] Now she was attempting to become that girl.

Yet she was not ready to settle. For Hillary, the "alienated academic" persona felt more comfortable. She yearned to be at the top of her class, and she spent long hours of the day and evening studying in the library. She had her first taste of rigorous academic study during the summer of her sophomore year when she worked as a researcher for political science professor Anthony D'Amato, who was later asked to leave Wellesley for his dissident views. Hillary adored him, breathlessly telling friends that he had a law degree from Harvard and was working toward a doctorate degree at Columbia. That summer, for three months, Hillary helped D'Amato with his research at a secluded house along the shore of Lake Michigan.[20]

The third persona that Hillary sampled was the "involved pseudo-hippie," an option that (as indicated by her *pseudo* prefix) became more of a fashion statement than a way of life. She settled for living vicariously through friends. She attended a beatnik wedding in June 1967 on Cape Cod and loved the experience.[21] In a letter to Peavoy, Hillary joked about a sizzling rumor making the rounds among her Park Ridge neighborhood's housewives that she had become secretly engaged while at Wellesley. "John," she wrote, "No — I am not engaged. I am married. Seriously, though, I'm only living in 'sin' for the Summer."[22] But this was all in fun; when it came down to it, Hillary followed the rules. While she adapted the carefree look of the "hippies," she never considered herself one.

The fourth category, "compassionate misanthrope," was really just a pipe dream. When the stress of college life became too much, she would fantasize about living a life of "withdrawn simplicity," preferably in some quiet place where she could devote herself to helping others and to reading books. "We're all here to help someone else," she often told friends.[23] But Hillary knew such work required a love of being with people and profound patience, and she was not a natural at either. This fundamental contradiction was not lost on her. "Can you be a misanthrope and still love or enjoy some individuals?" she asked Don Jones in a letter.[24]

Wrestling with these questions of identity, Hillary suffered a rare bout of depression. It arrived in February of her sophomore year, augmented by a stretch of cold weather. Suddenly, she didn't want to get out of bed in the morning. She began skipping classes and allowing her assignments to slide. Her professors became concerned about her. Consumed by a severe identity crisis, Hillary agonized over the same questions: *Who should I be? Who do I want to be?* The ensuing stress of not finding an answer made her bury her head under the pillows. "Thinking is a dangerous thing for me," she admitted in a letter to Don Jones.[25]

During this dark period, Hillary repeatedly asked her closest friends if they were happy, or she mused about what it took to be truly happy. She always wrapped the word *happiness* in quotation marks,[26] as if it were an ephemeral thing, something that happened to others through some elusive magic formula.

Hillary rescued herself from this funk by doing what she would end up doing again and again in her life: becoming less introspective. Even at this young age, Hillary was good at compartmentalizing—slamming the door shut on a room in her mind containing some unpleasant thought. If she concerned herself with advising people on how they could overcome their problems—and with helping friends and others hunt for their own solutions—then she would have much less time to spend on worrying about herself. And if she had no time to look inward, there was no chance of her discovering something within that she would be troubled by. This solution worked almost overnight.

The fifth and final identity, "political leader," is the one that Hillary devoted herself to pursuing after overcoming her depression. Her February angst hadn't been solely the product of an inability to find a path. In another letter, she had told Peavoy, "I have not yet reconciled myself to the state of not being the star."[27] She was committed to taking three carefully choreographed steps in college: First she wanted to be appointed a member of "Vil Junior," a club at Wellesley;[28] then she wanted to serve in the student senate; and finally she aimed her sights on the presidency of the Wellesley College Government Association.

Despite her freshman Young Republicans triumph, Hillary's memory of losing her high school class election was still fresh and raw, and even as a Vil Junior, she meticulously laid the groundwork for a successful run for student government president. She took on every issue and adopted bold positions that would be popular with the majority of her classmates. For example, students disliked the mandatory prayer in the dining hall; Hillary campaigned to discontinue it. Students objected to rigorous curriculum requirements that they argued limited their options and academic flexibility; Hillary would eventually manage to persuade the administration to relax those rules. A majority of students wanted a pass-fail grading option; Hillary lobbied hard for that. Her classmates and professors wanted Wellesley to become a more diverse place; Hillary aggressively campaigned for more minority students and faculty members.

But nothing annoyed the young women of Wellesley more than the college's insistence that it was a surrogate parent obliged to protect and, at times, discipline them. The college had a strict in loco parentis policy, which the students believed was a relic from the 1950s that treated them as if they were immature schoolchildren. Remembered Hillary, "We couldn't have boys in our rooms except from 2 to 5:30 P.M. on Sunday afternoons, when we had to leave the door partly open and follow what we called the 'two feet' rule:

two (out of four) feet had to be on the floor at all times. We had curfews of 1 A.M. on weekends, and Route 9 from Boston to Wellesley was like a Grand Prix racetrack Friday and Saturday nights as our dates raced madly back to campus so we wouldn't get in trouble."[29] Hillary declared that it was time to change all that. She had political and, eventually, personal reasons for doing so. Hillary had two serious boyfriends while at Wellesley, Ivy League men. At various times, both boys made the trip back to Park Ridge with Hillary to meet her parents, but "given my father's attitudes toward anyone I dated," the meetings were "more like a hazing than a social encounter."[30]

Hillary's political life extended beyond campus. By 1968, there were far fewer bitter debates among students about the war's merits, particularly after the Tet Offensive. The nightly news was filled with harrowing images of the Vietcong and the North Vietnamese inflicting casualties against American troops in the heart of Saigon, and print journalists were now explaining the war in increasingly worrisome ways. By then, Hillary was no longer trying to reconcile conflicted feelings about the war, or the leftward drift of her own politics. She was already beginning to call herself a "former Goldwater Girl," demonstrating her newfound political beliefs most dramatically by supporting the anti-war campaign of Senator Eugene McCarthy of Minnesota in his bid to displace President Lyndon B. Johnson as the Democratic nominee. Along with a few classmates, Hillary traveled to Manchester, New Hampshire, on weekends to stuff envelopes and campaign on Senator McCarthy's behalf.

Hillary might have initially felt intimidated by her classmates, but by now they were completely dazzled by her hard work, organizational skills, and unflappable determination. Liberated by focusing ahead instead of within, Hillary was remarkably adept when it came to helping her fellow students set goals and meet them. Most of her classmates do not remember Hillary talking openly about running for public office someday—but she didn't have to, because so many of them did it for her. She was a natural. "Other people around her talked about it on her behalf," said classmate Jan Piercy.[31] Karen Williamson, the student Hillary had attended church with, said the young, privileged Wellesley students used to say that if a woman was going to be elected president of the United States during their lifetimes, they just knew that it would be Hillary Rodham, Class of '69.[32]

*   *   *

IN THE SECOND SEMESTER of her junior year, Hillary ran against two classmates for the presidency of the student government. She spent three weeks going from dorm room to dorm room to describe for students how she intended to improve their college lives.

At a debate hosted by the *Wellesley News*, Hillary faced off against her opponents, Francille Rusan and Nonna Noto. Wearing a black turtleneck, a white sweater-vest, and big black-framed glasses, Hillary answered each question directly, stringing together complete sentences until they formed smart, glittering paragraphs. Her poise was impossible to miss. Among those impressed with her pragmatism and no-nonsense way of communicating was one of her political science professors, Alan Schechter, who was then in his early thirties. Schechter noticed that she spoke as effortlessly with senior administrators as she did with students.[33]

On a bitterly cold day in February 1968, Hillary Rodham won the presidency. "I can't believe what has just happened!" she told one of her professors. "I was just elected president of the student government. Can you believe it? Can you believe that happened?"[34] But of course it wasn't really much of a surprise at all.

She had about six weeks to enjoy her victory. On April 4, Martin Luther King Jr. was shot and killed on the balcony of a Memphis motel, where he was speaking to a group of supporters. The assassination shattered Hillary. One of her first heroes and role models was gone. Moments after hearing the news, she burst into the room of a friend, hurled her book bag against a wall, and screamed, "I can't take this! I can't stand it anymore! I can't take it!"[35] She was crying and shaking.

More bad news arrived in the middle of the night shortly after Hillary had returned home to Park Ridge in early June. She was awakened by her mother, who told her, "Something very terrible has happened again."[36] Robert F. Kennedy had been shot and killed in a Los Angeles hotel ballroom. A bereft Hillary consoled herself the next day by talking for hours on the telephone with a friend named Kevin O'Keefe, an Irish-Polish Chicago boy who loved the Kennedys. They both spoke about their worries about America now that Jack and Bobby Kennedy were gone.

Though "unnerved" by the assassinations, Hillary soon after traveled to Washington to serve for nine weeks in the Wellesley Internship Program. The program placed students in congressional offices and government agencies to see "how government works." Alan Schechter, the program's director, decided to assign Hillary to the House Republican Conference. He knew that she was beginning to move away from her Republican upbringing and her father's influence, but he "thought this internship would help me continue charting my course—no matter what I eventually decided," Hillary said.[37] She objected to the assignment but proceeded to report to a group headed by then Minority Leader Gerald R. Ford and Congressmen Melvin Laird and Charles Goodell. On their first day, the interns posed for a photograph with members of Congress. The photo of Hillary with the Republican leaders pleased her father immensely.[38] Hillary noted in her autobiography that he had it hanging in his bedroom when he died.

Hillary, the head of the Wellesley delegation, wanted to soak up as much national politics as possible. She became close to Goodell, who represented western New York and who had been appointed to the Senate by Governor Nelson Rockefeller to replace Robert Kennedy until a special election was held. As the internship wound down, Goodell asked Hillary and a few other interns to accompany him to the Republican National Convention in Miami Beach, to work on behalf of Governor Rockefeller's last-gasp attempt to wrest the party's nomination from Richard Nixon. Despite her shifting political allegiances, it was too good an opportunity to pass up.

Hillary was dazzled and unsettled by her first peek under the big top of American politics. In Florida, she stayed in the Fontainebleau Hotel, the enormous beachside art deco hotel that has been visited by every American president since Eisenhower. It was the "first real hotel" that Hillary had stayed in;[39] until then, she had been accustomed to roadside motels during vacations. It was a whirlwind week—among those she met were Frank Sinatra and John Wayne—and her head spun from it all. The excitement was tempered somewhat by the inevitability of Rockefeller's failing in his final bid to thwart Nixon. In many ways, Hillary stopped thinking of herself as a Republican the night Nixon accepted his party's nomination in Miami Beach. "The nomination of Richard Nixon cemented the ascendance of a conservative over a moderate ideology within the Republican Party, a dominance that has only grown more pronounced over the years as the party has continued its move to the right and moderates have dwindled in numbers and influence," Hillary wrote in her autobiography. "I sometimes think that I didn't leave the Republican Party as much as it left me."[40] In effect, that summer, the GOP became only her father's party, no longer one that the two shared. If the moderates had not dwindled in numbers and influence, the party might not have lost her — not as quickly, anyway.

A few weeks after Hillary returned home from Miami Beach, the National Democratic Convention opened in Chicago, and her friend Betsy Johnson called her and said, "We've got to see this for ourselves."[41] Once again, this was a chance to have a front-row seat to history, and Hillary instantly agreed.

Neither Hillary nor Betsy told their parents the truth about where they were headed. Instead, they said they were going into town to the movies. On the last night of the convention, they visited Grant Park, the site of much of the trouble that had occurred that week. "You could smell the tear gas before you saw the lines of police," Hillary recalled.[42] The police officers' brazen display of violence against young protesters stunned her. But she was also turned off by the other side: young people who attempted to change the world through violence masquerading as "civil disobedience." After long talks with her friend Kevin O'Keefe that summer, Hillary decided that despite her disillusionment with where the country was headed, politics "was the only route in a democracy for peaceful and lasting change."[43]

This sentiment was reinforced back at Wellesley that fall, when Hillary decided for her senior thesis to analyze the activities of a colorful Chicago community activist named Saul Alinsky, whom she had met the previous summer. Unlike Hillary, Alinsky believed that the way you changed governments and corporations was from the ground up, through grassroots organization and confronting the powerful with the facts. Conservative commentators would later cite the Hillary-Alinsky link as evidence of what they perceived as her hidden radical agenda. But although she admired his argument that people should be empowered to help themselves, Hillary did not change her belief that it would be difficult to change things from the outside. Instead, she concluded that "the system could be changed from within."[44]

Despite their disagreements, Alinsky offered Hillary a chance to work with him after she graduated. It was a kind gesture, but to accept would have been antithetical to Hillary's sense of power and politics. Instead, she chose the inside track: she would go on to law school.

Hillary was accepted by both Harvard and Yale. She couldn't decide which to choose until she attended a cocktail party at Harvard Law School. A friend introduced her to a professor who she said appeared to be "straight out of *The Paper Chase.*" When the professor heard that Hillary was trying to decide between Harvard Law and "its closest competitor," the professor said dismissively, "Well, first of all, we don't have any close competitors. Secondly, we don't need any more women at Harvard."

"I was leaning toward Yale anyway," Hillary recalled years later, "but this encounter removed any doubts about my choice."[45]

ALL THAT WAS LEFT was graduation from Wellesley, which Hillary assumed would be uneventful — an assessment that turned out to be far off the mark. A classmate and friend, Eleanor "Eldie" Acheson, the granddaughter of Dean Acheson, President Truman's secretary of state, had the idea that a student should address the graduating class at commencement for the first time in the college's history. Wellesley president Ruth Adams quickly rejected the proposal.

Acheson refused to take no for an answer, however, declaring that she would stage a counter-commencement that weekend and that she was certain her famous grandfather would attend. Hillary, as student government president, was summoned to see President Adams in her house on the shore of Lake Waban on campus.

"What is the real objection?" Hillary asked.

"It's never been done," Adams replied.

"Well, we could give it a try."

"We don't know whom they are going to ask to speak," Adams said.

"Well," Hillary said, "they asked me to speak."

"I'll think about it."

Adams finally approved the request, probably relying on her faith in Hillary. Hillary later admitted, "I didn't have a clue about what I could say that could fit our tumultuous four years at Wellesley." Friends made suggestions, dropping off poems and observations. On the eve of her speech, however, Hillary was still not sure what she was going to say. Many students advised her to talk about "trust, about the lack of trust both for us and the way we feel about others." She hurriedly cobbled together a speech overnight, her final "all-nighter" of her undergraduate career.[46]

ON THE MORNING OF MAY 31, 1969, more than two thousand parents, administrators, professors, and students gathered in the bright sunshine on the green lawn between the chapel and the library for Wellesley's ninety-first commencement exercises. When President Adams had seen Hillary earlier that morning, she had asked her what she was going to say. Hillary had said the speech was still "percolating."

In the audience was Hillary's father, Hugh Rodham, who had flown from Chicago to Boston late the night before and taken the MBTA to campus. Hillary's mother, who was not feeling well, could not be there, which disappointed Hillary. "In many ways, this moment was as much hers as mine."[47]

Hillary, fatigued from no sleep, was a bundle of nerves. The mortarboard made a riot of her hair, making her appear, in her words, "truly scary."[48] The commencement speaker was Senator Edward Brooke of Massachusetts, a Republican and the Senate's only African American member. Brooke acknowledged "profound and pressing social problems" confronting the country, but he criticized "coercive protest."[49] His speech "sounded like a defense of President Nixon's policies," Hillary said.[50] She was disappointed that the senator did not mention Vietnam, civil rights, or Martin Luther King or Bobby Kennedy. "The Senator seemed out of touch with his audience: four hundred smart, aware, questioning young women," she recalled.[51]

When Brooke completed his remarks, President Adams stood up and said, "In addition to inviting Senator Brooke to speak to them this morning, the Class of '69 has expressed a desire to speak to them and for them at this morning's commencement. There was no debate so far as I could ascertain as to who their spokesman was to be — Miss Hillary Rodham." Adams ticked off Hillary's academic and extracurricular achievements, and then said, "She is also cheerful, good humored, good company, and a good friend to all of us. And it is a great pleasure to present to this audience, Miss Hillary Rodham."

Hillary began, "I am very glad that Miss Adams made it clear that what I am speaking for today is all of us — the four hundred of us — and I find myself in a familiar position, that of reacting, something that our generation has been doing for quite a while now. We're not in the positions yet of leadership and power, but we do have that indispensable task of criticizing and constructive protest, and I find myself reacting just briefly to some of the things that Senator Brooke said."[52]

Nearly four decades later, Brooke recalled that Hillary used the speech "to her own advantage....I was there representing authority and she was there representing the frustrations of her generation, which she did most effectively."[53]

Hillary's rambling address touched on issues of trust of public officials and American institutions, mutual respect between young people and their elders, and the challenges that awaited the graduating seniors. When they arrived at Wellesley, Hillary said, her classmates found "there was a gap between expectation and realities. But it wasn't a discouraging gap and it didn't turn us into cynical, bitter old women at the age of eighteen. It just inspired us to do something about that gap."

She concluded with a poem written by a classmate named Anne Scheibner. Its last few lines were:

> Earth could be fair. And you and I must be free
> Not to save the world in a glorious crusade
> Not to kill ourselves with a nameless gnawing pain
> But to practice with all the skill of our being
> The art of making possible.

Her speech was greeted with a standing ovation from her classmates, but President Adams was deeply disappointed with the message, and especially with Hillary's spontaneous decision to rebut comments by the official commencement speaker. It was, she thought, disrespectful.

Later that day, Hillary said good-bye to Wellesley by breaking its rules. She jumped into Lake Waban near her dorm, an area where swimming was strictly forbidden. She left her cut-off jeans, T-shirt, and aviator-style sunglasses on the shore. "I didn't have a care in the world as I swam out toward the middle, and because of my nearsightedness, my surroundings looked like an Impressionist painting."[54] When she returned to the shore, her clothes and glasses were missing. A campus security guard told Hillary that President Adams had seen Hillary swimming from her house and ordered them confiscated.

Hillary may have provoked President Adams's ire, but her speech nevertheless attracted national attention. Highlights from it, as well as her photograph, appeared in the June 1969 issue of *Life* magazine, and she gave an interview to a Chicago TV station. Hillary's mother basked in the media attention lavished on her only daughter, saying she had heard the full gamut of reactions, from salutations like "she spoke for a generation" to criticism like "who does she think she is?"[55]

"The accolades and attacks," Hillary later reflected, "turned out to be a preview of things to come."[56]

CHAPTER 3

Following the Heart to Fayetteville

BEFORE LEAVING CAMPUS for a summer in Alaska, where she would work in a factory in Valdez sliming the guts from fish, Hillary had confided to her friend John Peavoy that she was still bedeviled by self-doubt. Yes, she was going to law school. But then what? What would she do with her life? "I wonder — who is me?" she told him. "I wonder if I'll ever meet her. If I did, I think we'd get along famously."[1]

An idealistic Hillary entered Yale Law School in September 1969 filled with a desire to become a citizen-activist who might just change the world. Her own decision to attend law school was motivated in large part by the disquieting events in America in the late 1960s. "In the end, the decision to apply and attend law school for me was an expression of [this] belief: the system can be changed from within," she told *Newsweek* in an online interview done thirty-five years after she graduated. "The law can be an incredible vehicle for social change — and lawyers are at the wheel," she added. "By sheer strength of argument you can right wrongs, protect society against abuse and serve the public good."[2]

For Hillary, Yale Law School presented itself as the perfect venue to accomplish such goals. Yale was in the throes of a revolution in the American legal profession and also in the way the institution itself dealt with the whirlwind of social and cultural change. Although many young women might have found the law school's imposing Gothic architecture and old-school, male-dominated ethos intimidating, Hillary found it appealing, even welcoming. The glacial movement toward gender equality in the law profession had barely begun, but Yale was one of its most aggressive and influential trailblazers. Of the students entering Yale Law School in September 1969, Hillary was one of twenty-seven women — barely more than 10 percent, though, as Hillary observed, "it was a breakthrough at the time and meant that women would no longer be token students at Yale."[3]

The first year in law school — mastering contracts, property, and torts — is often the most academically demanding for students. But in April 1970, as Hillary's One-L experience was nearing an end, the students at Yale became preoccupied with a far more intense challenge. Perhaps unsurprisingly, Hillary inserted herself in the middle of it.

That spring, eight Black Panthers, including party leader Bobby Seale, went on trial for murder in a New Haven courtroom. The city was invaded by thousands of angry activists who believed that the Panthers had been set up by law-breaking and overzealous FBI agents and federal prosecutors. The unrest spilled onto the leafy New Haven campus. On April 27, an arsonist, furious about the trial, set fire to the International Law Library, located in the basement of the law school. "Horrified, I rushed to join a bucket brigade of faculty, staff and students to put out the fire and to rescue books damaged by flames and water," Hillary recalled.[4]

At a meeting about the torching, Hillary became the impromptu moderator, urging the angry students to remain calm and bridging the gap between their needs and those of the school's administrators. "Hillary did what would nowadays be called international summitry — flying back and forth between both sides," said Kristine Olson Rogers, a classmate at both Yale and Wellesley. "She's always been one who sees the need for balance."[5]

Four days later, a May Day rally was held on campus. The crowd size swelled beyond the organizers' expectations, fed by President Nixon's announcement the day before that he was sending

American troops into Cambodia—a sudden, dramatic, and, in the minds of many, illegal expansion of the war. Yale had avoided much of the chaos that had overwhelmed many college campuses over Vietnam, in part because its president, Kingman Brewster, and the university chaplain, the Reverend William Sloane Coffin, had publicly challenged the escalation of the war. Coffin, in particular, had become a leader of the national anti-war movement, and many anti-war students at Yale admired the fact that both Brewster and Coffin not only listened to them but often agreed with them.

But the calm could last for only so long. On May 4, National Guard troops shot and killed four student protesters at Kent State University in Ohio, and the news of the shooting sent Hillary running out of the law school in tears. One of the first people she bumped into was Professor Fritz Kessler, who had fled Hitler's Germany. "He asked me what the matter was and I told him I couldn't believe what was happening," Hillary recalled. "He chilled me by saying that, for him, it was all too familiar."[6]

The following morning, the front page of most American newspapers published the iconic photograph of a horrified young Mary Ann Vecchio kneeling over the facedown body of a slain Kent student named Jeffrey Miller. Vecchio's arms are outstretched as she tearfully pleads for help. Hillary saw the photograph as a symbol of "all that I and many others feared and hated about what was happening in our country."[7]

The moderate radicalism that had been a Yale hallmark began to waver with the Kent State killings. Hillary had a choice. She could join the Black Panther supporters who wanted to burn down the campus and the government buildings, or she could take on the harder job of attempting to "change the system from within." "True to my upbringing," she recalled, "I advocated engagement, not disruption or 'revolution.'"[8]

On May 7, Hillary spoke at a convention marking the fiftieth anniversary of the League of Women Voters in Washington, DC. The invitation was extended to Hillary in large part because of the national publicity that her commencement speech at Wellesley had attracted the previous spring. Hillary's "emotions were close to the surface" as she delivered her speech, in which she argued that the American military's push into Cambodia was illegal and unconstitutional. Her fellow law students had recently voted 239 to 12 to join more than three hundred schools in a national strike to protest "the unconscionable expansion of a war that should never have been waged." Hillary had moderated the meeting when that lopsided vote had been taken, and it was marked by a "thoughtful, albeit lawyerly" debate.[9]

Joining Hillary on the dais that May at the League of Women Voters was Marian Wright Edelman, the convention's keynote speaker and a woman who would become one of Hillary's most important and influential friends. After graduating from Yale Law School in 1963, Edelman had become the first black woman admitted to the bar in Mississippi, and she was a tireless worker for children's rights. A few months earlier, at a conference in Colorado, Hillary had also met Edelman's husband, Peter Edelman, a Harvard Law School graduate who had clerked for Justice Arthur J. Goldberg of the Supreme Court and worked for Bobby Kennedy. The Edelmans were lobbying Congress to pass an amendment to the Constitution that would lower the voting age from twenty-one to eighteen. Hillary endorsed the change. "If young people were old enough to fight," she said, "they were entitled to vote."[10]

At the conference, Hillary was also introduced to the director of the Voter Education Project of the Southern Regional Council in Atlanta. His name was Vernon Jordan and, like the Edelmans, he was an aggressive advocate of the lower voting age. (In 1971, the voting age was lowered to eighteen when the Twenty-sixth Amendment was passed.) Hillary's friendship with Jordan would become one of the most important and influential of her life — and of her future husband's too.

Hillary learned from Peter Edelman about his wife's intention to begin an anti-poverty advocacy organization in Washington, DC, to be called the Washington Research Project. It would later be renamed the Children's Defense Fund. That summer, with the help of a private grant, Hillary worked for the Washington Research Project, beginning her devotion to many of Marian Wright Edelman's causes. Also that summer, Senator Walter F. Mondale of Minnesota decided to hold hearings investigating the working and living conditions of migrant farmworkers, especially those toiling in the sugarcane fields in the Florida Everglades. The hearings would mark the ten-year anniversary of Edward R. Murrow's award-winning documentary *Harvest of Shame,* and the idea was to investigate whether things had improved since Murrow had exposed the plight of the workers to the nation. Hillary was specifically assigned to research the education and health of migrant workers' children.

It was a remarkable experience. Hillary was touched by the bright, hopeful children who gushed with enthusiasm when their dirt-covered fathers and mothers returned home in the evening after a long day working in the fields. She became particularly close to a seven-year-old girl named Maria. The girl was preparing to receive her First Communion when her family returned home to Mexico after the harvest, but her family did not have enough money to buy a dress for their daughter to wear on her special day. "I told my mother about Maria, and she took me to buy a beautiful dress," Hillary recalled years later. "When we presented it to Maria's mother, she started crying and dropped to her knees to kiss my mother's hands. My embarrassed mother kept saying she knew how important it was for a little girl to feel special on such an occasion."[11]

Hillary was stunned to discover that the farmworkers and their children were routinely deprived of basic necessities like housing, food, and sanitation. At Mondale's committee hearings in July 1970, witnesses blamed the corporations that owned large farms in Florida for the squalid and unsafe conditions, which, it turned out, had barely improved since Murrow's documentary. Several of Hillary's fellow students were working that summer at law firms on behalf of the corporations that owned those farms. Her fellow students were "learning how to rehabilitate a corporate client's tarnished image," she wrote. "I suggested that the best way to do that would be to improve the treatment of their farmworkers."[12] Trying to persuade colleagues to resist working for deep-pocketed corporate clients was an idealistic goal and even, perhaps, a far-fetched one. And it was a goal that Hillary would abandon soon enough.

HILLARY'S EXPERIENCE THAT SUMMER inspired her to focus her studies at Yale on children's rights. At the time, this was a fledgling area of the law, as the rights of children had been traditionally covered by family law. Even that was not particularly complicated: Most judges deferred in courtrooms to whatever a child's parents decided would be best, and when the parents disagreed, the judges usually sided with the mother. Beginning in the early 1960s, however, several courts began carving out case law that decreed that children possessed a number of limited legal rights that were beyond the influence of their guardians.

Through her volunteer work at the New Haven Legal Services, which provided legal services to the poor, Hillary learned that children often needed their own advocates when they were victims of neglect and abuse. New Haven's industrial base had begun to crumble, and the once pleasant Connecticut city was slipping toward a state of increased poverty, segregation, and blight. No one felt the impact of such decline as shatteringly as New Haven's children. During her second year in law school, Hillary worked at the Yale Child Center, where a child development case that she helped litigate made a lasting impression.[13] A young legal-aid lawyer named Penn Rhodeen filed a lawsuit on behalf of a black woman in her fifties who had been the foster mother of a two-year-old mixed-race girl since birth. The foster mother sued the Connecticut Department of Social Services, attempting to overturn its decision that foster parents were not eligible to adopt children. Hillary assisted Rhodeen, and together they argued that the only mother the toddler had known was the foster mother, and the trauma of separating them would trigger lasting psychological damage to the child. Hillary and Rhodeen lost the case, but it introduced Hillary to a new calling. "I realized that what I wanted to do with the law was to give voice to children who were not being heard," she said.[14]

Hillary's resolve was deepened by the children she had encountered at the Yale Child Center — young boys and girls who had been beaten or burned, and others who had been abandoned. Meeting them served as a generational bridge to Hillary's mother, who had been mistreated and neglected by her parents and grandparents, something that Hillary had learned as a girl. Dorothy Rodham had overcome the deep emotional scars with the unselfish help of other caring adults, and now Hillary knew she wanted to give this gift too. "I want to be a voice for America's children," she declared.[15]

In November 1973, Hillary published her first article, an argument about establishing legal rights for children. It was nothing short of pioneering. Entitled "Children Under the Law" and published by the *Harvard Educational Review*, Hillary's article forcefully claimed that the legal status of children as "minors" should be abolished. Instead, she argued, children should be granted the status of "child citizens," with access to all rights granted to adults under the Constitution. "Categorizing everyone under eighteen or twenty-one as a minor is artificial and simplistic; it obscures the dramatic differences among children of different ages and the striking similarities between older children and adults," Hillary wrote.[16]

Years later, Hillary's article was portrayed by right-wing Republicans as evidence of her radical, "anti-family" beliefs. A few critics incorrectly accused Hillary of saying children should be permitted to sue their parents to avoid having to do household chores like taking out the garbage or making beds. Such criticism deeply hurt her. "I couldn't foresee the later misinterpretation of my paper; nor could I have predicted the circumstances that would motivate the Republicans to denounce me," Hillary observed decades later. There was something else she didn't realize at the time: "I certainly didn't know that I was about to meet the person who would cause my life to spin in directions that I could never have imagined."[17]

BILL CLINTON REMEMBERS the precise moment when he first set eyes on Hillary Rodham. It was toward the end of the fall of 1970 and his first semester at Yale Law School, and Bill was sitting in the back of Professor Emerson's class on political and civil rights. Near the front of the classroom was a blond woman whom Bill did not recognize. He had not been attending many classes because he was busy running political campaigns that autumn, and he assumed that this young woman had attended even fewer sessions than he had. Why else had it taken nearly a full semester for him to notice her?

Bill was not initially attracted to Hillary's appearance; she remained uninterested in impressing young men that way, and on this day her thick dark-blond hair was tied in a bun and her face was partially hidden by oversize brown eyeglasses. But there was something else that Bill saw that he did like. It was Hillary's poise, the confident way she moved. It was an attraction to something less obvious and more irresistible. Bill later admitted that on that very first day he saw her, Hillary "conveyed a sense of strength and self-possession I had rarely seen in anyone, man or woman."[18]

Bill was so smitten and curious that he followed Hillary out of the classroom, fully intending to introduce himself to her. But when he came within two feet of her, a force larger than himself stopped him from tapping her on the shoulder. "It was almost a physical reaction," Bill recalled years later. "Somehow I knew that this wasn't another tap on the shoulder, that I might be starting something I couldn't stop."[19]

Bill and Hillary stole glances at each other over the next few months and finally met near the end of their first year on that evening in the law library when Hillary confronted Bill with a forward handshake. Bill was flabbergasted by her boldness, but afterward, he decided the next move would be his. A few days later, Bill spotted Hillary in the law school's lobby. Sporting a long, bright flowered skirt, Hillary was hard to miss, and for the first time, Bill worked up the courage to approach her. Hillary was on her way to register for that autumn's courses, and Bill offered to accompany her. They talked and shared a few laughs as they stood in line, but when they got to the front of the line, the registrar asked Bill, "What are you doing here? You registered this morning."

"I turned beet red," Bill recalled, "and Hillary laughed that big laugh of hers. My cover was blown."[20]

Hillary and Bill then decided to go to the Yale Art Gallery to see a Mark Rothko exhibit. A workers' strike had closed the museum, but Bill persuaded a guard on duty to let them in, in exchange for Bill's cleaning branches and litter in the museum's garden. After seeing the artwork (and after Bill had completed his price-of-admission chores), the couple sat together in the garden, beginning a conversation that continues to this day.

Hillary was dazzled by many things about Bill. Her infatuation with Bill fueled her fascination with details large and small, and she found an infinity in even his seemingly minor features. "His wrists are narrow and his fingers tapered and deft, like those of a pianist or a surgeon," she recalled. "When we first met as students, I loved watching him turn the pages of a book."[21]

Bill and Hillary were inseparable that first week. But over the weekend, Hillary left New Haven for a long-planned visit to Vermont to see a man she had been dating. In the years to come, it would be her husband whose affections roved, but at the beginning, it was Hillary who had trouble making up her mind. Bill spent the weekend fretting that he might lose her. When she returned to Yale on Sunday night, he called her, but she was "sick as a dog," he recalled.[22] Bill immediately brought her chicken soup and orange juice, and with that, neither one was interested in anyone else.

That spring, Hillary and Bill sat together in the kitchen of a beach house on Long Island Sound near Milford, Connecticut, where Bill was living with three roommates. While one of the typical parties whirled around them, they quietly discussed their post–law school plans. Hillary knew only vaguely that she wanted to do something involving civil rights or child advocacy. "Bill was absolutely certain: He would go home to Arkansas and run for public office," she said.[23]

Bill was certain about something else: Hillary. "With Hillary, there was no arm's length," Bill recalled. "She was in my face from the start, and, before I knew it, in my heart."[24] That summer, she intended to work for a small law firm in Oakland, California, and Bill said he wanted to go with her. He had an opportunity that summer to help organize the southern states for Senator George McGovern's presidential campaign, but that job no longer appealed to him.

Bill's idea thrilled Hillary, but it frightened her as well. "Why do you want to give up the opportunity to do something you love to follow me to California?" she asked.

"For someone I love, that's why," he said.[25]

On the fringe of a large park near the University of California at Berkeley campus, they shared a small apartment. Hillary spent most of the summer doing research and writing legal briefs on a child custody case, while Bill read books and explored the off-the-beaten-path neighborhoods of San Francisco, Oakland, and Berkeley. Years later, one night from that summer stood out in Hillary's mind. At a cozy restaurant in Berkeley, Bill waited for Hillary to join him, but she was late. When she arrived, Bill was gone, but another customer told Hillary that he had seen Bill waiting. "He was here for a long time reading," the man told Hillary, "and I started talking to him about books. I don't know his name, but he's going to be president someday."

"Yeah, right," Hillary said, "but do you know where he went?"[26]

Hillary's boss in California was a lawyer named Mal Burnstein. Burnstein was immediately impressed with Bill's intelligence, telling him, "Gee, you must have offers from all these big firms."

"No," Bill replied. "I'm goin' back to Arkansas, and I'm going to be governor."[27]

Hillary heard this, and she just shook her head and smiled, although she knew her boyfriend was serious and determined to do precisely as he said. From the beginning, Hillary accepted the fact that if she was going to remain with Bill, she was going to have to take a radical geographic and career detour. If they had any hope of a future together, she knew that she would end up settling down in a place about as far away from Park Ridge as one could imagine.

*   *   *

THE HAPPY COUPLE RETURNED to Yale that September of 1971, moving into the ground floor of a house at 21 Edgewood Avenue. The seventy-five-dollar-a-month apartment was modest; the floors were uneven, the wind whistled through the cracks in the walls, but none of that mattered. Although they had lived together over the summer, this place felt to both like their first home.

The apartment belonged to Greg Craig, a fellow student and friend from Yale Law School. (Craig would go on to become one of President Clinton's chief defenders during the Senate impeachment trial in early 1999.) Craig was a civil-rights activist at Yale, and he regularly traveled around New England and beyond to attend protests and rallies. Hillary, he recalled, sympathized with his causes, but she chose to remain "campus bound." At Yale, Craig recalled, she built coalitions between different campus groups, and developed "a network that was as large as anyone's."[28] He called Hillary "a critic within the system" whose friends and allies ranged from activists from "the hard left" to "the most conservative elements of the Yale School." "She was not an ideologue, not a true believer," Craig said, confessing puzzlement at how polarizing Hillary later became.[29]

After Christmas that year, Bill drove from Hot Springs, Arkansas, to Park Ridge to spend a few days with Hillary's family. Her parents had met him the previous summer, but Hillary was anxious about this trip because her father was customarily critical of her boyfriends. No one was ever good enough for Hugh Rodham's only daughter. "I wondered what he would say to a Southern Democrat with Elvis sideburns," Hillary wrote.[30]

Almost instantly, Dorothy Rodham approved of Bill, and her fondness for him only increased after he discovered she was reading a philosophy book for one of her college courses and he launched into an enthusiastic discussion with her about it for more than an hour. Bill also won instant fans among Hillary's brothers and her old high school classmates, even a few of her old friends' parents. The mother of one of Hillary's friends slapped a quick endorsement on Bill, whispering to Hillary, "I don't care what you do, but don't let this one go. He's the only one I've ever seen make you laugh!"[31] Perhaps not surprisingly, it was touch-and-go between Bill and Hillary's father, although they found some common ground at the card table and watching college football on television.

In the summer of 1972, Hillary returned to Washington to work again for Marian Wright Edelman. Meanwhile, Bill took a full-time job for the McGovern campaign and was in Miami when McGovern was nominated. Once the nomination had been secured, the next stage of the campaign began. Bill had no doubts that he would be part of the final push.

"Bill asked me if I wanted to go, too," Hillary recalled. "I did, but only if I had a specific job."[32] She was offered a stint organizing a voter-registration drive across Texas, and she jumped at the opportunity to work on the campaign by Bill's side. The national voting age had just dropped, and Hillary and her colleagues targeted this newly enfranchised group of voters. Their hope was that if they registered enough college-age students to vote for McGovern, they could put the state in McGovern's column. But this amounted to nothing more than a pipe dream, and as the weeks passed, McGovern's poll numbers worsened.

An upside of the assignment was the location; Bill and Hillary lived in Austin, a charming city with a small-town feel despite its being home to the state capital and the University of Texas. Bill and Hillary were stationed in the city's McGovern campaign headquarters, located in what had been an empty storefront on West Sixth Street.[33] Hillary met dozens of student leaders from several Texas universities and seasoned Texas political operatives. In that last category, no one would wind up being more important to Hillary and Bill than Betsey Wright, a whip-smart campaign worker from a small West Texas town named Alpine. Wright had worked for Common Cause and the Texas State Democratic Party. She was hard to miss: She was big, brash, liberal, loud, wise, and supremely confident. At thirty, she was already a mentor for many young women working on her campaigns.

Wright was immediately awed by Hillary's intelligence and ambition. "I was less interested in Bill's political future than Hillary's," Wright told Clinton biographer David Maraniss. "I was obsessed with how far Hillary might go, with her mixture of brilliance, ambition and self-assuredness. There was an assumption about all the incredible things she could do in the world."[34] (After Bill and Hillary were married, Wright, a feminist to the core, admitted she was disappointed that Hillary did not choose to pursue a political career on her own. Hillary seemed to be investing too much of her future in Bill, a decision that gnawed at Wright. "It was thirty-five years ago when I dreamed of Hillary running for President," Wright said in 2007. "I did not want her to move to Arkansas and marry Bill Clinton. She did and I abandoned the dream.")[35]

For the campaign's homestretch, Betsey Wright invited Hillary to work in San Antonio. While there, Hillary organized a campaign rally for McGovern in front of the Alamo, an event that occurred just two weeks before Election Day. It wound up being Hillary's first exposure to grassroots politics. She discovered that the advance team of local workers "operated under tremendous stress" and — perhaps more memorably — that the McGovern campaign was running so low on money that the local vendors nearly did not get paid.[36] The lack of funds was a stress and a distraction, making the opposite possibility — a huge war chest — extremely appealing.

Two weeks later, McGovern was trounced by Nixon. "That 1972 race was our first rite of passage," Hillary said.[37]

Back at Yale, Hillary and Bill teamed up for the Thomas Swan Barrister's Union Prize Trial, a moot court competition. Hillary did the pretrial preparation, and Bill did all the talking in the courtroom.[38] They lost but commanded a formidable one-two punch, allowing them to showcase the strengths they would demonstrate in their future political partnership.

After they both graduated from law school in the spring of 1973, Bill took Hillary on her first trip to Europe. He had been there before, as a Rhodes Scholar, and he easily assumed the role of tour guide. They began in London, where they were awed by the majestic beauty of Westminster Abbey and Parliament, before crisscrossing the United Kingdom, exploring Stonehenge and the green countryside of Wales.

One soft summer evening, in the sumptuous Lake District along the shores of Ennerdale Water, Bill asked Hillary to marry him. Without hesitation, she said, "No. Not now."[39]

Hillary has said that she was in love at the time with Bill, but she needed time and space to sort out her feelings. She had seen how dramatically her mother was affected by her own parents' divorce, and she simply wanted to figure out whether Bill was the one. "I knew that when I decided to marry, I wanted it to be for life," said Hillary, identifying two intangibles that in this case frightened her — commitment and Bill's intensity. "I thought of him as a force of nature," she explained, "and wondered whether I'd be up to the task of living through his seasons."[40] But there was something else too, something that she did not mention to anyone: Bill was going to Arkansas, and Hillary harbored deeply ambivalent feelings about following him there.

Bill, however, would not be denied. "He set goals," Hillary said, "and I was one of them." He kept proposing to Hillary, and she kept saying, "Not now."[41]

"Well, I'm not going to ask you to marry me anymore," Bill finally said, "and if you ever decide you want to marry me, then you have to tell me."[42]

AFTER YALE, BILL AND HILLARY traveled in opposite directions, but not for long. Bill returned home to Fayetteville for a teaching job at the University of Arkansas School of Law. Hillary moved north, to Cambridge, Massachusetts, to work at the Children's Defense Fund for Marian Wright Edelman. Hillary lived alone, atop a rented house in Cambridge, and worked on a project looking into the significant discrepancies between census figures of school-age children and school enrollments. As part of her research, Hillary went door-to-door and found children who were not in school because of physical disabilities, such as deafness and blindness.[43]

The Children's Defense Fund sent those results to Congress and lobbied hard for a law to make public schools accessible to all children. Two years later, Congress passed the Education for All Handicapped Children Act, which required the public school system to educate children with physical, emotional, and learning disabilities.

Hillary found this kind of work deeply satisfying, but she was lonely and missed Bill "more than I could stand," she recalled. That spring, she had taken the bar exams in Arkansas and Washington, DC. She failed the DC bar but passed the one in Arkansas. Hillary thought: *Maybe my test scores are telling me something.*[44]

Meanwhile, Bill was preparing to run for a seat in the Third Congressional District in the House of Representatives, representing northwest Arkansas, including Fayetteville and Hot Springs. For Bill, the Watergate scandal provided an irresistible opening, making the Republican incumbent's seat vulnerable. Hillary visited Bill in December 1973, and while the two of them were drinking coffee in his kitchen, the phone rang. On the other end was John Doar, who had been selected by the House Judiciary Committee to lead the impeachment inquiry of President Nixon. Both Bill and Hillary had met Doar at Yale, when he was a judge during their moot court trial. Doar was something of a hero to Hillary, who saw him as "a Gary Cooper type: a quiet, lanky lawyer from Wisconsin."[45] She admired his work on behalf of civil rights in Mississippi and Alabama during the sixties, and the leading role he played in federal courtrooms arguing voting-rights cases.

Doar told Bill that his name was at the top of a list of young lawyers to help him with the impeachment inquiry. Bill turned down the offer, telling Doar that he was running for Congress. Doar then offered a staff job to Hillary. The job might have seemed unappealing — it offered little money and long hours — but to Hillary, history was calling her name. "It was, as they say, an offer I couldn't refuse," she recalled.[46] Her move from Cambridge to Washington also postponed her and Bill's ongoing conversation about their future together.

Before the move, however, Bill visited his friend David Pryor, a lawyer in Little Rock who was just beginning his own campaign for governor, to ask if the job was right for Hillary — and, by extension, for his own political fortunes. Bill wanted Pryor to calculate how Hillary's work on the impeachment of Nixon would play in the conservative enclaves of northwest Arkansas. "He talked to me about Hillary going to work for the Watergate committee," Pryor recalled. "He asked, 'Is that a good idea?' It was a career consideration. He knew that his career would be in politics, and the question was whether Hillary's connection with the Watergate committee might have political ramifications."[47]

In the end, they concluded her work on the committee would not significantly damage Bill, and Hillary joined the House impeachment inquiry as one of forty-three staff attorneys and one of just three women. It was a plum assignment that placed her, at the age of twenty-six, squarely at the epicenter of the fiercest, most important legal battle of her time. The lawyers, most of them in their late twenties and early thirties and all with glittering Ivy League pedigrees, worked seven days a week, often twenty hours a day, in the old Congressional Hotel on Capitol Hill across from the House office buildings. Most of the work was mind-numbing; Doar insisted that every fact — a memo's date, a meeting's topic — be typed on an index card and then cross-referenced with the other cards. By the end of their work, more than five hundred thousand cards had been created. Hillary first researched American impeachment cases, then helped draft procedural rules to present to the House Judiciary Committee. Hillary sat to Doar's left at the counsel's table during a committee meeting.

Hillary was also tasked with putting together an internal memorandum that laid out the organization of Nixon's White House. The memo concluded that despite the hierarchical nature of the White House, Nixon was a detail-oriented president, his hands directly involved with the stirring of many pots (and plots). To help figure out who was doing what, Hillary spent hours listening to the subpoenaed tapes received from the Watergate grand jury. In a windowless, musty second-floor room in the hotel, she struggled to make sense of Nixon's words. As she did, she got an intimate view of a president practicing the dark art of Washington politics, doing whatever necessary to maintain his grip on power. She was particularly astonished when she heard what the staff lawyers called the "tape of tapes" — Nixon listening to the sound of his voice on his own tapes, justifying his recorded comments in an attempt to minimize his role in the cover-up of the Watergate break-in. Hillary listened, like a fly on the wall, as the president attempted to rewrite history, saying, "What I meant when I said this was..." or "Here's what I was really trying to say..." "It was extraordinary to listen to Nixon's rehearsal for his own cover-up," Hillary recalled years later.[48]

Doar presented proposed articles of impeachment on July 19, 1974, and the House Judiciary Committee approved three of the articles, citing abuse of power, obstruction of justice, and contempt of Congress. Nixon resigned the presidency less than a month later, on August 9, sparing the nation an impeachment vote in the House and a trial in the Senate.

At a farewell dinner for the staff lawyers on the committee, everyone talked about their future plans. Hillary told a colleague, Bert Jenner, that she was going to be a trial lawyer like him.

"Impossible," he said.

"Why?" Hillary asked.

His answer stunned her: "Because you don't have a wife."

"What on earth does that mean?"

Without a wife at home attending to her personal needs, Bert Jenner explained, Hillary would not be able to cope with the extreme career demands of a trial lawyer. Years later, Hillary wondered if Jenner had merely tried to warn her, in his clumsy way, that the law was not a suitable place for a young, single woman.[49]

*   *   *

NOW OUT OF WORK, Hillary turned her attention to Bill and their future together. In August 1974, she decided to join Bill in Arkansas. "I had fallen in love with Bill in law school and wanted to be with him," she wrote in her autobiography. "I knew I was always happier with Bill than without him, and I'd always assumed that I could live a fulfilling life anywhere. If I was going to grow as a person, I knew it was time for me — to paraphrase Eleanor Roosevelt — to do what I was most afraid to do."[50]

She certainly feared Arkansas. It was as far away as possible from the life she had imagined for herself. To go there meant turning down jobs at white-shoe law firms in Washington, DC, or New York, and a job as the special counsel at the Children's Defense Fund. Sure, there was a job waiting for her in Arkansas — a job teaching law at the University of Arkansas. But professionally, it was a monstrously big detour. So this was not about work. She went to be with Bill, and to help Bill. He was running for Congress, and he needed her help.

On a humid mid-August evening, Hillary arrived in Fayette-ville. That day she watched, enthralled, as Bill gave a campaign speech before a good-size crowd in the town square in Bentonville. He was impressive.

Still, the odds were very tough. By the 1970s, the South was undergoing a political transformation. It had always been conservative, but Democrats had dominated the electoral landscape. Now Republicans had begun chipping away at the Democratic monopoly, and they would eventually replace it with one of their own. Northwest Arkansas was largely conservative, except for the university enclave in Fayetteville. Bill was running against John Paul Hammerschmidt, the first Arkansas Republican elected to Congress in one hundred years. Elected in 1966, Hammerschmidt was a lumberman who was extremely popular, a master at catering to his constituents' every need.

Before she had even arrived, Hillary had been on the phone with Bill, sometimes four times a day, giving advice, mentoring him. When she arrived, she took over, and she quickly discovered that the young female college students who volunteered on the campaign were deeply devoted to him; some were even pining to sleep with him.[51]

Though still unwed, Hillary and Bill had already made a secret pact of ambition, one whose contours and importance to the two of them has remained their secret across all these years. They agreed to embark on a political partnership with two staggering goals: revolutionize the Democratic Party and, at the same time, capture the presidency for Bill. They called it their "twenty-year project," an auspicious timetable for two young people in their midtwenties. And they agreed that the only way they would be able to achieve these goals was to do whatever it took to win elections and defeat their opponents. Bill would be the project's public face, of course. And Hillary would serve as the enterprise's behind-the-scenes manager and enforcer.[52]

In a personal letter she wrote to Bill sometime before she arrived in Arkansas for good, Hillary laid out some of the details. One of Bill's ex-girlfriends, Marla Crider, accidentally stumbled upon Hillary's letter sitting atop Bill's desk in his house in Fayetteville. As Marla Crider scanned the words, she was stunned by what she was reading. This was hardly the usual love letter. It was all about their mutual ambition, a game plan for reaching their shared calling.

"The note talked about all of their future plans...political plans; that is the best way to put it," Crider said. The letter "had everything to do with their careers," and Crider found it "so unusual that there was no talk of a home, family and marriage."[53] Having glimpsed the missive, Crider had not been at all surprised to see Hillary running Bill's first campaign for Congress.[54] Others might have raised an eyebrow at how comprehensive her role was. Hillary did everything. She wrote Bill's speech for the state party convention that September. She helped him hone his message, and she encouraged him to attack Hammerschmidt's morals and his judgment. She even sold sandwiches to help raise money for the campaign. But her domineering presence proved unsettling to a number of the men, including a local political operative who was used to being in charge.[55]

In the campaign's final weeks, the operative was contacted by a lawyer connected to the dairy industry. He was willing to give $15,000 to be used in Sebastian County, which would "ensure that you are able to win the election." The unspoken message was that in some parts of northwest Arkansas, such funds could be used to buy votes. And if Bill won, the dairy interests would expect political payback. At a late-night meeting, the operative explained the proposed deal to Bill and Hillary. The money was already waiting for them at the lawyer's office. Hillary listened to his pitch in silence, then shouted at Bill, "No! You don't want to be a party to this!"

The operative asked Bill, "Look, you want to win or you want to lose?"

Before Bill could respond, Hillary answered for him. "Well, I don't want to win this way," she said. "If we can't earn it, we can't go [to Washington]."[56]

And that was that. On election night, November 5, 1974, Hammerschmidt won by just six thousand votes. "It was the goddamn money!" the operative shouted late that night.[57]

THE DEFEAT DISAPPOINTED but did not deter Bill and Hillary. A few mornings later, he was in Fayetteville, thanking supporters with handshakes and plotting his next campaign.

Meanwhile, Hillary was teaching criminal procedure and advocacy at the law school. That spring, she went back to Chicago and the East Coast to meet with old friends, including potential employers. On the way to the airport in Fayetteville, Bill and Hillary had passed a modest redbrick house located on California Street, near the university campus. A "For Sale" sign was out front, and Hillary had mentioned casually that it was "a sweet-looking little house." She did not think about it again until she returned to Arkansas a few weeks later. When Bill picked her up at the airport, he asked her, "Do you remember that house you liked? Well, I bought it, so now you'd better marry me because I can't live in it by myself."[58]

This time, Hillary said yes.

CHAPTER 4

Personal Calculations

IN THE LIVING ROOM of their little redbrick house, on the afternoon of October 11, 1975, Bill and Hillary were married by the Reverend Vic Nixon, a Methodist minister whom Bill had met on the campaign trail. Hillary wore a lace-and-muslin Victorian dress she had bought with her mother the night before.

"Who will give away this woman?" Reverend Nixon asked.

Everyone looked at Hugh Rodham, but he wouldn't let go of his little girl's arm. "You can step back now, Mr. Rodham," the Reverend finally said.[1] And Hugh did.

The newlyweds took a peculiar honeymoon trip two months later. Accompanying Bill and Hillary to Acapulco, Mexico, was Hillary's entire family, as well as one of her brother's girlfriends. All stayed in the same penthouse suite.[2]

THE ELECTION IN NOVEMBER 1976 was a milestone for Bill and Hillary's twenty-year project. A Georgia governor named Jimmy Carter demonstrated that Democrats could take back the White House, after eight long years. More to the point, Carter proved to the Clintons that a little-known southern governor could win enough electoral votes to become president. Perhaps most important for the Clintons, after narrowly losing his first campaign for a House seat two years previous, Bill scored his first electoral victory in 1976, winning the race for attorney general of Arkansas. With his victory, the Clintons left behind the ivory towers of academia and the small-town comforts of Fayetteville and moved to the state capital, Little Rock, a city of about 150,000 people. Despite its size, large for that part of the world, Little Rock felt small, insular, and a bit old-fashioned; a close-knit, even gossipy town where it was not easy to keep a secret — something Hillary would soon find out.

The Rose Law Firm, Hillary's new employer, traced its history back 150 years and was established as a standard bearer of the state's business elite. It, far more than any other firm in the state, lay at the intersection of power and commerce. Arkansas may rank among the country's poorest states, but it does not lack superwealthy corporate citizens. The Rose Law Firm represented the state's biggest bank, Worthen; the largest brokerage outside Wall Street, Stephens Inc.; the poultry giant Tyson Foods; and a rapidly growing national retailer called Wal-Mart. Gaps between the haves and the have-nots were dramatic and would get all the more so in the years to come.

The clashing interests of the well-to-do and the rest of Arkansas were in evidence in the 1976 ballot box in the form of a populist initiative. For Hillary, the initiative quickly and painfully illustrated the political and personal calculations inherent in her decision, on arriving in Little Rock, to join the Rose firm.

The ballot initiative had been launched by advocates for the poor, a group called the Association of Community Organizations for Reform Now (ACORN). The group's founder, Wade Rathke, had set up shop in Arkansas in 1970 and become good friends with Bill Clinton. Before long, Rathke was introduced to Hillary. They both seemed to share a common political perspective: helping those on the lower end of society's totem pole.

"She understood community organizing," Rathke recalled.[3] Hillary was particularly interested in how ACORN's philosophy compared to the preachings of Saul Alinsky, the leftist-leaning community organizer who was the subject of her senior thesis at Wellesley.[4] With utility rates in Arkansas skyrocketing in 1976, ACORN pushed through a ballot initiative requiring utilities to lower rates for residential users in Little Rock and to increase them for business customers. The measure passed.

For its part, the business community was not going to allow

such a change to be implemented without a fierce fight. It argued that higher utility rates might discourage other businesses from coming to Little Rock. An electric cooperative, with a tiny presence in Little Rock, First Electric Cooperative Corporation, quickly filed a lawsuit challenging the ballot measure. So did several other industries.

The engine driving the challenge was the Rose firm, which enlisted its new and only female litigator to help its courtroom team face off against the attorneys for ACORN and other proponents of the measure.

"I was surprised and shocked to see her there," Rathke said. Rathke, based on his conversations with Hillary, had assumed she would be "an ally if not a friend."[5]

Lawyers are obligated to vigorously represent their clients, and the firm took pride in its "tradition of zealous and effective advocacy of our clients' interests."[6] So Hillary could hardly decline to fight her old friends, especially so early in her new career. And of course this was the predictable by-product of Hillary's choice to join the Rose Law Firm. She would be an advocate for clients who would be on the opposite side of the causes she had formerly championed.

"She was intricately involved in the formulation of the company's position," ACORN's founder said.[7] Hillary came up "with the research and authorities" that persuaded the judge to nullify ACORN's initiative, a friend recalled.[8] The winning brief was crafted by Hillary and a colleague over a late-night pizza dinner in the firm's law library.[9]

The judge embraced Hillary's legal theory—that the ordinance amounted to an unconstitutional taking of property—deeply angering ACORN.[10] "It's a sad day for democracy when big business can get a court of law to overturn a vote of the people," its chairman said in a statement.[11] The biggest losers were the poor and middle-class citizens of Little Rock, who were now left without assistance.

Hillary's role in the case won her praise from within Rose, but it instantly soured her friendship with Rathke, who still works for ACORN, now based in hurricane-ravished New Orleans. "I never had a personal conversation with her after that case," he said. Asked to explain, if not reconcile, the different paths he and Hillary had chosen, Rathke simply said, "She was involved in a different series of calculations."[12]

Those calculations did not stop Hillary, the politician, from later maintaining an alliance with ACORN when it was convenient. Thirty years later, she and ACORN worked together on increasing the minimum wage and on electoral reform. In 2006, Hillary received a warm reception at ACORN's annual meeting in Columbus, Ohio, after talking passionately about those issues. In addition, during both campaigns for senator, Hillary ran as the candidate nominated not only by the Democratic Party but also by the Working Families Party, which ACORN had helped create. For both sides, Arkansas was water under the bridge. But as Hillary would later discover, some of those she disappointed would not be so accommodating. Youthful idealism, she would later say, doesn't always "appreciate the political and social restraints that one faces in the world."[13]

THE LEAD ATTORNEY in opposition to ACORN's initiative, Herbert C. Rule III, was one of two Rose partners who had offered a job to Hillary after the 1976 election. The other lawyer was Vincent Foster, who had come to know Hillary while she was running the legal clinic of the University of Arkansas in Fayetteville.

Rose described itself as the oldest law firm west of the Mississippi. But the firm was just beginning to hire female lawyers. And Bill and Hillary were a profound oddity in Little Rock; a two-lawyer married couple was "unheard of" in Arkansas at the time, one of her former partners, Allen W. Bird II, recalled.[14]

Foster and Rule had introduced Hillary to their partners, a number of whom were "specifically interested in recruiting a woman" who was well qualified.[15] (Most female lawyers in Arkansas at the time practiced family law.) Hillary certainly met that test — as well as some others. Joseph Giroir, the firm's rainmaker, "made me look at his smelly feet during my interview," Hillary later complained, because he had come from a game of tennis, removed his shoes, and deposited his sweaty feet atop his desk.[16] Going to work on behalf of corporations was a long way from teaching law school or setting up a law clinic to help indigent clients. "Representing private clients," Hillary later explained, was "a career choice I had resisted before."[17] But her pragmatic style and traditional values made it easier to compromise.[18] She quickly concluded that a job with the firm "would be an important experience and would help us financially since Bill's salary as Attorney General would be $26,500."[19]

"If Hillary were doing what she most wanted to do in this world, she would not be a partner in a corporate law firm," her Wellesley friend Jan Piercy explained many years later. But a job in the big firm, she went on, was "what she's had to do" because she was the family's chief breadwinner.[20] Hillary, who had decried the "competitive corporate life" as "not the way of life for us" at her Wellesley commencement speech, was now ready to step firmly into the establishment.[21]

BY 1979, HILLARY — now First Lady of the state following Bill's election to governor the year before — was elevated to partner, the first woman to be granted such a promotion in the history of the firm.[22] During this time, she continued to pursue some pro bono work on issues such as child advocacy, including helping to reverse a state rule that barred foster parents from adopting their foster children[23] (the firm prided itself on its commitment to public issues and civic leadership).[24] But Rose's work litigating on behalf of commercial clients meant that the distance between the idealistic Hillary and the businesslike Hillary continued to grow.[25]

In one lawsuit she successfully handled, filed in 1979, her client was the Coca-Cola Bottling Company of Arkansas and its employee retirement plan. A worker, Ronnie Weeks, had sued the company in federal court, claiming he was permanently disabled and had been improperly denied retirement benefits.[26]

It was quite a turn for Hillary. Earlier in the 1970s, she had lashed out at a prominent Washington attorney for representing Coca-Cola, a company she felt mistreated workers in its Minute Maid subsidiary. At a hearing on migrant farmworkers, in the Russell Senate Office Building, one floor below where she would later set up her own office, she had confronted Joseph Califano Jr., Coke's lawyer. "You sold out, you motherfucker, you sold out," she had told him.[27]

A decade later, in her first trial before a jury, Hillary represented a canning company that had been sued by someone who opened a can of pork and beans and discovered the rear end of a rat in the can. She gained a moral victory when the plaintiff won just a token award. (Hillary became the butt of her husband's jokes for years over what he called her "rat's ass" case.)[28]

Though her colleagues thought her defense of the canning company was "flawless," she admitted that she was "amazingly nervous" before the jury and that from then on she "began steering her practice toward non-jury matters."[29] Years later, Arkansas legal reporters would say that they rarely saw Hillary in the courtroom; one survey found she had "tried just five cases in her career."[30]

One of those trials, an obscure case in 1984 involving the condemnation of land at Little Rock's airport, would raise questions about Hillary's abilities as a litigator. She represented the Little Rock Municipal Airport Commission, a longtime client. The airport was expanding, and the commission had condemned nearby property owned by the Rolf family.

The family rejected as too low the commission's offer to buy their land, and on February 23 of that year the case went to trial. Hillary's client had a serious weakness: The commission's longtime appraiser, George Fox Jr., had initially come up with an estimate for the Rolf property that the commission had deemed too high. Fox had quit in protest, and the commission had then found another appraiser who provided a lower estimate.

One of the Rolf family attorneys, Randy Coleman, knew all this and hoped to use Fox as his key witness. But he faced what seemed like an insurmountable legal hurdle. In 1979, the Arkansas Supreme Court ruled that landowners could not use the testimony of condemnation appraisers like Fox if they were identified in court as having worked for the governmental agency doing the condemnation.

As a result, Coleman proceeded gingerly in his opening statement to see how far he could get before Hillary objected. To his great surprise, she and Foster, her cocounsel, never spoke up.

"I told the jury I was going to call the appraiser, and I thought to myself, *I'm fixing to catch an objection,* but nobody said a word," Coleman recalled. He realized Hillary and Foster "were totally unaware of the case law that set out that precedent."[31]

Coleman quickly called Fox as his first witness and put on record his crucial testimony.

Fox told the jury that a commission official had tried to get him to lower his estimate of $542,500, but that he had refused and then resigned. The "dictatorial" order by the commission official, Fox testified, violated the independent principles of the appraising profession.[32] The jury quickly sided with the Rolf family.

"It was so obvious what the airport commission had done," the jury foreman, Andrew Cobb, remembered decades later. It looked, Cobb said, like they were "trying to steal the property."[33]

The jury awarded the Rolfs an amount in line with Fox's original estimate, $558,000.[34] Hillary quickly filed notice of an appeal, but a few months later she called Coleman and told him she was abandoning it. "We're going to pay the judgment" entered at trial, she explained.[35] Coleman told her, "You finally found" the 1979 case, figuring "that's why you're fixing to settle."[36] It was a safe assumption. Since Hillary had not raised the 1979 supreme court ruling during the trial, she could not use it to challenge Fox's testimony on appeal, and it would be embarrassing for her and the firm should anyone find out about her blunder. Coleman recalled, "She sloughed it off and went on."[37]

Foster was Hillary's cocounsel in many of her cases in Arkansas. The litigation section was located on the first floor of the law firm's brick building, which had once housed a YWCA. Foster and Hillary had offices across the hall from each other, and they shared a secretary for a while.

It was not easy being a woman with a career in Little Rock.[38] The first time Hillary went to a restaurant with Foster and another Rose Law Firm attorney named Webster Hubbell, a troublemaker called the men's wives to point out that they had eaten lunch with a woman.[39] "In Little Rock, at that time," Hillary wrote, "women did not usually have meals with men who were not their husbands."[40]

Still, the trio's lunches became a habit. They often frequented the Villa, an out-of-the-way Italian restaurant where they talked shop or about their families.[41] The laconic but courtly Foster became one of Hillary's best friends, and Hubbell, the former offensive tackle for the University of Arkansas Razorbacks who "looked like a good old boy," was a loyal supporter.[42] For their part, the two guys "were mesmerized by her."[43] Sometimes, after a few drinks, the three lawyers pretended to be in Italy; Hillary dubbed Foster "Vincenzo Fosterini."[44]

In 1980, after Chelsea was born, Hillary stayed away from her full-time job for four months. "Hillary really felt this would be the most important thing in her life as a woman," a friend said.[45] Her leave prompted quiet complaints from some of the men at the firm,[46] an indication of the firm's deeper divisions over women,[47] but soon after Hillary returned, she was asked by Joseph Giroir to take on greater managerial responsibility by becoming managing partner, a job then held by Foster.

"In 1981, I suggested Hillary do it," Giroir said, "but because Bill was running for reelection she couldn't spend time on it."[48]

Missed opportunity was a recurring theme during Hillary's years at the Rose Law Firm. Her political support for her husband and her bevy of outside causes prevented Hillary from working full-time. She told a reporter that in 1982 and 1983, as she worked on behalf of her husband, "I had no time to practice law and that's also been a financial disadvantage."[49]

Meanwhile, within the firm, an inevitable complaint around the water cooler was that "Hillary's not billing enough."[50] Rose has never made public what its partners were paid. But by 1986, about halfway through her tenure as a partner at the firm, Hillary was the lowest-paid partner, according to internal records.[51] Her share of the firm's profits was 2.04 percent, less than half the draw of her friends Hubbell and Foster and just one-fifth that of Giroir, the highest-paid partner.[52]

Between 1985 and 1989, Hillary averaged about $80,000 per year in salary from the firm, reaching a high of $98,000 annually, according to the Clintons' tax returns. That was certainly a comfortable income for Arkansas, but still less than that of her fellow partners. She told a local newspaper in 1990 that her salary was in the six-figure range, which was true, depending on one's definition of range.[53]

The biggest blemish for both Hillary and her firm involved now-famous work they did during the 1980s for troubled savings and loans, lending institutions that focus primarily on real estate lending. One federal inquiry into the firm's potential conflicts cost Rose money; another resulted in the criminal conviction of a partner. Hillary's involvement was investigated in both instances.

Arkansas gave early warning to the nation of the forthcoming troubles in the savings and loan industry; ultimately, the state would earn the dubious honor of having the highest percentage of thrifts that failed.[54] In late 1986, the state's largest thrift, FirstSouth, experienced one of the biggest collapses in the industry to that point. Federal regulators, who took control of FirstSouth, thought they had a malpractice claim against Rose. That's because Giroir, the firm's top partner, had been both a borrower and a lawyer on transactions resulting in large losses for FirstSouth.[55]

Hillary "worried that a $10 million claim would finally put the oldest law firm west of the Mississippi out of business," Hubbell recalled. "Years later, she would tell me that the years 1987–88 were the two hardest years of her life."[56] A decade after choosing to join the Rose Law Firm to make money, Hillary was confronted with the real possibility that the firm might go out of business for question-able conduct, with her career as collateral damage.

In early 1988, after protracted negotiations, the firm agreed to pay the government $3 million: $500,000 to be paid by the part-ners and the rest by the firm's insurance carrier. In addition, the firm and Giroir parted ways. (The FirstSouth settlement was kept confidential and did not become public for years, until after the Clintons went to Washington.) Rose soon found a new insurance carrier, and, the slate now viewed as clean, Washington regulators hired the firm for millions of dollars in new business.[57]

That was not the end of savings and loan trouble for the Rose Law Firm. It was routine firm practice to do inventory on closed files to see whether they should be kept, microfilmed, or destroyed. Six months after the FirstSouth settlement, Hillary had twelve sets of closed files destroyed, including four involving a troubled sav-ings and loan she had been the billing partner for, Madison Guar-anty Savings and Loan.[58] Later, numerous investigations would try to figure out how Madison came to retain Rose, why Hubbell and Foster failed to fully disclose the firm's prior work for Madison, what the firm actually did for Madison, and why Hillary destroyed her Madison files. Those inquiries would eventually lead to Hil-lary's appearance before a grand jury and the drafting of a possible indictment against her.

Madison was seemingly a minor piece of the Rose portfolio, using another Little Rock law firm for most of its legal work. It also paid a small retainer to Rose, $2,000 a month, regardless of the level of work, including no work at all. This was unusual, for both the firm and Madison.

Ultimately, Rose performed a smattering of tasks for Madison, dealing with state regulations, real estate deals, and loans. Hillary, as the lead partner, generated a modest amount of related bill-ing hours. But by July 1986, fifteen months after the account was opened, Hillary closed it down. She returned the prepaid monthly retainer without even using it against an existing debt that Madison owed Rose.[59] Only later would the curious relationship between Hillary and Madison become apparent.

When she launched her run for president in 2007, Hillary said almost nothing about her professional life down South. On her Web site, the story of her years in Arkansas was titled "Mother & Advocate." Her fifteen years of work at the Rose Law Firm, the longest chunk of her professional career, was mentioned in passing and without reference to the firm's name: "She also continued her legal career as a partner in a law firm."[60] The reasons for her reticence become apparent when one looks more deeply into what happened at Rose with regard to Madison Guaranty. The investigation surrounding Madison would lead to Hillary's law office — and a failing real estate venture in a rural pocket of Arkansas that became known as Whitewater.

CHAPTER 5

Investing 101

TO UNDERSTAND WHAT HAPPENED between Madison Guaranty and the Rose Law Firm, it is necessary to go back to Bill Clinton's ascendancy to the governorship of Arkansas. Bill's victory in the 1978 Arkansas primary had virtually ensured he would become governor that fall, given the state's large Democratic majority. But the governor's annual salary never exceeded $35,000, which left Hillary, the family's chief moneymaker, in a state of perpetual financial insecurity.

Inherently frugal, a trait handed down to her by her father, Hillary aimed to fortify the family nest egg. Hugh Rodham also taught his daughter to be ferociously risk-averse when it came to money, but that year she decided to shed that caution and to embrace two dicey investments. Both required little or no money down and relied on the expertise of close friends. Both also exposed the Clintons to hundreds of thousands of dollars in potential liabilities at a time when their total annual income was only $54,000.[1]

For all their similarities, the forays yielded vastly different financial results. One, trading in commodities, was a spectacular success, producing a return of almost 10,000 percent in nine months. For that Hillary could thank a savvy friend, Jim Blair, who was the outside counsel for poultry giant Tyson Foods. The other, a failed real estate deal known as Whitewater, was a financial disaster, cost-ing the Clintons $36,862. For her real estate losses, Hillary blamed Bill's political chum and her client, Jim McDougal.

In reality, both ventures proved to be more complicated than a simple profit or loss. McDougal engaged in unlawful transactions to prop up Whitewater, and Hillary's commodity brokerage firm ignored established trading rules. Hillary was unaware of these questionable activities, but they would haunt her for years to come, both politically and financially, as the legal fees that resulted from Whitewater mushroomed to millions of dollars.

As it happened, the losing investment came first. McDougal ran into Bill and Hillary in the spring of 1978 at the Black-Eyed Pea Restaurant in Little Rock and casually offered them "a sure thing deal." Specifically, it involved a partnership with McDougal and his wife, Susan, in the purchase of 230 acres of undeveloped land astride the White River in northern Arkansas.[2]

The plan called for subdividing the land into smaller parcels that would then be sold to retirees or vacationers. To Hillary, "the attraction was obvious," because the forested countryside lots would appeal to northerners looking for recreational property and low taxes.[3] The Clintons never actually visited Whitewater, as the development was named; they let the McDougals manage it, and "if all had gone according to plan," Hillary stated, she and Bill "would have turned over the investment after a few years and that would have been the end of it."[4]

The two couples entered into a joint venture that later became a corporation, the Whitewater Development Company. Neither couple invested any money of their own: the purchase price of $203,000 was financed by bank loans. One of the participating banks concluded the credit risk was "minimal" because McDougal had past business ties with former senator J. William Fulbright.[5] (Thus did many things in Arkansas work.)

For the first two years, the Clintons—Hillary wrote all the checks—paid money to McDougal to cover interest payments to the bank. But by the summer of 1980, it had become "pretty obvi-ous" to McDougal that the Clintons expected him to handle all of Whitewater's finances and management.[6]

THE 1980 PRESIDENTIAL ELECTION had been a heartbreaker for the Democratic Party. Ronald Reagan's defeat of President Jimmy Carter launched a twelve-year Republican reign in Washington. As if that outcome were not depressing enough for the Clintons, Bill had lost his reelection bid for governor that November, a humbling defeat that he would later describe as a near-death experience.[7] Her husband's failure left the thirty-three-year-old Hillary in tears; Dorothy Rodham would tell a reporter in 1992 that it was the only time she saw her daughter cry as an adult.[8] Bill's defeat must have seemed an unimaginable roadblock, one that neither he nor Hillary had envisioned when they set off on their twenty-year project. Hillary was shedding tears not only for Bill's future but for her future too.

For months after his defeat, Bill wallowed in bouts of depression and self-absorption. At only thirty-four years old, he seemed listless and adrift. It was Hillary's job to buck him up and try to reignite his political adrenaline. Hillary had "an uncanny knack for keeping me focused on the present and the future," Bill observed years later, and that job may never have been as difficult as it was during the first few months of 1981.[9] As recalled by McDougal, Hillary herself put it more bluntly: "Bill wouldn't have amounted to anything if I hadn't kicked his ass."[10] Bill would later be labeled the "Comeback Kid," but it was Hillary who carefully plotted, then orchestrated his political resurrection.

Bill's stunning loss might not have happened in the first place if Hillary had been able to devote more time and attention to his campaign that year. After giving birth to Chelsea on February 27, 1980, Hillary remained largely on the sidelines until the final few weeks of the campaign.

Reporters rarely saw her at events on the campaign trail that year. When she finally joined the fray, she immediately tried to take charge to turn things around, but by then it was too late. Voters resented Bill for raising the tax on car registrations, and Arkansas had become a dumping ground for Cuban refugees who had come to the United States in the Mariel boatlift and whose riot and escape from a federal resettlement camp provided fodder for Bill's Republican opponent, Frank White. During the campaign's closing weeks, White had aired a series of negative ads that Hillary had initially downplayed.[11] Though she eventually tried to play defense by going on offense, hoping to "hit back" and not let the charges "go unchallenged," the damage had been done.[12] With the wounds, Hillary said that she came to understand "the piercing power of negative ads to convert voters through distortion."[13]

In the last ten days of the campaign, Hillary attempted to orchestrate the media's coverage of her husband by trying to get a local reporter, John Brummett, to cover Bill's appearance at a crucial campaign stop.[14] Brummett had already been following Clinton while another reporter had been on the campaign trail with White. Brummett felt uncomfortable with "Hillary's controlling nature."[15] "I didn't need to have my assignment dictated by the governor's wife," he said, relaying his unease to his editor, who then assigned the other reporter to the event. Near the end of the campaign, both Clintons "were scared to the point of making sure they got the friendliest reporters."[16]

A fearful Hillary made a last-minute plea to Dick Morris, the political strategist, who had been sitting out this campaign, to conduct a quick survey of the bleak landscape.[17] Morris had first worked for Bill in 1978, helping him win the gubernatorial race. But he was not popular with Bill's more idealistic staff. One of them, Nancy Pietrafesa, confronted Hillary in the kitchen of the Clintons' house, demanding to know why she and Bill were relying on Morris. "This guy is poison," Pietrafesa told Hillary.

"If you want to be in this kind of business," Hillary replied, "this is the kind of person you have to deal with."

Pietrafesa replied, "Are you kidding me?" Pietrafesa later recalled, "Her attitude was, 'Get over it.'"[18]

Two years later, only Hillary and Morris recognized how poorly Bill was really doing with the voters in Arkansas. "I couldn't persuade anyone to ignore the polls that showed Bill winning," she wrote in her autobiography.[19] As a result, the election night gloom was made worse for many of Bill's supporters, who had remained in blissful ignorance.

The day after Bill's defeat, Hillary made the call to bring back Dick Morris to resuscitate her husband. In addition, she contacted Betsey Wright, the Democratic operative she knew from the McGovern campaign in Texas, to ask her to help organize Bill's files for a political comeback.[20]

Hillary also saw more clearly than Bill that if his political career was going to be rebuilt, it would have to happen in Arkansas, not Washington. Recognizing the strategic merit of this, Bill became counsel to a Little Rock law firm, a job that was not too taxing while affording him the flexibility that he would need to return to the political game.

It wasn't all Bill in terms of the changes to come. The fact that Hillary used her maiden name was increasingly perceived as an issue in the Clinton camp, where some saw it as a political strait-jacket for Bill. A few months after the election, over a breakfast of instant grits, in the tiny kitchen of the new house they bought in Little Rock after leaving the governor's mansion, Hillary heard a pitch from Vernon Jordan, by then a confidant of the Clintons. Jordan told her, "You're in the South. And in the South, you're not Hillary Rodham, you're Mrs. Clinton."[21] Hillary did not argue with that blunt assessment.

"I learned the hard way," she recalled years later, "that some voters in Arkansas were seriously offended by the fact that I kept my maiden name."[22] Ultimately, she decided to change her name to Hillary Rodham Clinton. "I decided it was more important for Bill to be governor again than for me to keep my maiden name," she wrote in her autobiography.[23] Whatever Hillary may have personally felt as a feminist who came of age in the 1960s and 1970s, her devotion to Bill's political ambitions — which also meant her own political ambitions — outweighed all else. "There's an irony in all of this," mused Pietrafesa. "Talk about a supportive spouse. There wasn't a minute in her life she didn't support his efforts."[24]

The comeback attempt worked brilliantly, and by 1983, Bill and Hillary were once again living in the governor's mansion. Governor Clinton quickly asked the legislature to let Hillary head an effort to improve the quality of the public education system, one of the state's most intractable problems.

Bill acknowledged that his selection of his wife guaranteed he would "have a person who is closer to me than anyone else over-seeing a project that is more important to me than anything else."[25] Hillary said she viewed the education job as "politically risky" because it would mean having to push for an increase in taxes. She was reluctant to do it, she wrote in her autobiography, but "eventually I relented" after "Bill wouldn't take no for an answer."[26] That was her version. When asked years later how Hillary wound up leading the panel, Bill told an opposite story. He said it was Hillary's idea to chair the committee. "She said, 'I think I'd like to be it,'" Bill recalled, adding that he was not convinced it was a smart idea. He reminded Hillary that she had just taken off eight months from her law practice to help get him reelected. But she stood her ground. "Yeah, but this may be the most important thing you ever do," she told him, "and you have to do it right."[27]

"Doing it right" to Hillary meant putting Hillary in charge.

Almost immediately, she had her hands full. In nearly every national measure of economic and social status, Arkansas ranked at or near the bottom, and education was no different.[28] When Hillary's committee released its first report in September 1983, she did not try to sugarcoat the state's problems. "Our schools are not doing as good a job as they must," she said at a press conference. "We Arkansans have to quit making excuses and accept instead the challenge of excellence once and for all."[29]

As a solution, Bill proposed a one-cent increase in the state sales tax, coupled with a controversial recommendation that had come from Hillary and her committee: teacher testing. Hillary appeared before a special session of the legislature and defended her panel's work, including the proposal for competence testing. She received enthusiastic reviews. One representative, Lloyd George of Yell County, said at the time, "It looks like we might have elected the wrong Clinton."[30] Few paid attention to the fact that her original standards committee had not actually suggested imposing teacher testing "but had only addressed the issue in vague terms."[31]

One group that did pay attention was the Arkansas Education Association, which tried to block the measure in the Arkansas Senate. In the end, however, the legislature gave the Clintons what they wanted, and the effort was widely seen as a success. Along the way, Hillary had shown political acumen by wooing and then winning over one of her chief critics in the press, John Robert Starr, the managing editor of the *Arkansas Democrat*. Starr even told another Arkansas journalist that he "reassessed" Bill Clinton after meeting Hillary and becoming "so impressed" by her in 1982.[32] Starr came to believe, if somewhat crudely, that Hillary had "been the balls behind Bill Clinton quite often."[33]

Hillary gave herself high marks on the education effort: "Arkansas had a plan in place to raise school standards, tens of thousands of children had a better chance to realize their learning potential, and teachers got a desperately needed raise in pay."[34] Even her one-time ally, then relentless critic, Dick Morris, found her education effort praiseworthy, saying she "was never finer" and distinctly moderate.[35] Hillary herself would showcase her education work in Arkansas on her presidential campaign Web site, twice citing her role in helping to "transform the schools" in her former home state.[36]

Hillary soon turned her attention to other causes, as well as to her work at the Rose Law Firm, and, said Starr, not much happened after she moved on.[37] The reform effort, one report later found, had bypassed teachers, and teacher testing was seen as the "least effective reform by far."[38] Still, Hillary's leadership on the education committee would be one of the reasons that Bill would choose her to lead his health care task force in the first week of his presidency.[39]

BY THE TIME BILL HAD LEFT the governor's office in early 1981, after losing reelection, the Clintons were asking few questions of McDougal, and he was offering them little information. The news, as it turned out, was all bad: Lot sales were sluggish, and interest rates were soaring. The last big check that Hillary wrote for Whitewater, $9,000 in August 1980, was left blank in the "pay to the order of" line. McDougal apparently used it to pay down the principal of a Whitewater bank loan, but the Clintons took the $9,000 as an interest deduction on their tax returns that year, citing McDougal as the payee.[40]

"We gave whatever money we were requested to give by Jim McDougal," Hillary later told reporters. "We just assumed whatever he needed, he would ask for."[41] Asked whether she and her husband should have paid more attention to Whitewater's debts, she replied, "Shoulda, coulda, woulda...we didn't."[42]

In January 1982, McDougal borrowed money and bought a small savings and loan in Arkansas that he renamed Madison Guaranty. He began using it as his personal piggy bank, to illegally foot the bill for Whitewater and other numerous real estate ventures.[43] The Clintons were unaware of McDougal's fraudulent conduct but benefited to the extent that his reductions of the Whitewater loans lowered their liabilities.[44]

By 1985, Madison had brought in the Rose Law Firm and Hillary to do some of its legal work, at a time when the thrift's finances were deteriorating. In 1986, after McDougal was thrown out of his savings and loan by federal regulators and plunged into a deep depression, Hillary assumed control of Whitewater's management, ensuring that the company's taxes were paid on time.[45] That year, McDougal made one last effort to take the Clintons off the hook, offering, in a letter to the couple, to buy them out "because of the high potential embarrassment for you."[46] One incentive for McDougal was to use the losses as a write-off on his taxes. But Hillary said no, taking her usual conservative course. As long as the Clintons remained liable for Whitewater's bank loans, she reasoned, it made no sense to sell the company's stock back to McDougal for him to use as a tax write-off.[47]

Hillary did, however, ask McDougal to remove the Clintons' names from the mortgage.[48] He refused. Hillary then asked for the corporate records, since she and Bill were still liable for any losses. She found them in disarray. Hillary subsequently asked herself why she and Bill had invested so much trust in McDougal and so little actual oversight of the venture itself. "I had no reason to question McDougal," she wrote in her autobiography, adding that "I kept paying whatever McDougal said we owed and tended to the more important demands in my life."[49]

Soon after taking over the company's books, Hillary managed to squeeze a little more money from Whitewater, a profit of $1,640 for her and Bill, by selling a small lot that had been used for a model home.[50] But she soon realized that "Whitewater was a fiasco" the couple needed to escape.[51]

It took nearly five years, until 1990, to gather the necessary paperwork and pay the relevant taxes.[52] Not surprisingly, Hillary's dim view of McDougal only intensified over that time. In 1990, she "talked Bill out of" being a character witness for McDougal at a federal criminal trial, where he was charged with bank fraud tied to Madison.[53] Later, as the possibility of buying up McDougal's share in the venture was being discussed, Hillary complained bitterly about paying anything more to someone who had brought her such bad luck. "I'm not paying a dime to that guy," she told one associate.[54]

The investigations of Madison subsided by 1991, and McDougal was acquitted. Whitewater, by all accounts, had ended up a money-losing venture for everyone. But the firestorm over McDougal's business activities would soon reignite.

IF HILLARY WAS DOWN on her real estate partner McDougal, she had nothing but praise for her commodities guide, Jim Blair. "She loved Jim Blair," recalled a friend of Hillary's. "Blair was her money man."[55]

Hillary and Blair had become good friends back in Fayetteville. Blair, a dozen years older than Hillary, was a top-notch attorney and someone with a knack for making money. He spent most of his life in politically conservative northern Arkansas, but he considered himself a "limousine liberal."[56] Blair and Hillary once won a tennis trophy playing together in a doubles tournament at Fayetteville Country Club.[57]

Despite all his success, Blair woke up one day in 1977 and said to himself, "This is not how I want to spend my life."[58] At the time, he was doing legal work for Tyson Foods, among other clients, and later became the poultry giant's outside counsel. He decided to try commodities trading as an exit strategy to "make enough money to quit," a sum that he put at $4 million.[59] About that time, a colorful commodities broker and client of Blair's, Robert "Red" Bone, called Blair and told him to stop by the office he ran in nearby Springdale — Refco — so he could fill him in on a hot tip.

Under Bone's direction, the Refco branch office had become a "money machine for everyone," including brokers who made tens of thousands of dollars a month in commissions.[60] A disparate band of clients, from farmers to lawyers and bankers, frequented the office. Now Bone had some "good information" relating to the cattle market that he wanted to share. He initially told Blair that in all his "years of trading, which by now had been eight or nine, this was the hottest deal he had ever seen."[61] A convinced Blair stepped into the game, if at first "very gingerly," he'd later recall.[62]

Bone had an unusual résumé. He had played professional poker in Las Vegas. He had held various jobs at Tyson, including a stint as the chairman's bodyguard. And he wasn't afraid to throw money around. Blair once recounted a story to a reporter about a night when Bone and his wife showed up at a pizza parlor just as the employees were putting up the "Closed" sign.[63] He asked for a pizza but was told the oven was shut down. Bone insisted he'd really like a pizza but again got the same answer. Then he offered $500 for the pizza. The answer: "OK, we're open for business."[64]

Bone's poker-playing experience and character extremes, it turns out, were good training for playing the commodities markets. But with commodities you can lose more than just the chips stacked in front of you; you can also lose chips you don't have. Commodity investing is placing a bet on future prices, hence the name: futures markets. The volatile game is not for the risk averse; three out of four investors lose money trading in the commodities markets.[65]

The reason for all the risk is that you have to put up only a small fraction of the price for a contract, say $1,000 for $25,000 worth of beef. A smart—or lucky—bet can pay off handsomely. If, when it comes time to bring your beef to market, its price has gone up 10 percent, to $27,500, you have made $2,500. That's a 150 percent return on your $1,000 investment. But if the price at market has dropped by the same amount, you lose your $1,000 stake and you owe an additional $1,500, or 150 percent of your original investment.

As a result of this leverage, brokers are supposed to require customers to deposit collateral known as "margin" to ensure the broker against being stuck for possible losses on future contracts. But at Red Bone's shop in the late 1970s, things were going so well that they didn't pay close attention to the margin rules.

By the fall of 1978, Blair himself was up $2 million and closing in on his goal of $4 million. "In 1978, I was on a very, very hot streak," Blair later recalled, "and I encouraged my law firm to follow my advice, and I encouraged my friends to open accounts and follow my advice. One of the people I encouraged to set up an account was Hillary Rodham."[66]

By then, Hillary and Bill had developed a very close personal relationship with Blair and his wife-to-be, Diane Kincaid.[67] At their 1979 marriage in Fayetteville, Jim and Diane asked Hillary to stand up for both of them, instead of a best man and a matron of honor. The politically correct Blairs referred to Hillary as their "best person."[68]

Hillary took Blair's advice and opened an account at Refco's Springdale office in October 1978 with a modest $1,000. Things were so loose that her account records even show her name was misspelled as "Hilary Rodham."

In her book, Hillary explained her decision to invest in the commodities market this way: "I was willing to risk $1,000 and let Jim guide my trades through" Red Bone.[69] But Hillary's close friend at the time, Nancy Pietrafesa, found Hillary's eagerness to gamble hard to fathom. "You don't throw a bunch of money into commodities at the age of thirty," Pietrafesa said.[70] But, she added, the investment was a "Blair thing," and Hillary "always touted Blair as someone who could make a lot of money."[71]

Asked by a reporter in April 1994 why she had embarked on such a risky investment, Hillary refused to accept the questioner's premise. "I didn't think it was that big a risk," she said, because Blair "and the people he was talking with knew what they were doing."[72]

She was also at a loss to explain why she had written only a $1,000 check for her first cattle trades when the margin rules at the time required her to deposit far more with her broker. Not only was her opening deposit abnormal, but "on occasion she traded with insufficient margin."[73] The futures trading expert who noted this also pointed out that the firm, not Hillary, had violated the margin rules.

Still, few could dispute the fact that for an investor with so much at risk, given her overall annual income, Hillary was remarkably disengaged. She simply gave the money to Blair and left it at that. Hillary's lawyer confirmed "she was under margin," but denied she received any preferential treatment and noted that "margin is for the protection of the broker."[74]

While disengaged, Hillary was remarkably successful. In the end, over a period of nine months, Hillary parlayed her $1,000 into almost $100,000, an outstanding though not unprecedented run.[75] (When people hit it big in commodities bets, they can hit it really big.) Her trading profits in 1978 and 1979 were duly reported on the Clintons' tax returns, and there was never any official finding that Hillary had done anything wrong. Still, the story of her trading activities would take on a larger life while the Clintons were in the White House. And, as Hillary moved on to the national stage, she would have to play a far more active role in attempting to distance her private business dealings from her public image.

CHAPTER 6

Influence

FOR MOST OF AMERICA'S HISTORY, the world of the female lawyer was a lonely one. At elite law schools, the existence of gender caps was widely suspected during the 1960s, though they were officially and repeatedly denied.[1] Even in 1973, as Hillary was graduating from Yale Law School, she was one of only 29 women in a graduating class of 178.[2] Nationwide, women made up an even smaller percentage of law school graduates, about 7 percent.[3] As late as the early 1970s, the percentage of practicing lawyers who were women hovered around 3 percent.[4] And in Arkansas, the prospects for female lawyers were even grimmer. In the late nineteenth century, the state bar banned women from joining it, meaning they could not appear in courtrooms. The ban lasted forty-four years, until it was lifted in 1917.[5]

By the 1960s and 1970s, as social unrest challenged established norms everywhere, a revolt also swept the American legal community. One of the revolt's trailblazers was Brooksley Born, a young attorney at Arnold and Porter, a pillar of the Washington establishment. In the early 1970s, Born and others founded a women's caucus at the American Bar Association, an organization she considered "very male and patriarchal."[6]

The determined band of women, who had been pioneers at their law schools and were part of the larger social movement sweeping the country, turned to Washington for help. In 1972, Congress passed a series of educational amendments, one of which, Title IX, banned sexual discrimination in higher education, including at professional and graduate schools. These laws are best known for creating an explosion in women's participation in collegiate sports, but they quietly changed the face of the legal profession. (By 2006, for example, the percentage of female students enrolled in the first-year class at Yale Law School was 46 percent.)[7]

Brooksley Born spent much of the 1970s and early 1980s spearheading women's issues within the bar association. Through the work of the caucus, she helped pave the way for the bar association's adoption in 1986 of Goal IX, a resolution intended "to promote full and equal participation in the profession by minorities and women."[8] Encapsulated in the resolution's passage was the belief that it was time for a new generation to lead the next stage of the effort.

Given her activist background and take-charge disposition, Hillary would have seemed a natural to take up the baton. Yet at first she was ambivalent about helping to lead the fight against her profession's glass ceiling.

In a sign of how far the revolution had come, the entreaty for Hillary to join the cause came in the second half of 1986 from a most unlikely source: Eugene Thomas, a conservative Republican lawyer from Boise, Idaho, who was then president-elect of the American Bar Association. With the adoption of Goal IX, Thomas was looking for someone to chair a follow-up commission. He viewed Hillary as a "strong leader and a bright woman.... I thought that was a fit."[9]

But when he offered her the chairmanship, she declined it.[10] He was disappointed with her decision, but he said he understood. Although Hillary never explained why she turned down Thomas, he had his own theory: He had wanted the commission to cover both minorities and women, but many women wanted separate inquiries. "To be candid with you," he explained twenty years later, "the leaders of the women's movement in the ABA, and she was one, didn't like being homogenized into Goal Nine's pot and stew."[11]

Thomas knew Hillary from her tenure at the Legal Services Corporation, a federally funded corporation that distributes grants to local programs that provide free legal services to the poor. President Carter had nominated her to the corporation's board in 1977, and she went on to become its first chairwoman the following year. Hillary had already worked on behalf of lower-income clients, but her work for Carter's 1976 presidential campaign was also a key factor behind her nomination for the chairmanship.[12]

Some Republicans in Congress viewed the corporation with deep suspicion, believing some of its local programs had strayed too far into social and political activism. But Hillary helped the Legal Services Corporation win budget increases from Congress. After Ronald Reagan became president in 1981, the corporation had to confront an uncertain future. Reagan had cut state funding for the program when he was governor of California. Thomas had used his Republican contacts in the White House and on Capitol Hill to help fend off the corporation's most vehement opponents, which was how the Boise conservative and the Little Rock liberal came to know each other.[13]

Years later, conservative biographers of Hillary would cite her tenure at the Legal Services Corporation, which ended in 1982, as proof of her leftist agenda. One author called her activities a "skillful bureaucratic manipulation from inside" the establishment in pursuit of her "radicalism."[14] But Hillary defied easy or short labels. She sometimes advocated causes opposed by liberal lawyers working for legal services, such as enlisting the private bar to donate more of its services to the poor, displacing nonprofit groups.[15] One board member who later became her friend, Mickey Kantor, initially saw Hillary as a chairwoman who was too mainstream and cozy with the establishment.[16] "From my perspective, she was very moderate," Kantor said. "I was a flamethrower."[17]

AS BILL GEARED UP to face reelection in 1986, this time, thanks to changes in the Arkansas state constitution, seeking a four-year term, he saw Hillary's work on education as an important part of his platform.

The 1986 campaign was the first one Chelsea was old enough to understand. Hillary told her six-year-old daughter that people might "be saying terrible things about" her father, even "lies."[18] But it was Chelsea's mother who would be the target of most of the sharpest attacks by Bill's opponents.

Hillary's rejuvenated law career had become an occasional sticking point. Specifically, questions about her income at the Rose Law Firm and the firm's business dealings with the state were raised by Clinton's opponents, first in the Democratic primary and later in the general election. With Bill's help, Hillary would manage to dodge the bullet.

In 1984, the Public Service Commission, mired in a protracted and expensive legal battle over the costs to Arkansas ratepayers of a nuclear power plant, had retained the Rose Law Firm to help litigate the case. Over the next two years, the firm signed five contracts with the Public Service Commission, netting Rose fees of just over $150,000.[19]

In September 1986, Frank White, once again the Republican candidate for governor, began running radio ads that tried to make the case that the Clintons had a conflict of interest because Hillary was a member of the law firm that her husband's administration had hired. Bill and White then argued about the issue in a televised debate.

"The money the state paid to the Rose firm was subtracted from the firm's income before Hillary's partnership profits were calculated," Bill stated, "so she made no money from it."[20] Bill also deflected White's attacks by asking him if he wanted to run for First Lady instead of governor.[21]

These arguments resonated. Based on her percentage of firm profits at the time, Hillary would have made only a few thousand dollars, at most, from the work. In addition, White had his own potential conflict of interest; he had worked for Stephens Inc., the company that had long dominated the state's bond business. And Bill's line about running for First Lady prompted bumper stickers and buttons saying, "Frank for First Lady."[22] White was further "embarrassed when the facts established that other Arkansas law firms had received significantly more business from the state while Bill was Governor," Hillary later wrote.[23]

Others quietly grumbled. Jim Guy Tucker, a longtime adversary and Bill's successor as governor after he became president, told investigators that he and other lawyers in Arkansas believed that Rose enjoyed an unfair advantage with state agencies such as the Public Service Commission.[24] In the eyes of the voters, the relationship became a nonissue, but after White's unsuccessful potshot in 1986, Hillary decided to deal with it once and for all. Her public account of how she did so is misleading, if not incorrect.

In her autobiography, she wrote that "after Bill became Governor again in 1983, I asked my law partners to calculate my share of profits, without including any fees earned by other lawyers for work done for the state or any state agency."[25] Some of Rose's top lawyers believe that the firm's policy of walling off Hillary from state fees was actually adopted in 1979, after Hillary became a partner and Bill became governor.[26] Vince Foster, Hillary's close ally, reported to Bill's presidential campaign in 1992 that "segregating State fees" had "always been the firm policy."[27]

In fact, law firm records show that Hillary didn't ask the firm to segregate her share of the state business until a few years after the date she claims in her book and only two months after White's unsuccessful attack. In a previously undisclosed memo to the Rose Law Firm partners, Hillary asked that the firm "segregate all fees earned in 1986 and hereafter" and distribute them "so that I do not share in them directly or indirectly."[28] The memo also disclosed that she had benefited in the past from fees earned from state-related business while Bill was serving as governor, a finding contrary to what some of her colleagues thought was the case. The criticism by White, Hillary explained in her memo, was unfair because the firm had done state business long before her husband was sworn in as governor. "While I do not even do state-related business, and have never done any paid work of any kind for the State, I do not want to be used as a reason for denying the Firm business it is qualified to perform," she wrote her partners.[29]

Eventually Hillary rectified the situation by repaying her share of past state fees "in any year Bill served as Governor," which she calculated as $12,235.83.[30] She also signed a promissory note for another $10,510.03, which was her share of fees earned by the firm as underwriter's counsel for state bond issues.[31]

In the scheme of things, spread across several years, the total sum was modest. But the issue was not just money. It gnawed at Hillary that she was coming under fire because of whom she was married to. And her reluctance to disclose minor unpleasantness would be a recurring habit — in Arkansas and in Washington.

DESPITE THE SIMMERING QUESTION of just how much of Hillary's work at Rose had been either inspired by or constrained by her being married to the governor, by 1986 Hillary's future was nothing if not bright. She had helped her husband win reelection. She joined the board of directors of Wal-Mart. And she became chairman of the Children's Defense Fund, the liberal advocacy group based in Washington. By the next year, 1987, she was named to head a prestigious national commission on women in the law. She had clearly parlayed a less-than-full-time practice in Arkansas into a national platform that transcended ideology and geography.

By 1987, as Thomas assumed the ABA presidency, his successor-in-waiting became Robert Mac Crate, a moderate, Rockefeller Republican. Born and raised in Brooklyn, Mac Crate had worked early in his career as counsel to New York governor Nelson Rockefeller. By then, it was clear that a separate commission that would study only women lawyers, and not minorities, would be created. Mac Crate set about that spring to find someone to chair the group. First he turned to Shirley Hufstedler, a former federal judge and President Carter's secretary of education. She turned him down. "Bob," she said, "you need a younger woman. You want a role model."[32]

So Mac Crate went back to the drawing board. He asked the director of the office of the president, Harriet Wilson Ellis, who worked for Thomas, for suggestions. She quickly recommended Hillary.[33]

"I don't know who she is," Mac Crate told Ellis.[34]

"She's the First Lady of Arkansas, and I worked with her at the Legal Services Corporation," replied Ellis. "She's going to go far."[35]

Mac Crate soon warmed to Ellis's suggestion after researching Hillary's credentials in Legal Services Corporation circles. His final reassurance was the Rose Law Firm connection: Rose's founder, Uriah Rose, had been one of the organizers of the bar association in 1876.

After completing his due diligence, Mac Crate thought the appointment of Hillary amounted to a "ten strike," but he still had some selling to do.[36] "I called Hillary on the phone," he recalled. "We had never met. We had never talked. I said I was forming this commission and wanted her to head it. She said, 'I've never done anything like that. I've been devoted to children and education.'"[37] Hearing her hesitancy, Mac Crate suggested she talk to several people that he was considering for the commission.

Meanwhile, Ellis weighed in with Hillary. "I don't think I want to do it," Hillary told her former colleague.[38] The time commitment worried her. There was a lot going on in Hillary's life. Her responsibilities included practicing law and raising her seven-year-old daughter. She was also serving on the boards of two liberal non-profit groups based on the East Coast: the New World Foundation and the Children's Defense Fund. Indeed, the fund had just picked her to be its chairwoman. She regularly attended fund board meetings, even though the trip from Little Rock to Washington was time-consuming and exhausting.[39] She had founded the Arkansas Advocates for Children and Families. She introduced a home-instruction program for preschool youth. She led legal aid efforts on the state and national level, directed prison projects, and chaired a rural health initiative in Arkansas.

Hillary even managed to insert her causes into corporate board-rooms, no small accomplishment. On the Wal-Mart board, she became the company's first female director and one of the few partners at the Rose firm to accept an outside position. As a Wal-Mart director, she pushed for nondiscriminatory hiring practices and increased sensitivity to the environment.[40] (Later, as a senator, Hillary kept her distance from the company and its critics after it became more controversial.)[41]

While Hillary was presented with this offer, Bill was also mulling over a run for president. But, in July 1987, he decided to take a pass. "Much has been written about the reasons for his decision not to run," Hillary observed. "But it finally came down to one word — Chelsea."[42]

Chelsea was a major concern for Hillary, too, as she was deliberating whether to accept the bar association job. But even with all her other responsibilities, friends like Ellis advised her that she would just have to find a way to do it all. "I said to her, 'You can make a big difference, and it wouldn't take up as much time as you think,'" Ellis said.[43]

Chelsea was the reason that Bill didn't run for president, but she was not reason enough for Hillary to turn down the bar association job, which would, not incidentally, get her out of Arkansas and allow her to assume a prestigious national platform that was not connected to her husband while continuing her pursuit of a lifelong cause.

Hillary finally told Mac Crate she would do it. When he advised Brooksley Born, who was still an activist on the issue, of his selection, she drew a blank on Hillary's name, as he initially had. She asked him: Hillary? Who is Hillary? Mac Crate described her as "the wife of the governor of Arkansas."[44] Born found herself appalled at hearing a professional woman described as someone's wife, as if that was the sole reason for her appointment.

It wasn't until a few months later, in October 1987, that Mac Crate met Hillary for the first time. The commission had gathered for its initial meeting in Chicago, the bar association's home. Mac Crate began by reading a speech his father, a congressman, gave in 1919 in support of woman suffrage. The Rockefeller Republican and the Arkansas Democrat immediately hit it off. (Mac Crate later changed his voter registration from Republican to Democrat, contributed thousands of dollars to Hillary's Senate campaigns, and put framed photos of Hillary in his New York office.)

The commission quickly got to work, holding hearings and examining the practices of law firms on issues like hiring patterns and maternity leave. It found widespread discrimination and after one year issued a report urging the bar association to publicly recognize that gender bias exists in the profession and to begin to eliminate it.[45]

At its annual convention in Toronto in 1988, the American Bar Association responded to the work of Hillary's commission by adopting a resolution that committed the association and its 346,000 members to "refuse to participate in, acquiesce in, or condone barriers to the full integration and equal participation of women in the legal profession."[46] The voice vote of approval was virtually unanimous. Hillary told the delegates that the commission's work was far from done. "Despite the progress that has been made," she said, "there still exist instances of subtle discrimination against women."[47] So in 1991, near the end of Hillary's chairmanship, the group created the Goal IX Report Card, an annual accounting designed to measure the progress of women in the association. For Born, this was "a wonderful device" to measure diversity within different sections of the ABA.[48] For conservative critics, the report card became an ideological hot button and was even seen by some as a surreptitious attempt to institute "quotas."[49]

WHILE HILLARY WAS FIRING on all cylinders, the same could not be said for her husband. The notion that Bill Clinton could run out of political gas seems inconceivable today, given what is known about his passion for official life, his zeal for the spotlight, and his almost invincible ability to overcome the greatest of controversies. But in 1987, Bill seemed to be on the ropes. And because of it, or perhaps despite it, Hillary was poised for the first time to dip her toes into the political waters.

Bill had already decided in 1987 to forgo a presidential run the next year. Before his decision, Betsey Wright had gone over with Bill a list of women with whom he had allegedly had affairs; she asked Bill for the truth and what the women might say. After hearing his response, she recommended that he not run.[50] There were rampant rumors in Arkansas about Bill's affairs, and Hillary was aware of them.[51] Bill recalled that "Hillary was relieved" and "happy" at his decision not to run because she thought he should finish his work in Arkansas and that George H. W. Bush would win anyway.[52]

By 1990, two years after he bombed on national television during a speech at the Democratic National Convention in Atlanta, Bill still had not decided whether to run for reelection in Arkansas. Enter Hillary, who told Dick Morris that she said to Bill, "If you're not gonna run, I wanna run."[53] Morris talked about it with a sympathetic Bill. "She's always deferred to my career," Bill told Morris. "Now it's her turn."[54]

But when Morris did two polls for Hillary, the results were not encouraging. "I came to the conclusion that she could not win because at that point nobody felt that she was separate from Bill," Morris recalled. Arkansans didn't see the Clintons as they saw themselves. Hillary was "very offended" by the notion of being Bill's surrogate, so "from that moment on, she determined that she would carve out her own identity in her own political image."[55]

This tension between the benefits of being so closely associated with her husband and Hillary's own desire for an independent career would remain a central dilemma for her and Bill. She might have been a bit audacious to imagine that she could become governor of his native state, but no one could begrudge her desire to escape his large shadow. She did not want to always be known as the "First Lady of Arkansas."

Realizing that, whatever he thought, the voters were not ready for his wife, Bill finally threw his hat in the Arkansas voters' ring one more time. His popularity by that point made his primary victory a pretty sure thing. Hillary managed to engineer the "only dramatic moment" when she showed up unannounced at a press conference in the state capitol rotunda that was called by Bill's main Democratic opponent, Tom McRae. At the beginning of the press conference, McRae showed a cartoon of a nude Bill Clinton, his hands covering his crotch, with the title: "The Emperor Has No Clothes."[56]

"All of the sudden, I hear these loud heels coming up the marble steps — it was her," recalled Ron Fournier, who covered the press conference for the AP. "All the cameras swung around to film her. She took over McRae's press conference."[57]

"Get off it, Tom!" Hillary shouted at McRae.[58] Waving a sheaf of papers, Hillary read out a number of McRae's previous statements praising Bill's record as governor. "I went through all your reports,"

Hillary told him, "because I've really been disappointed in you as a candidate, and I've been really disappointed in you as a person, Tom."[59]

Hillary's surprise attack caused a splash in the Arkansas press, and it triggered more than a few ripples in a state where voters assumed that a governor's wife should be satisfied by remaining behind the scenes. But it worked. "She came in at the right time, swinging the ax, and not just a little," Fournier recalled.[60] Bill wrote about the episode in his memoirs, acknowledging that Hillary's attack helped him cruise to victory in the primary by breaking "McRae's momentum."[61]

The McRae confrontation proved Hillary had learned an important lesson from the 1980 loss to White: the need to counterattack aggressively, fearlessly, and immediately. Her sudden appearance at the press conference was far from spontaneous. She had talked about it with her husband the night before,[62] and she knew that showing up would "get a lot of publicity."[63]

The McRae confrontation also proved another lesson, one Hillary would have a much harder time learning: Try as she might, to many she came off as grating, a schoolmarm snapping about undone homework.

Bill's 1990 reelection campaign would end up being relatively uneventful. But it sowed seeds of resentment among Bill's enemies that would dog the Clintons for years to come.

Bill's Republican opponent in the general election was Sheffield Nelson, a lawyer and wealthy businessman. His last-minute ads attacking Clinton's tax and budget policies forced Hillary and Bill to personally borrow $100,000 to help mount a media counterattack.[64] Nelson later told a television interviewer that his 1990 campaign had gathered information about Clinton's moral character, but he had declined to use the material in the campaign.[65] Hillary, on the same show, replied that Nelson had "been out beating the bushes trying to stir" up questions about Bill's womanizing,[66] calling Nelson "a very bitter man" who, after his defeat in 1990, had done everything possible "to try and get even."[67] All of that might have been true, but further agitating someone willing to spend his own money to dig up dirt on Bill was not necessarily the wisest strategy—especially when there was, at least when it came to women, plenty of Arkansas dirt to till.

Hillary helped create another foe during the 1990 campaign when she convinced Bill not to testify as a character witness in Jim

McDougal's savings and loan fraud trial that year.[68] McDougal was acquitted, and he subsequently threatened Hillary in connection with their Whitewater business deal.[69] It was hard to know how much damage he could do. McDougal was a deeply troubled man, taking medication for depression. He remained somewhat loyal to Bill, but after his acquittal his views about Hillary darkened.[70] She could hardly imagine in 1990 what McDougal and Nelson and the other enemies of the Clintons would do "to try and get even." It wouldn't be too long before she would find out.

BIAS AGAINST FEMALE LAWYERS remained a problem through the 1980s and 1990s, but during that stretch, Hillary became one of the "most influential or powerful" members of her profession in part because of her gender. In 1988, the *National Law Journal*, a small but prestigious and influential newspaper, named Hillary to its "Profiles in Power," a list of the one hundred most influential or powerful lawyers.[71] She was only one of four women to be honored. (Shirley Hufstedler, Mac Crate's first choice to head the bar association commission, was another.) In its preface to the 1988 profiles, the paper said that its list honored only lawyers "actively involved in the practice or teaching of law."[72] The editor and reporter responsible for the 1988 list are deceased, so a definitive reconstruction of the selection process is not possible. But another editor involved in compiling the list says that Hillary was specifically selected because the journal was looking for a woman involved in corporate litigation. In fact, by Hillary's own account, she was a part-time corporate litigator. Her trial record was sparse and certainly not stellar. She was the lowest-paid partner at a firm in a city located far from the commercial centers of America. Peggy Cronin Fisk, the reporter who wrote the *National Law Journal*'s 1991 profiles, acknowledged later that the label didn't fit. "She was not what I consider to be a topflight litigator or what anybody would consider to be a topflight litigator," Fisk said.[73]

"It was because she was a woman who was a corporate lawyer, and there weren't a lot of women doing that," recalled Anthony Paonita, now an editor for another legal publication, *The American Lawyer*.[74] "We were looking for juice," he explained. Plus, he added, "She just wasn't a political lawyer doing abortion or children's rights cases, the typical things women attorneys did then."[75]

Three years later, the newspaper again chose America's one hundred most influential lawyers. Again, Hillary made the list. Fisk said that by then Hillary's inclusion was based largely "on her work with the ABA, and the work she did on behalf of women's issues in the law."[76] Her editor, Doreen Weisenhaus, concurred with that view. "She played a role on the national stage for the legal profession and for children's and women's rights," Weisenhaus said. "That satisfied me."[77] However it was that she wound up being chosen as one of America's most powerful lawyers, Hillary skillfully used the law journal listing to burnish her résumé for the political world, beginning with her husband's 1992 presidential campaign and later in her 2000 bid to become a senator from New York. Occasionally, both Hillary and the press would misidentify the law journal's list as the "best" or "top" one hundred lawyers, even though the journal carefully explained that the list was not that kind of a survey. One 1992 campaign memo told aides, "HRC wants to make sure we are prepared to cite her *National Law Journal* Best Lawyer list."[78] By 2000, after Hillary's campaign biography again boasted that she was selected as one of the one hundred "top" lawyers in the nation by the *National Law Journal*, the paper's editor in chief chided her for the mistake. "Our quibble is with her use of the word 'top,'"[79] wrote editor in chief Patrick Oster, during Hillary's 2000 Senate campaign. "To us," Oster explained, the word *top* "implies 'best' or 'smartest,' but Mrs. Clinton was instead rated one of the most 'influential' lawyers" based on the "notion of power or impact."[80] (The final insult for Oster was that Hillary's own Web site misidentified the ranking as being compiled by a sister publication, *The American Lawyer* magazine.)

Such differences might seem trivial to outsiders, but they spoke to a larger trend: Hillary's career as a practicing lawyer had been, by many standards, underwhelming, but it would not have been politically convenient to admit so. Yet her exaggeration was ultimately unnecessary, more a sign of her own insecurity and calculation. In the end, while far from the "best" corporate litigator, Hillary certainly proved that she did have the influence that the *National Law Journal* had ascribed to her in 1991. Indeed, the next year, she helped her husband defeat an incumbent president. Eight years later, she easily won a United States Senate seat from an adopted home state.

The 1991 survey was prescient in another way: Joining Hillary on the list was a bespectacled Washington lawyer named Kenneth W. Starr.

PART TWO

First Lady

I think you can bloom wherever you're planted, if you put enough effort into it.

— Hillary Rodham Clinton

CHAPTER 7

The Defense Team

JAMES CARVILLE'S CAMPAIGN ANTICS during Bill Clinton's presidential run in 1992 were turned into political legend by *The War Room*, the documentary that was primarily filmed at Clinton's campaign headquarters in the old Arkansas Gazette newspaper building in Little Rock. The film's codirector, D. A. Pennebaker, a master of the cinema verité style, brilliantly captured the strategy sessions at the center of Governor Clinton's chaotic bid for the White House. Among the film's highlights were Carville's down-home bonhomie — "The country is going 'el busto," the Ragin' Cajun drawls gleefully — and a scene in which a fresh-faced George Stephanopoulos snaps, "You will be laughed at," into the phone at a political blackmailer who, on the eve of the election, threatens to reveal one of Bill's sexual indiscretions.

But not far from the cameras, in a simple one-story, flat-roofed cinder-block building, just a quick jaunt across a back alley, the campaign's real high-stakes action was taking place. Inside that building, nicknamed "the bunker" by campaign aides, the most perilous assignment of Clinton's presidential quest fell to a handful of mostly anonymous workers, many of whom were women.[1] They were known simply as "the Defense Team." It was an appropriate label for a group whose mission included defending Bill Clinton's twelve-year record as the governor of Arkansas, though that qualified as one of their easier tasks. The team was also expected to help defend Clinton from attacks against his personal behavior, including his alleged affairs with women and his careful avoidance of the military draft and the Vietnam War. The team was additionally charged with an equally delicate assignment: defending Hillary's professional record and her ethical conduct as a partner at the Rose Law Firm. The Defense Team was to act like a hard-boiled PI — find the clues, gather the facts, be unafraid to throw a hard punch — with one distinction: they were to do all of this stealthily, invisibly, without anyone except a tiny group of Clinton insiders ever knowing what they were up to. Their secret work would be overseen by Hillary.

A previously undisclosed campaign memo, prepared on March 25, 1992, identified more than seventy-five "issues facing the defense team," ranging from Bill Clinton's "personal hits" to problems in state-related legal work done by Hillary.[2] Her presence on the list was more than noticeable: Roughly two-thirds of the issues were matters relating to both Hillary and Bill or to Hillary alone. Many of the joint issues involved tax returns and financial disclosure reports. Eighteen of the issues solely involved Hillary's work at the Rose firm, some under the heading "Appearance of Influence through HRC."

The overwhelming nature of the task became immediately clear to Diane Blair, an early member of the Defense Team and Hillary's closest friend in Arkansas. Blair was a fifty-three-year-old political science professor at the University of Arkansas. Years later, Blair said she believed that Hillary considered her to be the sister that she never had.[3] For her, then, defending the Clintons was virtually a family matter.

There was much to defend, and not enough time, or people, to do the defending. When David Ifshin, the campaign's counsel, went to the governor's mansion in the fall of 1991 to discuss the possibility of preempting the press by disclosing a number of potential liabilities, Bill's rejection of the idea stunned him. Ifshin remembered Bill telling him, "I can't open my closet.... I'll get crushed by the skeletons."[4] Thus the job at hand became not one of calculated exposure but of diligent burial.

In March 1992, the campaign also put out an SOS to Betsey Wright, Bill's former aide, to come back to Little Rock from Harvard, where she was a fellow at the John F. Kennedy School of Government. Inside the Defense Team bunker, Wright established a special "box room" stocked with towers of the most sensitive files, including Bill's personal records and material from his years in public office.[5] In the bunker, Diane Blair assembled a hardworking, dedicated team of researchers, mostly recent college graduates, whom she dubbed, irrespective of gender, the "Box Boys."

Wright had a key to the room, but both Bill and Hillary ultimately controlled her work, as well as that of Blair and the others inside the bunker.[6] No one knew her husband's strengths and weaknesses better than Hillary, so it was a foregone conclusion that she would manage the Defense Team's handling of questions raised not only about Bill's public and private life but also about her own professional career. All of this was part of a wide-ranging and groundbreaking portfolio for the spouse of a presidential candidate. "She was a major player in that campaign, not just another staff person, but as a personality in her own right," the campaign's chairman, Mickey Kantor, said.[7] He added that "decisions were not made without her input because she had a clear view of him and what he wanted to accomplish."[8]

Less by choice than by necessity, Hillary was forced to turn campaign protocol on its head. Traditionally, a candidate's wife deferred to a candidate's senior strategists, especially when confronting difficult questions posed by reporters. But Hillary tightly controlled her own movements and message, assembling her own personal staff of several paid aides and simultaneously seeking the advice of dozens of close friends from around the country. "I was different," she later wrote of her oversize role in the 1992 campaign, "something that would become increasingly apparent in the months ahead."[9]

Hillary's defense activities ranged from the inspirational to the microscopic to the down and dirty. She received memos about the status of various press inquiries;[10] she vetted senior campaign aides;[11] and she listened to a secretly recorded audiotape of a phone conversation of Clinton critics plotting their next attack. The tape contained discussions of another woman who might surface with allegations about an affair with Bill. Bill's supporters monitored frequencies used by cell phones, and the tape was made during one of those monitoring sessions.[12]

A lot had changed since the moment eighteen years earlier when Hillary had been aghast at the suggestion that the Clinton campaign use underhanded means to garner votes in rural Arkansas.

Yet again, Bill Clinton's chances were being jeopardized by rumors of his womanizing. And yet again, it was up to Hillary to minimize the threat—and if that meant listening to a tape that had been obtained under questionable circumstances, then she would just deal with it.

The two most worrisome issues facing Bill Clinton were women and the draft. Hillary, publicly and in private, immersed herself in both. A few weeks before Bill's announcement in October 1991 that he was running for president, the couple met quietly with a group of reporters at a Washington ritual called the Sperling breakfast, named after Godfrey Sperling Jr. of the *Christian Science Monitor*. The idea was to do a preemptive strike on the womanizing issue. Hillary had come up with the idea and had also devised the talking points for Bill to use when answering questions about their marriage.[13]

The session was held in September at a Washington hotel. Hillary was there, for what one reporter later called a "model inoculation,"[14] as Bill told reporters "our relationship has not been perfect or free of difficulties."[15]

Soon enough, in January 1992, conversations between Bill and a former lounge singer named Gennifer Flowers surfaced in a supermarket tabloid, the *Star*. Flowers, who had secretly recorded the conversations, claimed she and Bill had had a twelve-year affair. When he learned of the impending publication, Bill quickly called Hillary, who was campaigning in Georgia and staying in the governor's mansion there. He "told her what was going on," he later wrote.[16] The allegations, while denied by Bill, "hit with explosive force."[17]

Hillary worried far more about the potential political impact than her husband did. When the recorded tapes surfaced, Hillary was in Pierre, South Dakota. She quickly reached Bill by phone. Bill, somehow still confident, thought no one would believe Flowers's story, especially because the *Star* had paid her for it. But Hillary shot back: "Bill, people who don't know you are going to say, 'Why were you even talking to this person?'"[18]

She was correct: The Gennifer Flowers allegations were prime fodder for the news media, and the scandal metastasized with remarkable alacrity. Soon, the campaign's Defense Team hired a private investigator who proposed "to impeach [Flowers's] character and veracity until she is destroyed beyond all recognition."[19] But no matter the tar, the spotlight remained on the governor, not on Gennifer.

On January 26, the Clintons appeared on the CBS News program *60 Minutes* to defend their marriage and defuse the scandal. The interview was taped Sunday morning, in a suite at the Ritz-Carlton hotel in Boston, and broadcast to a large audience that night, immediately following the Super Bowl. There was little doubt in the mind of the interviewer, Steve Kroft, and his colleagues at CBS that Hillary was in charge, from her review of camera angles to her domination of the interview.

But the planning went beyond what was evident on-screen. From secret focus groups done during the scandal's unwinding, the couple had learned to stop short of using the word *adultery.*[20] (The groups revealed that older women in particular reacted negatively to any discussion of adultery or cheating.)[21] Armed with careful language scripted for maximum political benefit, Bill and Hillary were prepared to speak euphemistically about Bill's past infidelities. In a memorable remark, Bill simply acknowledged "causing pain in my marriage."[22]

Hillary's most quoted line from the interview was a disaster, and it took a Hollywood star to help clean it up.

When Kroft suggested that their marriage seemed to some like "an arrangement," Bill quickly denied it, insisting, "This is a marriage."[23] Hillary too was incredulous and voiced her outrage.

"You know, I'm not sitting here, some little woman standing by my man like Tammy Wynette," Hillary said, her voice rising and eyes blazing. "I'm standing here because I love him and I respect him and I honor what he's been through and what we've been through together. And you know, if that's not enough for people, then heck, don't vote for him."[24]

The reference to the famous country-and-western singer quickly provoked a firestorm. After watching the show, Wynette immediately called her publicist, Evelyn Shriver, and asked, "Can you believe what she said?"[25] The next day, Hillary's aides phoned Wynette to try to arrange an apology, but the singer wouldn't take the call.[26] Desperate to put the flap behind them, Hillary's people called the actor Burt Reynolds to get through to the singer.[27] Reynolds "told Tammy you have to talk to her," and she relented and accepted Hillary's personal apology.[28] In her autobiography, Hillary admitted that she was careless with her choice of words, saying that she had intended to refer to Wynette's famous song "Stand by Your Man" and "not to her as a person."[29]

For millions of Americans, the *60 Minutes* interview was their first exposure to the Clintons. Bill, the apparent sinner, took a few punches but stayed on his feet. Hillary, the apparent victim, did not. It would take years for her to repair some of the damage to her image caused by her first national appearance on prime-time television. She would later blame former president Richard Nixon for being the one to launch the serious national attacks against her. A few days after the appearance on CBS, Nixon told Maureen Dowd of the *New York Times* that "if the wife comes through looking too strong, it makes the husband look like a wimp."[30] Hillary later explained, "Either he was getting even with me because I was on the impeachment staff — because he has a very long memory — or it's because he's laying the groundwork for an attack on me, which has turned out to be the case."[31]

Back in Little Rock, some of the young, out-of-state campaign workers were depressed by what they saw as Hillary's calculated, poll-driven embrace of her husband on national television.[32] They understood that Hillary's decision to stick with Bill was strongly affected by her desire to do what was best for Chelsea,[33] something Hillary herself would later acknowledge.[34] But to some of the campaign workers, it still didn't add up. So one night not long after the *60 Minutes* interview, in the campaign's offices inside the old Arkansas Gazette newspaper building, one of the young aides asked Diane Blair to explain Hillary's reasoning for sticking with Bill. "Hillary knew what she was getting into when she married him," Blair replied.[35]

Blair then turned to the challenge at hand. "Your job is to make him win," she said, "so get back to work." Capturing the presidency, Blair concluded, "will make it all worthwhile." That philosophy, the aide felt, was "too much of a Faustian bargain," but the aide too went back to work.[36] Hillary had long ago made a pact of her own with Bill; no allegations of Bill's womanizing, accurate or not, would stand in the way of reaching their shared goal. And if she was OK with it, why should anyone else object?

BILL'S PROBLEMS, OF COURSE, didn't go away with the disappearance of Gennifer Flowers. Questions about his military draft experience soon bedeviled the campaign. Hillary helped coordinate the handling of this issue as well, keeping a close eye on the campaign's management of it, even down to the level of figuring out how the campaign should approach former Selective Service System officials.

The contours of Bill Clinton's draft history are well known. Like others of his generation, he faced an agonizing dilemma: the prospect of having to fight in an unpopular war that he did not believe in. Bill had attended Georgetown University as an undergraduate and then went on to Oxford as a Rhodes scholar, but hanging over his head was the very real danger of a draft notice. In July 1969, after his first year at Oxford, Bill agreed to join a ROTC program at the University of Arkansas. Doing so helped him gain a deferment. Once his induction notice was canceled, he returned to Oxford and — being several thousand miles away from Arkansas — never actually joined ROTC. Nothing was done to force him home, but he remained in England knowing that he was far from in the clear.

On October 30, several weeks before a draft lottery was instituted, Bill was reclassified as draft-eligible. In December, after receiving the high lottery number of 311, he formally withdrew from the ROTC program he had never actually joined and applied to Yale Law School. Like some members of his generation, but not everyone, Bill had managed to navigate the draft maze.

But many questions about that journey have remained unanswered. Those questions have endured because important documents are missing from government and university archives; several crucial witnesses have died; aides have imprecise recollections; and Bill has been reluctant, on the campaign trail in 1992 and even in his bestselling autobiography, *My Life*, to be fully forthcoming.

Bill's murky draft status burst onto the campaign stage in early February 1992, on the eve of the crucial primary vote in New Hampshire, when the *Wall Street Journal* reported on his dealings with the university's ROTC program.[37] Not long afterward, ABC TV's *Nightline* discovered a 1969 letter from Bill to Colonel Eugene Holmes, the head of the University of Arkansas ROTC program, describing Bill's opposition to the war and his gratitude for "saving me from the draft" with a deferment.[38] Hillary was involved in the meetings about how to handle the new disclosure and was kept abreast at nearly every stage of how the campaign was dealing with persistent questions about Bill's draft status.[39] When, for example, Bill thought about bringing the letter with him for his appearance on *Nightline*, she scotched the idea.[40]

Hillary's preference for obscurity over exposure consistently characterized the campaign's reaction. As the Holmes letter was surfacing, Jim Wooten, an ABC correspondent, asked Bill whether he had received his draft notice before applying for ROTC. The candidate denied doing so. Wooten suspected this was not the truth but only later realized that Bill had told him a "flat-out lie."[41] That was not the only misleading statement Bill gave while running.

More than a decade later, he conceded that it was a "misstatement" for him to have claimed on the campaign trail, "I had never had a deferment."[42] Bill steadfastly denied dodging the draft, but voters were suspicious. Pummeled by that issue and by fallout from the Gennifer Flowers allegations, he dropped quickly in the polls. Still, he and his campaign fought back, and he finished third in the crowded New Hampshire primary. That he did not finish lower was seen as a great triumph, and the campaign continued with a sense of renewed momentum.

The draft issue, however, lingered. Bill had never fully addressed the question of whether he had received an induction notice. If he had been ordered to report, how was that order seemingly canceled? And was Bill indebted to anyone else besides Colonel Holmes for saving him from the draft?

The questions were pursued by the press and Clinton's opponents, but with limited success. They were not the only ones kept in the dark; so too were the campaign's public faces, like James Carville and George Stephanopoulos. At a meeting at the governor's mansion on December 27, 1991, Stephanopoulos raised the draft issue as a potential problem for the campaign, telling the Clintons, "We need some tighter answers."[43] Hillary became enraged and snapped, "Bill's not going to apologize for being against the Vietnam War."[44]

This too was personal. Like many draft-eligible men and their lovers, Bill and Hillary had long agonized over Vietnam. "When I first met Bill," Hillary wrote in her autobiography, "we talked incessantly about the Vietnam War, the draft, and the contradictory obligations we felt as young Americans who loved our country, but opposed that particular war."[45] She added that Bill "would have served if he had been called."[46] But he had been called, and he never served. The question that reporters were pursuing was why.

By 1992, almost all of Bill's draft records in official archives had been destroyed, dating back to an order in the mid-1970s by the Selective Service System, which administered the draft.[47] But unknown to any reporters at the time, his campaign possessed copies of many of the critical documents that had been destroyed. They included an "Order to Report for Induction" dated April 1, 1969, from the Hot Springs draft board; an induction postponement dated May 16, 1969; and a notice of cancellation on July 23, 1969, a few days after Bill had agreed to join the ROTC program.[48]

Within the Clintons' inner circle, only a handful of people knew that the campaign had access to Bill's original April 1 induction order.[49] The July 23 cancellation notice contained another piece of crucial information — the name of the official who wrote the letter canceling Clinton's induction.[50]

In April 1992, reporters' hunt for these documents intensified after Cliff Jackson, an Arkansas friend of Bill's at Oxford who later became an active foe, leaked a 1969 letter that he wrote indicating that Bill had indeed received an induction notice.[51] Hillary attended several meetings in New York that were called to figure out how the campaign should respond to the Jackson letter.[52] Belatedly, and for the first time, the campaign acknowledged that Bill had indeed received an induction notice. However, the campaign decided not to release the notice, despite numerous requests from the press.[53]

Meanwhile, Hillary and Bill were growing anxious about the Defense Team's draft research, including their efforts to ascertain what records were still in government archives. On April 20, 1992, a campaign aide reported in an e-mail message that "Bill and Hillary are impatient" and "want documentation of where we asked for records pertaining to Bill Clinton and documentation of what we were told; that is the priority."[54] Bill was told in an internal campaign memo that his draft and ROTC files were likely destroyed, but the campaign could not be sure, and it could hardly afford for the issue to become even bigger than it already was.[55]

Hillary and the rest of the Defense Team secretly weighed whether Bill should come clean about the records he did possess. A proposed statement had him saying: "Apparently any records that existed have been destroyed. I then searched my old records, and I came up with the attached documents which I did not know I had."[56] But because the statement was fraught with risk,[57] it was never released.[58] Instead, Bill assured reporters that, after having written "everybody in the whole wide world," he and his aides "didn't find anything out from any of the people we wrote to that hadn't been written in the press already."[59] His remarks were true, because the archive files were virtually empty.

Meanwhile, the disclosure that Bill had indeed received an induction letter created a new problem for the campaign. The ROTC official in charge of the program that accepted Bill told a reporter they "wouldn't have taken him" if they had known about the induction order.[60] Under the direction of Bill and Hillary, campaign aides consulted outside lawyers who told them that it was legally possible for Bill to join ROTC even after he received an induction.[61] But campaign aides weren't so sure; in a memo to Bill in April 1992, they wrote, "Under no set of circumstances can we see a way in which the Governor was eligible to enroll in a ROTC program with a pending induction notice."[62]

Their conclusion, however, left open the possibility of a "special exception or exemption" that might have allowed Bill's induction notice to have been "successfully circumnavigated."[63] Induction orders were issued by local Selective Service draft boards, but these boards were autonomous, so standards varied, and outside pressure could be applied. In Arkansas, like other states, a key pressure point to influence a decision was the state Selective Service director.

The campaign knew that Bill's induction order had been postponed on the authority of the Arkansas state director, Colonel Willard Hawkins,[64] and canceled at the request of Hawkins's deputy, Major Middleton P. Ray Jr.[65] Hawkins was dead, but Ray was still alive and living in Little Rock. At that time, Hillary was personally involved in approving conversations with draft experts and screening access to sensitive documents like Bill's personal diary from his student days.[66] She insisted that the campaign try to speak with Ray before the Republicans or the press did. "Hillary thinks we should get a written statement from Middleton Ray before somebody else gets to him," Betsey Wright told an aide on May 6, 1992.[67]

Based on conversations the campaign had already had with Ray, they felt comfortable that Ray would not speak to the press about Bill's draft record.[68] Still, the staff wanted to do additional research so if Ray was approached, "he'll come to what we want him to say."[69] The right sort of statement could essentially kill the story.

In the end, their concern was for naught: Ray was virtually ignored by Bill's opponents and the press. He was quoted briefly in one news account in September 1992, telling the *Los Angeles Times* that state directors could ask a local board to reconsider a draftee's eligibility, and that induction cancellations were most common when army draftees enlisted in the navy or another military branch.[70] Ray theorized that Bill's draft order must have been canceled, since he was never compelled to report for induction.[71] But the *Los Angeles Times* reporter who wrote the September article, William Rempel, never discovered that Bill's induction order had been canceled by Ray himself. Rempel wrote, "No record of a formal cancellation of Clinton's draft notice has been found in draft board files reviewed by *The Times* or, according to (Betsey) Wright, in Clinton's papers."[72] And that was it for Ray. (The most detailed published account of Bill's draft experience — a fifty-six-page narrative in David Maraniss's acclaimed biography *First in His Class* — does not even mention Ray's name.)[73]

The *Los Angeles Times* article, and another published by the *New York Times*, attempted to punch holes in an additional story that the campaign had told about the role Senator J. William Fulbright's office played in getting Bill into ROTC, thus saving him from having to comply with his induction order. While he attended Georgetown, Bill had worked as a clerk for the senior senator from Arkansas. The young student, like many others, was influenced by Fulbright's historical role in turning public opinion against the Vietnam War. Bill himself had repeatedly denied getting special treatment from draft officials. "I certainly had no leverage to get it," he claimed.[74] But the campaign gave widely varying accounts of whether Bill had contacted Fulbright, and maintained that any requests that might have been made dealt strictly with determining "what his options were."[75]

Academic researchers and reporters pored through Fulbright's papers at the University of Arkansas, some of which were still restricted. The *Los Angeles Times* obtained, through an unofficial leak, a note from Fulbright's top aide, Lee Williams, to Colonel Holmes, the ROTC chief, thanking him for making room for Bill in his already filled unit.

A letter from Fulbright to someone was not, however, the same thing as a letter from Bill to Fulbright, asking for help. A professor at the University of Arkansas, Randall Bennett Woods, who was writing a biography of Fulbright, found one letter from Bill inquiring about a summer job. But Woods publicly dismissed the letter as insignificant.[76]

Still, the Woods discovery prompted Bill to emphatically deny, to a local alternative weekly newspaper published in Little Rock, that he had ever written a letter to Fulbright or his staff requesting help to avoid the draft. "I am positive I never asked anyone for that," Bill told reporters on the campaign trail. "No. Never, never."[77]

Hillary and the members of the Defense Team knew Bill was not being honest. Bill had in fact written a few remarkably candid letters to Williams in 1969 and 1970 — letters that were missing from the Fulbright collection at the University of Arkansas.[78]

In a March 8, 1970, letter that the campaign did not release, Bill thanked Williams for opening the door with Colonel Holmes but expressed his regret that he had broken his promise to serve in ROTC.[79] Bill confided that he had "joined ROTC because it seemed the only way to do military service without going to Vietnam, immediately at least."[80] After he got a high number in the draft lottery, the note to Williams went on, Bill's stepfather, with his knowledge, had asked Holmes about releasing his stepson from his commitment. Holmes agreed, even though "he felt I owed the country two years of service" and considered Bill "intelligent but confused."[81]

"Two things still bother me," Bill, who was twenty-three years old, wrote, referring to his failure to honor his commitments to Holmes and Williams to serve in ROTC.[82] Letting down Williams bothered him the most. "I'm afraid that you may think I've gone back on my word to you and in fact undermined your word, since you made the initial contact with Col. Holmes for me."[83]

Williams, almost four decades later, recalled the letter. "I remember receiving some kind of an apology from him," Williams said. Clinton, he added, was just "one of many" opponents of the war he helped to avoid the draft.[84]

On March 21, 1970, Williams wrote Bill to relay a message from Colonel Hawkins about the likelihood of his being called up despite his draft number.[85] In his autobiography, Bill mentioned Williams's note to him, but he neglected to mention his frank letter to Williams written two weeks earlier.[86] And during the campaign, he acknowledged neither.

Another letter sent by Bill to Williams, dated May 8, 1969, was also too revealing for the campaign to disclose.[87] After telling Williams "I have been drafted," Bill turns sarcastic and even bitter: "Looks like my turn has finally come to take part in the wholly holy justifiable killing of the Vietnamese to prevent the odious germ of world commie-nism from spreading to them. It is wonderful what these powerful new drugs can do."[88] This letter, like all the others, remained a secret, as did most of the draft-related documents possessed by the campaign.[89]

Internally, as the campaign's Defense Team updated its draft material, it occasionally noted in memos the "inconsistencies" between what the campaign had told the press and what the campaign knew to be true.[90] In September, the Bush campaign tried to attack Bill for not being truthful about his draft experience. One such attack was made by Vice President Dan Quayle during a television interview.[91] But a few days later, Quayle's own Vietnam-era service with the National Guard came under sharp scrutiny after the *New York Times* found a "striking pattern of favoritism" surrounding his enlistment in the Indiana National Guard.[92] These reports helped quell the criticism of any favoritism extended to Bill.

As the campaign neared its dizzying climax, a yearning for posterity struck the Defense Team. Pennebaker's camera crews had long been following the work of the War Room, but there was no lasting record of all they had done for the campaign; despite helping Bill win the White House, the Defense Team remained practically invisible.

Hillary's dear friend, Diane Blair, conceived of the need to write a final chapter for history. She broached the idea with the Clintons, and they immediately agreed.[93] Exchanging her campaign strategist hat for the one she wore as a political science professor, Blair diligently interviewed senior campaign aides, including members of the Defense Team. Her questions, based on extensive preparation, elicited candid remarks from aides who trusted her. She chronicled the highs and lows of a dogged campaign and quickly generated a mountain of insightful information. In the end, she compiled her lengthy report — the introduction alone numbered thirty pages — into "big bound volumes."[94]

Only two copies of the Blair report were made. She gave one copy to Bill and Hillary when they visited the Blair family at their lakeside house in Arkansas in August 1993. She kept the other copy for herself.[95]

Diane Blair knew the Clintons were not likely to want to publish her report. "I just knew what was going to happen" after the Clintons had read it. "Basically, they said, let's wait."[96] During his long first summer in Washington, President Clinton endured withering political attacks from Republicans on Capitol Hill and from activists around the country. Bill and Hillary confided to Diane Blair that they were nervous about the project they had authorized just ten months earlier. The campaign had faced a dedicated group of Clinton haters, and it had fought back with hardball tactics of its own. It seemed to the new president and First Lady that the world would be better off not knowing what the Defense Team had been up to — and why they had been up to it.

As Blair described her project in a May 2000 interview for an oral history archive at the University of Arkansas, she was interrupted by a phone call from Hillary. Blair was fighting lung cancer and the side effects of chemotherapy, and Hillary, who was campaigning for the Senate at the time, stopped what she was doing every day to check in with her old friend.

Diane Blair died the following month, in Fayetteville. Hillary conducted the memorial service, delivering an eloquent address after an exhausting flight to Fayetteville with Bill from Asia. Blair's study has never been made public. Even Bill's campaign chairman wasn't aware of its existence until he was asked about it in 2007.[97] For almost everyone, the 1992 campaign's legacy remains the documentary *The War Room*. Only a handful of people know the debt that Bill Clinton owed to the stealthy work of Hillary and her Defense Team.

In the end, voters cared most about their own finances and the state of the economy, not the private lives of the candidates. As a result, Bill Clinton defeated a once-popular president, George H. W. Bush, assisted in his efforts by the presence of a surprisingly popular third-party candidate, H. Ross Perot.

The aggressive tactics that had helped the Clintons weather the campaign trail were not left behind in Arkansas when they headed to Washington. Indeed, during the next eight years, politics in Washington would get nastier than it had been in a long time, catalyzed by a particular cast of characters and the rise of the twenty-four-hour news cycle. Bill and Hillary realized quickly that the campaign trail they thought had ended with his election was in fact perpetual. At times, that perpetuity resembled a road with endless forward potential; at other times, it was more like a dreadful loop. When stuck on the latter, the Clintons found that events of the past returned to haunt them. One of those ghosts was Whitewater.

CHAPTER 8

The "Only Stupid Dumb Thing"

BILL AND HILLARY'S losing real estate venture, Whitewater, was so remote and unprofitable that they paid little attention to it for years. The property, nestled along the White River in rural northern Arkansas, near the town of Flippin, was hard to find. Despite the land's remote location, Bill and Hillary had initially believed it would be a profitable venture. But by the late 1980s, as the Clintons' partner, Jim McDougal, came under federal scrutiny, Hillary began to worry that their investment was a financial mess that needed to be cleaned up. She told one of her law partners, "We've got to straighten up Whitewater," but even her closest friends at the firm didn't know what the word *Whitewater* meant.[1] Bill never concerned himself with Whitewater — at one point he mistakenly told an aide he was no longer invested in the real estate project — so it fell to Hillary to worry about the couple's liabilities.[2]

After Governor Clinton became President Clinton, Hillary's worries about the money-losing land deal would be realized.

Ironically, Bill and Hillary's cursed partnership with McDougal began with Lee Williams, the aide to Senator Fulbright whose introduction had helped save Bill from the draft. It all started, innocently enough, in the early summer of 1968. Fresh out of Georgetown

University, Bill was twenty-one years old, and he was working as a volunteer in Arkansas for Fulbright's reelection. At the campaign headquarters, in the Marion Hotel in Little Rock, Williams, the campaign manager, introduced Bill to Jim McDougal, a colorful politico who was also working for Fulbright.[3]

Bill and McDougal's relationship was profitable, at first. In 1977, after he became attorney general of Arkansas, Bill bought some real estate from McDougal and from then–former senator Fulbright. He quickly resold it at a reasonable profit.

A year later, Bill and Hillary invested with McDougal and his wife, Susan, in the Whitewater land deal. The Fulbright tie sealed the Whitewater deal, just as it had helped Bill avoid Vietnam: The Clintons were impressed with McDougal's record of financial success, but it was his connection to "the impeccable Bill Fulbright" that had been "reassuring to both of us," Hillary wrote years later.[4]

A few years after the Whitewater investment, McDougal had also acquired a bank and a savings and loan, Madison Guaranty. Both institutions were supervised by state and federal officials, but no one in Arkansas raised concerns about the propriety of the real estate partnership between the governor and First Lady of Arkansas and McDougal, even after McDougal was indicted and acquitted of fraud involving Madison.

But what might have been seen as an unremarkable tangle in a small state did not seem so minor when presented on the national stage. Bill's financial disclosure form in Arkansas in 1991 had listed the land deal as an asset. Not long after he announced he was running for president, Hillary once again grew anxious about Whitewater's taxes and finances and asked her law partner, Bill Kennedy, to help.[5] It was not just Whitewater she was concerned about: The list of seventy-five worrisome issues identified in March 1992 by the campaign's Defense Team had included possible conflict-of-interest questions because Hillary did legal work for Madison Guaranty while at the Rose Law Firm.[6]

McDougal, once an influential man about town, had fallen on hard times and was living in a trailer in Arkadelphia, about an hour's drive southwest of Little Rock, by the time Bill began his run for president in October 1991.[7] In a series of interviews, McDougal claimed that Bill had asked him to hire Hillary and the Rose Law Firm. He said he did so reluctantly because he already had a law firm representing his savings and loan. (As mentioned earlier,

Madison ended up retaining Rose for $2,000 a month, regardless of services rendered.) McDougal also said that he believed there were documents demonstrating Hillary doing legal work on his behalf with the Arkansas Securities Department, the agency that regulated state-chartered thrifts like Madison Guaranty.

On February 11, 1992, one of the authors of this book (Jeff Gerth, then an investigative reporter at the *New York Times*) went to the Securities Department in Little Rock and lodged a request to review Madison's file under the state's Freedom of Information Act. A clerk found the records and left Gerth alone at a microfiche machine to review the file. He soon found two 1985 letters from the Rose Law Firm and the Securities Department with Hillary's name on them.[8]

Later that day, the Arkansas securities commissioner, Joe Madden, alerted the governor's office and the campaign of Gerth's discoveries. Madden told them that among the documents that Gerth had obtained was a letter from his predecessor that began, "Dear Hillary."[9] The campaign and the Rose Law Firm quickly scrambled. By 8:41 a.m. the next day, someone at the firm had retrieved a copy of billing and payment records for Madison.[10]

Several days later, Gerth called Webb Hubbell, the Rose Law Firm partner assigned to handle media inquires. Hubbell had reviewed the billing records but declined to discuss either the firm's work for Madison or how Rose came to be retained by the savings and loan. He did, however, promptly relay Gerth's questions, and his answers, to a member of the campaign's Defense Team.[11] By now, the issue had become serious enough that Hillary had limited the media's access to a small handful of campaign aides and attorneys and enlisted one of her closest friends, Susan Thomases, a New York lawyer, to specifically deal with Gerth and the *New York Times*.[12] Thomases, having talked with Hillary, called Gerth on February 20 and told him that one of the younger Rose attorneys, Rick Massey, was prepared to say that he had been responsible for landing Madison as a client.[13] Gerth followed her lead and called Massey in Little Rock. Massey promptly declined to take credit for bringing in Madison, saying he didn't know how it had come to the firm.[14]

Internally, the campaign, which at the time was already dealing with the draft and womanizing issues, saw Hillary's involvement with Madison as what it referred to as a potential "third strike."[15]

The concern, campaign aides later recalled, was political embarrassment, not legal liability: Hillary's reputation as a top-notch lawyer
with a career independent of her husband could be tarnished by
disclosures that she had worked for someone like McDougal, had
dealt with regulators appointed by her husband, and had been
hired because of a personal request by her husband, who was then
the governor.[16]

Gerth, meanwhile, was nearing the end of his reporting and
was set to meet with Thomases and Loretta Lynch, a member of the
Defense Team, in Thomases's New York office. By then, McDougal,
having searched his records at Gerth's request, had stumbled across
a few check stubs misplaced in a filing cabinet. He had thought
those stubs had been burned years earlier, but "by accident," they
had been mislaid with other financial records.[17] The newly found
stubs, which McDougal gave to Gerth, showed that the Whitewater
venture had written checks on an account at Madison Guaranty
with insufficient funds to pay its bills. Other records revealed that
Madison Guaranty did not bounce the checks. Someone had somehow provided the funds to cover the amounts due.

At the meeting at Thomases's law office, Gerth shared the new
documents with Thomases and Lynch. He then asked Thomases
about Whitewater's finances, but she had little to say about it.[18]
Just a few days earlier, Bill and Hillary had told her that Whitewater was an embarrassing mistake — in Hillary's words, the "only
stupid dumb thing we ever did."[19] Bill said he regretted the investment, in part, because it created the appearance of a conflict of
interest.[20]

On Sunday, March 8, the New York Times published a 1,785-
word article that disclosed the real estate partnership between the
McDougals and the Clintons, the connections to the failed savings
and loan, and the existence of Hillary's name on her law firm's filings on behalf of the savings and loan before state regulators.

The summary paragraph of the piece raised questions about
two possible conflicts of interest — a governor being in business
with someone whose company was regulated by the state, and the
governor's wife being involved in representing that business partner before state regulators that the governor had appointed. By citing McDougal's newly found bank records, the article also reported
that McDougal's savings and loan had been subsidizing the unsuccessful real estate venture with the Clintons. The article pointed

out that the Clintons had been "under little financial risk" because McDougal had been making most of the payments for a supposedly fifty-fifty joint venture.[21]

By Saturday night, the campaign had received a faxed first version of the story, helping strategists write a lengthy rebuttal for reporters the next morning; Hillary helped review and approve the statement.[22] The timing was important: In just two days, eight states were scheduled to hold presidential primaries, an event called Super Tuesday. One point of attack by the campaign was the headline on the article, "Clinton Joined S&L Operator in Ozark Real Estate Venture," which could be read as implying that the couple had made the investment while McDougal owned the savings and loan, though the article noted that the thrift acquisition had come a few years later.

Clinton campaign aides emphasized that Whitewater had never made the Clintons any money. They also complained that the article neglected to mention that the couple "were at substantial risk" and "continue to be personally liable for outstanding corporate loans."[23] Internally, however, the campaign realized the latter point was less than bulletproof since Bill had failed to list the Whitewater loan liability on his financial disclosure report filed with the Federal Election Commission.[24] Inside the campaign, a debate ensued. Should Whitewater be listed as an asset, which an aide recalled would "look like a sweetheart deal" because McDougal put more into the venture than the Clintons? Or should the campaign list it as a liability and look like a "victim"?[25] In the end, the Clintons chose the latter course of action and listed the Whitewater loan as a liability on an amended disclosure report filed a few weeks after the *Times* story was published.

Even though Bill had been the one to sign all the disclosure forms under oath, Hillary managed the campaign's response. Hillary also insisted that aides run all questions by her first. "She says she does not want us talking to anybody about any generic or specific tax question until she's heard the question herself," an aide wrote in a campaign memo.[26]

Soon other newspapers picked up the Whitewater story and raised additional questions about Hillary's role in landing the Madison account, as well as about her law firm's influence in Arkansas.[27] On March 15, the topic became a target during a Chicago debate among the Democratic presidential contenders on the eve of the

Illinois primary. Before the debate, Hillary urged Bill to "defend my honor,"[28] and he got his chance when Jerry Brown, the former California governor, accused the Clintons of a "conflict of interest" and charged Bill with "funneling money to his wife's law firm as state business."[29] Bill defended Hillary and attacked Brown for "jumping on my wife," adding, "you're not worth being on the same platform with my wife."[30]

Later that night, Andrea Mitchell, the Washington-based reporter for NBC News, decided to try to follow up with some questions of her own. Mitchell wanted to directly ask Hillary about the conflict-of-interest allegations, but she knew it would not be easy to gain access to her. The couple was scheduled to meet early-morning commuters the next day, between 6:30 and 7:00 a.m., at the Busy Bee diner, under Chicago's elevated rail tracks. "The only way to get a question to Hillary was to get up earlier than anyone else, hightail it to the diner, and plant myself on a stool as just another paying customer before the Secret Service and the advance men roped it off," Mitchell later recalled.[31]

After countless cups of coffee, Mitchell was well positioned and sufficiently awake to make the query. When Hillary passed by, Mitchell asked about Brown's charges of funneling and then "about a possible conflict of interest."[32]

She called Brown's charges "pathetic and desperate."[33] To the second question, Hillary replied: "I suppose I could have stayed home and baked cookies and had teas," but, she continued, "what I decided to do was fulfill my profession, which I entered before my husband was in public life."[34]

Her aides immediately knew the remark was going to touch a nerve. Clinton campaign strategist Paul Begala told her that her comments could be perceived as "an attack on stay-at-home moms."[35] Hillary, with a "wounded and naïve look on her face," disagreed, saying "no one would think that."[36] Hillary explained that she would have loved to have been a stay-at-home mom but couldn't afford to because of Bill's meager salary.[37] "You worry too much," she told Begala.[38]

Nonetheless, she went back outside the diner to clarify her remark. There, reporters were herded "with a rope like cattle" outside the coffee shop, according to Mitchell, and "lined up as a newly politically correct Hillary came out to declare that of course she was not demeaning women who worked at home."[39]

"But it was too late," Begala later said.[40] Her remarks were already on the wires and would be widely quoted nationally.

Her mistake proved to be a bonanza for the Republicans, as Hillary herself belatedly acknowledged. The criticism she received stemmed, she believed, from her role as "a symbol for women of my generation" and the personification of "a fundamental change in the way women functioned in our society."[41]

Her two different explanations for her remarks were classic Hillary; in neither of them did she actually accept blame. Such reluctance has been an almost reflexive response by her whenever confronted with criticism for a gaffe. Her reticence to admit a mistake, even one as simple as misspeaking on the campaign trail, lies in part in her own idealized view of herself, that she can do no wrong, as long as whatever mistake she made was in the pursuit of a larger good cause. Along with that comes the confidence that in any room she enters, she is the smartest.

But there is another reason why Hillary is reluctant to take full responsibility for her own mistakes: To do so would arm her enemies. Hillary has endured a great deal of public attack and media-promoted humiliation. She is a pioneer — but a cautious one. What might once have been a minor defensiveness has been amplified over time, a mounting frustration with having to answer for herself to those she feels are out to get her. Of course, every famous politician probably feels some of this, but few have had to sit alongside their spouse on national television while he effectively confesses adultery; few have had their political enemies call them and their child ugly; few have had to deal with hurtful gossip regarding their private life. And all this at a time when the nastiness and feedback loops of cruel gossip and modern media can be remarkably harsh and relentlessly quick. What is surprising for someone so smart, however, is how tone-deaf she sometimes seems, as in Chicago. And what's ultimately revealing is that she behaved this way before reaching national prominence. The Busy Bee diner under the L tracks was not that many miles from Park Ridge, where Hillary had once learned from her mother that the way to respond to a bully was to punch back.

Not surprisingly, the campaign, in its own polling and research, found that Hillary specifically struck voters as too aggressive and abrasive. In April 1992, top advisers wrote a memo reporting that she was seen as a wife intent on "running the show" and recommended a strategy to lower Hillary's profile for a while.[42]

The recommendations by the advisers were mostly adopted. However, as their confidential memo had predicted, Hillary became a staple in Republican attacks on the Clintons and their values, especially at the GOP convention, where Pat Buchanan attacked her as a "radical feminist" who likened marriage to slavery.[43]

By late March, the Whitewater investment had faded as an issue after a campaign lawyer released an accounting report showing that the Clintons had lost money in the venture, though nowhere near as much as the McDougals had lost.[44] But the lawyer's report did not address legal work done for Madison or any other client by Hillary or her firm; such questions were still being pursued by the Defense Team and numerous journalists.

At the same time, Hillary, Susan Thomases, and Loretta Lynch were trying to figure out what to tell the *New York Times* and the *Washington Post* about Hillary's involvement with Madison and other clients with matters before state regulators.

Hillary had initially stated inaccurately that she did not represent clients before state regulators.[45] The campaign's subsequent responses, which Hillary helped draft, were less absolute, saying she had "tried to avoid such involvement and cannot recall any instance other than the Madison Guaranty matter in which I had any involvement, and my involvement there was minimal."[46] In fact, Lynch's notes show that the campaign knew the billing records indicated "at least one conversation" between Hillary and the state securities commissioner.[47] The campaign never disclosed this fact. In addition, with the help of Vince Foster, Hillary drafted a statement defending her representation of Madison that cited her blemish-free record as a lawyer in Arkansas. Mixed into the statement was a concession that it was wrong for Hillary to speak with the state securities commissioner on behalf of Madison. "I can see how in retrospect that to avoid even the appearance of conflict I should not have become involved at all," she wrote.[48] But that statement was also not released to the public — for an obvious reason. "She didn't like admitting a mistake," campaign head Kantor said, in part, "because it will open her up to attacks" by Bill's opponents.[49]

Fifteen years later, in another presidential campaign, Hillary's quest for near infallibility (or the appearance of it) would surface again. This time the campaign was hers, and the mistake she refused to admit was her vote in 2002 for the war in Iraq.

*   *   *

HILLARY PRESENTED A NEW CHALLENGE to campaign reporters. The last time a spouse's finances had been a major issue in a presidential election was back in 1984, when Geraldine Ferraro, the Democratic vice presidential candidate, had to respond to questions about her husband's business dealings. And ethics were very much in the air in 1992 in Washington. The Speaker of the House, Jim Wright, a Democrat from Texas, had recently resigned after an ethics committee complaint was launched by a brash Republican congressman named Newt Gingrich, and Hillary was not immune to the new climate of suspicion. According to Hillary and Bill, Madison was an exception, and a limited one at that, to the general rule that Hillary did no work before state regulators. "I don't do any regulatory work for banks," Hillary emphatically said in March 1992.[50] In fact, some senior campaign aides, a few insiders at the Rose firm, and Hillary all knew that just such a case existed. The evidence related to this case was not disclosed to reporters and was later removed from the law firm's files by Hubbell.[51] The client was the Southern Development Bancorporation, a bank holding company that owned a rural development bank, Southern Development Bank, based in Arkansas. Hillary was a Southern Development director and outside counsel. During the six years Hillary served as their lawyer, Southern Development paid the Rose Law Firm between $100,000 and $200,000.[52] Moreover, at Bill's direction, a total of $300,000 in state-appropriated funds was invested in the bank after it was set up in 1986.[53] After he became president, Bill even boasted that "Hillary and I, when we were in Arkansas, helped to set up the Southern Development Bank in Arkansas" — neglecting to mention that Hillary's role was not pro bono but compensated in billable hours.[54]

The reason for the state subsidy was that Southern Development Bank intended to provide credit to many who otherwise would not have had access to it. But in many ways it was a bank like any other — including its desire to expand. As the primaries continued, the Clinton campaign learned that reporters from the *Washington Post* had been talking to Southern Development officials about Hillary's possible involvement in the acquisition of another bank, Elk Horn, and her work regarding the approval of that purchase by the state banking commissioner.[55]

Loretta Lynch interviewed Hubbell on May 11 after he had

reviewed Rose's files on Southern Development. Hubbell told her she wasn't going to be pleased with what he had found.[56]

The banking commissioner, appointed by Bill, had written Hillary a letter suggesting a bank Southern Development might buy.[57] Even more troubling, Hubbell told Lynch, was a separate transaction involving Southern Development.[58] The law firm files showed that Hillary had "conversations with" the state securities commissioner about a routine exemption Southern Development needed in order to issue stock.[59]

The next day, Lynch called the securities commissioner to find out what their files on Southern Development's stock transaction showed about Hillary. "Hillary is all over this file," the commissioner told Lynch. "Anyone can see that."[60]

On May 16, Lynch relayed her findings to Hillary and Betsey Wright. In an attempt to respond to the *Post*'s reporting, Lynch wrote that Hillary's dealings with the state securities commissioner "should not be public."[61] (After the election, the files documenting those conversations — such as the law firm's original copies of the Southern Development bank files — were removed from the Rose offices by Webb Hubbell and taken to his new home in Washington, DC.)[62]

Hillary's stonewalling worked. Her discussions with regulators, as well as the rest of Lynch's findings, never reached the public. When the *Post* piece was finally published in late July, it dealt with the development bank in passing, and the article garnered little attention. Reporters never discovered the securities connection, nor did they learn about the banking department correspondence.

Hillary had one last business deal she wanted to keep under wraps in 1992: her lucrative commodities trades of the 1970s. Here too, she succeeded.

The need for privacy about the Clintons' financial matters was paramount inside the campaign. Betsey Wright reminded another campaign worker about it in a memorandum. "Please do not discuss the Clintons' taxes beyond you and me and I will decide a need to know basis; Hillary is planning a little bit of privacy in front of the staff," Wright told Lynch.[63] Hillary was even more emphatic in a meeting that spring. She warned Lynch that if the tax returns showing the commodity trades were released, there would be serious consequences: "You'll never work in Democratic politics again," Hillary told her.[64]

Bill had released his tax returns going back to 1980, but not the returns that showed Hillary's gains from trading in commodities. Reporters who were curious about an unexplained jump in the couple's net worth around that time were given an alternative explanation: The money came from a gift from Hillary's parents and from savings from prior earnings.[65]

"It was a bad cover story," a former aide explained, but it worked, and the press interest "went away."[66]

As 1992 drew to a close and the Clintons prepared to move to Washington, they hoped to leave behind the mistake of becoming involved with Jim McDougal and Whitewater. They turned to their trusted friend Jim Blair — husband of Defense Team regular Diane Blair — to clean up the mess.

On December 22, 1992, the Clintons officially ended their investment in Whitewater when McDougal bought them out for $1,000. Jim Blair provided the money, writing a check to McDougal's lawyer, who, in turn, wrote a check to the Clintons.[67]

Blair, who later described his Whitewater work as "janitorial services," was slated to fly to Little Rock from Fayetteville to personally handle the closing at the offices of McDougal's attorney, but bad weather prevented him from attending.[68] So, at the last minute, a substitute was found to represent the Clintons — Vince Foster, who had once clerked for Blair. At the meeting in Little Rock, not far from his Rose Law Firm office, Foster turned over some Whitewater tax records to McDougal, saying "in a mournful tone of voice" that he was "simply a messenger."[69] McDougal, for his part, gave Foster a document filled with "inaccuracies" — purported minutes of a Whitewater board of directors meeting scheduled to take place that day. Foster accepted the concocted document in silence.[70]

Already, the McDougal connection was weighing on Foster's mind. Earlier that year, he had assumed control of Whitewater files and other records pertaining to Hillary that belonged to the law firm.[71] At some point, and without telling anyone, he had stashed away some of those records in a briefcase that wound up in his Little Rock attic.[72]

For Foster, McDougal was a door best left unopened. On a checklist of things to do before leaving Little Rock for Washington, Foster wrote, "Get out of Whitewater."[73] Getting out of Whitewater meant separating the new president and Hillary from the entanglements of the past, including a business partner who had been indicted on fraud charges.[74]

Unbeknownst to those trying to cut the rotten Arkansas cord that December, federal regulators were far from finished with McDougal and Madison. Blair had recognized, perhaps presciently, that McDougal's turning over the records to the *New York Times* had been a mistake.[75] But neither he nor Foster could have imagined how a few canceled check stubs would ultimately impact Bill and Hillary's lives in the White House.

CHAPTER 9

"Welcome to Washington"

ON INAUGURATION DAY, January 20, 1993, Bill and Hillary's "twenty-year project" was realized, right on schedule. Given the project's history, it was a certainty that Hillary would play a crucial, behind-the-scenes role in her husband's presidency. The question swirling around Washington was what formal role, if any, would she assume?

Five days after reciting the oath of office, Bill ended the speculation by announcing the formation of the President's Task Force on National Health Care Reform, to be chaired by the First Lady.

The health care crisis confronting America was not invented: 37 million Americans were uninsured and unable to afford the spiraling cost of health insurance. It was clear from the outset that a solution would not come easily. At lunch, just before the announcement, Bill, Hillary, and Ira Magaziner, who would help manage the effort, discussed the obstacles. Magaziner, a consultant, was a friend of the Clintons and shared a common career path with Hillary. He had gone from being a student activist to working with corporations, staying within the system. He had also delved into public policy, developing an ambitious economic blueprint for Rhode Island. The plan was soundly rejected by the state's voters, a lesson that went unheeded by the Clintons.[1] Just as Magaziner had done in Rhode Island, Bill and Hillary, with Magaziner's approval, set two extremely ambitious goals — rewriting the complex rules that governed 14 percent of the American economy and meeting the deadline of delivering a proposal to Congress within one hundred days.

From the moment Hillary was appointed, people in Washington wondered whether she was the right person for the job. "I decided Hillary should lead the health care effort because she cared and knew a lot about the issue," Bill later wrote, adding that she had both the time and the talent to be an honest broker for the American people.[2] But in June 1993, Hillary conceded that she was not a master of the subject. "I'm not an expert on health care," she later told Katie Couric. "I'm not somebody who has studied it." Her qualifications for the job, she said then, were her willingness "to immerse myself in all of the hard decisions" and her perspective as a consumer "who has to use the health care system."[3]

Whatever her qualifications, a large portion of Americans living beyond the Beltway embraced Hillary's quixotic role. The country seemed comfortable with the historic decision to put a First Lady in charge of a major policy challenge. One poll, taken the day after the president's announcement, found that 64 percent of those surveyed supported Hillary's appointment, and only 26 percent of those surveyed disapproved.[4]

But there were plenty of warnings about how difficult her job would be. Ira Magaziner estimated that the task force would need at least four years to persuade Congress to overhaul the system. "I'm hearing the same thing," Bill said. "But we have to try. We just have to make it work."[5]

Others saw the task as impossible, a fool's errand. "What did you do to make your husband so mad at you?" Mario Cuomo, then the governor of New York, asked Hillary during a White House visit.

"What do you mean?"

"Well, he'd have to be awfully upset about something to put you in charge of such a thankless task," Cuomo replied.[6]

Despite those warnings and predictions that the task force was doomed to fail, Hillary basked in the spotlight, determined to make history. A few days after the task force's creation, an old friend from Arkansas stopped by the Clintons' living quarters at the

White House to say hello. The friend found Hillary looking "radiant" and enjoying her new home and job so much that she let out a "happy laugh."[7] She seemed thoroughly unbothered by the assignment laid at her feet.

She hired a staff of twenty, soon dubbed "Hillaryland" by an aide. She took an office in the coveted West Wing of the White House, something no other First Lady had done. And she ensured that her chief of staff was named an assistant to the president, also a first.

Not everyone was thrilled. In one poll, 36 percent felt she had assumed "too large a role."[8] Hillary's large footprint also worried some of her closest advisers. Vernon Jordan, the man who helped convince her in 1982 to change her name and whose wise counsel was valued as much by Hillary as it was by Bill, had advised her not to take an office in the policymaking West Wing. Too symbolic, Jordan said. He told her to instead settle down in the more ceremonial confines of the East Wing.[9]

But Hillary saw things differently. "These physical and staff changes were important," she wrote, "if I was going to be involved in working on Bill's agenda, particularly as it related to issues affecting women, children and families."[10]

It didn't take long for her honeymoon to end.

"Welcome to Washington," an anonymous "federal lawyer" cynically told the *Washington Times* a few days after the formation of the task force, in an article headlined "First Lady's Task Force Broke Law on Secrecy."[11] The newspaper, which is openly conservative in its reporting and editorial stance, claimed that reporters had been barred from the first meeting of the task force — an apparent violation of a 1972 law because Hillary was not a federal employee and the law allows outsiders to be kept out of advisory committee meetings only if all the participants are federal employees. The unnamed "federal lawyer" was the main expert cited in the piece.[12]

The White House counsel, Bernie Nussbaum, a friend of Hillary's from their days together on the House Judiciary Committee's impeachment staff, quickly countered that the act was not intended to cover the First Lady. But three private groups, two involved in health care and one oriented toward conservative policies, sued for access to the task force's deliberations and records. Years later, Hillary described the lawsuit as a "deft political move, designed to disrupt our work."[13] Indeed, the mainstream press began referring to the task force as secret or secretive,[14] a strategic coup cited with pride a few months later by one of the conservative architects of the lawsuit. Handling of the case was delegated to Vince Foster, now the deputy White House counsel, adding to a workload that was already more than daunting. The litigation was not resolved until the summer of 1994 — after the task force had completed its work. By then, the partial victory awarded to the Clinton administration by the court of appeals felt sour.

In hindsight, Hillary concluded that she moved "too quickly" on health care. She also acknowledged that she overlooked a "giant red flag" on Capitol Hill indicating that Congress wanted to slow down the process. In an attempt to jump-start the health care initiative, Hillary tried a parliamentary maneuver, attempting to include it in the budget reconciliation act. But the chairman of the Senate Appropriations Committee, Robert C. Byrd, was a stickler for following the rules.[15] He didn't want his budget bills entangled with extraneous items, so putting health care on a fast track would require a waiver. In the end, Byrd decided that any debate about health care couldn't take place in the short window allowed for considering reconciliation — twenty hours — and he refused to grant a waiver. For some, Hillary's attempt to slip the bill through rubbed the wrong way. Politics in Washington, as longtime participants know, involves deliberation, analysis, and compromise. "You need to be able to sit back and look at all the players and see where you're going to get blown up along the way," said Leon Panetta, a former congressman who became President Clinton's first budget director and second White House chief of staff.

"Part of it comes from their being from Arkansas; they controlled a lot more there," Panetta continued. "In a small southern state like Arkansas, you not only know all the players — you can control the players. But in Washington, there are too many power centers and you can't control them all."[16] In Little Rock, there was one daily newspaper by the early 1990s and only a handful of public-policy groups. Washington, however, was home to thousands of local, national, and international news organizations, trade groups, and watchdogs of all kinds, many with very different needs and conflicting interests. On the day her husband took office, Hillary told James A. Baker III, the Bush family confidant, that the Clinton administration was determined to work with Republicans.[17] But reaching out "was a hard thing for [the Clintons] to learn," especially on health care.[18] Hillary would later acknowledge that her biggest mistake was a failure to understand "the way that Washington worked and the way the White House worked and [not] having a clear sense from the beginning about what was possible and what wasn't possible."[19] It was an acknowledgment that only partially accepted responsibility as it pointed the finger at others. Hillary's fault, as she saw it, had been that she was more ambitious and daring than the people who held her back.

CONSCIOUS OF A NEED to soften her image, the new First Lady, for her first newspaper interview after the inauguration, chose a well-known food writer for the *New York Times*, Marian Burros, who, like Hillary, had graduated from Wellesley. The First Lady's staff established strict ground rules: Burros was not permitted to ask Hillary any policy questions or details about the workings of the health care task force. Instead, the interview introduced Hillary in the more traditional role as First Lady, focusing on her plans for White House social events and changes she had already implemented to the kitchen's menu.[20]

In her dealings with the press, Hillary had a first rule: respect for the privacy of Chelsea, who was a teenager by now. Chelsea enrolled in Sidwell Friends, an exclusive private school several miles north of the White House, not far from the National Cathedral. Hillary and Bill regularly attended events at Sidwell as well as Chelsea's ballet performances at another nearby school.

Several months later, Hillary invited a broadcast journalist, Katie Couric, to interview her from time to time.[21] The two women bantered effortlessly and seemed to form an easy bond. Couric, for her part, found Hillary "incredibly disciplined" and "a tough nut to crack about admitting any vulnerability about herself or her husband."[22]

The few times that Hillary did engage with the media during those first few months in 1993 were superficial, to say the least, and they did little to accommodate the audience that was most important—the 535 men and women of the Congress. Although she met repeatedly with Congress on her health care work, she relied more on old friends like Nussbaum and Vince Foster to serve as emissaries with those on Capitol Hill. As she continued her work on the task force, she rejected most requests for interviews with the media. She retreated even more from the spotlight in April of 1993, after her father died.

But if Hillary was taking a media holiday, the pause was far from reciprocal. And it wasn't long before the first Clinton scandal, real or imagined, began.

An audit had uncovered several troubling accounting problems at the White House Travel Office. The audit of the travel office had been prompted by complaints to Hillary that the office failed to use competitive bidding when it chartered jets to fly reporters accompanying the president.[23] Subsequently, on May 19, the seven-member staff was fired. There would eventually be six separate inquiries into how the firings were handled. Ultimately, the head of the travel office was indicted but acquitted, and no one connected to the episode was convicted of a crime. In turn, four administration officials were reprimanded for exercising bad judgment, including William Kennedy, a former Rose Law Firm partner who had joined the White House counsel's office and had made the decision to bring in the FBI after the accounting problems had come to light.

According to previously undisclosed documents, including a 347-page memo presented in 1996 to Kenneth Starr, the independent counsel, Hillary had argued that her involvement in the matter was minimal, "at most, fifteen minutes of conversation."[24] Yet, the memo also found, the issue was somehow important enough for several others, including Vince Foster, to tiptoe around the precise nature of her role when the matter blew up.[25] David Watkins, who headed the White House Administrative Office and helped fire the travel staff, later told prosecutors "that he and Foster agreed to be protective of Mrs. Clinton in their White House Review Team interviews."[26] When initially questioned on June 3 by White House aides who were reviewing the matter, Foster declined to identify anyone else who might have been involved in the firings. His own notes on a conversation with Hillary said she "wanted to know what was being done about" possible improprieties at the travel office.[27] In a second interview, on June 30, Foster acknowledged that the First Lady "had expressed concern."[28]

Between the two interviews, on June 17, the *Wall Street Journal* published an editorial entitled "Who Is Vince Foster?" The overtly anti-Clinton *Journal* editors criticized the administration for its "carelessness about following the law."[29]

Foster's own notes are fragmented, but they clearly show his desire to defend the decision to fire the employees and the First Lady's role, whatever it may have been: "Defend management decision, thereby defend HRC role whatever it was in fact or might have been misperceived to be."[30] That misperception seemed to be the biggest problem. During his second conversation with the White House review team, Foster and his questioner "mutually exchanged views that HRC is perceived as being involved in decisions and events in which she has no participation."[31] That entry, the prosecutors concluded, was "highly damaging evidence to any prosecution of Mrs. Clinton."[32]

For Hillary, the travel office case, and its partisan nature, "became the first manifestation of an obsession for investigation that persisted into the next millennium."[33] But it revealed another obsession too: the Clintons' hypersensitivity to an overreactive media. Their conviction that the press assumed the worst led them in some cases to hunker down and not put out all the facts.

Part of the reason the Clintons were so wary of revealing anything about the inside workings of the White House was that, unbeknownst to the public, the new First Lady stood near the top of the administration's hierarchy. That point was made clear early on to the first outsider to join the White House team, David Gergen, a political strategist for Presidents Nixon and Reagan. In his first hours on the job, in late May, Gergen asked the chief of staff, Thomas "Mack" McLarty, to describe the White House organizational chart.

At the top was a single box. McLarty explained that there were "three people in that top box: the President, the Vice President and the First Lady. All three of them sign off on big decisions. You'll just have to get used to it."[34]

Hillary had to get used to it too; she had never had to compete for her husband's attention on policy matters. Gore shared her passion for policy, though his interests — technology, the environment, and government efficiency — were different from hers. But, a senior Clinton administration official recalled, they were "both alike in some ways" in public, "too rigid and they don't like to be challenged."[35]

The two "never had a good relationship" and vied over access to Bill. Hillary was upset that Gore had too much influence over her husband. Gore, for his part, saw Hillary "as too much involved" in presidential decision-making. The bad chemistry between the two was obvious to White House insiders: "You can be around them and feel it."[36] Before long, Gore would present an additional rivalry: The Tennessean had been aiming for the presidency as long, if not longer, than Bill Clinton. He had his own plans, and they certainly did not include waiting for Hillary to run.

Hillary never became tight with Gore, but she believed Gergen might help her mend fences with the press. "They've been tough on us from the start," she told him, "but we need to repair relations. You can really help us with that."[37] At first he did. Reporters' access had been curtailed when a door had been added between the press room and nearby West Wing offices. (Gergen says that Hillary and Susan Thomases initially wanted to move the press's quarters out of the West Wing to an adjacent building.) "In our first conversation," Gergen recounted in his memoirs, "I asked Hillary to have the door removed and she immediately agreed. She even wondered why it had not been done before!"[38]

Hillary had long been a fighter who — in the smaller Arkansas pond, at least — had relished political combat and usually prevailed. And her steadfast devotion to her husband and their twenty-year project had certainly continued in large part because she and Bill were able to fend off attacks from their few antagonists in Arkansas and produce results. As long as she could do something good, she felt she could ignore her critics. Not surprisingly, Hillary's most ambitious goal — her insistence that a health care bill be submitted to Congress within one hundred days — turned out to be the most unrealistic one, rejected by Senator Byrd, a fellow Democrat. Perhaps it was merely because Hillary was no longer thinking like a cautious lawyer; she was now the client, and an exacting and demanding one at that. (In a number of travel office documents, White House aides referred to Hillary as "TC," an acronym for "The Client."[39] Her former colleague Webb Hubbell described her as "a very demanding client indeed."[40])

The man at the other end of those demands was often Vince Foster, who struggled mightily to cope with this new, high-stakes environment. He was also thrown by a dramatic role reversal in his relationship with Hillary. No longer was Vince either the close buddy or the wise, patient teacher, as their relationship had been at the Rose Law Firm. Now Hillary was the boss, and Vince was quite often her punching bag.

According to Hubbell, "Hillary had snapped at [Foster] about the health care task force. 'Fix it, Vince!' he said she had hissed. It hurt him deeply." Earlier, Foster had told Hubbell that "Hillary and others were quizzing him daily about the capabilities and loyalty of the career Justice Department lawyers who were handling the case."[41]

Hubbell described the shift Foster experienced as subtle. Friends of Foster saw his transformation more dramatically: He was upset at playing the role of "second fiddle" to Hillary.[42] But Foster's anguish was both personal and professional. His diary-like notebook, the details of which have not been made public until now, contained an entry recounting the deep hurt he felt because Hillary spurned him once he got to Washington.[43] Hubbell said he and Foster both loved Hillary in a platonic kind of way, what he describes as a kind of familiar "workplace intimacy."[44] But in Washington, it seemed, Hillary had no affection to spare. Even though his West Wing office was located just a few short steps from Hillary's, by Hillary's own recollection, she did not speak with Foster a single time during the final thirty-one days of his life.[45] And their last conversation prior to that stretch was disappointing to Foster, perhaps even heartbreaking. A dinner date was arranged at the White House on Saturday afternoon, June 14, when Hubbell, Foster, and Hillary linked arms at the president's announcement of his selection of Ruth Bader Ginsburg to succeed Justice Byron White on the Supreme Court.[46]

"When are we going out, guys?" Hillary asked, quickly answering her own question with, "Let's go eat Italian,"[47] a reminder of their frequent lunches at their favorite red-sauce joint in Little Rock. Hubbell suggested they first stop by his house for drinks; his family had just moved into a stately home in the tree-lined Cleveland Park section of Washington. Hillary agreed, and the two big guys wrapped her in a bear hug.[48]

By sundown, Hubbell was ready: He had stocked up on Diet Coke, Hillary's favorite soft drink. But then the First Lady called to tell him that the *Washington Post* was preparing to publish a story about Bill's birth father and the fact that Bill had a half brother "who had just surfaced."[49] Hillary learned that the article was going to disclose that Bill Blythe, Bill's birth father, had been married at least twice before he had met the president's mother, Virginia. This fact, Hillary wrote years later, was "something nobody in the family had known."[50]

That was not true. In fact, in the first months of 1992, one of the Clinton campaign's private investigators had quietly reconstructed Bill's genealogy and personally briefed him on the tangled history of his true father and the existence of a half brother.[51] Hubbell had inherited the files on Bill's family tree. Bill was out of town, and it was left to Hillary to manage what she perceived as yet another potential obsession of the press.

Hillary told Foster, "I've got to find Bill. Then we have to find his mother."[52] The threesome's planned reunion, scheduled for the posh I Matti restaurant in downtown Washington, would have to wait.

"Oh, I'm so sorry," Hillary recalled Foster as replying.

"So am I," she told him. "You know, I'm just so sick of this." That would be the last time Hillary Clinton would speak to Vince Foster.[53]

That Saturday night, with Foster's help, Hubbell searched the boxes in his basement, but the two men could not locate the file. Hubbell called Hillary with the bad news. She told him it could wait and asked him to bring it to her office on Monday. He managed to locate it the next day.[54]

Foster's reaction to Hillary's cancellation of the dinner was palpable.

"Vince hardly said a word the rest of the evening," sulking and pulling his chair away from the table, Hubbell recalled.[55] Hubbell's wife said Foster behaved like "a child who had been promised quality time with a parent, only to have the parent renege when business had called him away."[56]

The next day, Foster unburdened himself, telling Hubbell that the reason he and the First Lady rarely spoke of late was because "she's so busy." When they did talk, it was nothing like those days back in Little Rock, Foster said. At the White House, Hillary only had time to bark orders at her mentor, telling him, "Handle it, Vince."[57]

Even that was about to end. Hillary's painful reconstruction of their last month of silence focused not on her inability to meet with him but on his failure to find the time to reach out to her. Though their offices were near each other in the West Wing, "Vince was busy," she recalled.[58]

FOSTER'S DESPAIR INTENSIFIED during the last few weeks of his life. After Congress authorized a further inquiry of the travel office firings, Foster sought advice from several private attorneys. He scribbled a deeply bitter note, which was torn into pieces but was later found, scattered at the bottom of his briefcase, by police. In it, he faulted himself for making "mistakes from ignorance, inexperience and overwork." He lashed out at the editors of the *Wall Street Journal* for lying "without consequence" in the editorial they had written about him. And he defended the "innocence of the Clintons and their loyal staff." The note's most quoted passage summed up his predicament: "I was not meant for the job in the spotlight of public life in Washington," he wrote. "Here, ruining people is considered sport."[59]

On July 20, shortly after 6:00 p.m., a U.S. Park Police officer found Foster's body in Fort Marcy Park, a federal park in Virginia. He was still holding his father's Colt pistol, and gunshot residue was found on his hand. An autopsy determined that he was shot a single time in the mouth. In one handwritten note he left behind, Foster called the Whitewater tax matter "a can of worms you shouldn't open."[60] Foster's death was investigated by prosecutors on two separate occasions, and each time they concluded he had committed suicide. Hillary said the official reports should have ended the efforts of "a cottage industry of conspiracy theorists and investigators trying to prove that Vince was murdered to cover up what he 'knew about Whitewater.' "[61] And indeed, the first report, by independent counsel Robert Fiske, found no evidence of murder or that the Whitewater inquiry was a factor in Foster's depression. But Fiske made that determination without the benefit of documents, specifically withheld by the White House, showing that Foster was working on tax issues related to Whitewater in his final weeks. Fiske's focus was to rapidly solve the issue of how Foster died, not why. "There was a public interest in answering as quickly as we could the threshold question of whether it was a homicide or suicide," he said in an interview.[62] And without those documents, he had no way of knowing how deeply tied Foster was to Whitewater, the link between the two going back to the December 1992 closing in Little Rock, when Foster had acted as a last-minute "messenger" for Hillary and Bill.

The withheld Foster Whitewater documents were obtained by Fiske's successor, Kenneth W. Starr, whose prosecutors conducted a lengthier, more exhaustive investigation. In his report, Starr listed the multiple stresses in Foster's life, mentioning his work for "The Client" and including the health care task force, the dismissal of the travel office employees, and tax issues relating to Whitewater as possible contributors to the depression that led him to kill himself.[63]

Starr now says his report on Foster's death could have been much more critical of the Hillary-related issues that consumed Foster before his death. "I could have dumped on her," Starr says.[64] But because Foster's involvement in the Madison and Whitewater matters was still under investigation, Starr's 1997 report said that it was "not an appropriate forum" to elaborate on Foster's involvement in those events.[65]

IN THE END, it was impossible to say for sure why Foster decided to take his own life. A suicide expert retained by Starr, Dr. Alan Berman, concluded that Foster was preoccupied with "themes of guilt, anger and his need to protect others."[66] An additional clue can be found in a conversation that has never been made public before.

In the last weeks of his life, Foster offered some advice to Loretta Lynch, a member of the Clinton campaign's defense team. Lynch had come to Washington to discuss a possible job in the White House counsel's office, where Foster was the deputy.

After chatting with another White House lawyer, Lynch found herself in Foster's small office in the West Wing. The conversation turned to questions of morality and ethics. Foster and Lynch had worked together on issues related to Madison and Whitewater in 1992, and Lynch knew that Foster "always tried to do the ethical thing."[67] When the subject of taking a job in the White House arose, Foster urged Lynch to turn it down. She would, he warned, lose her moral compass. "Don't come to Washington," Foster said. "You'll lose your soul."[68]

Foster was buried in his hometown of Hope, Arkansas. After the funeral, at her mother's house in Little Rock, Hillary confided to Webb Hubbell, "We shouldn't have asked him to come to Washington."[69]

Foster may have found hope in a passage he highlighted before he took his life. It read: "From all that dies new life springs eternal." The line, part of a book of quotes obtained by the independent counsel a few years after Foster's death, had the comment "Pretty thought," in Foster's handwriting, next to it.[70]

By the summer of 1993, the ways of Washington, sometimes called Potomac fever, had not dissuaded Bill or Hillary. According to one of their closest friends, Taylor Branch, they still planned two terms in the White House for Bill and, later, two for Hillary.

Branch described the plan to two Washington friends, John

Henry and Ann Crittenden, over a barbecue dinner at a rodeo in Aspen, Colorado, that summer.[71] The president would frequently talk with Branch, a well-respected historian and author, about his place in history, and shortly after he was elected president, Branch said, Bill asked him to begin recording "diary sessions"[72] as part of an oral-history project.

Branch had just come from one of those sessions, a marathon late-night chat with Bill at the White House, where the two men had talked as they stood on the back balcony, looking toward the Washington Monument. Now in the cool mountains of Colorado, Branch told his friends about the Clintons' presidential plans. The bold goal of sixteen years in the White House took Henry's breath away. "I was shocked," he said.[73]

AS THE SUMMER TURNED INTO FALL, Hillary continued her practice of not doing any substantive interviews with reporters. She later came to realize that she should have adopted an "off-the-record, bring-people-along strategy"[74] to keep reporters informed, but at first it had not seemed as if there would be a need to do an aggressive sales job with the press. Hillary testified before Congress about health care five times over three days in September 1993, a dramatic and "triumphant"[75] performance that received almost uniformly glowing media coverage.

"During the past months, as I have worked to educate myself about the problems facing our nation and facing American citizens about health care, I have learned a great deal," she told the House Ways and Means Committee on her first day of testimony. "The official reason I am here today is because I have had that responsibility. But more importantly for me, I'm here as a mother, a wife, a daughter, a sister, a woman. I'm here as an American citizen concerned about the health of her family and the health of her nation."[76]

The Clintons' approach to health care, a concept called managed competition, fit squarely within the New Democrat or Third Way message that Bill had featured in his campaign. (Some commentators offered a less idealistic label, calling his philosophy "triangulation.") The plan called for the government to prod employers into providing health insurance for everyone and use competition among health care providers to keep the costs down. Ideologically, it fit in between the two main bills proposed in Congress. It was not as far to the left as the liberal-backed single-payer proposal, modeled on Canada's health system. But it was more ambitious and reliant on the government than a bipartisan measure supported by large businesses.

If Bill and Hillary felt comfortable in the pragmatic center, they had taken radically different routes to arrive there. He had cut his teeth in politics before becoming a policy wonk. She had gravitated first to social policy, arriving in Washington as a relative novice in politics and with scant expertise in health care. Still, she took the helm of a political assignment that would have been a difficult test for even the most seasoned veteran.

And she dazzled commentators. She spoke earnestly, almost never referring to notes, her mastery of the subject clear. This too was classic Hillary: brilliantly book smart, a fantastically quick study when it came to policy—but sometimes jagged when it came to practice. The positive press notices that resulted from her testimony gave Hillary and her colleagues a "false sense of momentum and support," said Mickey Kantor, a member of President Clinton's cabinet at the time. As a result, "she got isolated" and continued to work with a "group of people, all of whom were off in the same direction," Kantor recalled.[77] Instead of reaching out, Hillary's aides told her they needed "to keep substantial control in the drafting" of the health care legislation, even though the bill being drafted required "thousands of modifications, revisions and conforming amendments."[78] (The proposed legislation, submitted one month after Hillary's successful appearances before Congress, came in at 1,342 pages.) Even senior members of the administration who expressed doubts about aspects of Hillary's plan were not taken seriously.[79] Meanwhile, her testimony energized her opponents, a formidable group that included the insurance industry, the pharmaceutical companies, and doctors' organizations.

And Hillary's stewardship made many Americans uncomfortable as the effort wore on. When an anxious health insurance agent asked Hillary how her plan, if passed, would affect the agent's job, Hillary coldly advised, "Find something else to market."[80] The abrasive response left the agent shaken and quickly became national news. At home in charts and binders and numbers, Hillary was adrift when it came to the human touch, which seemed superficial but was absolutely essential given the politics of health care reform. White House polling data showed that the public saw health reform as a personal issue and didn't give "a fuck about the national interest," White House aide Harold Ickes recalled. "The critical element in carrying the day on this" was "trust in the Clintons."[81] And this trust was lacking, partly as a result of Hillary's overall inability to radiate emotional warmth, partly as a result of the ongoing criticism.

The attacks against Hillary were extremely personal. Some of them had a basis in policy and politics, but others went well below the belt. Hillary initially accepted such assaults as part of the territory, but there was no precedent for them, both because the relatively new phenomenon of twenty-four-hour cable news created a new arena for mudslinging and because there had never been someone like Hillary in the White House before. "Heat comes with anything," she said.[82] She also traced some of the criticism to her "partnership" with President Clinton and the fact that it was "threatening" to some Americans. "But," she explained, "I can only be true to myself." She added that it was "better to get heat trying to do something important for people."[83] Once again, she chose to do things her way, which, she believed, was the right way. Such fortitude might have been admirable when facing cruel attacks from outside, but it also defined an inflexibility and I-know-what's-best mind-set on the inside. And as the health care reform effort began to flatline, Hillary's involvement became a fatal component.

Years later, Hillary conceded in her autobiography that she had "underestimated the resistance I would meet as a First Lady with a policy mission." She also admitted that the failure was partially caused by her "own missteps" in "trying to do too much, too fast."[84] But many of these rationalizations ultimately pointed the finger at others: those who had opposed her and those who were unable to keep up with her. In years to come, those two forces would again and again be blamed by Hillary when things didn't go her way.

CHAPTER 10

The School of Small Steps

HILLARY'S FIRST YEAR in the White House was hardly the dream life she had envisioned. By the time the holiday season of 1993 rolled around, Hillary was struggling to overcome a deep malaise; a few friends even worried that she was clinically depressed.[1] She had personal and political reasons for the blue mood: In Hillary-land, they were trying to "control the fallout" from a series of recent articles about Bill's womanizing.[2] Hillary was slated for a holiday appearance on the *Today* show, but the interview was scrubbed after the network refused to agree to a request by her staff that she not be asked about the new allegations that Bill had fooled around in Arkansas, including with a woman named Paula.[3]

On a bitterly cold morning between Christmas and New Year's, Hillary and her chief of staff, Maggie Williams, sat down for coffee in the West Sitting Hall of the White House. Before a fan-shaped window, their favorite spot in the residence, the two friends flipped through the newspapers and tried to be upbeat about the coming year. "Hey, look at this!" Maggie Williams said, handing her a copy of *USA Today.* "It says you and the president are the most admired people in the world."[4]

Everywhere else they looked, however, the news was grim.

There were stories about Whitewater and the anticipated troubles awaiting the First Lady in the year ahead. Hillary was hopeful that Americans would maintain a spirit of fair-mindedness, even as she struggled to maintain her own.

That struggle would prove to be a formidable one, for Hillary and for Bill.

Certainly their political opponents would show them no quarter. On January 6, 1994, Bill's beloved mother, Virginia, died of cancer at her home in Hot Springs. A few hours after learning she had passed, Bill and Hillary happened to hear the news flash on the *Today* show: "The president's mother died early this morning after a long battle with cancer." Right after the report, Newt Gingrich and Senator Bob Dole appeared for a previously scheduled television interview. There were no condolences that morning. Instead, the two Republicans turned to Whitewater. "It, to me, cries out for the appointment of a regulatory, independent counsel," Dole said.[5]

Hillary noticed that Dole's remarks devastated Bill. "Bill was raised by his mother to believe that you don't hit people when they're down, that you treat even your adversaries in life or politics with decency," Hillary recalled.[6]

Two weeks later, Attorney General Janet Reno appointed Robert Fiske, a moderate Republican and former United States attorney in Manhattan, to be a regulatory independent counsel. Fiske assumed control of the inquiry into Whitewater and Madison Guaranty already under way at the Justice Department. Hillary had vigorously opposed the appointment of an outside lawyer to investigate the Whitewater mess, but Bill had ignored her advice — something he later regretted as much as any decision that he made during his presidency.[7] Recalled Bill in his autobiography, "It was the worst presidential decision I ever made, wrong on the facts, wrong on the law, wrong on the politics, wrong for the presidency and the Constitution."[8]

For her part, Hillary wished she "had fought harder and not let myself be persuaded to take the path of least resistance." Over time, however, she would begin to view Fiske as "impartial and expeditious,"[9] a more benign view shaped by Hillary's opinion of his successor, Kenneth Starr.

Starr took over from Fiske after eight months. Unlike Fiske, however, because of statutory changes, Starr was appointed not by Reno but by a panel of judges headed by a Republican. The First Lady viewed him as a deeply partisan Republican whose sole intention was to prolong the nasty investigation at least through the 1996 presidential election.[10] But many of Starr's controversial inquiries actually grew out of actions taken by Fiske. It was Fiske who had personally rewritten crucial language of his charter as originally drafted by Justice Department lawyers. Fiske's editing included revising a clause to broaden his authority to investigate any allegation that arose during the inquiry.[11] Fiske said he created the "extremely broad clause" because, as a veteran prosecutor, "it was very important to me" to have that discretion. That open-ended clause would eventually become "a huge issue,"[12] Fiske understandably recalled.

Starr, Fiske's successor, acknowledged that the rewritten clause "certainly helped set the stage"[13] for his office to investigate Bill's affair with White House intern Monica Lewinsky. Both Starr and Fiske would also use the clause to investigate Webb Hubbell.

Hubbell's problems were apparent early in Fiske's tenure. Two months after Fiske's appointment, Hubbell resigned as associate attorney general to deal with a dispute with the Rose Law Firm over his billing practices. That dispute would eventually lead to his imprisonment after investigations by Fiske and Starr revealed that while at Rose, Hubbell had defrauded his clients and his partners.[14] On hundreds of occasions he used Rose Law Firm checks to pay his personal expenses.[15] Hillary had not believed the problem was serious, mainly because Hubbell had assured her it wasn't, so she had joined a group of his friends and supporters to try to find work for her old law partner prior to conviction.[16]

"At the time," Hillary told an interviewer inquiring about Hubbell, "we had no reason to disbelieve his denials of wrongdoing, and he unequivocally just looked us in the eye and said, 'I didn't do anything wrong, this'll blow over, this is all being taken care of.'"[17]

But prosecutors came to see the matter far differently, and they wondered whether the consulting jobs that Hillary and others helped Hubbell get after he left the Justice Department were intended to buy his silence about Hillary's legal work for Madison.[18] Hillary was aghast at the prosecutors' "hush money" theory, viewing it as the latest far-fetched assault in "the never-ending fictional conspiracy that, honest to goodness, reminds me of some people's obsession with UFOs and the Hale-Bopp comet some days."[19]

Bill was in Boston at a fund-raising dinner at the Park Plaza Hotel when the news broke that Hubbell had resigned as associate attorney general. Bill was stunned. Hubbell's resignation was "hard to believe....He's one of the most widely esteemed people I've ever known," the president said grimly.[20] Later at the dinner, Bill spoke about the need for a renewal of cooperation and even trust between Republicans and Democrats. With Hubbell clearly on his mind, Bill said the Republicans in Washington were "dedicated just to being against everything we are for, and dedicated to the politics of personal destruction." His face reddening, he said the Republicans would "rather take off after" Hillary than debate her on the merits of health care reform.[21] He posed this rhetorical question: "Why...are we confronted in this administration with an opposition party that stands up and says, 'No! No! No! No! No! No! No! No! No!'?"[22] With each *no*, Bill's voice got louder and he banged the podium harder. The audience was stunned; the president seemed to be losing control before their eyes.

No charges were brought in connection with the consulting jobs, but Hubbell pleaded guilty in late 1994 to cheating his former clients and partners—including Hillary—out of at least $394,000. His guilty plea "shocked" Hillary, who "found it hard to take."[23] She had called Hubbell a week before the plea, having heard a news report that he might be indicted. She told him, "You've got to fight this, Webb" and "You've got to get tough."[24] That was Hillary's final conversation with Hubbell,[25] ending a relationship that began nearly two decades earlier with the ACORN utility case.

The Rose Law Firm trio—Foster, Hubbell, and Hillary—was now down to one.

A FEW DAYS AFTER Hubbell's resignation, the *New York Times* ran a lengthy story about Hillary's commodity trades. Her aides and lawyers had finally provided financial records to the *Times*, but only after the newspaper made clear that it was preparing to publish a detailed account of her trading profits.

Initially, senior aides to the Clintons said in March 1994 that Hillary "based her trades on information in the *Wall Street Journal*."[26] That explanation was subsequently dropped.[27] An aide to Hillary then said she had withdrawn from the market in the fall of 1979 because she had found trading too nerve-racking in the final months of her pregnancy.[28] But another White House aide quickly declared that excuse "inoperative"[29] after it was disclosed in April 1994 that Hillary made $6,500 in a commodities-trading venture in 1980 but failed to report that profit to the IRS.

Shortly after that, Hillary took responsibility—in her standard combination of singular acknowledgment and plural blame—for her aides' confusing answers to reporters, saying they stemmed from her being away, working on other issues. "I probably did not spend enough time, get as precise," she explained, "so I think that the confusion was our responsibility."[30]

Soon after the commodities-trading story was published, Bill and Hillary tried to improve their relationship with the media. They had their friend Susan Thomases reach out to a prizewinning journalist, James Stewart, a contributing writer for *The New Yorker*. The Clintons, Thomases told Stewart, wanted someone to fairly present the story of Whitewater and Foster's death, and to investigate the couple's ideological enemies. Stewart, intrigued by the overture, then flew from New York to Washington, where he met Hillary in the Map Room of the White House.[31]

After some pleasantries, Stewart recalled, Hillary "railed against the tactics of the right-wing media and think tanks" and expressed amazement that statements of fact from her and Bill were "not accepted at face value"[32] by reporters.

Hillary insisted she had nothing to hide, so Stewart continued his project. He had subsequent discussions with Hillary's aides. Believing the First Lady "would cooperate with me,"[33] he began writing a book about the Clintons and their adversaries.

But neither Hillary nor Bill cooperated.[34] Hillary's attitude toward the mainstream press stayed consistent from Little Rock to Washington—distrusting and wanting control. The Clintons were also somewhat naïve to think that if they simply pointed Stewart in the direction they preferred, he would walk dutifully ahead. Eventually his book, *Blood Sport*, drew wide praise, but not from the Clintons, and added to a torrent of stories about Hillary's professional life in Arkansas that continued to tarnish her reputation.

By mid-April, Hillary's approval ratings had dropped from 56 percent the year before to 44 percent, a historically low mark for a First Lady.[35] Aides knew that Hillary's stubborn reluctance to speak with the press was one of the sources of the public's displeasure with her. For weeks, her aides and friends had urged her to confront the negative reports and innuendos in an open, candid way.

It was one thing to stay in the background, but by not providing Americans with an example different from her initially off-putting public appearance, she was leaving it to her political enemies to define her.

In late April, Hillary told her chief of staff, Maggie Williams, "I want to do it. Let's call a press conference."

"You know you'll have to answer all questions, no matter what they throw at you," Williams responded.

"I know. I'm ready."[36]

The press conference took place in the State Dining Room, a less formal setting than the East Room, but the atmosphere was supercharged with drama and expectations.[37] At the last minute, Hillary decided to wear a pink sweater and a black skirt, which led the sixty-eight-minute session to be dubbed the "pink press conference." (Some reporters speculated that Hillary's choice of wardrobe was an attempt to "soften" her image,[38] the sort of fashion analysis a male political figure would never have been subjected to.)

At the outset, Hillary acknowledged that she had failed to make herself accessible to the press. She explained that her desire for a "zone of privacy" for her family and her habit of doing things her own way "led me to perhaps be less understanding than I needed to [be] of both the press and the public's interest, as well as [their] right to know things about my husband and me."

She attributed her reticence with journalists to the lessons she had learned as a child. Her parents had repeatedly told her, for example: "Don't listen to what other people say. Don't be guided by other people's opinions. You know, you have to live with yourself." It may have been good advice then, and she had certainly followed that advice since moving into the White House, but now, Hillary explained, it was time she began to open up and be "rezoned," as she put it. The reporters laughed.

A reporter asked whether her criticism of the Reagan era as a decade of unabashed greed appeared hypocritical in light of her recently disclosed commodities-trading windfall.

"I think it's a pretty long stretch to say that the decisions we made to try to create some financial security for our family and make some investments come anywhere near" the "excess of the 1980s," she replied. Inverting reality, she claimed that it was her father's stubborn frugality and quest for financial security that had helped her succeed at trading commodities.

She acknowledged that her refusal to release her 1979 tax returns and her steadfast opposition to the appointment of an outside counsel to investigate Whitewater had created the impression that she was trying to hide something. "I think that is probably one of the things that I regret most and one of the reasons why I wanted to do this," she said.[39]

Afterward, Hillary's aides and friends assured her that she had done quite well. But she was unconvinced. She told one friend that a one-hour press conference would not end this kind of siege. "They're not going to let up," she said. "They're just going to keep coming at us, no matter what we do."[40]

ON MANY MORNINGS in the spring of 1994, Hillary woke up feeling sad and alone. She recalled "aching for all the close friends, associates and relatives who had passed out of our lives or had been unfairly attacked."[41] The list included her father; Bill's mother, Virginia; and Vince Foster. She felt "down in the dumps"[42] and incredibly lonely.

Part of her melancholy was based on the Whitewater saga. (One morning in March, the Dow Jones average dropped twenty-three points because of "rumors" about the scandal.) An even larger part of Hillary's disappointment was rooted in her strong sense that the health care gambit was doomed. Yet another aspect had to do with the diminished role she was playing in the West Wing. The unprecedented policy position that Hillary had assumed on inauguration day was being downsized, drip by drip. She was going from an all-powerful copresident to a junior partner—albeit one with outsize influence and access to the boss. The shift was all part of the White House's perpetual campaign. Most Americans—62 percent in one poll—said they did not want Hillary involved in policymaking, though they approved of her performance as First Lady. This suggested strongly that a majority of Americans expected Hillary to stay within the boundaries of the traditional role of First Lady and not meddle in the official business of the country.[43] That would not be possible—she was too smart, too strong, and too proud for that, and her husband trusted her judgment on most things—but some adaptation was, and Hillary found herself edged toward the sidelines.

That summer, Hillary concluded that the whole Whitewater hubbub was nothing more than an attempt at "undermining the progressive agenda by any means....If you believed everything you heard on the airwaves in 1994, you would conclude that your President was a Communist, that the First Lady was a murderess and that together they had hatched a plot to take away your guns and force you to give up your family doctor (if you had one) for a Socialist health care system," she wrote.[44]

Her sense of persecution was only going to get worse. Hillary found the decision to appoint Kenneth Starr troubling and a confirmation of her fears of a politically inspired inquiry.[45] In turn, the lawyers and investigators who worked for Fiske, including agents from the FBI and the IRS, were worried that Fiske's departure would weaken the investigation. As a result, shortly after Starr was named to replace him, Fiske convened a meeting in Little Rock.

"There was a lot of concern among the FBI and the IRS about what was going to happen to the investigation," Fiske explained. "So I set up a meeting of about forty people from the FBI and the IRS. I said, 'Don't worry about this.' Ken Starr is a very fine person. We were ready to bring eight indictments against twelve people in the fall of 1994 and the spring of 1995. I said I was confident these indictments [would] happen. And every single one of those charges was brought and resulted in convictions." Fiske concluded, "Everything I would have done, he did."[46]

Starr mirrored that assessment, declaring, "Everything in Little Rock we inherited from the wonderful Bob Fiske." Of course, Starr would subsequently expand Fiske's investigation in ways that no one could have foreseen. Starr, shortly after taking office, was told by Fiske to "be prepared to move your family to Little Rock; you're going to be here for a long time."[47] That turned out to be another Fiske understatement. The independent-counsel investigation of the Clintons would stretch on for years, cost more than $50 million, and inflict terrible damage on the president and his wife, and, depending on whom you asked, the country.

Regardless of who was in charge of the investigation, the anger at the Clintons that summer across America was palpable. In Seattle, in late July, during a West Coast bus tour to rally support for the health care bill, Hillary was stunned when an angry mob of hundreds of protesters screamed vitriolic slogans at her about health care, gun control, and abortion rights. Most of the protesters were men who had been energized by local talk show radio hosts.[48] Hillary wore a bulletproof vest,[49] and she later recalled it was one of the first times that she had felt her life was truly in danger. "I had not seen faces like that since the segregation battles of the sixties," she told friends after returning to Washington. "They had such hatred on their faces."[50]

When Hillary returned to Washington, the last Republican senator who had backed the health care bill, John Chafee of Rhode Island, withdrew his support. Twenty-two months after Hillary's quixotic crusade began, it was over. The bill was not even introduced on the floor of the House or the Senate by the Democrats for a vote, a damning footnote—though by then hardly a shock. Although some advisers of Hillary's had urged her to try to work out a compromise with the Republicans, she had concluded that any deal would mean only that insurance premiums would go up. And then Bill and Hillary would be blamed, an eventuality that was unacceptable heading into the midterm elections that fall. As a result, Hillary had consistently rejected advice to compromise on the measure.

Hillary was devastated. Bill tried to console her by saying there were bigger mistakes in life than "getting caught red-handed" trying to provide health insurance to 40 million Americans who were without it. He chalked up the defeat to the $300 million spent by the health insurance industry and other lobbies with a keen interest in killing the bill. And he harbored deep resentment for the Republicans, especially for the way they had successfully turned his wife into the target.[51]

"Someday we will fix the system," she later wrote. "When we do, it will be the result of more than fifty years of efforts by Harry Truman, Richard Nixon, Jimmy Carter and Bill and me. Yes, I'm still glad we tried."[52] But for now, Hillary, whose ambition was always the engine of her life, had to set big plans aside and lower the expectations she had for herself.[53] She would describe her new role this way: "I now come from the school of small steps."[54]

FOR ALL ITS SETBACKS, the Clinton presidency had also seen remarkable successes in its first two years. Bill's budget bill had laid the fiscal groundwork for wiping out the deficit. That in turn helped grow the economy and create more than 10 million new jobs. In 1994, North Korea agreed to freeze and eventually dismantle its nuclear weapons program, Jordan signed an unprecedented peace treaty with Israel, and Haiti restored its elected president to power.

Hillary saw these as "Bill's milestones,"[55] and later, in her run for president, she referred to these accomplishments as something "we did."[56]

But 1994 also saw the low point of Bill's years in the White House — the genocide in Rwanda, which resulted in the loss of an estimated 800,000 lives in just a few weeks. Despite knowing what was happening in Rwanda, Bill effectively did nothing — as did his peers in other countries. While they postponed taking action and pretended not to be aware of the genocide going on, hundreds of thousands of men, women, and children died.

Predictably, Hillary did not blame Bill for the inaction, but rather "the failure of the world, including my husband's administration."[57] Bill later claimed that he and the other world leaders "did not fully appreciate" what had been going on in Rwanda.[58] In fact, his intelligence agencies and numerous newspaper, radio, and television journalists had made it all extremely clear to the world. Hillary would have had to ignore the news for weeks, as well as the frantic pleas of human-rights activists and some members of Congress, not to know what was happening. There is no evidence she did anything substantial to help.

When good things happened, they happened because of Bill and Hillary. When bad things happened, Hillary often found the fault in others.

As the Washington spring gave way to an unusually humid summer in 1994, Stan Greenberg, the White House pollster, organized a focus group. He gave the people assembled a list of phrases and asked them to pick the ones that best described President Clinton. "Over his head" was the most-stated phrase to describe Bill. Second most popular was "indecisive," followed by "immature."

This was no way to approach the midterm Congressional elections that fall. Greenberg delivered the bad news directly to Bill and Hillary in a memo written for their eyes only. "The administration, the Democrats in Congress and the party face a disaster in November unless we move urgently to change the mood of the country," Greenberg noted. To the public, the Clintons appeared to be overwhelmed and overmatched by Washington. An image of a chaotic White House, with its steady, unflattering press leaks and bumbling on issues ranging from homosexuals in the military to the nomination of an attorney general (his initial nominee, Zoe Baird, had been forced to withdraw after it was disclosed she had not paid taxes on household help), had gained traction with voters around the country, Greenberg had found. "This is about being young and inexperienced, from a small, backward state, and failing to master the bad forces at work in Washington," he wrote. "A few months ago, Whitewater was interpreted as gridlock, but now it is evidence of being over-his-head. This is about Bill Clinton personally, to devastating effect."[59] Bill Clinton and the Democratic Party had also been hurt by the widespread perception that Hillary had been out of her league on health care reform.

Hillary had sensed the bad feelings about her husband's presidency as she traveled around the country to promote the administration's health care bill, and now she tried to do something about it. In September, she called Dick Morris, the political strategist who was representing more Republicans than Democrats at the time. "The president needs you," Hillary told him.

The plan was that Morris would "rescue" Bill one more time, just as he had back in Arkansas. But despite the tinkering that Morris did — getting Bill to act more like the president and less like a stumping, desperate candidate — the polls failed to improve. Four days before the midterm elections, Morris delivered the bad news to Bill by telephone. "You're going to lose the Senate and the House," Morris told the president.

"Not the House," Bill replied. "No way."

"And the House, and by significant margins," Morris said.

"No way, no way. Not the House," Clinton replied. "Not the House. You're wrong. You really think so? You're wrong."[60]

Morris was right. It was a rout, the biggest Republican sweep into Congress in four decades. The Republicans captured control of the House by 26 seats; the Democrats lost a total of 54 seats. The Republicans also gained control of the Senate, 52 to 48. And not a single Republican incumbent lost in any reelection contest for a job in the House, the Senate, or a governor's mansion.

Georgia Republican Newt Gingrich became the Speaker of the House and the enforcer of the Republicans' "Contract with America," a series of position papers they hoped to transform into a legislative agenda. Almost immediately, Gingrich was mentioned as a presidential contender in 1996. (His wife, Marianne Gingrich, said she was not interested in the job of First Lady. "Watching Hillary has just been a horrible experience," she told journalist Gail Sheehy.)[61]

On the morning after the election, Hillary stayed out of sight. Bill faced the press, but he refused to blame one single thing, or person, for the sweeping defeat. "I think [the voters] were saying two things to me," the president said sheepishly. "Or maybe three...maybe three hundred."[62]

Dick Morris spoke with Hillary a few days later. "You know, Dick," she said, "I'm just so confused. I don't know what works anymore. I don't trust my own judgment."

"Well," Morris told her, "you know you had gone very far left."

By the end of the conversation, Hillary confided to Morris that she was lost: "I don't know how to handle this. Everything I do seems not to work. Nothing goes right. I just don't know what to do."[63]

One evening in the fall of 1996, during a game of hearts aboard *Air Force One*, the president was asked by Leon Panetta, his chief of staff, why he had put up with Morris all these years. The president, trying to unwind after a grueling day on the campaign trail, was "taken aback" by the question.[64] He paused a moment to think and then told Panetta that in politics "you need to hear from the dark side, and Morris represented that." In other words, Panetta later explained, "in order to win they needed to have someone like Morris to guide them, to understand the Gingriches of the world."[65] And Morris was part of that larger strategic plan, conceived, Bill said, by Hillary and him more than two decades ago, their "twenty-year project." The project, Panetta went on, "had begun in Arkansas with the goal of establishing a long-term change in where the Democratic Party was heading" and "included capturing the presidency."[66] Victory was the aim, and poll-driven policies were the means.

CHAPTER 11

The Discipline of Gratitude

THEY WERE DUBBED "the Chix"—a support group of ten women whom Hillary counted as her closest confidantes and dearest friends. Each week, they met with the First Lady to offer her a smile, a joke, a hug, and, if needed, a shoulder to cry on. The group included her scheduler, her speechwriter, her chief of staff, and the White House social secretary, as well as a longtime pal (Susan Thomases), a trusted media consultant (Mandy Grunwald), and a veteran Democratic activist (Ann Lewis). The "Chix" nickname had been coined by Evelyn Lieberman, the White House deputy chief of staff at the time. Their usual meeting place was the Map Room on the first floor of the First Family's White House residence. In that historic chamber, Franklin Delano Roosevelt had met with his top military men to plot bombing runs during World War II. Hillary adored the room and worked hard to refurbish it, placing a framed map of Europe, showing the Allied positions that FDR had consulted in 1945, above the fireplace.[1]

It was certainly an appropriate setting in late November 1994 for the Chix to help Hillary plot her comeback. With the Republicans preparing to take over both houses in Congress—in part because of her failed health care reform effort—and the president still personally reeling from the election results, the First Lady needed the group's support and advice now as much as at any other moment in the White House.

When Hillary walked into the room, the Chix were already assembled around a square table. Seeing their expectant faces unleashed a burst of emotion from Hillary. With her voice cracking, she apologized for letting everyone down. Then, stifling tears, she promised her friends that it would not happen again. The reason was simple: She was going to quit the public-policy part of her job, she told them. The copresidency experiment had failed.

"I told them I was considering withdrawing from active political and policy work, mainly because I didn't want to be a hindrance to my husband's administration," she recalled years later.[2] That night, at George Washington University, a forum on First Ladies was scheduled. Hillary told them she intended to cancel her appearance at that event too.

It was not a secret that Hillary's policy role had been scaled back, but it still was remarkably substantial — indeed, unprecedented — for a First Lady. The women sat in stunned silence. Then, each one told Hillary that she could not give up or back down. Their message: "Too many other people, especially women, were counting on" her — not just to move forward, but to succeed.[3]

Lissa Muscatine, Hillary's speechwriter who later served as the ghostwriter of *Living History*, told the First Lady, "Young people look to you for guidance in their own lives." Muscatine added, "You're a role model. What kind of message would you be sending if you stopped being actively involved?"[4]

Urged by her friends, Hillary attended the forum that night at the Mayflower Hotel in downtown Washington. An enthusiastic response from the audience gave her a much-needed emotional boost. Afterward, for the first time since the health care reform gambit ended, Hillary felt prepared to climb back into the arena. She recalled the words of encouragement of her heroine Eleanor Roosevelt: "If I feel depressed, I go to work." That's what Hillary did. Bill needed her, after all.

FOR AS LONG AS HILLARY could remember, her job was to work on her husband's behalf. Her confidence in her own judgment was badly shaken; she was "unsure" how helpful she could still be to Bill.[5] But she knew that Bill's confidence was also shaken. And so Hillary reached out again to the one person in politics that she knew who possessed the intelligence, temperament, and ego to help Bill be Bill.

That person was Dick Morris, and he sat down for a secret meeting that December, in the White House Treaty Room, with the president and Hillary. Hillary had been the "principal link" between her husband and Morris,[6] a political strategist who relished his role as the president's secret, indispensable man. He even had a code name, "Charlie." No one else inside the Clinton inner circle knew he was there.

It was no surprise that Hillary was inclined to enlist Morris to help Bill. From 1992 through late 1994, she and Morris had spoken once or twice a month by phone. "I had tried to offer her advice on her own work and on her own political style, advising incremental steps in health care and urging greater stress on cost-containment measures," Morris recalled. "Much of the time I passed ideas on to the President through the First Lady."[7]

Before Morris even had a chance to sit down in the Treaty Room, he looked Bill in the eye and said, "So, you want me to do basically for you what I did in 1980 or '82?"

"Yep," Bill said. "I want you to come back and do the things for me here that you did back in Arkansas. I need new ideas and a new strategy. I'm not getting what I need here, and I want you to come in. I've lost confidence in my current team."

With a half smile, Hillary told Bill, "You know, you have to stop asking us to rescue you every time."

The semiserious remark forced the president to raise his hands. "Last time," Bill said. "I swear."[8]

Not long afterward, Morris met privately with Bill in the Oval Office. Morris was armed with an alarming set of polling data that had gauged the president's popularity. About one-third of those polled believed Clinton was "immoral," and another third saw him as "weak." Morris was convinced that Bill had the power to change the "weak" perception, but it would take some bold action. Then Morris broached a subject that almost no one dared bring up with Bill: His weakness, Morris said, was Hillary.

"The more she seems strong," Dick Morris told the president, "the more you will inevitably be seen as weak."

Bill blanched at the remark once made by Nixon before quickly changing the subject. But Morris returned to it a moment later. "Look," he said, "you and I know the reality of your marriage. Your strengths feed on each other. But people don't get it. They think either she's wearing the pants or you're wearing the pants."[9] Morris urged Bill to show Hillary the polling data and discuss their dilemma and try to come up with a solution. (It is almost certain that Bill rejected Morris's advice, a friend said.)[10]

Unaware of Morris's conclusions, Hillary felt sure that the president would be in good hands. Several of her friends said returning Morris to the inner circle was Hillary's way to disengage herself from most of the day-to-day policymaking and the whirlwind of the West Wing. She needed some time and distance to focus on herself, her needs, and her goals.[11] "I really believe it took her a long time to get used to the way she was savaged in the health care thing—that seared her memory forever," a friend said. "And it gave her a reason to be much more indirect in the use of power in the White House. She was far less out there afterward."[12]

Christmas brought her two identical gifts, each of which would prove to make a powerful impression on the First Lady. A member of Hillary's prayer group, made up of women who reached out to Hillary, a group that included some Republicans,[13] and a friend from Arkansas each gave her a copy of a book entitled *The Return of the Prodigal Son*, written by a Dutch priest named Henri Nouwen. Hillary was touched by Nouwen's exploration of the parable that Jesus Christ told about the younger of two sons who had left his father and brother and then led a wayward life. When the son finally returned home, he was embraced by his father but resented by his responsible older brother. Hillary recalled that "one simple phrase in Nouwen's book struck like an epiphany: 'the discipline of gratitude.'"

She had been feeling sorry for herself—all the disappointments of the past two years had ensured that emotion—and as a result, she recognized that gratitude for all the good things in her life would not be easy. "I had so much to be grateful for, even in the midst of lost elections, failed health care reform efforts, partisan and prosecutorial attacks, and the deaths of those I loved," she recalled years later. "I just had to discipline myself to remember how blessed I was."[14]

Bill had his own advice for how Hillary should get out of her funk. "When you're confronted with a deal like this, it's not just whether you rebound from it politically, externally," he told her. "I mean, internally it has an impact on you. It either shrinks you up and makes you narrower or it makes you bigger and better and you grow from it."[15]

On a grim day not long after the midterm elections, Hillary stopped by her office and paused to look at a framed photograph of Eleanor Roosevelt on a table. She was struck by the apparent contradictory emotions of calmness and determination etched in Eleanor's face. She recalled Eleanor's get-on-with-it philosophy for a woman on the ropes. "A woman is like a teabag," Eleanor Roosevelt famously said. "You never know how strong she is until she's in hot water."

"It was time for another talk with Eleanor," Hillary decided.[16]

Since the beginning of Bill's presidency, Hillary had "communed" with Eleanor, holding imaginary conversations with her heroine as a way to draw inspiration and guidance from her life. Hillary devoured scores of books about her, finding strength in her courageous example. When she was confronted with a difficult decision, Hillary literally asked herself, "What would Eleanor do? How would Eleanor handle this?"[17]

On January 26, 1995, Hillary delivered the keynote address at the dedication of Eleanor Roosevelt College in San Diego, an event that she had anticipated for months. The First Lady was generally effusive about her heroine's courage, but the speech also revealed much about Hillary's own thinking during those dark days. Hillary's theme was about making right choices and the importance of resisting the temptation to allow detractors, critics — yes, even enemies — to turn you into something that you are ashamed of.

"Eleanor Roosevelt also understood that every one of us every day has choices to make about the kind of person we are and what we wish to become," she said. "I would say that every day you have the opportunity to demonstrate courage. You have a choice. You can decide to be someone who tries to bring people together, or you can fall prey to those who wish to divide us. You can be someone who stands against prejudice and bigotry, or you can go along with the crowd and tell the jokes and point the fingers. You can be someone who believes your obligation as a citizen is to educate yourself and learn what is going on so you can make an informed decision. Or you can be among those who believe that being negative is clever, being cynical is fashionable, and there really is nothing you can do anyway."[18]

Her friends knew that this speech was an intensely personal one.[19] Hillary had already figured that she had a choice to make — more than one choice, actually.

THE FIRST WAS to basically stop attending the weekly Wednesday-night meetings held upstairs in the residence with the president, Dick Morris, and other political strategists. In fact, from January 1995 until Morris's exile from the Clinton camp in August 1996 (following disclosure of his tryst with a prostitute at the Jefferson Hotel in Washington), Hillary attended only a handful of sessions.[20] One administration official said he recalls Hillary attending a key fund-raising meeting in late spring 1995, her appearance noteworthy because she had been absent for months.[21] There was nothing subtle about this decision; it communicated clearly to everyone that she was backing off.

If anyone had missed the message, Hillary made preparations to put thousands of miles between herself and the White House. She decided it was time to get out of Washington and explore the world.[22] It felt to some in the West Wing like Hillary was making her escape.

On March 25, 1995, seventeen hours after lifting off from Andrews Air Force Base outside Washington, Hillary's military jet approached Islamabad, Pakistan, on her first lengthy trip overseas without her husband. Her large entourage included Chelsea.

In some ways, Hillary was following in the footsteps of a less ambitious First Lady, Jacqueline Kennedy, by traveling to five countries in South Asia. Jackie had visited India and Pakistan in March 1962, and Hillary's itinerary was bound to recall the earlier voyage.[23] But her journey was also a personal one; she needed to find her bearings, and she was returning to familiar ground — women's rights.[24] Perhaps, a friend said, the trip abroad was Hillary's first, tentative step toward her own political resurrection.[25]

Her first day in Islamabad included a lunch in her honor hosted by president-elect Benazir Bhutto, the first woman in Pakistan's history to ascend to the top post. Other Pakistani women of accomplishment attended the luncheon, including a police deputy superintendent and a pilot. It was rare for women to achieve that kind of success in a Muslim country, and Hillary found it ironic that South Asia yearned for female leadership. "Pakistan, India, Bangladesh, and Sri Lanka have all been governed by women elected as Presidents or Prime Ministers," she observed, "in a region where women are so devalued that some newborn girls may be killed or abandoned."[26]

Bhutto declared that "women who take on tough issues and stake out new territory are often on the receiving end of ignorance." These remarks resonated with Hillary.[27] (Bhutto, too, had a husband with legal problems; he eventually went to jail in Pakistan on corruption charges.) A decade later, as Bill contemplated the possibility of his wife running for president, he would study Bhutto's life and career as an example of the power of family political legacies.[28]

The next day, Hillary visited the American embassy in Islamabad to console employees grieving over the assassination two weeks earlier of two colleagues in Karachi. The killings were an apparent retaliation for the recent extradition by Pakistan to the United States of the mastermind of the 1993 World Trade Center bombing. A few days before Hillary's trip, some in Congress had called on the United States to do more to curb Pakistani schools that were training terrorists.[29] But Hillary's visit was not about the politics of terrorism.

From Islamabad, Hillary flew to Lahore, the capital of Punjab. There, she focused her attention on the plight of women. Sitting under a tree outside Lahore, she heard a woman with ten children — five boys and five girls — describe how her daughters had less of an opportunity to attend secondary school than her sons. "I know my girls have hearts and minds too," the woman told Hillary, "and I want to give them the same chance my boys have."[30] At Lahore University of Management Sciences, Hillary exhorted the audience, proclaiming that, "if women don't thrive, the world won't thrive."[31] She also told a story about a man trying to find his identity. The anecdote carried universal meaning. "We are all struggling to find our bearings," she said.[32] The words applied as much to the man in her story as they did to her.

From Pakistan, Hillary traveled to India, where she made a speech on women's rights at the Rajiv Gandhi Foundation. Gandhi was a former prime minister, as was his mother, Indira Ghandi, and his grandfather. Indira, like Benazir Bhutto, had been a female leader with a family legacy, another example Bill Clinton would study years later in helping Hillary mull a run for president.[33]

In New Delhi, Hillary was smitten by a poem written by a young student at the Lady Shri Ram College. She ended her speech with it.

Too many women
In too many countries
Speak the same language
Of silence... [34]

The verses touched the reporters traveling with the First Lady — a further sign of her new comfort level with the press, at least those who had joined her on the trip to Asia. "The transformation that took place in my relationship with the press was one of the pleasant surprises of the trip," Hillary recalled. [35] That improved relationship was partly based on the fact that Hillary's contemporaneous remarks were, by trip rules, off the record and went unreported, encouraging her both to talk and to travel more. [36]

IN SEPTEMBER 1995, Hillary traveled to China to attend the fourth annual United Nations World Conference on Women. She was just the honorary chair of the American delegation, but her role turned out to be an active one. She hoped "to push the envelope as far as I can on behalf of women and girls," and her speech, in Beijing's Plenary Hall, was a loud call for women's rights to be finally equated with human rights, "once and for all." [37] Secretary of Health and Human Services Donna Shalala, who as a cabinet member sat at the U.S. table in Beijing, thought Hillary had "captured the moment in a single phrase." [38] Hillary's self-doubts after the ugly events of 1994 seemed thoroughly extinguished by the time she completed her twenty-one-minute address.

But Hillary's idealistic aims were tempered by her pragmatic politics. She did not name the host country or any other country in her speech, even though she was well aware of China's efforts to muzzle opponents, including forcing nongovernmental groups to hold forth in exile, forty miles from the conference. [39] Even after the Chinese government blacked out her speech on the closed-circuit television in the Beijing Plenary Hall, she said nothing to upset them. [40]

Hillary subsequently told CNN that she had in fact been referring to violations by China. [41] But Bill, eager to improve ties with Beijing, insisted "there was no attempt to single any country out." [42] And whatever she said later, in her speech Hillary had certainly not named names.

The Beijing speech became, she wrote, "a manifesto for women all over the world." [43] Indeed, her message was beamed all over the world, if not in the Beijing Plenary Hall itself. Her speech lifted her "from being a really first-rate First Lady," observed Donna Shalala, "to being an extraordinary one."[44] Perhaps even in Eleanor Roosevelt's league, though Hillary always refused that kind of high praise. "I hesitate to draw any comparisons," she said, "because I don't think there will ever be anyone like her."[45] But hesitation was different from refusing.

ON THE SURFACE, Hillary appeared much less active, even chastened by the health care debacle.[46] She attended no cabinet meetings and fewer White House policy meetings. And she became "extremely careful," Donna Shalala said, to "not be at the table developing policy."[47] But although she adopted a lower profile, Hillary remained a "firm, clear advocate," said Shalala.[48] Robert Reich, the former secretary of labor and a longtime friend of the Clintons, said it was "impossible to overestimate her influence."[49] Reich recalled sending messages to the president through Hillary, which he called a "very simple back door."[50]

Formally, the downsizing of Hillary's West Wing was accelerated after the resignation of the White House chief of staff, Thomas "Mack" McLarty, a childhood pal of Bill's from Arkansas and a close confidant of Hillary's. The new boss was Leon Panetta, the former budget director and an old Washington hand.

Under McLarty, Hillary had been more powerful than Al Gore, the traditional number two. But after Panetta arrived, the First Lady was knocked down a notch to Gore's level.[51] The First Lady and the vice president had already been constant rivals for the president's attention, and now that contest intensified. One Clinton aide recalls Hillary telling her husband to ignore Gore's advice. "Remember," Hillary told Bill, "he's not the president...*you* are."[52] With the advantage of proximity, Hillary owned the last word, but Gore had his resources — and allies — too.

On a range of issues, the First Lady continued to weigh in firmly but quietly. "On budget issues, where she felt a program was not being sufficiently funded, she would say it, in a small staff meeting or in the Oval Office," Panetta recalled.[53] Indeed, on Capitol Hill, Hillary was still seen as the White House go-to person on budget issues. "When I want to get the child care numbers improved in the White House's budget, I don't call the Office of Management and Budget; I don't call the chief of staff. I call the First Lady," said

Christopher Dodd, the Democratic senator from Connecticut.[54] And after the health care defeat, Hillary had come "back at it through other issues, like the health of veterans returning from the Gulf and women's issues," Panetta said.[55] On a multibillion-dollar child health program, Hillary was "very active," according to her former top aide, in lobbying Congress and then stayed with the issue after it became law to ensure it was implemented properly.[56]

Publicly, Hillary portrays her years as First Lady as totally subordinate to the president. "I supported his agenda," she wrote in her memoir, "and worked hard to translate his vision into actions."[57] That was true in many cases, but not always. Indeed, as her husband increasingly bent in response to polling data and Republican discontent, it was Hillary who attempted to hold the line. On what was perhaps Bill's signature issue, civil rights, Hillary worked hard to prevent him from retreating too far when faced with Republican opposition or some of Morris's inclinations. Polls showed that a majority of Americans were opposed to affirmative action. Panetta tried to tell the president that "it's more than polls."[58] Hillary, too, urged her husband to keep fighting for affirmative action. "You can't back off on this issue," she told Bill. On civil rights, according to Panetta, Hillary was "the voice of conscience — her voice was the voice of what's right; her voice was the strong voice."[59]

Hillary's reception abroad had resuscitated her self-confidence and her commitment to her core issues — including a willingness to take a principled stand against the two poll mavens closest to her: her husband and Dick Morris.[60] Increasingly this voice was heard outside of Washington. Once again the model was Eleanor Roosevelt, who had been given a high-profile Civil Defense post in 1941 only to resign the following year after suffering withering attacks from critics. She had then reinvented herself, embracing a softer approach to issues she cared about, such as women, minorities, and immigrants, through radio interviews and a regular newspaper column. It did not take long for her popularity to soar. Hillary's adaptation of the "Eleanor Roosevelt way" was not lost on strategists from both parties. She began writing a book, *It Takes a Village*, and a syndicated newspaper column. Both book and column were decidedly accessible affairs, without sharp edges, and designed to be hypoallergenic in every way. Hillary certainly saw her book on children as an attempt to counter the Dickensian pronouncement of Newt Gingrich, the Republican Speaker of the House, and his allies, especially the "reactionary pundits and TV and radio personalities."[61] But it was political in an extremely subtle sense.

This public softening was not matched in private. Around the time of the book's publication, Leon Panetta first realized how animated Hillary could become about the steady stream of attacks launched against her and Bill by the Right. During a helicopter ride from the White House lawn to Andrews Air Force Base, in an attempt to make conversation, Panetta casually said something about someone in Arkansas, and Hillary suddenly lashed out.

"Let me tell you," Panetta recalled her saying, "the right wing has been going after us since Arkansas. They haven't let us alone. They are dishonest."[62] Hillary's sudden outburst "went on till we landed at Andrews," Panetta recalled.[63]

Yet Hillary also found ways to accommodate the Gingrich crowd, on issues like welfare reform. Along the way, she caused a permanent rift with her oldest ally in the cause of children's rights. In 1996, as Hillary was promoting her book, Gingrich forced the president to confront a possible third veto of welfare legislation that had passed Congress. The groundbreaking measure that ultimately emerged from the Republican-controlled Congress was designed to move welfare recipients off the rolls and into the workplace by imposing time limits on their benefits. Initially, Bill had proposed the welfare reform effort, but aspects introduced by Gingrich and his allies had altered the bill in ways that the president found disconcerting. A key opponent of the legislation was Marian Wright Edelman, the founder of the Children's Defense Fund, and the woman who Hillary credited with inspiring her in 1970 to commence a lifelong advocacy for children.[64]

Twenty-five years later, however, Hillary was no longer an idealistic advocate. She had become, like her husband, a calculating, pragmatic politician. Advocates such as Edelman, Hillary concluded, "were not bound to compromise."[65] She contrasted their refusal to bend with the conciliation frequently sought by her and her husband.

Publicly, Hillary denied compromising her principles or values when she endorsed her husband's support of the welfare legislation, which came as he was facing reelection. She believed, she claimed, that the third bill passed by Congress went far enough in its guarantees of medical benefits, child care, and food stamps to warrant her and Bill's support.[66] (Others, both liberals and conservatives,

noted that the third bill was almost the same as the previous two
Bill had vetoed.)[67] "Strategies and tactics must be flexible enough
to make progress possible," she wrote, "especially under the difficult political conditions we faced."[68] In a private discussion about
welfare reform a few months before the bill passed, Hillary told a
White House associate: "We have to do what we have to do, and I
hope our friends understand it."[69] Though she was not yet an openly
practicing politician, Hillary's explanation signaled how she would
operate when she became one — taking the road of short-term electoral advantage when necessary and without expressing regret.

Years later, the welfare reform bill was viewed by many as a
success; others considered it an abandonment of the truly needy
for the sake of scoring political points. In her book *Living History*,
Hillary found the space to acknowledge more than four hundred
friends, colleagues, and supporters. Marian Wright Edelman was
not one of them.

CHAPTER 12

"Off to the Firing Squad"

FOR HILLARY, the month of January 1996 marked a sudden and dramatic turn of events. Until then, things had again been looking up. Her foreign travel had been a success, helping to heal the wounds from the collapse of the health care effort. The manuscript for It Takes a Village was finally complete. And Bill's reelection prospects were looking up after he stood down the Republicans during an ill-advised, Gingrich-inspired government shutdown.

Even the endless inquiries seemed manageable, nearing a favorable outcome. Just weeks earlier, in late November, Jean Lewis, the investigator who had started the federal investigation of Madison Guaranty in 1992, acknowledged being a conservative Republican.[1] Suddenly the Clintons' claims of political witch hunt seemed more credible. Then in late December, a law firm, Pillsbury Madison and Sutro, completed a report for federal regulators finding no reason to sue various parties, including the Clintons, for losses stemming from the collapse of Madison. The Clintons and their supporters heralded the report, saying its conclusion that they had been passive investors in Whitewater with Jim and Susan McDougal reaffirmed what Bill and Hillary had maintained from the outset: They were not aware of Jim's stewardship of the real estate company. Hillary and Bill later wrote, somewhat bitterly, that the news media down-played or ignored the law firm's findings.[2]

Something that had begun with a few canceled checks for several thousand dollars had produced a $3.6 million report that the Clintons saw as exoneration. But the decision not to sue them did little to remove the cloud of suspicion hanging over the president and First Lady.

"A CONGENITAL LIAR."[3] That was the phrase used by *New York Times* columnist William Safire to describe Hillary at the start of 1996, and the label walloped the First Lady, dropping her into a deep funk.[4] Her husband was furious. If Bill Clinton were not the president, White House press secretary Mike McCurry said, "He would have delivered a more forceful response to the bridge of [Safire's] nose."[5]

"The first word I had in mind was *prevaricator,* which means liar, and the second one was *dissembler,* which also means liar," Safire (a former Nixon speechwriter) explained on national television after his column was published. "And then I said to myself: I'm in the opinion business. Why can't I express my opinion with the simple English word that everybody understands?"[6]

Safire's phrase was precipitated by the discovery of Hillary's law firm's billing records for Madison Guaranty; he believed the records contradicted her recollection of having done minimal work for the Arkansas savings and loan. He also did not think that she had been truthful about other matters under investigation, such as her commodities trades. Safire's comments ricocheted all over America; conservative commentators, like Rush Limbaugh, gleefully parroted the words "congenital liar" for weeks. Later that month, a majority of people polled said they thought Hillary was a liar.[7]

On that Sunday, January 14, when Safire explained to a national television audience why he had chosen those two words, and commentators repeated the president's threat to punch Safire in the nose, Bill Clinton phoned Monica Lewinsky at her mother's apartment in the Watergate complex in Washington, DC. By then, Bill and Monica had been carrying on a sexual relationship for about six weeks. He invited Monica to meet him that afternoon in the Oval Office, where he said he'd be working.

She was enthralled that her "first date" with the president was in the Oval Office. They spent about thirty minutes together in the president's bathroom, where she performed oral sex on him.[8]

Less than one week later, Hillary returned to her alma mater, Wellesley College, on Friday, January 19, to speak about her lifelong passion for children's issues. In introducing the First Lady to the standing-room-only audience, the college's president, Diana Chapman Walsh, reminded the audience that twenty-seven years earlier, Hillary had beckoned her fellow students to "throw ourselves into the tumult."[9] Her return to the bucolic women's college along the shores of Lake Waban would mark the beginning of Hillary's most tumultuous week yet, one in which she would reach the nadir of her distress.

EARLIER THAT SAME FRIDAY, the First Lady's lawyers in Washington were informed by the independent counsel that she had been subpoenaed to appear before a grand jury in connection with the recent discovery inside the White House of her law firm's billing records. Carolyn Huber, Hillary's longtime assistant, said she first discovered the records in August 1995 in Room 319A, part of the White House personal residence.[10] The documents showed the number of hours that Hillary had billed a decade earlier to Madison Guaranty, the failed institution at the center of the counsel's investigation. Unaware of their significance, Huber put them in a box in her own office in the East Wing and didn't examine them again until January 1996.[11] Previous searches had failed to locate the files.[12]

The command by Kenneth W. Starr, the independent counsel, that Hillary appear before a grand jury, an unprecedented demand for a First Lady, signaled a dramatic shift in his team's tactics. Hillary's previous interrogations by Starr were held at the White House, away from the press. "This time there would be no quiet deposition in the White House," Hillary recalled.[13]

Her lawyers argued for a change in venue. But "Starr insisted on summoning me to the courthouse," she said.[14] Starr and his deputies proposed allowing Hillary to enter the courthouse by using a back entrance, as a way to avoid the television cameras.[15] Hillary rejected the offer because she said it "would make me look as though I had something to hide."[16]

Hillary's mood was further spoiled by another Whitewater matter. Earlier in the week, she had appeared on Diane Rehm's talk show on National Public Radio. Rehm asked her about a 1993 recommendation by David Gergen, a White House aide, to turn over

Whitewater-related documents to reporters at the *Washington Post*, a suggestion that Hillary had opposed.[17] Hillary replied, "We actually did that with the *New York Times*. We took every document we had, which again I have to say were not many. We laid them all out."[18]

Inside the White House, aides knew that Hillary's remarks were inaccurate; in fact, the *Times* had not been given many documents. "We all knew what Hillary said wasn't true," one said.[19] One staffer who had to help correct the record didn't relish the task. "I thought I'd get sacked," the aide remembered, after Hillary "went bat shit" and hung up the phone with another underling dealing with the problem.[20]

Finally, Jane Sherburne, a White House lawyer, called Hillary to resolve the issue. The First Lady poured out her distress. "I can't take this anymore," she said. "How can I go on? How can I?"[21]

IN THE END, another White House counsel released a partial mea culpa. The statement said Hillary had "mistakenly suggested that the *New York Times* was provided access to all of the Whitewater-related documents in the possession of the 1992 campaign."[22] In addition, it suggested that campaign staffers, not Hillary, had withheld the documents. Hillary, who almost never publicly acknowledged a mistake for fear of arming her opponents, was not about to concede ground at such a crucial moment in her war with Starr.

Hillary "believed," the statement went on, "that the campaign had turned over all of the documents," but "she had since learned that the campaign would not provide reporters with certain records."[23] In reality, Hillary herself had been actively involved in the 1992 decision to withhold documents from the *Times*.[24]

By January 19, 1996, the day of her subpoena, her Wellesley speech, and the mea culpa, Hillary's approval ratings had dropped, in a span of just two weeks, from 59 percent to 42 percent.[25] Hillary worried that she was in danger of losing "whatever credibility I retained."[26] Her anxiety was so palpable that she hardly slept or ate for the next week, until her testimony was completed.[27]

On a cold winter day, one week after getting her subpoena, Hillary appeared before the grand jurors. A moment before she entered the courtroom, she broke the ice with a quip: "Cheerio! Off to the firing squad!" she told her lawyers.[28]

Inside the grand jury room, she explained to the jurors (mostly women and African Americans) and the lawyers from the independent counsel's office (all white and male) that she did not know what had happened to the billing records after she moved from Little Rock to Washington.[29] She also said she did not know how they wound up in Room 319A. She was asked about her never-released statement from 1992 in which she acknowledged that she "should not have become involved at all" in helping represent Madison before state regulators.[30]

Afterward, a throng of reporters waited for Hillary in the dark outside the courthouse. They asked her how she was feeling. "It's been a long day," she said.

Another reporter wondered, "Would you rather have been somewhere else today?"

"Oh, about a million other places."

When asked about the long-missing, suddenly found billing records, Hillary said, "I, like everyone else, would like to know the answer about how those documents showed up after all these years. I tried to be as helpful as I could in their investigation efforts."[31]

As they had done at the pink press conference, reporters noted that Hillary wore an embroidered black wool coat to the grand jury, "emblazoned on the back with a gold dragon."[32] Her wardrobe caused several commentators to dub her "the dragon lady," and Hillary's office put out a statement noting that the coat, made by Hillary's friend, the Little Rock designer Connie Fails, had been worn by the First Lady during the inaugural events in January 1993.[33]

Hillary returned to the White House after her court appearance and entered the Diplomatic Receiving Room, where Bill and Chelsea embraced her with big hugs.[34] Bill then dashed off to a black-tie fund-raising event. Later that night, after being debriefed by the lawyers, Hillary retired upstairs to the private residence, and a profound loneliness set in. This was not how it was supposed to have been. When Senator Chris Dodd phoned that evening to lend his support and ask how she was feeling, Hillary told him he was the only caller she had heard from.[35]

THE INDEPENDENT COUNSEL never charged anyone in connection with the tardy production of the legal documents. But the saga of the missing billing records marked a turning point in how the Clintons and Kenneth Starr viewed each other.

Prosecutors were suspicious about why documents under subpoena for nineteen months had suddenly turned up. Despite Hillary's professed lack of knowledge, Starr's suspicions deepened because, among other things, his investigation had found three workers inside the White House who had seen Hillary carrying a cardboard box, possibly containing billing records, on the third floor of the residence in July 1995.[36] There were suspicions in Hillary's camp too. One White House lawyer said that she began to see Starr not as a truth seeker but as someone "out to do harm" to Hillary.[37]

On a cold Friday in January 1996, late in the afternoon, copies of the 116 pages of billing records were made available to reporters at the offices of Hillary's lawyers in Washington. The reporters had little time to analyze the records—ultimately a disadvantage for the Clintons, since it turned out that the media's first accounts framed the issue for years to come.

On their face, the records showed that Hillary had billed sixty hours of work for Madison in 1985 and 1986. Her fee ranged between $125 and $140 per hour. The biggest chunk of hours was in connection with a Madison-backed real estate development, called IDC in the records but more commonly known as Castle Grande. Hillary had billed for fourteen conferences with Seth Ward, a key figure in the real estate development. Her supporters explained that the records, which showed she had worked roughly four hours a week over a fifteen-month period, were consistent with Hillary's long-expressed recollection that she had done minimal work for Madison.

But her Republican critics saw the records as directly contradicting her previous statements of having little or no involvement, especially in connection with transactions involving Ward and Castle Grande.[38] To them, the records revealed a regular, weekly allocation of nearly half a day of work, over a year and a half period.

Meanwhile, the press, in hundreds of news stories, focused on Hillary's billings for Seth Ward and IDC,[39] in part because the Castle Grande transactions, especially those involving Ward, were quickly found to be a sham meant to hide from bank examiners that Madison was breaking federal lending rules.[40]

The billing records seemed to link Hillary not only to a troubled client, Madison, but to a questionable transaction—the Castle Grande real estate deal. That connection fueled suspicion among Starr's prosecutors about the motive for removing the billing records from the Rose Law Firm in the first place and why they had been unavailable to investigators for so long.

The inquiry, in part, was mired in semantics. Hillary, her defenders said, remembered the matter as IDC, the title on the billing records, and so she understandably had not recalled the matter as Castle Grande when asked about it by investigators. But there was another possibility: Hillary did not or could not have done some of the work she billed for. When one looked closely, it was possible to see that her invoices were undocumented, inaccurate, or padded, albeit in small ways. Hillary, it turned out, wasn't guilty of facilitating nefarious transactions — she was guilty of doing less work than she took credit for.

Hillary added her single biggest allocation of time in working for Madison, 14.5 hours, to the firm's bill after the fact, in her own handwriting and without any documentation or explanation. When asked by prosecutors about the handwritten "time added in," she testified that it happened once in a while "because of the way I didn't always keep my records or I wasn't always in the office."[41] In one internal memo, investigators said they were "unable to reconstruct the basis (if one exists) for Mrs. Clinton's $1,818.75 increase" in her billings;[42] Hillary, like other partners at her firm, had wide latitude in the 1980s to charge the client.[43] (The Rose Law Firm, which prided itself on its ethical practices,[44] tightened its procedures after Hubbell's fraud was discovered in 1993.[45])

On two other entries, Hillary slightly increased her billable hours through handwritten additions. Her explanation was that the firm's secretaries had in all likelihood forgotten to enter the proper time, and she simply corrected the bill after the fact.[46] Hillary also billed for meetings and discussions that others did not remember or said didn't happen. Hillary billed for fourteen conversations with Seth Ward involving Madison, but Ward did not remember any of the fourteen conversations with Hillary, even though he knew her well and remembered other legal dealings with her that were reflected in her billings.[47] She also billed for several meetings with other Rose Law Firm lawyers who did not bill for the same meeting on their own time sheets.[48] On a real estate option related to Castle Grande, for which she billed two hours, Hillary utilized the wrong legal description for the property, and it had to be corrected after the mistake was discovered by others.[49]

On April 25, 1998, when prosecutors from the Independent Counsel Office questioned Hillary about her billing from May 1, 1986, to prepare the real estate option, she went out of her way to minimize her role. "I don't believe I drafted the option agreement," she testified.

"But," one of the prosecutors shot back, "you billed for it."

"It, it was billed for," Hillary replied. "That is correct, along with several other activities in a two-hour period....I do not believe I drafted this option from scratch. That would not be something I would do."[50]

By 1997, the idea that Hillary did not do all the work she had billed for came to be quietly embraced by several aides to Starr's and even some members of Hillary's legal team.[51]

"Hillary wanted fee credits so she padded the bill," including, "specifically Castle Grande," one of Starr's investigators explained at the time. "But Hillary also can't acknowledge that she didn't do the work" because it would undermine her public image as a top-notch corporate lawyer.[52] Though not flattering for Hillary, the likely truth in this case also raises doubts about many of the criminal theories entertained for years by investigators and the media. Her likely indiscretions were altogether modest; but the scandal that would result from Hillary's attempt to cover up sins of the past would be enormous.

JIM MCDOUGAL BEGAN cooperating with Starr after he was convicted of fraud in a 1996 jury trial in Little Rock, and suggested to investigators that the Rose billing records were inaccurate. Ward had never mentioned any discussions with Hillary on IDC matters to him, McDougal told investigators. Furthermore, "Hillary Clinton could not have handled the option because she didn't understand it," McDougal said.[53]

When the independent counsel gathered evidence that Hillary had billed another client for work she did not do, it lent credence to the possibility that her Madison bills were inflated. "It is possible that Mrs. Clinton increased the amount of the [Madison] invoice without doing any additional work," prosecutors concluded. "There is evidence that she did that in an unrelated matter Rose handled."[54] This evidence, gathered in secret by the grand jury, was never made public.

To some of the hawks in Starr's office, "the billing records put her in the middle of bank fraud"[55] or "suspicious transactions,"[56] so Castle Grande was "the key to everything."[57] And yet, the question of what her billing records really demonstrated — evidence of fraud, of overbilling, of sloppy billing, or nothing of significance — was impossible to answer because investigators for both Starr and Fiske never found Hillary's time sheets for 1985 and 1986, the years she worked for Madison, a former investigator explained.[58] Hillary's secretary had removed her time sheets from storage in 1992, as press questions about her work swirled around Bill Clinton's first presidential campaign, and they had vanished.[59] The possibility that Hillary had padded her bills became nothing more than a footnote for Starr's inquiry — literally.[60]

Soon after Hillary was interviewed under oath on July 22, 1995, Starr's point man for investigating Hillary's role in Madison, Hickman Ewing Jr., had met with a small group of staffers. Ewing believed Hillary had lied, but wasn't sure whether it was to protect her billing irregularities or to hide criminal conduct.[61] Because Hillary had testified she did not recall matters about fifty times, Ewing told the group that he gave her a grade of "F minus."[62]

Ewing's assessment of the First Lady's performance, made at a restaurant named the Faded Rose in Little Rock, "kind of shocked" Starr.[63] Starr found her to be cold and aloof,[64] but he thought she had done better.[65] Following the meal, Ewing and Starr took a car ride together during which Ewing, a former United States attorney in Tennessee, lectured Starr on how to properly interview witnesses.[66]

Starr, then forty-eight and five years younger than Ewing, was a former federal appeals court judge and solicitor general with no prosecutorial experience. His career was steeped in arguing legal and constitutional issues, not interrogating witnesses. During the time Starr had been writing opinions and winning numerous awards and distinctions, Ewing had been busy prosecuting criminal cases. Despite those differences, the two men shared a religious kinship and an ideological bond, both having been nominated to federal posts by Republicans. And both shared a dedication to getting to the bottom of things with regard to the Clintons.

Ewing's theory went like this: Hillary and Hubbell had released "inaccurate stories" about Hillary's legal work on Madison in 1992, when the issue surfaced during Bill's presidential campaign. They were then "stuck with" these erroneous narratives when they were later questioned under oath by investigators, resulting in even greater inaccuracies and omissions.[67]

However, putting out inaccurate stories to the press and repeating them under oath is not a crime unless the stories are found to be willfully inaccurate — one of the obstacles that Ewing could not overcome.[68]

As Starr moved toward deciding whether to bring charges against Hillary, the billing records loomed large for investigators because they "revealed that Hillary Clinton performed much more work on Madison Guaranty than was previously known."[69] (Again, Hillary was trapped, in that if she admitted she hadn't done that work, she'd be off the hook in one instance but setting herself up for an entirely new problem.) In addition, the records showed that investigators had not known about Hillary's apparent involvement in the Castle Grande–related transactions.[70]

The Clintons' legal defense team also pored over the billing records. While they publicly maintained that the billing records exonerated Hillary, demonstrating she had done nothing wrong, privately some members of her legal team reached a more nuanced view: The bills did demonstrate small-time bill padding, but it was a practice knowingly tolerated by McDougal, the man who hired Hillary.[71]

"McDougal knew the bills were padded," said one member of the Clinton legal team. "There's documentary evidence of it, but McDougal couldn't admit the billing scheme."[72] That's because McDougal hired Hillary as a favor to Bill, and he was willing to close his eyes to Hillary's overbilling as part of the favor he was doing for Governor Clinton.[73] In any case, Hillary's lawyers had never been too concerned about what Jim McDougal might say: His credibility was already in doubt even before he was convicted of eighteen counts of conspiracy and fraud. It was the paper trail that the Clintons worried about.[74]

AMID IT ALL, Hillary began contemplating her own political future, most likely in the Senate. She saw being a senator as the most prestigious elected job in Washington other than the presidency, and it would serve as a launching pad to the White House.[75] Because Illinois had not been her home since she graduated from high school — and she had never felt comfortable living in Arkansas — she needed to adopt a state from which to run. As early as March 1996, New York presented itself as a surprisingly inviting and refreshingly open-minded place.

Her friend Sid Blumenthal, formerly the Washington correspondent for *The New Yorker*, who joined the White House as an aide to the president but would become one of Hillary's trusted confidants, suggested to the First Lady that she travel to Manhattan. Blumenthal assured her that the trip would provide a welcome respite from the scandal-driven hysteria and chaos of the capital. A luncheon in honor of Hillary was held at the Century Association in New York, on March 19, 1996. Several dozen editors and writers from influential magazines and book-publishing houses were present. Hillary did not arrive with prepared remarks, preferring instead to answer a wide-ranging series of questions from those present. (No one discussed the cloud hanging over Hillary until Sid himself delicately raised the matter of Whitewater, near the end of the luncheon. Hillary "spoke frankly," Blumenthal recalled, "explaining Whitewater's emptiness.")[76] The reception that Hillary received was enthusiastic.

Blumenthal said that the day in New York began changing Hillary's perception of a state that had turned her off during the Democratic presidential primary in 1992. She began to see New York as a place where people were savvy enough to reject the media-fed stereotype of her and instead accept her on her own terms. Blumenthal believed that the single day in Manhattan had made such a profound impression on Hillary that it had amounted to a critical first "step on the road that led her eventually to decide to run for the Senate there."[77]

Hillary had that future in mind when she prepared for her speech at the Democratic National Convention in Chicago in late August 1996. She knew that her heroine, Eleanor Roosevelt, had been the first First Lady to address a national political convention, but that had been back in 1940, long before television cameras had become a staple of such gatherings. And while she had never been out of the spotlight during the past four years, Hillary saw her speech as nothing less than her first opportunity to speak directly to the American people.[78] This would be her moment, in the spotlight and without filter. This was Bill's convention, to be sure, but the speech would be her chance to shine.

Yet, just as she had been before her graduation address at Wellesley, Hillary wasn't sure what to say. She was dissatisfied with the prepared text, and Bill, who was traveling with Chelsea on a train from West Virginia to Chicago, was not there to provide his usual smart advice and good cheer.[79]

On the morning of her address, Hillary panicked.[80] She did not know what to say, and her nerves were getting the better of her.

Her mind racing, she seized on a few sentences delivered by the Republican nominee, Senator Bob Dole, at his party's convention earlier that month. Dole had clumsily attacked Hillary's book *It Takes a Village*, saying that the village in the title was a metaphor for "the state." The Kansas senator had clearly missed the main argument of her book, that families bore the ultimate responsibility for children, while the "village" — her metaphor for society — shared "responsibility for the culture, economy, and environment in which our children grow up."[81]

Dole's critique became Hillary's muse. That night, nearly twenty thousand delegates, guests, and media members were in the arena. Millions of Americans were watching at home. When Hillary took the stage, she was extremely nervous, but the crowd greeted her with a wall of enthusiastic noise. "My motions to urge the crowd to sit down were futile," Hillary recalled in her book, "so I just waved and let the cheers wash over me."[82] She began by speaking about Chelsea, who was preparing to enter her senior year that fall at Sidwell Friends. Hillary went on to directly rebut Dole, saying that yes, it did take Bill and Hillary to raise Chelsea. But it took a lot more. "It takes teachers," she said. "It takes clergy. It takes business-people. It takes community leaders. It takes those who protect our health and safety. It takes all of us.... Yes, it takes a village. And it takes a president. It takes a president who believes not only in the potential of his own child, but of all children, who believes not only in the strength of his own family, but of the American family.

"It takes Bill Clinton!"[83]

The crowd roared its approval. Afterward, Hillary felt as if she had truly connected with an audience — and Americans around the country. For so long, she had stood alongside the object of the audience's affection. Now she was the one they were applauding. It was a rush like none other. "I knew then she was bitten by the bug," one friend recalled years later. "I could tell she wanted to hear those cheers again and again."[84]

THAT NOVEMBER, Bill Clinton cruised to reelection, easily defeating Senator Dole by 8 percentage points nationally. Hillary immediately began envisioning a far more visible but less active behind-the-scenes role for herself in Bill's second term, noting that she wanted to "speak out publicly to help shape White House policy on issues affecting women, children, and families."[85]

The first year of the second term was a time of more "pseudo-scandals," as Hillary called them. The Washington press corps focused on the fund-raising excesses of the Clintons — notably, Lincoln Bedroom overnights for big campaign contributors, and White House coffees sold to political donors. It was also a year of funerals — Princess Diana and Mother Teresa both died, within weeks of each other in the late summer, and Hillary attended both services.

But nothing was more traumatic for Hillary than the departure of Chelsea from the White House. In September 1997, Chelsea entered Stanford University as a freshman and a member of the Class of 2001. Hillary went to Bed Bath and Beyond and Linens 'n Things to prepare her for the trip. After the Clintons arrived in Palo Alto, California, they helped Chelsea organize her dorm room, which seemed overstuffed with bunk beds, two desks, and two dressers. Bill seemed to be moving in slow motion, insisting that he carry Chelsea's luggage and helping take apart her bunk bed with a wrench. By the end of the afternoon, it was time for the parents to say good-bye.

"What do you mean, it's time to leave?" Bill said, rather panicked. "Do we really have to go now? Can't we come back after dinner?"[86]

The next month, Hillary turned fifty, but she was so busy she barely noticed the rite of passage, she and her friends said. She was far more distressed by Chelsea's absence. The White House was not the same without her daughter, Hillary told friends.[87]

Throughout their time together in Washington, Hillary had always managed to make time for her daughter. Chelsea had joined her mother on several state visits. And she had provided a sort of ballast amid the scandals and attacks. Now she was on the opposite side of America.

After New Year's Day 1998, Bill and Hillary traveled to St. Thomas in the U.S. Virgin Islands for a quick four-day rest. At a house overlooking Magens Bay, Bill, Chelsea, and Hillary relaxed, played cards, swam, jogged, rode bikes, read books, and completed thousand-piece jigsaw puzzles. Bill also played golf while Hillary and Chelsea scoured the local shops. Midway through the trip, Bill and Hillary went down to the beach for a swim.

A photographer from Agence France-Presse was in the bushes on a public beach across the bay. With a telephoto lens, he captured a private, carefree, unguarded moment between Bill and Hillary, laughing and holding each other. The photograph was published in newspapers around the world. Mike McCurry, the White House press secretary, lashed out at the photographer for invading the Clintons' privacy, and the image also raised security questions.

Some commentators thought the Clintons had staged the photo with hopes that the photograph would dispel questions about the strength of their marriage. "Hello?" Hillary said. "Just name me any fifty-year-old woman who would knowingly pose in her bathing suit — with her back toward the camera."[88]

However unguarded the moment was, it would be one of the last that Bill and Hillary would share in public for a very long time. Within weeks of their joyful embrace on St. Thomas, Hillary would consider the possibility of leaving Bill for good.

CHAPTER 13

The Most to Lose

ON THE MORNING OF January 14, 1998, in the Treaty Room of the White House, Hillary was placed under oath, for the fifth time, by prosecutors from Kenneth Starr's office. Starr found Hillary's "frosty demeanor" to be a "vivid and stark" contrast to the graciousness displayed by the president.[1] But despite the chill, this session was nearly effortless and surprisingly painless; best of all, it lasted just ten minutes. The three prosecutors, all of them men, politely asked Hillary a few final, perfunctory questions about the last case Starr's office was pursuing against the Clintons. This latest investigation involved allegations that the Clinton White House had improperly obtained confidential FBI files, many of them files of prominent Republicans. When the session was over, the First Lady was so relieved that she would likely not have to answer additional questions under oath about some "non-scandal," as she called it, that she failed to detect a smirking smugness that had crept into the expressions on the faces of Starr's men.[2]

But her lawyer, David Kendall, noticed something odd, almost off-putting, in the demeanor of the prosecutors.[3] Rather than carrying the hangdog look of lawyers who watched helplessly as their last labyrinthine inquiry had unraveled, these men appeared to be energized by great expectations. "Like the cats who swallowed the canary" was the way that Kendall described the prosecutors' behavior to Hillary after they had left.[4] There was something in their manner and in the bounce in their step. They were acting as if they had a wild card hidden up their sleeves.

They did. What neither Hillary nor Bill knew was that just two days earlier, a forty-eight-year-old Pentagon public affairs employee named Linda Tripp had called Starr's office with a new set of allegations. Hers was a riveting and embarrassing tale of sex and lies, all captured on secretly recorded audiotapes that implicated the president in an affair with a White House intern and raised allegations of perjury and obstruction of justice. Tripp had originally volunteered her story to the lawyers representing Paula Jones in her lawsuit against the president. Jones, a former Arkansas state employee, had sued Bill Clinton in 1994 for sexual harassment over an alleged encounter in a Little Rock hotel in May 1991.

Tripp told Starr's prosecutors that since late 1995, Bill Clinton had carried on an on-again, off-again sexual relationship with Monica Lewinsky, a then twenty-one-year-old White House intern. Tripp also told the prosecutors that the president had helped Lewinsky find a corporate job in New York. And she said that the president had encouraged Lewinsky to lie, under oath, about the nature of their relationship in an affidavit to be given to Paula Jones's lawyers.

Here, Robert Fiske's rewriting of his charter came into play in a way that would badly burn the president. Starr and many of his troops were by now convinced that Bill and Hillary were hiding the truth, and they aimed to prove it. In Linda Tripp's secret tape recordings of conversations she had had with Lewinsky, they had found a key to a door they wanted badly to unlock.

Later that very week—on Saturday, January 17—the president was scheduled to be deposed by Paula Jones's lawyers. During that session, he would certainly be asked, under oath, about the nature of his relationship with Lewinsky.

The deposition by Jones's lawyers, coming just days after Starr's office began investigating the Lewinsky case, amounted to nothing less than an elaborate perjury trap designed to catch the president in an under-oath lie for political purposes. The trap by Jones's lawyers was intended at the very least to harm Bill politically and possibly drive him from the presidency.

That lawsuit, now four years old, had dragged on to this embarrassing and risky denouement because neither Hillary nor Bill had any desire to strike an out-of-court settlement with Jones, even after the Supreme Court had ruled that the president of the United States was not immune to standing trial in civil lawsuits. Bill's lawyers—and even Bill himself—were inclined to settle. But Hillary ultimately overruled them, saying that "the public would see a settlement as confirmation,"[5] declaring that if they paid Jones a single dollar, "the lawsuits would never end."[6] Hillary seemed to be suggesting that there were other women out there who would be encouraged to file a lawsuit against her husband, which may well have been true, but tactically her advice turned out to be disastrous.

"With the wisdom of hindsight, of course, not settling the Jones suit early on was the second biggest tactical mistake made in handling the barrage of investigations and lawsuits," Hillary observed years later. "The first was requesting an independent counsel at all."[7]

By the end of that week, Bill and Hillary's inaction on the Paula Jones lawsuit and his decision to name an independent counsel to investigate Whitewater had merged to create a volatile threat that endangered the things that mattered most to each of them—his legacy and her future.

ARMED WITH LINDA TRIPP'S tawdry tale and audiotapes, Kenneth Starr sought permission to extend the Whitewater inquiry into Tripp's allegations. Starr had already investigated whether friends of the Clintons had attempted to pay "hush money" to Webb Hubbell—an inquiry that had gone nowhere—but the thinking in Starr's office was that the president's alleged attempt to "buy" Monica Lewinsky's silence through a lucrative job in New York was tantamount to the same sort of obstruction of justice. There was a low threshold for an independent counsel to begin an investigation. Indeed, during the four years since he became independent counsel, Starr had taken on a number of unrelated inquiries, all of which consumed a lot of time and resources but never led to any charges against Bill or Hillary. Nevertheless, by virtue of the wording of the independent-counsel statute, he was well within his rights to follow nearly any lead. When the Lewinsky matter began in January 1998, therefore, it was not surprising that Attorney General Janet Reno granted Starr's request to investigate it. She had approved the request on Wednesday, January 14, the same day that Hillary was sitting for her last question-and-answer session with Starr's prosecutors — thus the grins in the Treaty Room.

At 1:00 p.m. on Friday, January 16, Monica Lewinsky arrived at the Pentagon City mall in suburban Virginia to have lunch with her friend Linda Tripp. Lewinsky was unaware of Tripp's betrayal. On that same evening, the president stayed up late with his legal team, rehearsing his answers during a marathon six-hour cram session to prepare for the Paula Jones deposition the following day. On a witness list, provided by Jones's lawyers, were the names of seven women. One of them, Monica Lewinsky, had signed an affidavit on January 7, swearing under oath that she had not had "sexual relations" with the president. Bill knew he would be asked a series of questions not only about Paula Jones but also about the seven women on the witness list, including Lewinsky. And, just as Monica had done in her affidavit, the president was prepared to lie.[8]

SATURDAY, JANUARY 17, 1998, was a thickly overcast, unseasonably mild day in the capital. Before Bill left the White House that morning for the deposition, Hillary gave him a warm embrace and wished him luck.[9] The president then took the short two-minute ride from the White House to the Skadden, Arps law office of Robert Bennett, Bill's gruff, blunt, and imposing defense lawyer.

After being sworn in, the president was handed a legal document by the Jones lawyers with a court-approved definition of "sexual relations." The definition was excruciatingly specific — "contact with the genitalia, anus, groin, breast, inner thigh, or buttocks of any person with an intent to arouse or gratify the sexual desire of any person."

Though the deposition was intended to deal with the alleged incident at the Excelsior Hotel in May 1991 between then-governor Clinton and Paula Jones, Jones's lawyer, James Fisher, began with a series of questions about a woman named Kathleen Willey, a former White House volunteer, and an encounter she claimed to have had with the president just a few short steps from the Oval Office. Then Fisher turned to Monica Lewinsky.

"Did you have an extramarital sexual affair with Monica Lewinsky?" Fisher asked the president.

"No," Bill replied.

"If she told someone that she had a sexual affair with you, beginning in November of 1995, would that be a lie?"

"It's certainly not the truth," the president said. "It would not be the truth."[10]

James Fisher quizzed the president for nearly ninety minutes about Monica Lewinsky, asking him repeatedly about whether he had "sexual relations" with her, as it was defined in the legal document. Each time, Bill said no. Near the end of the interrogation about Lewinsky, the president asked Fisher if there was something "more specific" that he wanted to ask him about his dealings with the former intern.

Fisher declined the offer. "Sir," he said, "I think this will come to light shortly, and you'll understand."[11]

Bob Bennett, Clinton's lawyer, later reminded Jones's lawyers that Monica Lewinsky had signed an affidavit ten days earlier, swearing under oath that she did not have sexual relations with the president. The Jones lawyers did not respond to Bennett's assertion, but they knew, from Linda Tripp's audiotapes, that Lewinsky had lied in her sworn affidavit.[12]

Late that afternoon, after a six-hour session, Bill left Bennett's office and returned to the White House. Hillary noticed that Bill looked tired and upset.[13] When she asked him how the deposition had gone, Bill snapped that the proceeding was "a farce" and said he deeply resented having to endure such an ordeal. The Clintons had planned to go out that evening for dinner with Erskine Bowles, Bill's chief of staff, and his wife, but Bill said he just did not feel up to it.[14] Instead, the president stayed in, spoke with a few friends on the phone, and went to sleep in the early morning hours. He had to sense that both his presidency and his marriage were in trouble.

SHORTLY BEFORE DAWN on Wednesday, January 21, 1998, Hillary was awakened by Bill in their bedroom in the White House. The president sat on the edge of the bed and told her, "You're not going to believe this but..."

"What are you talking about?" she said sleepily.

"There's something in today's papers you should know about."[15]

Bill explained that the *Washington Post* was publishing a story that morning describing an affair that he had with a former White House intern, and that Kenneth Starr was now investigating whether he had lied about it under oath or asked the intern to lie about it during the Jones deposition. The article also reported that Starr's prosecutors were actively investigating whether the president and his friend Vernon Jordan had obstructed justice when they had helped Lewinsky find a job in New York.[16]

Hillary sat astonished, listening but saying nothing.

About the allegation that he had carried on an affair with a woman young enough to be his daughter, Bill offered his wife this explanation: He had become friends with Monica two years earlier, while she was working as an intern for chief of staff Leon Panetta in the West Wing during the government shutdown in November 1995. Bill said that he had offered her some help to look for a job. She must have mistaken his friendship for something more, Bill speculated.

Whether Hillary had considered, even for a moment, that Bill's story was a pack of lies is unknown. Two close friends of Hillary said a few months later that they believed she suspected immediately that Bill probably did carry on an affair with the young woman,[17] because, as one friend said, "there were so many other affairs. This didn't come out of the blue."[18] Added a senior administration official, "You never quite knew what the truth was with the president. I suspected there was something to it, and I believe Hillary did too."[19]

This official added that immediately after hearing about the alleged affair and Starr's inquiry, Hillary was stunned and furious. An element of her anger, the official said, was this rhetorical question that she had posed to Bill: "How can you be so stupid to arm our enemy?"[20] Indeed, Bill had handed Starr a potent weapon. The official also said he was convinced that Hillary knew "something had happened" between Bill and Monica, adding, "I am certain that he let on that there was a trace of truth to this."[21] However, the official insisted that Hillary was "unaware of all the sordid details...she didn't learn about them until August. So the betrayal, for her, was about the details and how long the affair went on."[22]

Another friend and adviser to Hillary, who spoke to her within forty-eight hours of the scandal becoming public, said Hillary acted "as if she knew that Bill had to have had an affair with Monica...and she was still determined to beat it back, and win."[23] The friend went on to say that Hillary found it easier to set aside any feeling of betrayal because she perceived Starr's new inquiry "as an all-out assault on the presidency....Even if [the affair] was true, she was going to fight to the death to save his presidency."[24] Because the president had been "blindsided" by the perjury trap set by Jones's lawyers, with help from Tripp and in consultation with Starr's office, Hillary observed that she was deeply offended by "the unfairness of it all." It was that perceived unfairness that persuaded Hillary to be "more determined to stand with him to combat the charges."[25]

Years later, Hillary insisted that she had believed her husband's weak cover story from the very beginning. Hillary explained in her memoir that, despite his many previous affairs, Bill's story made sense to her because counseling a young woman "was completely in character for Bill."

"He said that she had misinterpreted his attention, which was something I had seen happen dozens of times before," she continued. "It was such a familiar scenario that I had little trouble believing the accusations were groundless."[26]

But Hillary knew that millions of Americans — millions of women, in particular — did not believe Bill Clinton as easily as she did. In her memoir, she acknowledged that most seemed perplexed by her steely determination to accept his explanation, carry on, and not leave her husband. Hillary knew that many people wondered, "How can she get up in the morning, let alone go out in public? Even if she doesn't believe the charges, it has to be devastating to hear them." It *was* both devastating and "isolating," Hillary acknowledged.[27] The Lewinsky allegations began the "loneliest and most difficult year of her life," one of her friends said.[28] From the very beginning, however, Hillary was determined to make her own choice about how to proceed. She decided to do "what was right for me," as she put it, "no matter what anyone else thought or said."[29] For Hillary, defending Bill was, in a very real way, an act of both self-defense and self-preservation. And she decided, as she had done many times before, to dig in and defend her husband. A friend said that it was easier for Hillary to think of Bill's carrying on an alleged affair as an ingeniously devised political attack than as a betrayal of their marriage vows.[30] Back in college, Hillary had regained her balance by refusing to look inward, by focusing her attention on helping others deal with their own issues. Now, rocked backward, she did the same thing.

In Hillary's autobiography, she writes only briefly about the hurt and shock of first learning about the affair. "A nuisance civil action had metastasized into a criminal investigation by Starr, who would undoubtedly take it as far as he could," she said. "Leaks to the media from the Jones camp and the Office of the Independent Counsel implied that Bill's testimony in his sworn deposition may have conflicted with other witness descriptions of his relationship with Lewinsky. It appeared that the questions in the Jones deposition were designed solely to trap the President into charges of perjury, which might then justify a demand for his resignation or impeachment."[31]

Privately, Hillary was hopeful that "people might start to understand" the argument that she had been making for years: She believed that the prosecutors were attempting to undermine the office of the presidency and her husband's agenda through an abuse of their power.[32] Omitted from her account was an acknowledgment of the peril endangering her own political career. Her friend and adviser Sidney Blumenthal observed, "For her, the stakes were greater than for anyone. They encompassed not only everything she had worked on politically for a lifetime, but her marriage. She had to defend both."[33]

A political future was by no means a vague hypothetical. She was nearly certain by early 1998 that she was going to seek a Senate seat, possibly in New York. And this scandal, it appeared in those early days, directly threatened that prospect. More immediately, the Clintons' reported plan for eight years for him in the White House, followed by eight years for her, was now in peril. Hillary was just furious that such a stupid, sad mistake on her husband's part now endangered all their plans — no, all *her* plans.[34]

Around the world, reporters spoke of the risk to Bill Clinton's legacy. But the view from Hillaryland was simple: She had the most to lose.

HOURS AFTER FIRST HEARING her husband utter the name "Monica Lewinsky," Hillary had to leave the White House to deliver a speech in Baltimore, at the invitation of Taylor Branch, the historian. It was a previously scheduled engagement, and she was determined to fulfill her commitment.[35]

Besides, what choice did she really have? She had to carry on. Hillary thought yet again of the words of wisdom of Eleanor Roosevelt, who had observed that a woman in political life had to "develop skin as tough as rhinoceros hide."[36] As she had done in the past, Hillary concluded "it was important to reassure the White House staff that we would deal with this crisis and be prepared to fight back. . . . The best thing I could do for myself and for those around me was to forge ahead."[37]

So that afternoon, Hillary was aboard an Amtrak train churning northbound toward tiny Goucher College in Baltimore. After her thirty-minute speech at Goucher, Hillary was confronted at the Baltimore train station by a throng of reporters and camera crews. It was the largest crowd of media she had seen in years, exceeding the one waiting for her outside the Whitewater grand jury room. "Do you think the charges are false?" a reporter yelled.

Hillary was sitting on a bench in the center of the train station. She paused, stood up, approached the cluster of microphones and cameras, and said, "Certainly I believe they are false — absolutely."[38]

Hillary was then asked how she was able to endure the questions, and she said, "You know, I wouldn't say that it's not hard, because it's difficult and painful anytime someone you care about, you love, you admire, is attacked and subjected to such relentless accusations as my husband has been. But I also have now lived with this for, gosh, more than six years, and I have seen how these charges and accusations evaporate and disappear if they are given even the light of day. So I feel the same way about all of this."[39]

Finally, she said that Starr's inquiry was bad for America. "All of this . . . it's something I wish that neither my husband, nor anyone associated with him, were subjected to because I regret it deeply, and it's something that I don't think is good for the country," she said. "It's not good for our country that political accusations and conflicts are turned into matters of legal concern," she added. "They ought to be fought out in the arena, but since my husband has been so successful in changing the direction of the country and accomplishing so much on behalf of the country, I think it has been very hard for his opponents to accept."[40]

While Hillary was in Baltimore, the president sat for three previously scheduled interviews with *Roll Call*, National Public Radio, and PBS television. Jim Lehrer of PBS asked him, "You had no sexual relationship with this young woman?"

"There is not a sexual relationship," Bill replied. "That is accurate."[41]

In newsrooms across the capital, the president's choice of the verb *is* triggered loud alarm bells. For Bill, whose legendary political skills included the artful parsing of language, this choice of tense was not at all subtle and even clumsy.

As it was becoming obvious to reporters and strategists around town that the president of the United States had engaged in a sexual relationship with a woman young enough to be his daughter, Hillary was back in her office at the White House, apparently oblivious to such a judgment. She was thinking less about Bill's possible guilt and more about her hatred of Kenneth Starr.[42] She called Sid Blumenthal, who was often derided by some of the political strategists because he frequently saw elaborate conspiracy theories between "the right wing" and its favorite target, the Clintons. (Rahm Emanuel, a Clinton political strategist, nicknamed him "G.K," for "Grassy Knoll.")[43] But Blumenthal would be invaluable to Hillary in the days ahead, primarily because he had maintained trusted relationships with a number of important Washington authors and correspondents, including, not incidentally, David Brock. Brock was the author who had been on the payroll of *The American Spectator*, a right-wing magazine backed by the conservative Richard Mellon Scaife, which led to his writing in 1993 about allegations by two state troopers who claimed they had set up sexual encounters for Bill while he was governor, a scandal dubbed "Troopergate."[44] Since then, however, Brock had quite publicly switched ideological sides. In the process, he had become one of Blumenthal's trusted confidants. Hours after the *Post's* scoop was published about Starr's inquiry into the Lewinsky affair, Brock had fed Blumenthal fresh information about the novel way that Starr had come to know about Monica Lewinsky and Linda Tripp, including the critical role played by several conservative lawyers, a group dubbed "the elves."[45] Those lawyers had given free legal help to Paula Jones, and one of them had tipped off Ken Starr's office that Linda Tripp would be bringing Starr her allegations and secretly recorded audiotapes.

Blumenthal told Hillary about his conversation with Brock. "We could see the lines of influence underlying the scandal, the cause and effect, intent and action—and they were political and familiar," he later recalled. "Thus, on the first day, both Hillary and I knew about what she would soon call the vast right-wing conspiracy."[46]

Blumenthal was struck by Hillary's calmness and determination while the scandal hysteria was consuming the capital and the country. "This was politics," Blumenthal later recalled, "perhaps a greater crisis than ever, but politics nonetheless."[47] But her steely demeanor was misleading; in the West Wing, "it was just chaos," said a former Clinton administration official. "For two days, we had a rolling meeting. We were in crisis. No one knew what to do."[48]

Forty-eight hours after the story broke, senior White House officials decided on the "rules of the road" going forward. This was a legal matter, and only a select few people would deal with the strategy and the details: David Kendall; Kendall's partner, Nicole Seligman; Cheryl Mills, a lawyer in the White House counsel's office; and Hillary. "Hillary was in all the meetings," the official said. "She had done this before, and she was going to do it again."[49]

Hillary confided to Blumenthal that the president also viewed this as a crisis that would be won or lost in the political arena. After sizing up the threat now aimed at his presidency and his place in history, Bill had told Hillary earlier that day, "Well, we'll just have to win."[50] There was nothing subtle about the president's choice of the word *we.* If he had any chance of escaping another very tough jam, Bill needed Hillary, as he always did. He knew it, and she knew it.

FROM HIS OFFICE on the CBS lot in Burbank, California, Harry Thomason had watched the president's shaky interview with Jim Lehrer on PBS. Like the journalists who had watched, Thomason, a television producer and an old friend of Bill, saw a president who was offering a legalistic, shady, and even clumsy defense. He put down his TV remote and grabbed the phone and called Hillary to voice his concerns about what he had seen.[51]

"When can you get here?" she asked.[52]

The next night, in the White House, Thomason urged the president and the First Lady to give the public a united and defiant front against the allegations, which continued to be the talk of the nation. On Monday morning, January 26, there was a press event scheduled in the Roosevelt Room of the White House about funding children's after-school care. This provided the perfect opportunity for Bill, with Hillary and Vice President Gore standing by his side, to knock down the charges with vigor.

Gore did not like what he was seeing.[53] The budding scandal had already created a gulf between him and the Clintons. The loyal vice president found the scandal distasteful, and he was surprised at how quickly Hillary went into battle mode, and how easily she seemed to set aside any astonishment at how Bill's dalliance had damaged the administration's agenda. For her part, Hillary was disappointed in Gore, sensing that he was not doing enough to defend the president.[54] One adviser explained that Hillary demanded "complete and total loyalty to the president. So when Al was upset with what happened to the president, I assume it added fuel to the fire."[55] That fire had been smoldering since the beginning. One adviser recalled that Gore and Hillary had had numerous heated disagreements that were not personal but political. "Sure, they clashed," the adviser said.[56] Another said: "They are completely different people. You can be around them and feel it."[57] (Years later, Gore acknowledged that there had been "a lot of water under the bridge" in his relationship with the Clintons.)[58] Hillary's reaction now struck Gore as odd and impersonal.[59] Her husband had betrayed her, humiliated her — what could be more personal? And yet her filter seemed to allow only the political to pass through.

In the Roosevelt Room that morning in January 1998, after completing his remarks about child care issues, the president hesitated a moment and shot a look of fury at the bank of three dozen television cameras. "I want you to listen to me," he said, though this was less of a request than a directive. "I'm going to say this again." And then, with a finger jabbing the air, and his eyes furious slits, the president said methodically, "I did not have sexual relations with that woman" — and he paused for a beat here — "Miss Lewinsky. I never told anyone to lie, not a single time — never. These allegations are false. And I need to go back to work for the American people." Bill then pivoted sharply away from the lectern; with a defiant-looking Hillary in his wake, he stormed out of the room.

In her autobiography, Hillary simply said this about Bill's performance: "I thought his show of anger was justified under the circumstances, as I understood them."[60] She said nothing about the fact that she had strongly urged her husband to knock down the charges and that she had insisted that she stand by his side as he did it.[61] That she would subsequently distance herself from Bill's remarks is understandable: Her husband's response was a lie, and he knew it, and in her heart, so did Hillary.[62] At the time, though, she had pushed aggressively for him to say the sort of thing he had said; Hillary Clinton was not about admitting a mistake, and neither would be her husband.

By his side that day, Hillary had been silent. But everyone in America, it seemed, wanted to hear from her. The following day was the president's State of the Union address, and Hillary had a long-standing commitment to appear on NBC's *Today* show in New York. "I would rather have had a root canal, but a cancellation would have created its own avalanche of speculation," she reflected.[63] Hillary was urged by her advisers and Bill's aides to say nothing about Kenneth Starr. The thinking was that an attack against him by the First Lady would "antagonize him" and simply make matters worse for the president.[64] However, lawyer David Kendall disagreed with that counsel; he quietly told the First Lady that she should say whatever was on her mind without any concern about the consequences.

A close friend of Hillary said that she had vowed on the night before her *Today* show appearance: "I'm going to war with Starr."[65] The friend said, "She knew the only way to win this thing was to put Starr on the defensive. And the perfect chance to do that was in New York on the *Today* show."[66]

Hillary spent the night of January 26 in a suite at the Waldorf-Astoria hotel, waking the next morning at five o'clock. On the short drive over to NBC at Rockefeller Center, Hillary was "very relaxed," her chief of staff, Melanne Verveer, recalled. "Not uptight. Not apprehensive."[67]

Ten minutes before seven, from the *Today* studio, Hillary spoke with Sid Blumenthal for a last-minute pep talk. Blumenthal suggested that she say, "There are professional forces at work whose only purpose is to sow division by creating scandal."[68]

That morning, Matt Lauer was alone on the somber set at Rockefeller Center; Jay Monahan, the husband of his cohost, Katie Couric, had died just three days earlier after a long battle with colon cancer. Hillary, looking exhausted, with deep circles beneath her eyes, sat directly across from Lauer, who began the interview immediately following the seven o'clock news.

"On 'Close-Up' this morning," Lauer began, "the First Lady of the United States, Hillary Rodham Clinton." Turning to Hillary, he said, "There has been one question on the minds of people in this country, Mrs. Clinton, lately. And that is, what is the exact nature of the relationship between your husband and Monica Lewinsky? Has he described the relationship in detail to you?"

"Well, we've talked at great length," Hillary said. "And I think as this matter unfolds, the entire country will have more information. But we're right in the middle of a rather vigorous feeding frenzy right now, and people are saying all kinds of things and putting out rumor and innuendo. And I have learned over the last many years being involved in politics, and especially since my husband first started running for president, that the best thing to do in these cases is just to be patient, take a deep breath, and the truth will come out."

This answer was remarkable for its avoidance of the question. The truth was she knew full well whether he had described the relationship and whether she believed her husband or not.

A moment later, Lauer tried a different approach, saying how James Carville had described the reinvigorated independent counsel's office inquiry as a monumental personal war between Bill and Starr. "You have said, I understand, to some close friends, that this is the last great battle. And that one side or the other is going down here."

Hillary shook her head and frowned. "Well, I don't know if I've been that dramatic — that would sound like a good line from a movie," she said. "But I do believe that this is a battle. I mean, look at the very people who are involved in this. They have popped up in other settings. This is — the great story here for anybody willing to find it and write about it and explain it is this vast right-wing conspiracy that has been conspiring against my husband since the day he announced for president. A few journalists have kind of caught on to it and explained it. But it has not yet been fully revealed to the American public. And, actually, you know, in a bizarre sort of way, this may do it."[69]

The First Lady's highly charged phrase to describe the Clinton enemies — "a vast right-wing conspiracy" — infuriated the men and women working in Starr's office on Pennsylvania Avenue, to whom the word *conspiracy* connoted criminal activity on their part.[70] Later that day, Starr took the unusual step of releasing a statement that described Hillary's allegation that he and his prosecutors were participants in a conspiracy as "nonsense."[71] But the First Lady's invocation reached its intended audience. One week later, a *Washington Post*/ABC News poll showed that 59 percent of those polled believed that "Clinton's political enemies are conspiring to bring down his Presidency."[72]

After the *Today* show interview, on her way back to Washington, Hillary had another brief phone conversation with Kendall. "I heard your words of wisdom ringing in my ear," she told him.

"And which words of incredible wisdom were you hearing?" Kendall asked.

"Screw 'em!" she said, laughing out loud.

"It's an old Quaker expression," replied Kendall, a Quaker.

"Oh," Hillary said, "like 'Screw thee?'"[73]

Hillary had not laughed so hard in a long time.

AS THE SCANDAL UNFOLDED, Hillary once again asked herself what Eleanor Roosevelt would have done in such an untenable position. The answer came easily: *Fight. Fight to the death.*[74] And that's what Hillary did. From the first day, she took control of the press operation and the legal strategy sessions from inside the White House.[75] An anti–Monica Lewinsky campaign began within hours of the *Washington Post* scoop, with whispers to reporters that the former intern was not just infatuated with the president but that she was the president's "stalker." A White House aide told reporters that the young woman was "unstable" and had battled a "weight problem." There were other catty nicknames ascribed to her by White House aides: "Elvira," for her long black hair and tight wardrobe, and "Clutch," because when the president or some other famous person shook her hand, she did not want to let go.[76] Right-wing critics of the Clintons had long made fun of Hillary's — and even Chelsea's — appearance. Those crude attacks had been deemed despicable by many. Now, the White House played that game too.

Three thousand miles away, Chelsea was in the middle of her freshman year at Stanford University. The embarrassing scandal was swirling around her, making the hardship of her first year away from home even more difficult. Hillary spoke often on the phone with Chelsea during those first few weeks. In late February, the First Lady made an unannounced trip to Palo Alto to be with her. Chelsea told her mother that she did not want her father to visit the campus, a decision that "crushed" him, a friend said.[77] She believed that her father had indeed had an affair with a woman only a few years older than she was. For Bill, who doted on his only daughter, Chelsea's verdict was as bad as it gets.[78]

IT WAS NOT JUST Monica Lewinsky whose reputation was trashed by aides at the White House. Kenneth Starr was going to become "a household name, and not in a good way," Carville predicted, with a large dollop of Cajun-spiked glee. "There's going to be a war."[79] Carville's cocksure vow was less a threat than a directive, and it was specifically intended for the Hillary loyalists.

Allies of the White House took aim at, among other things, Starr's religiosity, poking fun at the fact that he sang hymns every morning. Starr thought it was a "religious smear" to caricature him as being "a person of faith." He also believed that the religious attack by Clinton allies "redounded, not surprisingly, to my benefit in a number of communities, but not in the cultural elite."[80]

Still, Starr himself later conceded the attacks on him were ultimately successful with the American public, in part because "there was no one on the other side" to defend his record as a judge and an officer of the court. Starr faults himself for not going to Janet Reno, the attorney general, and asking her to defend him, since legally, he could not personally comment on the case.[81] When he eventually did sit with Reno many months later, she was investigating Starr's activities, including his earlier relationship to Paula Jones's attorneys before he became independent counsel. (He had offered one of Jones's lawyers advice on a matter of constitutional law before he had become independent counsel.[82]) Starr considered Reno's investigation "a declaration of war," and by then it was too late for him to ask her to defend his conduct.[83]

For Hillary, the performance of nearly everyone enlisted to defend the Clintons exceeded her expectations. For the couple, the first test of loyalty was the passion and commitment exhibited by friends in the midst of a full-blown crisis. "Everyone had a lot of practice, but this was an all-out war and everyone hunkered down and just did it," said a longtime friend of Hillary.[84]

In March, another miniscandal rattled the White House: Kathleen Willey, the former White House volunteer, told *60 Minutes* that the president had groped her and placed her right hand on his aroused penis in his private study just off the Oval Office. Bill saw her allegations as further evidence of prosecutorial misconduct on the part of Starr.[85] The day after the interview, he pronounced himself "mystified and disappointed" by Willey's account.[86] With Hillary's go-ahead, the White House then released nine fawning letters that Willey had sent to Bill after the alleged incident.[87] (Hillary is silent about Kathleen Willey in her book *Living History*.)

In late March, Bill and Hillary traveled to sub-Saharan Africa to tour six nations in eleven days. It was a welcome escape from the feeding-frenzy atmosphere in the capital, though they insisted the trip was not taken in response to the Lewinsky scandal.

While the Clintons and their aides were in Senegal, on April 1,

Judge Susan Wright granted the president's lawyers' motion for a summary judgment and threw out the Paula Jones case. The judge concluded that Jones possessed no credible evidence to support her claim. The twisted irony of this was not lost on either Hillary or Bill, who spoke privately about their astonishment that the Clinton presidency was endangered because he allegedly lied under oath in a civil lawsuit that a judge had thrown out of court.

"This is *not* Watergate," Hillary told friends.[88] She would soon learn that in some ways, it was.

CHAPTER 14

The Most to Gain

AFTER THE CLINTONS returned from Africa in late April 1998, a sense of routine nearly returned too. The Starr inquiry was relatively quiet through the spring months as prosecutors interviewed witnesses before the grand jury, including Linda Tripp. But behind the scenes, Monica Lewinsky was preparing to cut a deal with Starr's prosecutors that would grant her immunity from prosecution for lying under oath about her relationship with the president. On July 17, Starr took the extraordinary step of sending a grand jury subpoena to the president. It was the first time in American history that a sitting president would be required to appear before a federal grand jury in which he was the potential target.[1]

Now out of the way was Jim McDougal, who had died in federal prison in March 1998. Shortly thereafter, much of what he could have further testified about became irrelevant. Before Hillary's final interrogation had occurred on April 25, 1998, Hickman Ewing and several other prosecutors had prepared a blizzard of memos, laying out the evidence and a draft indictment. The possible indictment of Hillary and Webb Hubbell for obstruction of justice and making false statements had an underlying theory—the notion that the two had "knowingly or not provided legal services that facilitated" crimes, especially Castle Grande and the real estate option, "and exposed themselves, and the Rose Law Firm, to potential criminal and civil liability."[2] But on April 27, 1998, Starr's prosecutors, after a daylong meeting, decided not to bring any criminal charges against Hillary. The crucial question of whether Hillary knew that her legal work had facilitated crimes was skirted.

The decision not to charge Hillary was the result of a litany of factors: the staleness of the real estate transactions, the circumstantial nature of the evidence, the death of witnesses such as McDougal, the freshness of the Lewinsky case developing against Bill Clinton, and the sympathy that potential jurors would likely have for Hillary while also harboring antagonism toward Starr.[3] But while that antagonism was mounting, it did not prevent Starr from going forward in his attempt to investigate the president.

On July 27, Monica Lewinsky struck the immunity deal with prosecutors, sparing her a federal perjury indictment. The next day, as she prepared to appear before the grand jury, she turned over what would become the case's most important piece of evidence— a navy blue dress purchased at the Gap.

During that summer, Hillary had struggled to maintain a semblance of normality. In late July, she appeared at a battered women's shelter in Cincinnati and talked over lunch with several women being treated there.[4] That evening, she attended a fund-raising event. While there, Hillary got a call from an aide in Washington: Bill was going to testify before the grand jury.[5]

Since the president had agreed to testify voluntarily, Starr withdrew his historic subpoena. But Bill insisted on doing things partly on his terms. For instance, he did not want the indignity of walking into a federal courthouse. Starr agreed to this condition because the independent counsel had seen how the public reacted negatively to seeing Hillary endure such an indignity.[6] It was agreed that the president's question-and-answer session would be broadcast inside the grand jury room through live, closed-circuit video transmission. And it would be videotaped, just in case a member of the grand jury was absent that day.[7]

With Monica Lewinsky now cooperating with prosecutors, the president's lawyers were trying to find out what Starr had. A day after Bill agreed to testify, David Kendall got his answer when Starr informed him that prosecutors needed to draw a vial of the president's blood. For months, there had been press reports of a semen-stained dress. Such a request could only mean that Starr was going to use a DNA test to unravel seven months of the president's lies.

The blood test represented "a low point" for Bill, a moment that ranked as one of the worst of his presidency,[8] and he commented to friends on the dark symbolism of Starr literally taking his blood.[9] On August 3, in the Map Room of the White House, the president, his face flushed with anger, rolled up his left shirt sleeve. The White House physician, Dr. E. Connie Mariano, drew a vial of the president's blood, while an FBI agent, one of Starr's prosecutors, and David Kendall watched this first-ever event. For Bill, this episode was the ultimate indignity in a long year of humiliations. "When they took the blood from his arm," one of Bill's closest friends said later, "that's when it really hit home."[10]

Now, the president was confronted with the prospect that his baroque lies would be revealed to everyone — his wife and daughter, his friends and aides, and the American people. Bill had several options but none of them was attractive: He could invoke the Fifth Amendment before the grand jury, but that would amount to political suicide. He could testify and continue to deny the truth, but the public would likely not forgive him for lying in front of a federal grand jury. Such a strategy could get him indicted. Or he could acknowledge the truth, the most attractive option from a legal standpoint, but the worst option when it came to his relationships with Hillary and Chelsea.

"What's he going to tell Hillary?" one of his friends wondered shortly after the blood was taken from Bill's arm. "And what's she going to tell him?"[11]

HILLARY WAS AMONG the last to know the truth — or, at least, that is what she would have the readers of her autobiography believe. From late July to the middle of August, she relates in her book, she argued that Bill should testify before the grand jury. "I didn't think there was any reason to worry if he did," she wrote.[12] But, in fact, a friend of Hillary's noted, the First Lady had privately counseled the exact opposite, insisting that Bill resist testifying before the grand jury. He had overruled her.[13]

On Friday, August 14, the *New York Times* published an extraordinary article on its front page. Headlined "President Weighs Admitting He Had Sexual Contacts," the story's four authors wrote:

WASHINGTON, Aug. 13 — President Clinton has had extensive discussions with his inner circle about a strategy of acknowledging to a grand jury on Monday that he had intimate
sexual encounters with Monica S. Lewinsky in the White
House, senior advisers have said.[14]

At the time, a White House aide insisted that the article was
intended to alert Hillary that, in fact, Bill did have a sexual relationship with Monica Lewinsky.[15] But, as the article reported — and
aides at the White House confirmed — Hillary was intimately
involved in the meetings with Bill's lawyers, David Kendall and
Mickey Kantor, throughout August as they prepared for his testimony. A more likely explanation for the story was that it was
intended to prepare the public for the president's admission.

For her part, Hillary says nothing about the *Times*'s article in
her book. She is also silent about the important day-to-day role
that she played during the White House's damage-control operation
that year and the critical help she gave the president to prepare for
his testimony. Instead, Hillary recalls an intriguing conversation
that she had on the evening the story was published, Friday, August
14. In the Yellow Oval Room of the White House, Hillary met with
Bob Barnett, one of Washington's most influential and discreet lawyers, about an unrelated matter. As their meeting wrapped up, Barnett asked if Hillary was worried about her husband's date with the
grand jury, presumably because the *Times* had just reported that Bill
was preparing to change his story.[16]

"What if there's more to this than you know?" Barnett asked.

"I don't believe there is," Hillary said. "I've asked Bill over and
over again."[17]

A moment later, Barnett said, "You have to face the fact that
something about this might be true."

"Look, Bob," Hillary said, "my husband may have his faults, but
he has never lied to me."[18]

EARLY THE NEXT MORNING, Saturday, August 15, Hillary was
awakened by Bill, who was anxiously pacing the carpet in their
bedroom. "He told me for the first time that the situation was much
more serious than he had previously acknowledged," Hillary writes
in her autobiography. "He now realized he would have to testify
that there had been an inappropriate intimacy. He told me that what

happened between them had been brief and sporadic. He couldn't tell me seven months ago, he said, because he was too ashamed to admit it and he knew how angry and hurt I would be."[19]

Hillary recalled that she could hardly breathe. She said she started crying and screaming, "What do you mean? What are you saying? Why did you lie to me?"

"I'm sorry. I'm so sorry," Bill said. "I was trying to protect you and Chelsea."[20]

Hillary told her husband that he needed to tell their daughter the awful truth. And that's when Bill began to cry.

HILLARY WAS AT A LOSS; Bill had not only betrayed their marriage but had jeopardized his political future, and hers. She was unsure whether their union "could — or should — survive such a stinging betrayal." She knew that she needed time to sort out her feelings "carefully, on my own timetable."[21]

Bill, meanwhile, still faced a date with the grand jury that Monday. In the Map Room of the White House on Monday, August 17, 1998, he was confronted by Sol Wisenberg and Robert Bittman, prosecutors from Starr's office. Members of the grand jury watched, live, at the federal courthouse on closed-circuit television. Kendall was with the president. Wisenberg began the proceedings by reminding Bill that he was "under oath." If he provided false or misleading answers, Wisenberg reminded him, "you could be prosecuted for perjury and/or obstruction of justice."

"I believe that's correct," the president said.[22]

Bill gave them nothing. When asked directly whether he was "physically intimate with Monica Lewinsky," he read a written statement acknowledging "inappropriate intimate contact," but he repeatedly said that this "did not consist of sexual intercourse," nor did it "constitute sexual relations" under the three-pronged definition he had been given during the Jones deposition back in January.[23]

The president devoted much of the four hours allotted for the grand jury session to bitterly ripping his accusers and even the prosecutors. He seemed to be purposefully running out the clock. He seethed that the Jones case was less about alleged sexual harassment and more about a concerted effort to harass him for political gain. "They just thought they would take a wrecking ball to me and see if they could do some damage," he said.[24]

Bittman pointed to a passage in Bill's Jones deposition when his lawyer, Robert Bennett, had assured everyone that "there is no sex of any kind in any manner, shape, or form" between the president and Lewinsky. Bittman asked the president whether he agreed that this "was an utterly false statement."

With a wan smile, the president said, "It depends on what the meaning of 'is'…is."[25] That smile seemed to suggest that Bill knew the line was preposterous. "If 'is' means is, and never has been, that is one thing," he continued. "If it means, there is none, that was a completely true statement."[26] The quotation came to symbolize Bill's hairsplitting obfuscation (and it was later memorialized in *Bartlett's Familiar Quotations*). The answer infuriated Starr's prosecutors and strengthened their resolve to send a report on the matter to Congress, which they felt was their obligation under the independent counsel law.[27]

Starr's men left the White House that evening feeling as if it was clear that the president had lied under oath not only in the Paula Jones deposition but also that afternoon to the grand jury.[28] Meanwhile, Bill had stormed out of the Map Room at 6:35 p.m., burning with fury. After a quick meal and a shower, he carried that anger into the White House Solarium, where his top advisers were waiting—Charles Ruff, the White House counsel; his lawyers, David Kendall and Mickey Kantor; his strategists, Rahm Emanuel, Paul Begala, and James Carville; and his old friends Harry and Linda Thomason. The president's task was to prepare a brief statement to deliver to the nation that evening at ten o'clock eastern standard time. Chelsea was also in the Solarium, but Hillary was not there, and her absence was conspicuous.[29]

A Clinton administration official who insists Hillary knew "some of the truth" back in January said, "It was the details that she didn't know—all the details."[30] Now, she did.

"I didn't much want to help Bill compose his public statement on a matter that violated my sense of decency and privacy," she recalled years later. "Finally, though, out of habit, maybe curiosity, perhaps love, I went upstairs."[31]

Bill was furious with Starr. "*Hate* is not too strong a word," one of his closest friends said afterward.[32] Some of the advisers in the room had wanted the president to break the news to the country that he had misled the public, but to do so with a heartfelt apology. The statement written for the president by Paul Begala was carefully worded, mixing a confession with contrition. He needed to communicate that he had dragged the country through an awful ordeal. Even Carville, who had declared war on Starr back in January, thought it would be better for the president to simply admit he was wrong and not say anything to provoke the independent counsel.[33]

But Bill refused. His fury at Starr poured out of his pen as he began writing a new speech, longhand, on a yellow legal pad.[34]

His strategists continued to caution him about a message that would challenge Starr and possibly upset Americans. Bill paused a moment and asked Hillary for advice. "It's your speech, Bill," she said with a shrug. "Say whatever you want." A moment later, she snapped: "You're the President of the United States — I guess."[35]

At 10:00 p.m. sharp, as millions of Americans watched, Bill Clinton, looking exhausted, with dark circles under his eyes, confessed that he had carried on an "inappropriate relationship" with Monica Lewinsky that was "wrong." He apologized. But midway through the speech, he turned his fury on Starr. With his eyes narrowed into slits and his jaw angrily clenched, he suggested that Starr's long, winding criminal inquiry into his "private business dealings twenty years ago" — an inquiry that he added "found no evidence of any wrongdoing by me or my wife" — had led directly to this painful ordeal for the country. It was Starr's fault, the president argued.

Within minutes, the media's reaction to Bill's speech poured into the White House, and it was uniformly negative. The political strategists who had pleaded with the president to be more conciliatory and apologetic were proved right — the commentators wanted to hear a confession and an apology, not more venom for Kenneth Starr.

The following day, the Clinton family was scheduled to leave the White House for their August vacation on Martha's Vineyard. Before leaving, Hillary's press secretary, Marsha Berry, released this brief statement: "Clearly, this is not the best day in Mrs. Clinton's life. This is a time when she relies on her strong religious faith."[36]

As the Clinton family walked slowly in the bright afternoon sunshine toward *Marine One* waiting on the South Lawn, Chelsea was wedged between her mother and father, holding their hands and serving as a buffer between them. As he carried a slight grin, communicating a mix of embarrassment and guilt, Bill's left hand clutched a leash tied to Buddy, his dog. Hillary grimaced.[37] A poignant photograph of the Clintons' silent, slow walk, with Chelsea leaning ever-so-slightly toward her mother, was published in newspapers around the world. It instantly became an iconographic image of a family struggling publicly with heartbreak. Hillary's stoicism in the eye of the storm seized the attention of millions of women who, at last, seemed to relate to her troubles. Many of them had dealt with straying husbands or boyfriends, and the decision about what to do next was always bound up by concerns about children, money, the web of the past, and the uncertainty of future prospects.

On that day after the grand jury testimony, many American women asked themselves, *What would I do in her place? Could I be as tough and as strong as Hillary?* Other women wondered, *Why was she so forgiving of him? Why wasn't this affair the last straw?* Regardless of which camp the women belonged to, however, many agreed that there seemed nothing inauthentic about the predicament that Hillary now found herself in. Her courage in the face of her husband's betrayal seemed real, as did her pain. Her vulnerability, captured in that photograph, did not appear staged. For many of these women, Hillary's raw hurting emotions were hard to miss. At last, she appeared to be fallible and real.

WHILE THE PUNDITS may not have liked it, Bill's defiant, unapologetic speech did nothing to diminish his sky-high approval ratings with the public, though his standing with Hillary had "hit rock bottom," she observed.[38] Months earlier, a majority of Americans had decided that the Lewinsky scandal was not enough to drive Bill Clinton from office. The economy was booming, antipathy toward Gingrich's Republicans had grown, and most people felt the president's private sins were a secondary issue. Bill was fond of saying, "The American people always get it right."[39] By that logic, they had ratified Bill's long-shot gamble that a president's private behavior, as distasteful as it was, would not affect anyone's judgment about his job performance.

Another set of rankings was also being monitored in the West Wing — Hillary's merrily skyrocketing approval rating. By the end of the summer, her approval ratings had peaked at around 70 percent, even higher than Bill's.[40] This development must have struck Hillary as the oddest result of all. She had tried to win the public's respect and admiration to establish a political career of her own by immersing herself in policy development, from her universal health care attempt and onward, as both a public voice on her own and as Bill's most trusted adviser. And yet, at nearly every turn, much of the public had been unimpressed by her efforts and deeply distrustful of her motives. Now, suddenly, Bill's admission that he had had an affair with a woman half his age—after months of lying to Hillary—had presented her with the opportunity to be reconsidered by the American people. Not every American agreed with her apparent decision to forgive him and stay with him, of course. Many were perplexed by her reasoning, and some saw it as further evidence that Bill and Hillary had a partnership built on power, not love or fidelity. But a majority of Americans extended Hillary the chance to rehabilitate her image, to start anew. For the Americans who had disliked the First Lady, some seemed willing to accept and even embrace Hillary the victim, finding that role far more appealing than Hillary the lawyer or Hillary the strategist or Hillary the feminist or Hillary the health care savior.

"She isn't thrilled about being forced to play the wronged little wife, but it's working," said one of Bill's closest confidants in late August. "You stick with what works."[41]

ON MARTHA'S VINEYARD, in a borrowed house, Bill slept downstairs on the couch and Hillary slept upstairs in the master bedroom. Hillary barred Bill's golfing pal, Terry McAuliffe, from joining them on the Vineyard, which meant the president was forced to spend most of his vacation alone or with his dog, Buddy.[42] More than once, TV cameras captured the image of Bill walking Buddy down a long driveway. Bill returned briefly to the White House to announce that he had ordered a cruise missile attack against the pharmaceutical plant in Sudan and the terrorist training camps in Afghanistan belonging to a then little known terror financier named Osama bin Laden, who was believed to be behind the bombings of two American embassies in east Africa earlier that month.[43] Republicans immediately criticized the attacks, claiming the president had ordered them merely to take attention away from his own problems.

Back on the Vineyard, Chelsea visited friends. Hillary tried to sort out her feelings; she knew she needed time and space to untangle her conflicted emotions. She also knew she needed help. She reached out to Don Jones, her youth minister. Jones reminded

Hillary of a sermon by the theologian Paul Tillich, entitled "You Are Accepted," which he had read to Hillary's youth group thirty-five years earlier in Park Ridge. "Grace strikes us when we are in great pain and restlessness," Tillich preached. "It happens, or it does not happen."[44]

Hillary waited to see if grace would happen.

AFTER THE CLINTONS RETURNED to Washington, the choice confronting Hillary was simple: Run or fight. "I hadn't decided whether to fight for my husband and my marriage," she wrote in her autobiography, "but I was resolved to fight for my President."[45] Hillary recalled having trouble sorting through her jumbled emotions. Hillary and Bill decided to begin regular marital counseling "to determine whether or not we were going to salvage our marriage," she said.[46] As Bill's wife, "I wanted to wring his neck. But he was not only my husband, he was also my President."[47] Furthermore, the Clintons decided to give the media what it wanted: an apologetic president. The strategy was as much Bill's as it was Hillary's, and it would be played out in a weeks-long contrition tour, to be capped off in mid-September at a White House prayer breakfast. And Bill's audience was to be more than just the press corps: Hillary told him that if he wanted to be forgiven, he would need to keep apologizing to the public — and to her as well.[48]

At the prayer breakfast, in the East Room, with a bank of cameras covering it live, Bill quietly told the ministers there that he was seeking "pastoral counseling." "I don't think there is any fancy way to say that I have sinned," he said.[49]

A few hours later, two black vans from the Office of Independent Counsel delivered copies of the 110,000-word "Starr Report," along with thirty-six boxes of supporting documents, to the sergeant-at-arms of the United States Congress. In the report, Starr said there was a record of the president's "abundant and calculating lies" under oath, obstruction of justice, and an abuse of power that "may constitute grounds for impeachment."[50] That evening, the Republican-led House Rules Committee published the entire report on the Internet, a calculated embrace of technology that also conveniently spread the embarrassing details.

Hillary refused to read the report, but she noted in *Living History* that the word *sex* appeared 581 times in the 445-page report; *Whitewater* appeared only four.[51] "Starr's distribution of his report was gratuitously graphic and degrading to the Presidency and the Constitution," Hillary wrote. "Its public release was a low moment in American history."[52]

"A cheap, dime-store sex novel," was how one of Bill's closest friends described it.[53] Most Americans agreed; they did not blame Bill for the behavior that was described. Instead, they blamed the messenger. Sixty percent of Americans said that Congress should not pursue impeachment proceedings and that Bill should not resign. Starr's approval ratings sank even lower, and the president's inched further upward. Meanwhile, Hillary's approval ratings reached an all-time high.

In mid-September, Hillary met with a delegation of two dozen Democratic congresswomen in the Yellow Oval Room. As the women sipped coffee and nibbled on pastries, Hillary talked passionately about defending the president against impeachment proceedings. The women seemed buoyed by her words and asked Hillary to campaign for them.

"I'll help you in any way I can," she said. "But I also need you to help hold the party together, and to keep the Democratic Caucus members where they belong — behind the Constitution and the President."[54]

That fall, a few close friends of the Clintons noticed a new dynamic beginning to take shape in the couple's relationship. The change was not subtle, and it had everything to do with obvious expressions of Bill's worry and concern about the effects his conduct was having on his wife. Beforehand, whenever the couple's daughter, Chelsea, entered a room, Bill dropped what he was doing and focused entirely on her. Now, the same thing was happening when Hillary appeared. "His daughter had always come first, but now Hillary did too," one person close to Bill said. "In deed and expression, you could see he was trying to do everything he could to make it up to Hillary.... He feels he owes her.... It was like: 'Whatever Hillary wants, Hillary gets.'"[55]

At the same time that Bill needed to find ways to make amends, Hillary was busy mapping out her own life after the White House, contemplating a series of political steps that were just as ambitious as the ones Bill had taken. Yet Hillary also knew she would need Bill if she had any chance of realizing them.[56]

Throughout that fall, Hillary had a frenetic campaign schedule for the midterm elections, keeping her distance from Bill. Their evenings together in the White House were "awkward," she recalled. "I didn't avoid him as I had before, but there was still tension between us and not as many shared laughs as I was used to on a daily basis with my husband."[57]

Meanwhile, there was more good news that autumn for Hillary. She was invited to appear on the December cover of *Vogue* by editor in chief Anna Wintour. The First Lady accepted, saying it was a "counterintuitive" decision on her part, but she was pleased that she did. During the photo shoot in the White House Red Room, Hillary glittered as she wore a glamorous burgundy velvet Oscar de la Renta dress. Annie Leibovitz took the cover photograph, which was accompanied by an oversized compliment in gigantic italicized type: *The Extraordinary Hillary Clinton*.[58] Hillary's renaissance had truly begun.

CHAPTER 15

New York State of Mind

ON THE RECEIVING LINE at a White House Christmas party in December 1997, Judith Hope, the New York State Democratic Party chairwoman, clutched Hillary's forearm, pulled her aside, and whispered, "A lot of people think when you leave the White House, you ought to run for U.S. senator from New York!"

"You're kidding!" Hillary said, raising her eyebrows and chortling through one of her signature belly laughs.[1] The First Lady's reflexive response communicated a mixture of humility and surprise — and more than just a hint of interest.

The seat that Hope was eyeing for Hillary belonged to the beloved senior senator from New York, Daniel Patrick Moynihan. Although it was widely assumed he would retire in 2000, Moynihan was actually still mulling over a run for one more term. And as one of the grand old men of the Democratic Party, he certainly did not appreciate that Hillary's friends had decided she should try to succeed him. He already had a tense relationship with the Clintons, and it was strained further when it became clear that Hillary had not consulted with him regarding his retirement timetable.[2]

Judith Hope's whispered suggestion — leaked to the *New York Post* — was the first public hint that a "Draft Hillary" movement might be afoot.[3] But the thinking and planning had begun long before the winter of 1997. After Hillary and Bill had had preliminary discussions with a group of trusted advisers that included strategist Harold Ickes and fund-raiser Terry McAuliffe, they decided that it would be better if Hillary's interest in the Senate and New York appeared to be coming from outside the White House. This strategy was needed to squelch the inevitable speculation that Hillary was "a carpetbagger" interested in using a New York Senate seat as a launching pad for a later run for the presidency — which, of course, she was.[4]

In November 1998, despite the Lewinsky scandal and the impeachment inquiry, Democrats gained five seats in the House, narrowing the Republican margin to twelve (223 to 211). On the Friday night after the election, with Bill and the Democrats still flush from their surprising triumph, Hillary received an unexpected late-night phone call from Representative Charlie Rangel, the Harlem congressman and close friend of the Clintons.

"I just heard that Senator Moynihan announced he is going to retire," Rangel told Hillary. "I sure hope you'll consider running because I think you could win."

"Oh, Charlie," Hillary said. "I'm honored you would think of me, but I'm not interested. And besides, we have a few other outstanding matters to resolve now."[5]

"I know," Rangel said. "But I'm really serious. I want you to think about it."

Even as Rangel was pushing, Hillary feigned disinterest and impatience with the prospect of a Senate campaign. "I had other things on my mind," she said in her book.[6] Privately, she continued to encourage the "Draft Hillary" movement.[7]

AT THE TOP OF HILLARY'S LIST of "other things" was the looming impeachment of her husband, an irreversible black mark that would scar Bill Clinton's legacy. Despite the Democrats' favorable midterm election results, impeachment was gaining momentum in the lame-duck session of the House.

On December 11 and 12 of that year, the House Judiciary Committee voted along party lines to refer four articles of impeachment to the full House for a vote. Behind the scenes, Bill's lawyers attempted to persuade the House Republican leadership to forgo a full impeachment vote in favor of a formal censure of the president. It was a losing battle.

In the last weeks of 1998, Hillary was absent from some of the strategy sessions that Bill held with his legal team and his political advisers.[8] Her absence was not difficult to miss. She was now focused on herself, her own interests, and her own future. Bill was used to Hillary commandeering the troops in any crisis, and her lack of participation in this one distracted the president, making him even more moody and grumpy.[9]

"She's moved on," a friend said. "She's thinking of herself rather than him....It's the first time I have seen this happen....She wants the Senate, maybe run for president someday. He fucked up, and he knows it. Now he has to help her get what she wants....They both know it's time for him to do right by her."[10]

EARLY ON THE COLD, CLOUDY morning of Saturday, December 19, Hillary rode a black presidential limousine from the White House to Capitol Hill to attempt to raise the spirits of a glum group of House Democrats. Within hours, the House of Representatives was scheduled to consider the impeachment of a president for only the second time in American history. Standing before the House Democratic Caucus, Hillary said, "You all may be mad at Bill Clinton. Certainly, I'm not happy about what my husband did. But impeachment is not the answer. Too much is at stake here for us to be distracted from what really matters."[11] Hillary assured everyone that her husband had no intention of placating the Republicans by resigning from office. Her emotionally charged performance wowed the House Democrats, giving them hope on a dark day. She also said simply, "I love and care deeply about my husband."[12]

Loud cheers could be heard resonating from the packed caucus room during Hillary's private talk. And more than one person departed dabbing away tears.[13]

That afternoon, the House adopted two of the four articles of impeachment against the president — one for perjury before the grand jury and the other for obstruction of justice. As a result, in January, Bill would face a trial in the United States Senate that would determine whether he would be removed from office.

After the historic vote, a group of somber Democrats, led by Representative Richard Gephardt of Missouri, drove from the Capitol to the White House to stand beside the president in a demonstration of party solidarity. For a few brief panicked moments, several senior White House aides worried that Hillary would not join the president for the ceremony. She was missing, conspicuously, but everyone was relieved when the First Lady arrived and, without a word, put her hand through her husband's crooked arm. Bill and Hillary then walked slowly down a curving path from the Oval Office to the Rose Garden, where the House Democrats waited for them.[14]

Vice President Al Gore warmly introduced the president, saying, "I know his heart and his will." Bill appeared to well up with tears at those words. With Hillary standing beside him, Bill declared that he intended to serve "until the last hour of the last day of my term."[15] Despite the impeachment vote, the proceeding had the air of a pep rally, with Democrats seeming upbeat. Hillary, however, appeared both solemn and distracted; for long minutes, she gazed without expression into the distance. She looked at Bill fleetingly, with an expression signaling mostly sadness.[16]

On New Year's Eve, a Gallup poll named Hillary as the most admired woman in America. Twenty-eight percent of the respondents surveyed had ranked her first; in second place was Oprah Winfrey.[17] Maureen Dowd of the *New York Times* shrewdly observed that Hillary was finally being embraced by Americans not "for something that she has done, but for something she has endured."[18] In a way, Hillary had hidden behind a toughened veneer for so long that it was as if people needed to see her struggle with her own vulnerabilities before they gave her a second chance. "It's very good to see her held in such high public regard but rather sad to think about the reasons why," said Peter Edelman, who had quit the Clinton administration to protest Bill's signing of the welfare reform bill. "As she becomes more a traditional First Lady, more ceremonial, her poll ratings rise."[19] Indeed, it gnawed at Hillary that her role as the silent, aggrieved wife had earned her record approval ratings and the affection of much of the country.[20] And yet, as a politician, was she not supposed to make the most of it?

THE SENATE IMPEACHMENT TRIAL of William Jefferson Clinton began on January 7, 1999, and would last five weeks. Because sixty-seven votes were needed to convict the president and there were fifty-five Senate Republicans, it was a foregone conclusion that Bill would not be removed from office. Nevertheless, Republicans intent on further humiliating Bill and hoping to damage the Democrats saw no need to halt the proceedings.

Hillary purposefully avoided watching most of the trial, though she could not help laughing when she saw Chief Justice William

H. Rehnquist emerge at the Senate rostrum in a black robe with three gold braided bars stitched to his upper sleeves. Rehnquist told reporters that he had personally designed the special robes, getting the idea from costumes he had seen in a Gilbert and Sullivan comic opera, *Iolanthe*. "How fitting that he should wear a theatrical costume to preside over a political farce," Hillary noted in her memoir.[21] And indeed, the trial dwindled to its foregone conclusion with a combination of high school melodrama and B-grade movie.

It had been Hillary's idea to enlist Dale Bumpers, the former senator from Arkansas, to deliver a defense of Bill on the Senate floor.[22] There, Bumpers posed this question, which would deeply move Hillary: "Where were the elements of forgiveness and redemption, the very foundation of Christianity?"[23] Faith, the fundamental underpinning of Christianity, had helped Hillary get through that long year, she told friends. She thought often of an old saying that she learned in Sunday school: "Faith is like stepping off a cliff and experiencing one of two outcomes — you will either land on solid ground or you will be taught to fly."[24] There was no denying that the country seemed profoundly grateful to Hillary for standing by her husband. In the end, she not only saved their marriage; she also helped save his presidency. Now, it was her turn to fly.

THERE IS NOTHING WRONG with a public figure using raw political ambition as a personal engine to pursue higher office; anyone who has ever sought the presidency has relied on immense ambitions to propel him to win the ultimate prize in America's public life. On February 12, as the Senate was voting "not guilty" on both articles of impeachment against her husband, Hillary was at the White House, meeting with Harold Ickes, the blunt-spoken maven of New York politics whose unvarnished remarks were frequently laced with profanity. Hillary says Ickes had "persuaded me that I had to acknowledge the growing public pressure to run and take the question of a campaign seriously."[25]

Hillary had suggested as recently as 1997 that she and Bill intended to settle in Little Rock after leaving the White House. "We certainly will live in Arkansas," she said on C-SPAN.[26] Ickes now spread out a map of the Empire State on a table in Hillary's office: There were 54,000 square miles to cover, a dizzying array of small towns and midsized cities to visit, a lot of intricate local political issues to master. And then there was New York City, America's largest metropolitan center, its five boroughs a hodgepodge of clashing politicians and groups with competing interests that would be an immense headache to navigate.[27]

If all that wasn't daunting enough for Hillary, Ickes then ticked off a long list of political hurdles: She was not from New York; she had never run for public office; and her likely Senate opponent—popular New York City mayor Rudolph Giuliani—would be formidable. Ickes also warned that the Republican Party "would do everything in its power to demonize" Hillary and her politics. Then there was another vexing question: How could a First Lady even run for elected office? It had never been done before for a reason. It presented a logistical nightmare because she would have to run for a New York seat from the White House.

Several hours into the meeting, Ickes made this admission: "I don't even know if you'd be a good candidate, Hillary."[28] It was a legitimate worry. Though Hillary's approval ratings were higher than at any point during her husband's presidency, she remained a polarizing figure with no experience seeking elected office. Hillary recognized another potentially difficult problem: Democratic women, especially professional women "who normally would be my natural base," were "skeptical" about her ultimate motives and, more important, her decision to "stay married to Bill."[29]

Still, those warnings hardly stopped the momentum. With the impeachment trial finally behind Bill, her office announced on February 16, 1999, that she was considering running for the Senate. This merely confirmed what many political analysts had long assumed. But in *Living History*, Hillary insisted that until shortly before that announcement, she actually was undecided and even leaning against running. Many of her closest friends and advisers—including her scheduler Patti Solis Doyle; her former chief of staff, Maggie Williams; and Mandy Grunwald, the media consultant; among others—had urged Hillary against running, telling her that she would have far more influence on the issues she cared about if she worked outside the confines of the hundred-member Senate club. Doyle, in particular, had been her usual blunt self, blurting out, "Hillary, I just don't think you can win this race."[30]

"I needed a push," Hillary writes in her book, and she says she got it from an unlikely place.[31] On March 4, she visited the New York City Lab School in the Chelsea neighborhood of Manhattan; this was Hillary's tenth trip to New York since autumn. The audience at the school was assembled to salute female athletes and to watch an HBO-produced documentary entitled *The Struggle of Women in Sports.* Hillary appeared on the school's stage with tennis legend Billie Jean King, Olympic gold medalist gymnast Dominique Dawes, and WNBA star Nikki McCray. Above Hillary was a banner emblazoned with the words "Dare to Compete."[32]

A student at the school, Sofia Totti, who was also the captain of the girls' basketball team, introduced the First Lady. "Today we have a tennis star, an Olympic gymnast, a basketball hero," Totti said. Then turning to Hillary, with a sly grin, she added, "And, hopefully, a runner."[33] As Hillary took the podium, she shook Totti's hand. The teenager whispered in her ear, "Dare to compete, Mrs. Clinton. Dare to compete."[34]

It's an irresistible story, and its inclusion in *Living History* helped readers to believe that Hillary was much more undecided than she actually was. Totti's challenge, Hillary recalled, "caught me off guard," and the whispered words forced her to begin more seriously considering a series of tough questions about her life after the White House.[35] "Could I be afraid to do something I had urged countless other women to do?" Hillary said she asked herself. "Why am I vacillating about taking on this race? Why aren't I thinking more seriously about it? Maybe I should 'dare to compete.'"[36]

While this inner dialogue made for great reading, it was more consistent with Hillary's public version of her ascension than the truth, according to her confidants.[37] There's hardly a hint that Hillary had harbored any personal ambition for herself in the 531 pages of her autobiography. And although the title of Hillary's autobiography is *Living History,* she often avoided portraying herself as someone who aggressively sought a prominent place for herself in the greater American narrative. Of course, runs for the Senate and ultimately the presidency were dreams that she and Bill had talked about, even yearned for, for as long as they could remember.[38] A veteran U.S. senator put it this way: "She has a driving ambition that transcends her husband's. In fact, much of his ambition comes from her — and there's no question he has plenty."[39] But it made for a better story to say that Hillary had been summoned into the political arena by acclamation.

Hillary claimed that Sofia Totti's words of encouragement reminded her of a scene from one of her favorite films, *A League of Their Own,* about a 1940s women's professional baseball team. When the team's star catcher, played by Geena Davis, declares that she wants to quit the team to return home to be with her husband, the team manager, played by Tom Hanks, tells her she cannot give up.

"It just got too hard," Geena Davis's character complains.

"It's supposed to be hard," Hanks tells her. "If it wasn't hard, everyone would do it — the hard is what makes it great."[40]

The hard is what makes it great. Hillary loved the simple appeal of that line. Sure, a Senate run would be hard. But it would also be great. She knew it, and she knew she was going for it — even if she pretended otherwise.

BY THE SPRING OF 1999, Mark Penn, the pollster who remains one of Hillary's closest advisers, had taken his first poll about Hillary's potential campaign. He sent her a memo with the good news: New York residents who lived upstate were open to the idea of her running. Both Penn and Mandy Grunwald, the media consultant, encouraged Hillary to visit all sixty-two counties in the state. Penn coined the phrase "Listening Tour" to describe the way he believed the First Lady should introduce herself to a state where she had not lived.[41]

"If I proved to New York voters that I understood the issues their families faced," Hillary observed, "and was determined to work hard for them, I just might be able to do it."[42] There was no better way to prove that than to crisscross the Empire State and do far more listening than talking.

But before the Northeast trek came a quick southern vacation. In late May, Bill and Hillary spent five days in Florida. Nearly every night, they stayed up past midnight, talking about her run. Bill was energized by the prospect; he didn't have another campaign in his future, something that bothered him deeply, and some of the sting was removed by the prospect that he could live vicariously through Hillary's first.[43] Hillary was understandably insecure about how she would come off engaging in retail politics, shaking hands and clutching shoulders on the rope line, and, of course, speaking off-the-cuff to voters and reporters. The latter aspect, they both knew, had gotten her into much trouble during Bill's 1992 presidential campaign. Bill promised to serve as her coach.

Hillary knew she needed to improve and, as with everything else, was willing to work hard at it.[44] Bill made sure he was there to help. "There's one way for the president to get out of the doghouse — give your wife everything she wants," a close acquaintance said.[45] "He feels he owes her," said another longtime friend who knew them both well.[46] To their closest friends, it seemed obvious: It wasn't the counseling sessions or Bill's torrent of heartfelt apologies that would begin healing the breach created by the long Lewinsky year. Nor was Hillary's Senate run just giving them something fresh and exciting to talk about — it was saving their marriage.[47]

ON A WARM EARLY SUMMER NIGHT in June, Hillary hosted the thirtieth reunion of the Wellesley College Class of 1969 at the White House. As the dinner-dance continued past ten o'clock, she invited a half dozen of her closest college friends upstairs, to the third-floor Solarium, to finish their wine.

The group included Alan Schechter, the political science professor; Jan Piercy, Hillary's roommate in college, who was now the U.S. executive director of the World Bank; and Johanna Branson, a Boston art professor and historian and another Wellesley roommate of Hillary's.

Hillary quickly changed her clothes. Outside the tall Solarium windows, the capital city shimmered below. Hillary raised the subject everyone was thinking about but had not dared to broach. "Jan thinks this is a crazy thing I'm contemplating," Hillary said, baiting her friend.

Jan quickly said, "I never said that, Hillary, because I'd never give you political advice."

Branson's husband, Jock Gill, played devil's advocate, ticking off the reasons why Hillary might want to avoid the scrum of American politics. Wouldn't it be better for her to pursue her causes some other way?

Hillary said she had considered running a philanthropic foundation, which wealthy donors had offered to establish for her. And there had been many other options: assuming a college presidency, hosting a television show, or becoming a chief executive officer. "But," Hillary said, "I would always be viewed as *former First Lady*. It would be, 'former First Lady said such and such...'"

Her friends nodded. They understood. On various occasions, Hillary had used the term "derivative spouse" to describe herself. This run would erase that.

Gill pressed her: Hadn't politicians put her though enough misery? Why did she want to join their club?

"I just feel so committed," Hillary replied. "I'm not satisfied with what we've done. *I'm* not done."

Gill wondered why Hillary was fixated on the Senate rather than on some other more singular, effective bully pulpit.

"You know, for years — for *decades* — I have written legal briefs," Hillary explained. "I have given speeches. And I have lobbied Congress. I have been standing outside, knocking on the door, while they set policy and pass laws. I'd like to be on the inside making the case. I've been on the outside too long."

The next question: Why choose New York, of all places?

In a half-winking way, Hillary confided that she'd investigated "some other possible states, but they have a number of very qualified people running who had worked hard and long to be congressional candidates."

For Hillary, the first thing that was appealing about New York was that there was a historical precedent for a well-known nonresident: Bobby Kennedy won a Senate seat in 1964, and just four years later sought the presidency.

Hillary told her friends that the other thing that was appealing about a Senate run was that it would be a rare thing in American politics — a candidacy by acclamation. "I'm being drafted," she said. "It is so rare to be drafted in this way. The nature of politics is such that you have to seize the moment when and if it comes, or it may never come again."[48] She wanted to be wanted.

Now all that was left was to choose a time and place to announce her intention to run. The strategists decided the best spot would be Senator Moynihan's bucolic nine-hundred-acre farm in upstate Pindars Corners. Pulling off such a launch, however, proved to be a chore.

Moynihan was still quietly fuming over the roundabout way he had found out about Hillary's interest in his seat. Mandy Grunwald, a former Moynihan aide, was designated as Hillary's emissary to "soothe" the senator's feelings.[49] Even with her soothing, however, Moynihan seemed less than enthusiastic about embracing Hillary's candidacy. For example, he decided that the press could not go past a certain tree on his farm, a decision that would prevent the assembled TV cameras from actually getting an image of his house.

Nevertheless, on July 7, a warm afternoon, the retiring senior senator from New York by her side, Hillary walked down a dirt road toward a contingent of more than two hundred reporters, some from as far away as Japan. Moynihan spoke about *Plutarch's Lives* before finally saying flatly, "I think she's going to win."[50]

Hillary then announced that she had formed an exploratory committee for the purpose of running for the U.S. Senate and would begin a "Listening Tour of New York." "I suppose the questions on everyone's mind are: Why the Senate? Why New York? And why me?"

All pertinent questions, considering Hillary had still not purchased a house in the state. (Later that summer on a house-hunting trip, she would find a lovely old Dutch Colonial farmhouse and barn in Chappaqua, north of New York City, in Westchester County.)[51] As Hillary parried the inevitable round of queries, a few reporters detected that Moynihan seemed somewhat ambivalent, maybe even bored. "It was still very rough, even after getting him to allow her to come to his farm," Neel Lattimore, Hillary's former press secretary, recalled. "Moynihan was doing it more for the party and less for Hillary."[52]

For Hillary, that day marked a rite of passage. Besides finally standing on her own as a candidate (Bill was not there), she saw it as the first page of a new chapter in her life with Bill. Her decisions to stay with him, and run for office, were intrinsically linked in her mind.

Bill, for his part, was also gratified. Beneath a white tent, on a glorious summer afternoon on Martha's Vineyard that August, he confided to a crowd of contributors and friends that when Hillary decided to move down to Arkansas to be with him in 1973, he was terrified that he was depriving her of a banquet of exciting career opportunities. "I was so afraid that I was taking her away from her life — the most gifted person I had ever known up to that time," Bill said. "And so all she is really doing today is what I thought, for the benefit of the country...maybe she should have been able to do in 1973. I'm very glad she didn't do it then, and very glad she is doing it today."[53] He also confided to the crowd that he had recently told his wife, "For twenty years, we've gone where I wanted to go and done what I wanted to do, and I'll give you the next twenty years. And if I'm still alive after that, we'll fight over the rest."[54]

A person who watched it said, "Her expression, as he said those things, was one of pure bliss, of true love."[55]

*　　*　　*

OUT OF THE GATE, Hillary stumbled, more than once. At an event in the fall of 1999 in which Bill welcomed the world champion New York Yankees to the White House, manager Joe Torre handed Hillary a Yankees cap. The lifelong Cubs fan wasted no time slipping it on her head with an ebullient smile. Many New Yorkers, especially the tabloids, poked fun at the image. Hillary said at the time that the Bronx Bombers had always been her favorite American League team, and she remarked in her book that she was also a die-hard Mickey Mantle fan as a child. It might have been true, but in a state where her opponent was famous as a die-hard Yankee booster, it came off as phony.

Then, in November 1999, Hillary found herself making an even bigger gaffe. On a trip to Israel, she attended an event as First Lady with Suha Arafat, the wife of Palestinian leader Yasser Arafat. After Suha Arafat's remarks, in which she suggested that Israel had used poison gas against Palestinians, Hillary went to the podium to speak and lightly kissed Mrs. Arafat on the cheek. The Jewish community in New York was outraged. Hillary claimed later that Mrs. Arafat's "hateful words" had not been properly translated from Arabic to English in her earphones, and she denounced Mrs. Arafat's allegation.[56] The New York press had a field day with this story too.

Her response was to keep grinding her way forward. Hillary hoped to visit all sixty-two counties in New York and to meet as many small groups of voters, particularly women, as possible. Driving the state in a Ford conversion van (the press corps dubbed it the "HRC Speedwagon"), she followed Bill's Rules for Campaigning: Shake as many hands as possible; listen to as many people as possible; never stop smiling or asking questions. As she became more comfortable opening herself up, the voters reciprocated. A down-to-earth, even self-effacing Hillary was not what most people expected. Many New York residents were quoted in the local press saying something along the lines that the First Lady "seems like one of us." This early judgment along the back roads of upstate New York amounted to an enormous accomplishment for a woman born in Illinois who had spent the majority of her adult life living in Arkansas.

Not long after her New Year campaign began, Hillary appeared on the *Late Show with David Letterman*. She was nervous about the appearance, expecting that the acerbic Letterman would attempt to embarrass her. Letterman asked about the Clintons' house in Chappaqua, joking that since he mentioned it "every idiot in the area is going to drive by honking now."

"Oh, was that you?" Hillary asked.[57] Letterman laughed, and the crowd roared.

The official announcement of her intention to run came in February 2000. (Reporters joked that it was the fourth time that Hillary had signaled her intention to run.) At this event, in Purchase, New York, Hillary Rodham Clinton dropped not just one of her names but two from her campaign buttons, literature, and signs, becoming, simply, "Hillary."

The single name was a major part of her strategy to portray herself to New Yorkers not as the world-famous First Lady but as a friend and neighbor, who wants you to know her on a first-name basis. "Who needs the formality of a surname when your first name is relatively unusual and your fame is unparalleled?" observed Beth J. Harpaz, an Associated Press reporter who covered Hillary's 2000 campaign. "Elvis, Cher, Madonna, Oprah, and now, Hillary!"[58]

A few weeks later, it was Mayor Giuliani's turn to be excoriated by the press. When an undercover New York police officer shot and killed a black man named Patrick Dorismond in March 2000, Giuliani's already-strained relations with the city's minority community became a highly charged campaign issue, one that Hillary and her advisers knew they had to exploit. Many citizens in minority neighborhoods distrusted the police, and after Giuliani released Dorismond's sealed juvenile records, impugning the dead man's reputation, the city's minority communities became even angrier at the mayor's tactics. Hillary saw Giuliani's handling of the situation as "wrong" — and she said so.[59]

In Harlem, at the Bethel A.M.E. Church, Hillary pounced on the mayor, battering Giuliani with criticism for his handling of the case. "New York has a real problem, and we all know it," she said. "All of us, it seems, except the mayor."[60] The crowd reacted with sustained cheers. Giuliani was furious, saying Hillary and the Reverend Al Sharpton "are reading from the same script. What they're trying to do is take a difficult situation and try to turn it into a politically polarizing situation for her advantage."[61] But Hillary's advisers were convinced that her performance in Harlem was the turning point in her campaign; she believed that she had finally found her political voice, one that was simultaneously tough and compassionate.[62]

A few weeks later, Giuliani stunned everyone with his announcement that he was withdrawing from the race after being diagnosed with prostate cancer. Hillary was eight points ahead at the time. A new Republican candidate emerged — a young, fresh-faced U.S. congressman from Long Island named Rick Lazio.

That spring, as Hillary continued to campaign, she was devastated by the news that her best friend, Diane Blair, had been diagnosed with metastatic lung cancer. At sixty-one, Blair was Hillary's closest confidante, and Hillary had visited her at a hospital in Fayetteville several times. In June, Diane's husband, Jim, had called Hillary to say the end was near. Hillary, joined by Bill and Chelsea, flew to be at her bedside. Diane had undergone chemotherapy treatments that weakened her and caused her hair to fall out. But she beamed when Hillary entered her hospital room to say good-bye.

"Don't ever give up on yourself and what you believe in," Diane told Hillary. "Take care of Bill and Chelsea. They need you. And win this election for me. I wish I could be there when you do. I love you."

With Bill and Chelsea by Hillary's side, Diane Blair finally said, "Remember."

"Remember what?" Bill asked.

"Just remember."[63]

Five days later, Diane Blair died. The void left by her death is still a gargantuan one in Hillary's life; she still thinks of her old friend at least once every day.[64]

BACK HOME, HILLARY BEGAN to prepare for three debates against Rick Lazio. She had built a comfortable lead in the polls, anywhere from twelve to fifteen points. On the debate stage in Buffalo on September 13, Lazio chastised Hillary for the enormous soft-money contributions flowing to the Democratic National Committee, and he challenged her to ban her campaign from accepting any large Democratic Party checks. Hillary tried to respond, but Lazio kept talking over her, waving a piece of paper that he had called the "New York Freedom from Soft Money Pact." He left his podium and marched toward Hillary and shoved the paper toward her, but Hillary refused to sign it. He then pressed himself even closer to Hillary, slapping the document in front of her, and shouting, "Right here, sign it right now!"

Hillary offered to shake Lazio's hand, but he said, "No, no, I want your signature. Because I think that everybody wants to see you signing something that you said you were for. I'm for it. I haven't done it. You've been violating it. Why don't you stand up and do something—do something important for America. While America is looking at New York, why don't you show some leadership because it goes to trust and character."[65]

At first, most pundits and reporters thought Lazio's aggressive move on the soft-money issue had scored him a resounding victory. But many viewers, especially women, were offended by the way that Lazio had "invaded" Hillary's space in such an aggressive manner.

Lazio discovered how his confrontation was playing the next morning, during a campaign stop at a classroom in Rochester. A seven-year-old girl looked up at Lazio and asked, "I watched you on NBC last night—why were you fighting with Mrs. Clinton?"[66] A poll by the *Daily News* showed that by a margin of two to one, women voters believed Hillary had won the debate.[67]

Despite the backlash from his debate-night confrontation, Lazio continued to wage a largely negative campaign. Hillary fought back with pointed ads of her own, including one that featured former New York Mayor Ed Koch, who admonished Lazio by saying, "Rick, stop with the sleaze already."[68] Although Lazio closed the gap in October to a mere handful of points, Hillary went on to win 55 to 43.

Hillary and Bill were overjoyed. "After eight years with a title but no portfolio," Hillary said, "I was now 'senator-elect.'"[69] For Hillary, those two words carried a sweet ring. The second half of the Clintons' ambitious presidential plan was about to begin.

PART THREE

First Woman

Politics is more difficult than physics.
   —Albert Einstein

CHAPTER 16

The Mysteries of Hillaryland

A CAMPAIGN AIDE for Bill Clinton created the nickname "Hillaryland" in 1992, and the label appropriately defined an important subculture during the Clinton presidency. "My staff prided themselves on discretion, loyalty, and camaraderie, and we had our own special ethos," Hillary observed. Bill's aides, on the other hand, "had a tendency to leak," she noted. "Hillaryland never did."[1]

By the time Hillary began her Senate quest, Hillaryland had become a code word for discipline and devotion to its matriarch. Her devotees described "the cult around her" as rivaling a previous dynasty. "I haven't seen this kind of loyalty to Hillary since the loyalty shown to Bobby Kennedy," said a longtime Democrat who is very fond of Hillary.[2] But Hillaryland's power and reach eclipsed the empire built by the Kennedy clan. Today, no active political organization can match its depth, discipline, or devotion, according to Senate aides and political analysts.[3] And in many ways, the loyalty and secrecy that surround Hillary mirror the disciplined and secretive network built by President Bush, her political demon.

"Hillaryland is culturally closer to Bushworld than to Bill Clinton–land," one Senate adviser observed. "It is more principled, more focused. There is more discretion." Continued the adviser,

"The closer you are [to Hillary] the more loyalty there is to create and maintain that culture. If you are disloyal or indiscreet, there will be a price for the disloyalty. There is a fear of retribution that permeates the group."[4] Another longtime friend of the First Lady begged off talking about Hillaryland, saying half kiddingly, "She'll kill me if she catches me talking to you."[5]

UPON ENTERING THE SENATE, Hillary sought to seamlessly transfer Hillaryland from the White House to the Capitol. But the sixteen blocks up Pennsylvania Avenue would prove to be a more difficult transition than she had envisioned.

Hillary's payroll roster, after she launched her presidential campaign, totaled nearly two hundred people, roughly two-thirds working on the campaign itself and one-third serving as her Senate staff, working out of a dozen offices scattered throughout Washington, New York State, and the rest of the country.[6] As New York is a large state, senators are afforded more appropriated money to pay for larger staffs, and Hillary manages one of the biggest staffs in the Senate. (Under congressional rules, Senate business and political campaign work are generally required to be kept separate. Nevertheless, Hillary's staff, on at least one occasion, used an official Senate computer e-mail service in 2007 to invite Democratic senators to a kick-off fund-raising reception for her presidential campaign, featuring her and Bill.)[7] Beyond the people on her payroll, Hillary has hundreds of shadow advisers, academic experts, strategists, and consultants, all of whom are standing by, ready to serve at a moment's notice, even as they work elsewhere at full-time consulting jobs.[8]

Hillaryland's chief adviser, of course, is Bill, who often test-markets Hillary's positions or sound bites before she uses them herself to see how they play. Her team is constantly busy drafting speeches, legislation, and policy briefs. They also keep the media largely at bay, offering nuggets to favored journalists and arranging infrequent off-the-record sessions with select members of the press while mounting vigorous and aggressive counterattacks against errant reporters. They plan her travel and sort through thousands of scheduling requests. Last but not least, they solicit enormous sums of money—one fund-raiser estimated that Hillary will raise a record $125 million before the primaries begin in January 2008—in order to feed the machine.[9]

If elected president, Hillary promises "to replace secrecy and mystery with openness."[10] But her practices in running her Senate office have sometimes demonstrated a cavalier attitude toward the rules and a proclivity toward secrecy.[11]

For example, for six years, a few dozen of her employees who are called congressional fellows have labored as a shadow staff that the public rarely hears about. This retinue is both larger and more hidden than those of her colleagues, according to Senate aides and a review of public records. One reason for the obscurity is that Hillary has repeatedly failed to file the appropriate notifications with the Senate for at least a dozen of those fellows. In keeping these fellows off the books, Hillary has apparently violated Senate rules requiring the disclosure of temporary hires. In addition, in the case of some of her shadow employees, she has failed to ensure that they agree, in writing, to abide by the same Senate rules that apply to permanent staff.[12]

VISITORS TO CAPITOL HILL can easily find the office of their home state senator by touching a screen on the wall of the Senate's office buildings. For Hillary, the screen shows SR476, for the Russell Senate Office Building, the oldest and most prestigious of the chamber's three office buildings.

Each senator is entitled to a suite of offices. In the Russell Building, most suites have nine offices. Ideally, the offices are adjacent. Senators from states with large populations are allocated three additional offices.

Russell 476, the old Moynihan office, is on the top floor along the inner ring. To travel to the Senate floor to cast a vote, Hillary must walk some distance to reach the elevator that transports her to the basement. There, she catches one of the old, operator-driven trains that shuttle officials underground to the Capitol.

The afterglow from Hillary's relatively easy Senate campaign didn't last long. In the Senate, office space is one of the three pillars of empire — the other two being money and people. On Capitol Hill, a senior Senate official remarked, "Real estate is the be-all and end-all."[13]

Down the corridor from Hillary is the office of Senator Trent Lott, who in 2001 was the Senate majority leader, and, perhaps more important, a member of the Senate Rules Committee. Lott not only wanted some of the offices adjacent to Hillary's for himself but he also had his eye on a nearby spacious corner office that had served as Senator Moynihan's mail room and that Hillary hoped to inherit as part of her suite.[14]

Lott had given notice right after Hillary's election that she was in for a rough time. "When this Hillary gets to the Senate—if she does, maybe lightning will strike and she won't—she will be one of one hundred," Lott said in Mississippi after her election victory, "and we won't let her forget it."[15]

He didn't. "Hillary was getting screwed," one Senate official recalled. "It looked for a while like she might have to move."[16] A desperate Hillary turned to Senator Christopher Dodd, the ranking Democrat on the Rules Committee, who pushed back on Lott; a compromise was reached in which Hillary kept the old mail room, and Lott got a few offices that were situated next to Hillary's suite. To fill out her allocation, Hillary picked up some offices around the corner from her base suite.[17]

As Hillary settled into her new space, Karl Rove, President Bush's chief strategist, was setting up shop in the West Wing office that Hillary had used as First Lady. Rove later joked about finding a full-length vanity mirror inside his new White House home.[18] When Hillary bumped into Rove one day soon after, she insisted she had not put up the mirror.[19] Rove repeated the story a few weeks later, anyway.[20] Though he never explicitly said Hillary had been responsible for the mirror, if Rove was trying to tease or bait Hillary, it worked. When she ran into him again, this time at a stop for the Capitol's shuttle train, she tartly said: "I told you I didn't put the mirror there."[21]

AS HILLARY JOSTLED over Senate office space, she was also looking to buy a home in the District of Columbia. Some senators live a spartan life in Washington, occupying small, rented apartments, sometimes with fellow legislators as roommates. Hillary decided to go the other route. In many ways, her Washington home would become Hillaryland's most important venue, where money could be raised at night and loyalists could comfortably gather over weekends for brainstorming sessions.

To buy a suitable house, though, she needed a few million dollars. She and Bill had already stretched their finances to the limit by paying $1.7 million for a home in Chappaqua, a prerequisite to her run for office in New York. Bill, of course, was poised to make lots of money: Within a few years he would be earning $10 million to

$15 million annually from speeches and consulting work for two corporations.[22] But in early 2001, the couple was still saddled with significant legal debts of more than $5 million.[23]

On January 2, 2001, Hillary signed a book contract to tell her story. She was paid a record advance of $8 million by Simon & Schuster.[24] Two weeks after closing the book deal, Hillary and Bill paid $2,850,000 to buy a brick colonial in northwest Washington. The house, near the British Embassy, is named for the cul-de-sac it sits on, Whitehaven. Hillary would later spend more than $1 million to remodel the house, adding an elevator and a new pool house and expanding the residence from 6,260 square feet to 7,218 square feet. The elevator is used primarily by the only full-time resident of Whitehaven, Hillary's mother, Dorothy.[25]

In late 2006, Whitehaven served as a busy presidential campaign salon. Immediately after her landslide reelection as senator, Hillary hosted officials and political leaders from New Hampshire and Iowa in separate dinners at her home. (The video of a relaxed Hillary announcing her presidential bid in January 2007 would be shot in the sunroom of Whitehaven.)[26]

The scores of fund-raising events held at Whitehaven are closed to the public. Visitors are asked to check their bags, cameras, and cell phones at the door; pictures are taken by an authorized photographer. For even more discreet sessions, Hillary borrows the nearby houses of friends, heightening Hillaryland's invisibility.[27] In the Cleveland Park section of Washington, not far from White-haven, is the home of Evelyn Lieberman, who, as a White House aide during the Clinton presidency, was a "formidable presence in Hillaryland, where she ran interference on operations and logistics."[28] In 2006, Hillary occasionally attended strategy sessions at Lieberman's home,[29] and in early 2007, former Clinton administration officials met at Lieberman's house to discuss Hillary's presidential campaign strategy shortly before she officially announced her intention to run.[30]

Hillary has found other creative ways to leverage her considerable appeal and turn it into additional support. In 2003, she came up with the idea of establishing a small nonprofit foundation to promote job growth in New York, especially upstate. This branch of Hillaryland was based in New York City and headed by Roger Altman, who served as deputy secretary of the treasury under President Clinton and went on to become chairman of the boutique investment bank Evercore Partners. In early 2006, Altman quietly organized a group of experts on energy policy from academia, investment banks, and think tanks to prepare a lengthy written report and personally brief Hillary on its work.[31] Senators routinely seek advice and input from outsiders. But it is unusual to rely on a secret task force. Members of Hillary's group say they were asked not to discuss their involvement and assured they would not be publicly identified with her.[32]

Hillary did publicly announce another advisory group, a quasi-permanent committee of New York agricultural experts. That panel's creation traced back, in part, to a hidden staffing decision that led to Hillary's apparent violation of Senate rules.

The story begins in the summer of 2001, when Hillary was looking to fill a gap in the expertise of her staff. No one in her Washington office had much expertise in agriculture.[33] The need was urgent; a massive farm bill was coming up for consideration.

Hillary, in a conversation that summer with Susan Henry, the dean of Cornell University's College of Agriculture and Life Sciences, sought help. Specifically, Hillary "indicated that she wanted to increase her own agricultural expertise and that of her staff," as part of an effort to "speed up her understanding of New York State's agricultural interests" for the upcoming farm bill debate.[34] A few weeks later, Henry supplied Hillary with Lee Telega, a longtime Cornell staff employee involved in a statewide dairy program and, part-time, as a lobbyist in Albany, New York. Telega had been chosen by Cornell's government relations, or lobbying, arm.[35]

Telega rented an apartment in Washington for his six-month stint as one of Hillary's congressional fellows. Cornell continued to pay his salary and picked up many of his expenses for his "special assignment."[36] The fellowship appeared to be a win-win situation for Hillary and the university. "Cornell, for very selfish reasons, wanted a senator who understood northeast agriculture," said one Cornell employee who worked with Hillary, adding, "It's very important to us" because Cornell's agriculture school is one of the biggest in the nation and benefits from land grants.[37]

Historic land grants weren't the only government gifts Cornell depended on. The university has long been the recipient of numerous federal research grants.[38] Cornell, as well as northeast farmers, benefited from the 2002 farm bill. Indeed, the university's annual grants from the Department of Agriculture rose almost 40 percent from 2002 to 2005, including funds for new programs specifically created by the legislation.[39] Hillary was not a member of the Senate Agriculture Committee, but she supported the bill, actively lobbied fellow senators on benefits important to New York (and Cornell), including conservation programs, and said she and others "fought hard" to win increased funding for those programs.[40]

Hillary benefited from the arrangement as well, securing an in-house expert on an important subject at no cost to her. Telega prepared memos, cultivated sources inside the Department of Agriculture, met personally with Hillary and her staff, represented Senator Clinton in negotiations with other congressional staffers, reached out to farmers he knew for help, and was granted Senate-floor privileges the day the farm bill was passed.[41]

Hillary's circle of farm advisers quickly widened when her agricultural advisory group was formed in 2001; Telega played a key role in selecting its members, which included Dean Henry and a number of other Cornell officials and alumni.[42] "There's no conflict of interest in a land-grant institution putting a fellow in the senator's office," Telega said. He explained, "Senator Clinton told me in one of the first meetings" that his job was to "make sure that New York State gets its fair share of the farm bill."[43]

But the job of determining whether there is a conflict of interest is not left up to a senator or a fellow. Instead, the screening for such conflicts of interest is done by the Senate Select Committee on Ethics. Senators are advised to contact the committee before they use the services of a fellow because, by the practices of the chamber, "each fellowship situation must be analyzed on a case-by-case basis" for possible conflicts of interest.[44]

Senators are also supposed to file a report with the Ethics Committee if they use the services of an individual who is paid and works for more than four weeks.[45] (Only about half the Senate's members use fellows, mainly because it's nearly impossible to attract the extra help without the office space.)[46] The form called the "Supervisor's Report on Individuals Who Perform Senate Services" is supposed to be signed by both the supervisor (normally the senator) and the employee. The report discloses the employee's starting date and the source and amount of his or her compensation. Subsequent reports are required on a quarterly basis, as is a termination report.[47] For unknown reasons, neither Hillary nor her office filed a single one of these reports for Telega.[48]

Another rule applies when senators use the full-time services of any individual, including fellows, who work for more than ninety days, even if they are unpaid. This rule says, "No Senator shall utilize the full-time services of an individual for more than ninety days [in a calendar year] unless [the individual] agrees in writing to comply with the Senate Code of Official Conduct in the same manner and to the same extent as an employee of the Senate."[49] Hillary and Telega never completed any such agreement, either, which is to be filled in by the senator and then signed by both parties.[50]

As a result of these omissions, the public and the Ethics Committee were left in the dark about Telega.[51] And he was not an isolated example; a few dozen fellows worked for Hillary in her first term, including two other Cornell agricultural fellows. Some worked shorter terms than others; a few stayed on as permanent employees. The breadth of issues on which they worked was wide-ranging — from military and national security issues to health care, aging, the environment, stem-cell research, and other domestic topics. Their tasks included writing speeches, conducting research, drafting legislation, meeting with lobbyists and constituents, representing Senator Clinton at outside events, and preparing talking points for Hillary.[52] "These fellows are free labor," said the administrator of one program supplying a fellow to Hillary. They "expand organizational capacity," especially "in the context of a presidential campaign."[53]

But during Hillary's first term as senator, she filed only one supervisor's report for her full-time fellows, in 2003 — and even that report was inadequate because she never filed the other necessary documents, even though the supervisor's report that she had signed clearly indicated they were required.[54] The fact of the filing suggests Hillary was aware of the reporting requirements.[55] (Fellows are not expected to navigate the rules on their own.) But again and again she did not bother.

Then, beginning in late March 2007, Hillary and six of her fellows suddenly — and, in most cases, belatedly — filed the forms pledging to abide by the Senate Code of Conduct, and the initial supervisory reports.[56] The filings occurred after questions had been raised with the sponsors of some of her current fellows.[57]

Ignorance of the rules was certainly a possible excuse, albeit a bad one: Senators and Senate employees are regularly briefed by the Ethics Committee, so "everybody should know" the rules.[58]

However, the committee, lacking audit authority, does not have the ability to hunt for missing reports; it simply receives and files the forms. The lax enforcement practices of the Senate ethics panel have prompted critics, including Senator Barack Obama of Illinois, to propose an independent investigative body to look into the behavior and practices of members. Most senators, including Hillary, oppose the idea.

The laissez-faire enforcement of the rules by the Ethics Committee makes it difficult to determine how many reports Hillary should have filed for her fellows. (The number depends upon the duration of their work and whether they were compensated.) Still, over the course of six years, she appears to have neglected to file a few dozen reports for at least a dozen fellows. In eight cases, Hillary used fellows from the same sponsoring organization that supplied fellows to other senators; while those other senators filed correctly, Hillary did not.[59] In four other cases, fellows from other sponsors worked long enough with Hillary to fall under the reporting requirement.[60]

She may have been deferential when it came to matters of territory and seniority, but Hillary's lack of documentation of these workers seems careless at best and negligent at worst. A Senate ethics expert noted that Hillary's practices with her fellows were "unlike any other senator." Overall, the expert said, her office operated with a "we can do what we need to do" attitude.[61] Her failure to file reports on her fellows demonstrates something that has long complicated the political and professional careers of Hillary Clinton: an underlying sense that the rules of the game are up to her.

CHAPTER 17

The Longest Day

ON A SUN-SPLASHED September morning, Hillary Rodham Clinton stepped out of her neo-Georgian mansion in Washington for the twenty-minute drive to Capitol Hill. Eight months into her first job as an elected official, Hillary was still getting acclimated to the clubby corridors and the odd customs of the United States Senate. She had had even less time to settle into her $2.85 million home. After all, she had been able to observe the Senate with intimate attention during the eight years she had spent living in the White House. Getting used to a house not located on Pennsylvania Avenue was a challenge.

Dressed smartly in a black pantsuit and a sky-blue shirt, the junior senator from New York looked forward to attending that morning's hearing on education. It was a subject that she knew as well as any other senator did, and a forum that promised to accentuate her strengths.

Before climbing into the black Suburban waiting in her driveway, Hillary heard the news: A plane had crashed into the World Trade Center's north tower. Like most Americans who heard that first report, Hillary assumed it was a "terrible accident."[1] She settled into the seat, and as her driver was negotiating the vehicle through northwest Washington traffic, the radio reported that a second plane had crashed, this one into the World Trade Center's south tower.

She realized this was no accident.

Hillary's first impulse was to make sure that Chelsea was safe. Chelsea was living in Manhattan, where she worked as a consultant, and Hillary knew that she had planned to go for a jog around Battery Park early that morning and then stop for a cup of coffee, which she sometimes did near the twin towers. Her heart racing, Hillary frantically dialed Chelsea's cell phone number, but the sudden surge of phone usage had crashed Manhattan's cellular networks. In all likelihood, Chelsea was out of harm's way, but Hillary could not stop imagining the worst.[2]

Hillary then called her husband. The forty-second president of the United States was half a world away, in Australia, to deliver a speech. When Bill Clinton's phone rang, it was shortly before midnight local time, and he was in his hotel room, watching the live images of the burning World Trade Center. He immediately asked Hillary if Chelsea was all right.

Hillary hesitated. How could she tell him that she had no idea whether their daughter was safe?

"Everything's fine," Hillary fibbed. "Don't worry."[3]

At that moment, Chelsea was desperately trying to phone her mother from a friend's apartment in the Union Square neighborhood of Manhattan. Perhaps luckily, Chelsea had decided not to run that morning. After a friend called with the awful news of the first crash, Chelsea had watched the live television pictures of the second plane plowing into the World Trade Center. Each time she dialed her mother's cell phone, the call was disconnected. Bewildered by the television images, Chelsea left her friend's apartment. Immediately she saw hundreds of people racing full speed out of the Union Square subway station. Everyone, it seemed, was heading north, away from the besieged southern tip of Manhattan, but Chelsea began running south, against the crowd, searching for a pay phone to call her mother and father.

I am going to die, Chelsea thought to herself. For some reason the towers tumbling down reminded her of Humpty Dumpty. *It just seems as if the world is falling down, like Humpty Dumpty,* she thought.

After she stopped running, she started to pray, for America and New York City. She also said a prayer of hope for the nation's leaders — for President George W. Bush, New York mayor Rudolph

Giuliani, and, of course, her mother. "I thanked God that my mother was a senator representing New York," Chelsea later recalled, "and that Rudy Giuliani was our mayor."[4]

BY THE TIME HILLARY arrived on Capitol Hill, she still had not spoken with Chelsea. Joined by their staff members, Hillary and most of the other senators huddled around their office television sets and watched the horrific images. At 9:37 a.m., a third hijacked plane crashed into the Pentagon, just outside Washington, DC. Most of the one hundred senators, including Hillary, were eventually evacuated from the Senate office buildings.

Hillary and some of her colleagues were hurried into the Capitol Police headquarters, an older, seven-story building located several blocks from the Capitol. There were reports that another hijacked plane was on its way to Washington; some people speculated aloud that the next target was the Capitol dome or the White House. Amid the chaos swirling around her, Hillary heard her cell phone ring and quickly answered it. It was Chelsea. Her daughter was safe. The sound of her mother's voice brought tears to Chelsea's eyes.[5]

In less than sixty minutes, America's priorities changed, and along with them, Hillary's. The economy, the budget, tax cuts, education, health care, stem-cell research — none of these issues seemed to matter now. Hillary knew that foreign policy and counterterrorism, areas where she had relatively little experience, would now be paramount. As a freshman senator, Hillary had secured seats on committees covering a range of familiar domestic issues, like education and health care. She was elated with her assignments because they allowed her the opportunity to "continue the work I have been doing for over thirty years on behalf of children and families."[6] Those assignments were now far less important for a senator from a state that had just endured its worst attack since the Civil War.

For counsel, Hillary would turn to her husband. For nearly thirty years, Bill and Hillary had depended on each other for advice and support, especially during times of political crisis. This time, with no less than the security of the country at stake, Hillary knew instinctively that she would need to rely on Bill more than ever. "That September morning changed me and what I had to do as a senator, a New Yorker, and an American," Hillary later wrote.[7]

After speaking with Chelsea, Hillary phoned Bill a second time to reassure him that their daughter was safe. They then embarked on the first of many lengthy conversations that day about the past and the future — and about what the strategy should be to deal with both. Bill would recall two days later that he spoke with Hillary "quite often, all night long."[8] She was not just a senator from New York, but a female senator who had presidential ambitions in mind. Both Bill and Hillary intuitively grasped that a post–September 11 female candidate would be judged not only by her talk in the "war on terror," but also by the decisions she made.[9]

Her husband was not Hillary's only presidential counsel on this longest day. That afternoon, along with fellow New York senator Charles Schumer, she spoke by telephone with President George W. Bush, who was in an underground bunker at Offutt Air Force Base outside Omaha, Nebraska. The president promised them both that he would "do everything possible to help the rescue and recovery and what needs to be done in future years," Schumer recalled.[10]

Hours later, Hillary appeared live on CNN, just moments before Bush addressed the nation from the Oval Office. "We are united behind the president," she said. "This is an attack on America and we will support the president in whatever steps he takes. We can't let these evil acts deter us. We are going to support the president."[11]

Early that evening, as the sun began its slow descent behind the tall trees ringing the Capitol grounds, several hundred senators and House members gathered on the steps of the Capitol building's East Front. House Speaker Dennis Hastert and Senate majority leader Tom Daschle said a few words. There was a moment of silence for the thousands of victims and lost rescue workers. Then, as live television cameras scanned the grim and saddened expressions of the still-stunned lawmakers, they began to sing "God Bless America."[12] The song began spontaneously but every senator and representative was soon singing loudly and clearly. Irving Berlin's lyrics had never seemed more poignant, more urgent:

> *God bless America, land that I love*
> *Stand beside her, and guide her*
> *Through the night with the light from above.*

At least one camera lingered for a moment on Hillary as she sang. Her eyes shimmered with tears.

THE NEXT DAY, workers were still pulling bodies from the Pentagon, where the blistering impact of American Airlines flight 77 had left the western side of the military fortress in shards. In New York

City, a massive column of gray smoke cut through the sky, as if to signal to the satellites the horrors playing out below. Shaken and collectively grieving, Americans struggled to absorb the enormity of what had happened while their leaders tried to figure out how to respond.

Both Hillary and Bill knew that a vulnerable public needed its public officials to project an unwavering resolve. Already on September 11, Bill had been urging Hillary to make a bold statement to demonstrate that she possessed the toughness to help America wage a long war against a shadowy enemy.[13] The next day, on the floor of the Senate, Hillary heeded her husband's advice, delivering a fiery and emotional call to arms. She described the attacks on the World Trade Center and the Pentagon as an "attack on America" and called for swift and firm punishment for the terrorists who directed the suicide hijackers. Her rhetoric was decidedly more muscular than that of some of her Democratic colleagues. At one point, she vowed that any country that chose to harbor terrorists and "in any way aid or comfort them whatsoever will now face the wrath of our country."[14] Such remarks caught the attention of the Bush White House. "We were struck at the time," one Bush White House official said, "by how tough and supportive of the policy [her speech] was."[15] In a now-famous address before Congress, Hillary's threat would be echoed by President Bush eight days later.

And yet, for Hillary, who some of her friends say is the toughest person they know, the act of projecting toughness would prove to be an enormous challenge. Her lack of expertise in fighting terrorists further complicated matters. In the eight months prior to September 11, the freshman senator had delivered a total of nearly two hundred speeches, press releases, and statements, yet none of them had addressed counterterrorism issues.[16] Her staff still lacked the security clearances to see the most sensitive national security secrets, though, of course, Bill was privy to them.[17] And while her husband would be her most powerful asset — not only because of his experience but also because of his savvy and political acumen — in purely political terms, the events of September 11 would surely expose Bill and Hillary to a new array of attacks on his presidency. Given her position, it was inevitable that the job of defending Bill's legacy would fall primarily to Hillary.

Suddenly she was confronted with the most urgent of questions: As the former First Lady, how could she defend the Clinton

Hillary, seen here in a photo from her 1965 high school yearbook, left Park Ridge, Illinois, as a conservative "Goldwater Girl," but by the time she had graduated from Wellesley College, she had become an anti-war Democrat.

AP PHOTO/FILE

Bill and Hillary were married in Fayetteville, Arkansas, on October 11, 1975, the official start to one of the most powerful and enigmatic political partnerships in American history. WILLIAM J. CLINTON PRESIDENTIAL LIBRARY

Then-governor Bill Clinton and Hillary cuddle with their daughter, Chelsea, in 1980.

WILLIAM J. CLINTON PRESIDENTIAL LIBRARY

Hillary was largely absent from Bill's 1980 gubernatorial reelection campaign. Not coincidentally, he lost.

COURTESY OF THE *ARKANSAS DEMOCRAT-GAZETTE*

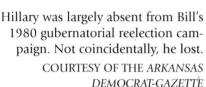

Hillary stands beside her exuberant husband after th "Comeback Kid" won the run-off Democratic election on June 8, 1982, putting him on the road back to the Arkansas governor's mansion. Bill was elected governor five times.

COURTESY OF THE *ARKANSAS DEMOCRAT-GAZETTE*

Wearing a three-piece ensemble of gold lamé in a baby houndstooth motif, Hillary prepares for Bill's inaugural ball on January 13, 1985.

COURTESY OF THE *ARKANSAS DEMOCRAT-GAZETTE*

Hillary, a Methodist, and Bill, a Baptist, share a hymnbook at Immanuel Baptist Church in Little Rock on January 16, 1985.

COURTESY OF THE *ARKANSAS DEMOCRAT-GAZETTE*

Despite all the turbulent times in their marriage, Bill and Hillary share a genuine love and respect for each other. Bill once said, "The tapestry of our marriage is deep, colorful, and well-woven—and nobody will tear it asunder."

COURTESY OF THE *ARKANSAS DEMOCRAT-GAZETTE*

A disappointed Hillary wipes away a tear as Governor Bill Clinton announces on July 15, 1987, that he will not run for president in 1988.

COURTESY OF THE *ARKANSAS DEMOCRAT-GAZETTE*

In 1993 and 1994, Hillary took her health care crusade across the country. Here, she addresses a rally at the University of Colorado at Boulder on March 14, 1994.
WILLIAM J. CLINTON PRESIDENTIAL LIBRARY

Hillary delivers a final word of support to President Clinton moments before she joins her husband, and Vice President Al Gore, at a rally of Congressional Democrats in the Rose Garden on the afternoon Clinton was impeached by the House of Representatives in December 1998. Bill was the second president in history to be impeached.
© SUSANA RAAB 1998

The Clintons share a private moment at a celebration of the 200th anniversary of the White House, held in the East Room on November 10, 2000, which was attended by all the living former presidents and their spouses, with the exception of President Reagan. © SUSANA RAAB 2000

Hillary listens to President Bush in the Oval Office on September 13, 2001. At this meeting, the president committed $20 billion in emergency 9/11 aid for the state of New York. AP PHOTO/THE WHITE HOUSE, ERIC DRAPER, HO

Hillary and Senator Bob Graham of Florida talk to reporters on March 10, 2004, collaborating on a voting bill. In 2002, Graham urged his colleagues to read all the Bush administration's intelligence about Iraq. He voted against the war resolution in October 2002; Hillary did not. AP PHOTO/MANUEL BALCE CENETA

Hillary and Senator Barack Obama chat at the annual convention of the National Association for the Advancement of Colored People in Washington, DC, on July 19, 2006. Less than a year later, they were vying for the support of the association's members in their respective campaigns for president.

AP PHOTO/EVAN VUCCI, FILE

Flanked by her close allies, Senator Carl Levin of Michigan *(left)* and Senator Jack Reed of Rhode Island, Hillary waits to address a news conference by Democratic senators who announced new national security legislation on Capitol Hill on September 7, 2006. PHOTO BY BRENDAN SMIALOWSKI/GETTY IMAGES

Hillary reviews information about Iraq during a Senate Armed Services Committee meeting on November 15, 2006.

PHOTO BY BENJAMIN J. MYERS

Hillary meets the press, on January 17, 2007, following her trip to Iraq and Afghanistan. Earlier that day, she videotaped the announcement of her intention to run for president, which was posted on her Web site three days later.

PHOTO BY BENJAMIN J. MYERS

"I'm not running as a woman," Hillary tells a forum at the University of Dubuque campus on March 4, 2007. "I'm running because I think I'm the best qualified and experienced person for president."

administration from the inevitable charges that it did not do all it could have done to prevent an attack against America? As a new senator, what could she do to help New York and the country heal and to prevent another attack?

HILLARY LEFT THE CAPITOL that afternoon and flew with her senior aides to LaGuardia Airport. She was accompanied on the flight by Joseph Allbaugh, a close ally of President Bush's and the director of the Federal Emergency Management Agency, and Schumer, whose complicated relationship with Hillary would be tested in the coming days. From LaGuardia, the threesome flew in a helicopter over Ground Zero.[18] The sight was staggering and terrible: Where there had once been soaring buildings, there was now rubble and smoke and the ghosts of thousands of innocents.

Both Hillary and Schumer later met with Giuliani, New York governor George Pataki, firefighters, FEMA officials, and hundreds of other Americans still attempting to rescue people from the smoldering pit. At Ground Zero, Hillary spent several hours talking with Pataki and Giuliani. "This has been, on a human level, one of the most gratifying experiences I've ever had," Hillary said two weeks later. "We've really bonded. I don't know how else to describe it."[19]

Afterward, Hillary huddled with Schumer. The two agreed that an initial request by the Bush administration to set aside $20 billion in emergency federal rescue aid for New York, Washington, and Pennsylvania was not nearly enough. They wanted the total package to be doubled to $40 billion, with half going to New York alone. The extra $20 billion figure for New York was pulled out of thin air, aides to both senators said. "If [the Bush administration was] going to give $20 billion to fight the [war on terror], I figured they could give $20 billion to help rebuild the city — and it's as good a number as any," Hillary later explained.[20]

The following afternoon, the two senators returned to Washington for a meeting with President Bush in the Oval Office. "We stand with you," Hillary told the president. "We stand with you united in Congress and united as a nation." Schumer asked Bush pointedly if he would be willing to double the federal rescue aid package, with $20 billion going to New York City.

"You've got it,"the president said, without hesitation.[21]

The generosity of Bush's instant agreement stunned everyone in the Oval Office. Hillary later recalled it as "one of the most emotional moments that I can certainly remember."[22] She added, "I've been in that room a lot of times, and I understand the power of the presidency to provide comfort in times of great need."[23] (In fact, Bush's quick response to the larger request was less spontaneous than it seemed at the time. Prior to the meeting, the president had been informed of the request, and after satisfying himself that it was reasonable, he gave the go-ahead to his aides. "We received a heads-up," a White House official said.)[24]

Still flush with emotion, Hillary left the meeting and told reporters on the White House lawn that she would stand behind President Bush "for a long time to come."[25]

At that moment, it was hard to find someone who didn't support the president. But for Hillary, her embrace of his presidency represented something truly extraordinary. When she first arrived in the Senate, she had quickly concluded that Bush and the senior members of his administration, along with their congressional allies, were "using every lever of power available to undo the economic, social and global progress achieved during my husband's presidency."[26]

"I admit I viewed that prospect dimly because I believe my husband was a very good president who left our nation well prepared for the future," Hillary recalled in her memoir. "Soon, though, I realized that the agenda wasn't about undermining Bill's work over eight years, it was about dismantling decades of policies, protections, and opportunities that had built the great American middle class at home and enduring alliances abroad."[27] And in the Senate itself, she had excoriated the administration on an array of issues, from environmental protection to health care.

But two days after the terror attacks, Hillary compartmentalized and pushed aside her previously harsh assessments. She was prepared to stand by the president, even if it meant she would have to begin figuring out how to deal with her husband's counterterrorism record.

That night, Hillary was scheduled to do three interviews on two television networks. On the *CBS Evening News*, Hillary told Dan Rather about the president's support that afternoon for the $20 billion in emergency aid for New York. Rather then quickly took a detour and asked her about her husband's attempts to deal with Osama bin Laden, the Saudi terror financier whose group, Al Qaeda, was already identified by intelligence officials as the organizer of the attacks.

It was a moment that Hillary must have anticipated, but it's likely that it arrived a bit sooner than she had figured. She paused for a moment before plunging in. "Well, Dan, I've always been very concerned about the threat of terrorism," she said. "I consider that our number one homeland threat."[28] It was an odd answer, considering her previous lack of public engagement on the topic. In fact, before September 11, Hillary had never spoken publicly as a senator about a homeland threat to the United States.[29] Hillary then recalled the Clinton administration's actions on counterterrorism. She talked about her husband's frustration with the "difficulty of getting good intelligence, of knowing where a suspected terrorist is, of having to count on people who—whose allegiances are not to the United States."[30]

Not long afterward, Hillary appeared live on CNN. Anchor Judy Woodruff asked her to comment on a news story that had just broken on the wires. It reported that during the final weeks of his presidency, President Clinton had considered an attack to kill bin Laden after terrorists had bombed the U.S.S. *Cole* in a Yemen port in October 2000. The wire report was based, in part, on information from a senior Clinton administration official.[31]

Hillary seemed to confirm the assertion of the wire story.

"Well, Judy, I'm not privy to all the information," Hillary said. "I know there was intelligence about his location. There was a plan that was put into place to try to pinpoint his location. It relied, as I recall, on human intelligence assets, namely people who were on the ground providing us with information. And my memory is that at the last minute those assets proved unreliable and were not able to form the basis for the kind of firm footing we needed for launching the sort of attack that we are considering."[32] In fact, the story later turned out to be incorrect. In its report, the 9/11 Commission concluded that President Clinton had last considered a military strike against bin Laden in May 1999, twenty months before the Clintons left the White House and well before the *Cole* attack.[33]

Hillary's last television appearance that evening was on CNN's *Larry King Live*. When King asked Hillary to talk about the wire report describing her husband's purported last-ditch attempt to have bin Laden killed, this time she sidestepped the question.[34] Instead, she reminded viewers of the Clinton administration's "attacks on some of Osama bin Laden's assets in Afghanistan" in August 1998. The U.S. military had bombed two of Al Qaeda's training camps and an alleged Al Qaeda chemical factory in the Sudan. Hillary characterized that attack as a partial success, though she was sensible enough to offer an obvious concession: "We were not successful in eradicating him and his network."

On Friday, September 14, 2001, Hillary sat down for another nationally televised interview, this one with Katie Couric on NBC's *Today* show. Her appearance this time was far more personal than the three interviews she had given on the previous evening, describing, for example, her anguish in the first hour after the attacks, when she could not contact Chelsea. She also seemed far less defensive about Bill's counterterrorism record as she forcefully — and, it turns out, presciently — described the challenge of fighting the long war on terrorism that would soon begin. America, she said, would be embarking on an unconventional, complicated war against a determined and resilient opponent. "It's an enemy unlike we've ever had before," she explained. "It's not like being bombed at Pearl Harbor and knowing immediately where that attack came from and what we need to do to try to defeat the state that brought it about."[35]

Leaving the NBC studio in northwest Washington, she drove to Washington Cathedral, where she met up with her husband to attend a national prayer service. (The day before, Bill had flown back to New York from Australia on an Air Force jet provided by President Bush.) With circles of sleeplessness under her eyes, she sat quietly in a pew near the front with her husband, their hands tightly clasped.[36] Later that day, Bill was asked what he would do if he were still president. "The important thing," he replied, "is that I'm operating as a civil servant and I'm going to support Hillary."[37]

That afternoon, Congress moved forward on the $40 billion emergency aid package. Hillary and other members of the New York congressional delegation proudly took credit for ensuring that New York would receive at least half of the appropriation for its recovery efforts.

IT IS NOT AT ALL UNUSUAL for a senator from New York to stand by the president at a time of crisis. But Hillary's positioning also worked in a subtle way to begin to distinguish her from her husband's record. Quickly separating herself from Bill's legacy was important and politically expedient.[38] In a poll that weekend, more Americans blamed the Clinton administration than the Bush administration for the terrorist attacks.[39] Without knowing much about how either administration attempted to deal with Al Qaeda, the public seemed to draw this conclusion from the fact that Bill Clinton had had eight years to stop the terrorists, while George W. Bush had had only eight months.

After the memorial service, Hillary went to New York, as did Bush. At Ground Zero, he made his iconic appearance, getting the firefighter's badge, rallying rescue workers, and telling the crowd through a bullhorn, "I can hear you...the rest of the world hears you, and the people"—Bush paused here for a moment as the crowd noise swelled—"and the people who knocked these buildings down will hear all of us soon." Hillary stood nearby and cheered the president's vow.[40]

With each passing day that week, Hillary seemed to grow more comfortable in her role as an energized street fighter for a shattered city. She had proved during her Senate campaign how good she was at retail politics, and that first week, every move she made seemed right. She was, of course, inevitably overshadowed by her former opponent Mayor Giuliani, who would be acclaimed as "America's Mayor" for his resolve in lower Manhattan in the hours immediately after the attacks and for his performance since then in holding the city together. And yet, for many New Yorkers, the images of Hillary fighting for the $20 billion in federal assistance for lower Manhattan, and standing atop the rubble with the president and Mayor Giuliani, dispelled any lingering doubts that she was a carpetbagger celebrity politician with few authentic ties to her new home state. "People now see her as a senator," said Bob Kerrey, the former Democratic senator from Nebraska and the president of the New School in New York City.[41]

Being in the spotlight, though, had its disadvantages, and Hillary was quickly reminded how merciless the glare could be. On September 20, President Bush addressed a joint session of Congress. He formally identified Al Qaeda as the perpetrator of the September 11 attacks. "Either you are with us or you are with the terrorists," Bush declared. "From this day forward, any nation that continues to harbor or support terrorism will be regarded by the United States as a hostile regime."[42] The president's comments were similar to Hillary's remarks delivered in the same chamber eight days earlier. Despite the unity of the two messages, however, nearly a dozen times during the speech, cameras showed Hillary rolling her eyes, clapping without enthusiasm, talking animatedly with Senator Schumer while the president spoke, and shaking her head while occasionally guffawing and appearing to feign interest in the president's speech.[43]

Around the country, there was swift and harsh reaction. An Atlanta schoolteacher named Kathie Larkin wrote in a letter to the editor of the *Atlanta Journal-Constitution*, "This is behavior I would not accept from my sixth-graders listening to a speaker, and I expected better of an adult from a state ripped apart by terrorist violence. Hillary needs to grow up." In a letter published by the *Washington Post*, James Gale of Silver Spring, Maryland, observed that Hillary "at times seemed bored and uninterested, clapping perfunctorily, and at other times she was talking during the speech. I thought her actions were unbecoming a senator at this difficult time."[44] For weeks, conservative commentators and columnists, spurred on by Republican operatives who sent out press releases detailing Hillary's televised reactions, ridiculed her odd array of facial expressions during the speech. The conservative weekly newspaper *Human Events* projected that Hillary's facial reactions reflected her feelings about a missed political opportunity: "A more cynical observer might surmise that perhaps Hillary is bitter that, as a wartime president, Bush's reelection chances have pretty well doused her own ambitions for 2004."[45]

A few days later, Hillary sat down in her Senate office with Nicholas Lemann of *The New Yorker*. Like most of her constituents, Hillary looked to her own past as a way to draw the emotional courage to get through the crisis. Lemann asked her how Americans would react to learning that they were on the "receiving end of a murderous anger."

"Oh, I am well aware that it is out there," she said. "One of the most difficult experiences that I personally had in the White House was during the health care debate, being the object of extraordinary rage. I remember being in Seattle. I was there to make a speech about health care. This was probably August of '94. Radio talk-show hosts had urged their listeners to come out and yell and scream and carry on and prevent people from hearing me speak. There were threats that were coming in, and certain people didn't want me to speak, and they started taking weapons off people, and arresting people. I've had firsthand looks at this unreasoning anger and hatred that is focused on an individual you don't know, a cause that you despise—whatever motivates people." Nevertheless, Hillary remained optimistic about the future: "I think we recognize that the sense of invulnerability that has been a hallmark of the American psychological experience has been shattered," she said. "We are now standing shoulder to shoulder with Israelis, who worry when they go to a pizza parlor. Or with Londoners, who got up every day and faced the bombs during the Battle of Britain. Or with most of the rest of the human race that has ever existed, and that exists now, whose lives are shaped by the hazards of life. But that should not be an excuse for either giving in to fear or giving up on life. The purpose of terrorism is to terrorize. And the only way that a terrorist ultimately wins is if you give him permission to defeat you."[46]

Two weeks later, on a mid-October evening at Madison Square Garden, "The Concert for New York" was held to raise money for victims of the terror attacks. The headline act was ex-Beatle Paul McCartney. Giuliani, Governor Pataki, and Bill Clinton made brief appearances, and each was greeted warmly by the capacity crowd of twenty thousand people, mostly New York firefighters and police officers. But when Hillary strode onto the stage, she was confronted with a hearty chorus of boos and heckling—an unsurprising response given both the fact that the firefighters and police unions had not endorsed her Senate candidacy in 2000 and the recent flak over her behavior during the president's speech.

"Thank you! Thank you for being here tonight!" Hillary began saying, but the cacophony of boos and heckling just grew louder. She then began shouting to be heard over the din. "Thank you for supporting New York! Thank you for your generosity!" In the crowd, police officers and firefighters yelled, "Get off the stage!" and "We don't want you here!" Hillary smiled, ignored the hecklers, and waved through it all.

Afterward, Hillary described the catcalls and boos as "almost part of the healing process" for the police officers and firefighters, adding that she did not take their reaction personally. "They can blow off steam any way they want to," she said with a shrug. "They've earned it."[47] A broadcast of the concert subsequently aired by VH-1 and later released on DVD replaced the booing when Hillary walked onstage with wild cheers.[48]

THAT FALL, HILLARY cosponsored a measure to release a specially priced first-class U.S. postage stamp that raised money for the families of rescue workers killed on September 11. It was the kind of modest, symbolic gesture that she spent much of the next few months making. She also spoke out on a number of issues related to the terror attacks — airport security, bioterrorism, and border security — but her involvement was largely limited to public statements made at press conferences and released by her staff, because her committee assignments had left her without much of a platform to engage legislatively on the issue. She supported Bush's invasion of Afghanistan to rout the Taliban, which had provided safe haven to Al Qaeda and its training camps. And on October 25, she voted for the Patriot Act, which gave new tools to law enforcement agents and intelligence officials to gather and share information. (Only one senator — Democrat Russ Feingold of Wisconsin — voted against the measure.) She remained decidedly hawkish, far closer to President Bush than most of her fellow Democrats were.

Before long, however, Hillary found her September 11 issue. Workers and residents had worked literally around the clock since September 11 at Ground Zero, and many had complained about the hazardous conditions. The Bush administration had assured the public that conditions were safe, but some workers were clearly suffering from breathing problems and other ailments. Hillary began lobbying to persuade Congress to approve money to monitor how the contaminated air around Ground Zero was affecting the lungs of recovery workers. She eventually hired one of the leading experts on occupational hazards and pulmonary health, Dr. William Rom of New York University, to be her legislative fellow. Rom proved conclusively that pieces of glass, asbestos fibers, and fly ash (a mineral residue that is used as a substitute for cement) had gotten into the lungs of rescue workers. His findings enabled Hillary to land more cooperation from the White House and the Environmental Protection Agency, which were reluctant to acknowledge that conditions at Ground Zero were contributing to workers' health problems. To further pressure the White House, she placed a legislative hold (a senator's privilege to delay a nomination) on the administration's nomination of Mike Leavitt to head the EPA. Her strategy worked, and a meeting was soon scheduled between Hillary and White House aides. Rom accompanied Hillary to the meeting, where he explained his study of September 11 rescue workers and the possibility that the asbestos fibers could cause them to develop cancer.[49] Hillary was able to persuade the EPA to agree to further study the issue. Eventually, research revealed that almost 70 percent of those who worked at Ground Zero had developed lung ailments as a result of the poor air quality following the September 11 attacks.

Taking on the air-quality problem was a brilliant move on Hillary's part. By highlighting health and the environment, she succeeded in carving out a post-September 11 issue that played to her strengths while meeting the needs of her constituents. Along the way, it also created some space between her and the Bush administration and an opportunity to return to the base of her party, who were not as supportive of Bush as she had been.

Not coincidentally, Bill Clinton's political philosophy had been rooted in precisely this sort of tactical triangulation: He would occupy the space between extremes, his positions neither liberal nor conservative, and his alliances convenient. So far, Hillary had done the same with 9/11, albeit with a tilt further right than some — including her opponents — had expected. But within a year of the attacks, she would be confronted with a new phase in the Bush administration's so-called war on terror, and she would have to grapple with what she described as "probably the hardest decision I have had to make." For this decision, the junior senator from New York would have to not only continue to defend Bill Clinton's record but also forge a record of her own that she knew would define her future presidential ambitions.

That "hardest decision" would involve a country that had caused her husband a good deal of annoyance but, despite intermittent moments of diplomatic crisis, had rarely if ever been a supreme challenge. The current administration felt quite differently. George Bush and his vice president, Dick Cheney, claimed Iraq's leader, Saddam Hussein, posed a direct threat to the United States.

Once again, Hillary would be forced to prove her toughness.

CHAPTER 18

"The Hardest Decision"

BY THE EARLY AUTUMN of 2002, the prospect of a U.S.-led invasion of Iraq was gaining momentum in Washington. The Bush administration was pushing its case that Saddam Hussein posed a direct threat to the United States and his neighbors in the Middle East because he possessed a cache of weapons of mass destruction — both chemical and biological — and was aggressively pursuing the development of nuclear arms. Bush and Vice President Dick Cheney declared repeatedly that there were strong ties between Saddam's regime and Al Qaeda, the perpetrators of the September 11 attacks. And the administration warned that the United States would no longer tolerate Iraq's thwarting the mission of UN weapons inspectors.

In early October that year, the Senate prepared to vote on a resolution that would give the president the authority to use military force in Iraq if his diplomatic efforts failed. For Hillary, it amounted to the most important vote of her public life. It would also turn out to be a box from which she would find it difficult, if not impossible, to escape.

Coming to a decision involved a knotty set of calculations, some of which seemed preordained. Hillary had put down, as she put it, a "pretty pugnacious" marker the day after September 11 by saying that those helping terrorists would face the "wrath" of the United States.[1] Retreating from that muscular stance would be tricky. On the other hand, if she voted yes, she would be giving President Bush the authority to launch a preemptive war—a concept that reminded her of the failed war in Vietnam, which she had so bitterly opposed.

Voting against the resolution would also mean retreating from the policies of another president—her husband. Bill Clinton had signed a law in 1998 that contained nonbinding provisions calling for regime change, and he also predicted that same year that Saddam Hussein would use weapons of mass destruction.

Only a year after the September 11 attacks, the fear of terrorism was so widespread in America that it was relatively easy for Washington to fold a confrontation with a tyrranical, anti-American dictator into the administration's overall "war on terror." Polls showed that most Americans believed there was a link between Saddam Hussein and September 11. Hillary surely was not unaware of all this.

Finally, there was Hillary's concern that she could never win the presidency if she didn't prove that she was tough enough. This had always been a worry. Female candidates had long suffered as a result of the stereotype that they could never be as strong as a man. Now the defense of the homeland had become such a paramount issue that Americans insisted that their president—man or woman—protect them from another terrorist attack. That was especially true for New Yorkers, her new constituents.

Of course, Hillary *was* tough. And she was experienced. But her insecurity about her public image, her knowledge that her nascent national security credentials might be perceived as insufficient by voters, and her and Bill's experiences of the past twenty years watching the Republicans trump the Democrats when it came to national security made it difficult for her to vote no.

Her vote was further complicated by her shifting relationship with the sitting commander in chief. If Hillary was going to support Bush, it would mean she would have to extend him the benefit of the doubt. She had hoped he would continue to pursue diplomacy with Iraq whether or not Congress gave him the power to wage war, a pledge the president indeed had made. But trusting Bush was difficult for Hillary, especially since, despite their alliance over 9/11, he had continued to aggressively unwind numerous domestic and foreign-policy measures implemented under her husband's administration.

Many other Democrats in the Senate had their own histories to redo. Most of them had opposed the 1991 resolution that narrowly gave the first President Bush the authority to attack Iraq following its 1990 invasion of Kuwait. Saddam Hussein had remained in power when the Persian Gulf War ended, but the UN Security Council had adopted a resolution designed to keep him and his weapons programs in check. Weapons inspectors tasked with enforcing the resolution had later left Iraq, complaining that Hussein made their jobs difficult. According to the Bush administration, Hussein had continued to develop weapons of mass destruction. Though the decision not to attempt to take Saddam out in 1991 had been made by President Bush's father when he occupied the Oval Office, conservatives pushed some of the blame onto the Democrats, many of whom had opposed that war in the first place.

If many in Congress were thinking hawkishly, the same could not be said for a number of American allies in Europe. Iraq, they argued, was not threatening its neighbors. Some felt that even without the weapons inspectors, Iraq was forcefully constrained by economic sanctions and overflight patrols. As heated debate gripped the United Nations and anti-war protests began playing out worldwide, Tom Daschle, the leader of the Democrats in the Senate, implored his divided colleagues simply to vote their conscience.[2]

For Hillary, that meant consulting Bill.

Explaining her vote, Hillary noted, "Perhaps my decision is influenced by my eight years of experience on the other end of Pennsylvania Avenue in the White House, watching my husband deal with serious challenges to our nation."[3]

It was not a coincidence that Hillary invoked her time in the White House, or her husband's record, as she explained her rationale. While Hillary was building her own record as a leader, Bill's behind-the-scenes role became a hypersensitive issue among Hillary's closest advisers, who steadfastly refused to discuss the matter publicly.[4] But just as he had engaged in most aspects of her Senate career, Bill served as her main counsel on the Iraq war vote.[5] He had personal experience to offer: While Bill was president in 1998, the United States, assisted by the United Kingdom, had launched more than 400 cruise missiles and flown 650 air attacks against suspected

WMD sites in Iraq after Saddam Hussein refused to cooperate with UN weapons inspectors. "Mark my words, he will develop weapons of mass destruction," President Clinton had said at the time to justify the attack. "He will deploy them and he will use them."[6] In his 2004 memoir, Bill defended his decision to attack suspected WMD sites in Iraq, though he did not repeat his ominous prediction. He also reminded readers that some Republicans had been "in a snit over the attacks," dismissing them as a "wag the dog" attempt to delay a pending vote in the House of Representatives on whether to impeach him.[7]

Several days before the vote was scheduled in Congress, President Bush made a televised speech from Cincinnati, leaving "no doubt" he was prepared to strike Iraq if Hussein refused to disarm.[8] The president, secondarily, spoke of one last try at diplomacy. Hillary gravitated toward this option and hoped that Bush was serious when he mentioned it.[9]

The day after the Cincinnati speech, she had a rare opportunity to explore whether he was. Hillary and a few other senators met privately at the White House with the president and some of his advisers.[10] The president had "no recollection of Senator Clinton asking a question" at the meeting.[11]

Afterward, according to Hillary, Condoleezza Rice, then the national security adviser, called Hillary and "asked if I had any questions." Hillary said she did: Would the president use the authority granted by Congress to go to the United Nations and "get the inspectors to go back into Iraq?" Rice, according to Hillary, replied, "Yes, that's what it is for."[12] But President Bush and Rice both recall saying that "one advantage of the authorization" by Congress was the leverage it gave them at the UN and in the Middle East, not that they needed the authorization to gain that leverage.[13]

Given the subsequent revelations regarding the Bush administration's inaccurate statements during the run-up to the Iraq war, it is impossible to know if the president and Rice were telling the truth about the exchange with Hillary. But both seem to agree that Hillary's opportunity to push the president regarding diplomacy — if for no other reason than to get it on the record that she had done so — was effectively squandered.

As she had always done, Hillary prepared for her decision on the war vote by doing her homework, or what she often called her "due diligence." This included, she later said, attending classified briefings on Capitol Hill concerning intelligence on Iraq. She also noted that she had consulted with national security officials from the Clinton administration whom she trusted.[14]

What she has not discussed publicly is whether she specifically read the classified version of the National Intelligence Estimate, the most comprehensive judgment of the intelligence community about Iraq's WMD, which was made available to all one hundred senators. The ninety-page classified report was delivered to Congress on October 1, 2002, just ten days before the Senate vote. An abridged summary was made public by the Bush administration, but it painted a far less subtle picture of Iraq's weapons program than the full classified report, part of which was later declassified. To get a complete picture, one needed to read the entire classified document.

Hillary still had no one on her staff with the security clearances needed to read the NIE and the other highly classified reports that pertained to Iraq.[15] This put more pressure on her to read these reports herself. Senators could easily access the NIE in a secure room on the fourth floor of the Capitol or in the offices of the Senate Intelligence Committee.

Rather incredibly, given the magnitude of the vote to come, only six senators personally read the report.[16] In 2007, on the presidential campaign trail in New Hampshire, Hillary was confronted by a woman who had traveled from New York to ask her if she had read the complete intelligence report. Hillary responded that she had been briefed on it. "Did you read it?" the woman screamed. And Hillary repeated that she had been briefed, though she did not identify who had briefed her or admit that none of her own aides could possibly have done so.[17]

The question of whether Hillary took the time to read the NIE is critically important. Unlike the abridged and sanitized summary, the longer, classified version of the Intelligence Estimate contained numerous caveats and dissents on Iraq's weapons and capabilities, making it sound less certain that the country posed a legitimate threat to the United States. The declassified version of the Intelligence Estimate, which was openly discussed by Congress and reported on by the press, omitted most of the questions and qualifiers about Iraq's alleged stockpiles of WMD. Indeed, one of Hillary's Democratic colleagues, Bob Graham, the Florida senator who was then the chairman of the Intelligence Committee, said he voted against the resolution on the war, in part because he had read the complete NIE. Graham said that it did not persuade him that Iraq possessed WMD. "I was able to apply *caveat emptor,*" Graham said later, adding regretfully, "Most of my colleagues could not."[18]

On Tuesday, October 7, 2002, Senate Democrats, including Hillary, held a caucus over lunch on the second floor of the Capitol. There, Graham "forcefully" urged his colleagues to read the complete NIE prior to making their final decisions.[19] Two days later, on the Senate floor, Graham again implored his colleagues to read the classified intelligence reports before casting such a monumental vote.[20]

In her own remarks on the Senate floor on October 10, 2002, Hillary paid her respects to Senator Graham's position and to that of others, noting the "differing opinions within this body." Then she went on to offer a lengthy catalog of Saddam Hussein's crimes. She talked about her husband's "intensive four-day air assault" in December 1998 on "known and suspected weapons of mass destruction sites." She cited unnamed "intelligence reports" showing that between 1998 and 2002, Saddam Hussein had "worked to rebuild his chemical and biological weapons stocks, his missile delivery capability, and his nuclear program." Both the public and secret intelligence estimates on Iraq had contained such analysis, but the secret assessment had also included a dissent by the State Department's intelligence arm that had concluded — correctly, as it turned out — that Iraq was not rebuilding its nuclear program. The classified report also contained additional conditional language in its description of Iraq's nuclear ambitions.

Hillary continued, accusing Iraq's leader of giving "aid, comfort, and sanctuary to terrorists, including Al Qaeda members."[21] This statement fit squarely within the ominous warning she had issued the day after September 11.

Hillary's link between Iraq's leader and Al Qaeda, however, was unsupported by the conclusions of the NIE, as well as by several other classified reports and unclassified documents that were available before the Senate vote. Indeed, there was but one document that supported Hillary's statement: a letter from the CIA to Senator Graham, which somewhat tepidly mentioned "growing indications of a relationship" with Al Qaeda by Iraq, based on "sources of varying reliability."[22] In fact, the classified reports concluded that not only was Iraq not allied with Al Qaeda, but that Saddam Hussein and Osama bin Laden were rivals who harbored feelings of deep mistrust and enmity toward each other. A Defense Intelligence Agency report in February 2002 concluded, "Saddam's regime is intensely secular and is wary of Islamic revolutionary movements. Moreover, Baghdad is unlikely to provide assistance to a group it cannot control."[23] A CIA report of June 21, 2002, said, "The ties between Saddam and bin Laden appear much like those between rival intelligence services, with each trying to exploit the other for its own benefit."[24] And, according to Graham, the complete NIE report, which remains classified, noted that Saddam Hussein had "few if any contacts with Al Qaeda and no particular interest in assisting Osama bin Laden."[25]

Nevertheless, on the sensitive issue of collaboration between Al Qaeda and Iraq, Hillary found herself adopting the same argument as the one aggressively pushed by the president and vice president. Bush, Cheney, and other administration officials had repeated their barely supported claim so many times that by early October 2002, two out of three Americans believed that Saddam Hussein had been involved in the September 11 attacks.[26] By contrast, most of the other Senate Democrats, even those who voted for the war authorization, did not make the Al Qaeda connection in their remarks on the Senate floor. One Democratic senator who voted for the war resolution and praised President Bush for his course of "moderation and deliberation," Joe Biden of Delaware, actively debunked the reports of Al Qaeda in Iraq and called them "much exaggerated" in his remarks.[27] Dianne Feinstein of California, who said she had read the complete classified NIE report, described any link between Saddam Hussein and Al Qaeda as "tenuous."[28]

In fact, the lone Democratic Senator who came close to echoing Hillary's hawkish remarks about Hussein's alleged assistance to Al Qaeda was Joseph Lieberman of Connecticut. Yet even Lieberman tempered his words on the Senate floor about the connection by noting that the "relationship between Al Qaeda and Saddam's regime is a subject of intense debate within the intelligence community."[29]

However, there was no debate among most of those who had served in the Clinton administration. According to Kenneth Pollack, who was a national security official under President Clinton and a leading proponent of overthrowing Saddam Hussein, any link between Saddam and Al Qaeda was "bullshit....We all knew that was bullshit." Pollack advised Hillary about Iraq prior to her war vote.[30]

The Saddam–Al Qaeda link, so aggressively pushed by the Bush administration, was later debunked as false. So, how could Hillary, described in 2006 by *The Washingtonian* magazine as "the brainiest" senator, have gotten such a critical point wrong? "My vote was a sincere vote based on the facts and assurances that I had at that time," she said, declining to characterize her vote as a mistake. "And I have taken responsibility for my vote."[31]

Hillary knew that her vote, in many ways, amounted to a test of her ability to make life-or-death decisions, which is a direct responsibility of the commander in chief. Just as she had intuited in the days after the terror attacks, she knew now that she had to exhibit even more toughness than her male counterparts.[32] Yet if she did not bother to read the complete intelligence reports, then she did not do enough homework on the decision that she has called the most important of her life. If she did read them, she chose to make statements to justify her vote for war that were not supported by the available intelligence. And if she read the reports, it seems bizarre that she would not have said so.

ON OCTOBER 11, 2002, the Senate voted 77 to 23 to authorize the Bush administration's war against Iraq. The result was shaped in part by the upcoming midterm elections. Some of the senators up for reelection did not want to appear weak on an issue that the administration had skillfully tied to America's "war on terror."[33] Hillary, having been elected two years earlier, had no such immediate worries. And yet electoral politics was a factor in her self-positioning and her vote.[34] Indeed, prior to the invasion, Hillary was far more prescient than many of her Senate colleagues about the potential difficulty of rebuilding Iraq. In a number of private meetings with top Bush officials, Hillary asked pointed questions about how the administration planned to deal with the inevitable challenges of governing the country after the invasion. In a secret briefing for senators in February 2003 on Capitol Hill, Hillary vigorously prodded Secretary of Defense Donald Rumsfeld on the subject, according to participants.[35]

For all the scrutiny of Hillary's vote, curiously, a central moment has gotten lost. It came on October 10, 2002, the same day Hillary spoke on the Senate floor about why she would support the Iraq war authorization. In her remarks, she stressed the need for diplomacy with Iraq on the part of the Bush administration and insisted she wasn't voting for "any new doctrine of preemption, or for unilateralism."[36] Yet just a few hours later, Hillary voted against an amendment to the war resolution that would have required the diplomatic emphasis Hillary had earlier gone on record as supporting—and which she now says she had favored all along.

The long-overlooked vote was on an amendment that had been introduced by several Senate Democrats who hoped to rein in President Bush's authority by requiring a two-step process before Congress would actually authorize the use of force. Senators knew full well the wide latitude that they were handing Bush, so some tried to put the brakes on his presumed march to war. The first proposed cautionary element in the amendment demanded a second UN resolution explicitly approving the use of force against Iraq. If his efforts at diplomacy failed, the amendment allowed Congress to demand that the president get a second authorization for war. It required him to return to Congress to "urge us to authorize a going-it-alone, unilateral resolution," said the amendment's author, Senator Carl Levin of Michigan.[37] In other words, the amendment was sending this message to Bush: Trust but verify. Levin's opponents, among them John McCain, argued that the amendment's requirement of a second UN resolution limited "our freedom of action."[38] That limitation, of course, was precisely what Levin and his cosponsors had intended.

For decades, there has been a highly contentious debate between Congress and the president over which branch of government has the power to authorize the use of force. The amendment, had it passed, might not have prevented President Bush from invading Iraq, but it offered an opportunity for senators to go on the record in favor of a more diplomatic approach.

The Levin amendment presented Hillary with the perfect chance to demand that Bush actively pursue additional diplomacy before going to war. But she chose not to do so, instead joining the significant majority of seventy-five senators who voted against Levin's proposal. Those seventy-five were largely the same ones who then voted the next day in favor of the war authorization. Three senators—Feinstein, Tom Harkin of Iowa, and Herb Kohl of Wisconsin—straddled the fence, voting yes on Levin's resolution before voting yes on Bush's war authorization. (After his amendment was defeated, Levin voted against the war authorization.) If Hillary had joined her three Democratic colleagues and supported Levin's amendment, she subsequently could have far more persuasively argued that she had worked toward a multilateral diplomatic approach. Instead of voting for Bush to pursue more diplomacy, she voted to give Bush the authority to invade Iraq.

THE RUSSELL SENATE OFFICE BUILDING is the oldest of the three buildings that house the chambers and offices of the nation's one hundred senators. Its corridors are lengthy; its offices are cavernous; and its ceilings are high. But on the morning of March 6, 2003, none of those bedrock structures could contain the loud sounds made by dozens of chanting and angry women dressed in pink who congregated outside Russell 476.

The protesters were members of a left-wing group organized a few months earlier in opposition to the war. Their name, "Code Pink: Women for Peace," was intended to ridicule the color-coded terrorism security alerts promulgated by the Bush administration. That morning, the group had brought their cause to the door of Senator Hillary Rodham Clinton.

The Code Pink women had decided to mount a last-gasp attempt to stop the war by confronting senators in the halls of Congress. Though they were earnest, their campaign was mostly symbolic. Five months earlier, members of Congress, including Hillary, had given President Bush all the authority he needed to wage war against Saddam Hussein's Iraq. By now, the military buildup in the region was nearly complete and the invasion seemed inevitable. (In fact, it was only days away.)

Hillary's senior staff members were stunned that such a large, raucous group was demanding to see the senator. Without hesitation, they rejected Code Pink's demand for a meeting, explaining that their boss was too busy conducting Senate business on the floor. (Senators generally do not meet people without a prior appointment.) Undeterred, the women camped outside Hillary's office, refusing to leave until they spoke with her. Apparently persuaded by the group's determination, Hillary's aides told Code Pink's leaders the senator would meet with them in about an hour. One of the ground rules was that no reporters were permitted to attend. Code Pink agreed and they were directed to a nearby room, where they passed the time singing peace songs and chatting.[39]

Suddenly, the big walnut doors were thrown open and Hillary, dressed in a bright blue coat over a black pantsuit, strode into the room. The women rose quickly from their chairs and applauded. Hillary smiled and took her place behind a table, facing the women. She thanked them, acknowledged their concerns, and paid homage to the group's trademark color.

"I like pink tulips," she said with a smile.[40]

Hillary then addressed the obvious gap between Code Pink's position on the war and her own. "I disagree on an aspect of those concerns," she said. Hillary then asked if the group had a spokesperson.

A tall woman dressed in pink approached the table. She was wearing a pink slip on top of her pink outfit, emblazoned with the words "Hilary [sic], you're not listening to the women. We say: NO WAR IN IRAQ." She introduced herself as Medea Benjamin and thanked Hillary for taking the time to meet with them.

Benjamin, a veteran of causes on the left, explained to Hillary that she had recently led a delegation to Baghdad, where she and her colleagues expressed their solidarity with Iraqi women and met with United Nations weapons inspectors, who said they needed more time.

Benjamin then touched on several of the signature issues of Hillary's career: "We want you to help us protect the Iraqi women and children and our children," she said, asking Hillary to work to ensure that federal money went to "child care, health care," but not to a war.

Hillary nodded but said nothing.

Benjamin continued with her polite approach. "We know you're a wonderful woman," she said, "and that deep down, you really agree with us."

Business being business, the Code Pink leader then cut to the chase. "There are two ways to go," she intoned. Her group could give Hillary a pink badge of courage if she supported their position. If not, the group was prepared to give her a pink slip.

Hillary struck a conciliatory note.

"I admire your willingness to speak out on behalf of the women and children of Iraq," she said, adding, "Those are causes on which I feel very strongly." She confided that her October 2002 vote to support the president on a possible invasion of Iraq was an "extremely difficult decision for me." Hillary then embarked on a lengthy and detailed explanation for her vote and her knowledge about Iraq. Not only was her explanation more detailed and revealing than the remarks she had delivered on the Senate floor prior to her vote, but her comments to Code Pink would surpass those made in her subsequent speeches, writings, and communications with her constituents on the matter.

In her memoir, *Living History*, Hillary makes no mention of a previous interest in Iraq and discloses only one conversation she had with her husband about it, in 1998. But now she told the women, "This is something I have followed for more than a decade." There was some truth to that, in that as president Bill had intermittently dealt with Iraq, and she had seen that from the inside. But if Iraq had been a particular interest of hers, she had certainly effectively hidden that fact while in Washington.

When asked by one of the women why the United States took on the responsibility to disarm a country like Iraq, Hillary replied that without "U.S. leadership" there would not be "a willingness to take on very difficult problems" because of the "attitudes of many people in the world community today." She cited her husband's muscular foreign-policy actions, at times taken unilaterally, as a precedent for the Bush administration's intervention in Iraq. "I'm talking specifically about what had to be done in Bosnia and Kosovo, where my husband could not get a UN resolution to save the Kosovar Albanians" from the ethnic-cleansing policies of Slobodan Milošević, Hillary told the women. "We had to do it alone."

Another Code Pink member then asked Hillary if she believed Saddam Hussein possessed weapons of mass destruction. "There's been no accounting (by Iraq) for the chemical and biological weapons," Hillary admitted. But she added that Saddam Hussein had "such a proven track record" that he could only be described as having "an obsession with WMD." She then suggested, but did not explicitly say, that she had read the secret intelligence reports on Iraq. "I ended up voting for the resolution after carefully reviewing the information and the intelligence that I had available," she said. Hillary told the Code Pink protesters that she had also done her due diligence by "talking with people" she trusted. She did not identify those trusted advisers.

Finally, Hillary took the opportunity to take a poke at the president, expressing "one hundred percent" solidarity with Code Pink's criticism of Bush's domestic priorities. They applauded. Then Hillary turned to leave.

"Sorry, guys," she added.

Just a few days before the Code Pink visit, Hillary had expressed a preference for a peaceful solution through diplomacy and weapons inspections, telling reporters in upstate New York, "It is preferable that we do this in a peaceful manner through coercive inspection."[41] But this was just rhetoric when matched up against her votes and her continued support of the president. The bottom line was that Hillary still supported the war. So, before she could make her exit, a Code Pink leader told her, "I heard that you were willing to give up the life of innocent people in Iraq to find Saddam Hussein, so I just want to give you my pink slip." The woman then tried to shove a pink undergarment into Hillary's hand.

Hillary would not touch it and shot a look of fury at the woman. "I'm the senator from New York," Hillary snapped, wagging her finger at the woman. "I will never put my people's security at risk. I resent that."

"You are! You are! You are!" several women shouted at Hillary as she swiftly turned her back to the Code Pink audience and walked out the door. One of the protesters shouted at her, "You're living in denial!" After the senator left, the women began singing:

Putting our bodies on the line,
Stop this war while there's still time,
Putting our bodies on the line,
Hillary's got to show some spine.

The "vast right-wing conspiracy" had attacked Hillary Rodham Clinton for decades, but never as "in her face" as this group of leftist women had. And apparently unbeknownst to Hillary, the women had video-recorded everything and, on the eve of the launch of her presidential campaign, they would post the video on YouTube.

The Code Pink protest was a sign that Hillary's vote had the potential to cause her some big problems. And the war itself hadn't even begun.

CHAPTER 19

The Club

THE UNITED STATES CONGRESS is an archaic institution that lags behind the rest of America. It is less diverse, more wealthy, and in its rules and customs a Jekyll-and-Hyde combination of quaint parliamentary procedure and ferocious partisan squabbling.

There are important distinctions, however, both between the two chambers and within the Senate itself, where seniority prevails. Senators, who face reelection every six years, look down on their colleagues in the House, who must win reelection every two years. The Senate, the so-called upper chamber, is seen as far more deliberative — unlike those of the House, its rules stipulate that 60 percent of its members must agree to end a debate — and the elitist culture has often encouraged a sobriety missing in the other chamber. It is also predominantly male; during Hillary's tenure, there were at most sixteen female senators.

The key to Hillary's success in the Senate was a combination of charm and commitment. "She was patient and diligent. She is wonderful with names, and remembering your birthday; she has a great gift [for] that," one Senate aide recalled.[1] One of the principal objects of her attention was Robert C. Byrd, the longest-serving senator and someone "who is not easy to charm," the aide added.[2] Hillary had crossed Byrd years earlier when she had tried to sneak her health care reforms through by adding them to other legislation, and she worked hard to win him over. "She was very cognizant of the rules of the Senate, the emphasis on seniority," said James Varey, who headed the Capitol Police during Hillary's first few years in the Senate.[3]

And of course Hillary was not just any elected official. Her experience as First Lady helped her work magic inside the anterooms of the Senate. "She spends that minute with you and makes you think you know her," the aide recalled.[4] Her good nature, her sense of humor, and her ability "to tell a good story" surprised some of her colleagues, according to Senator Barbara Mikulski of Maryland. "What so impressed the Republicans was how industrious she was, how serious she was, and how she was not judgmental," Mikulski said. "They came to respect her because she wasn't paparazzi oriented."[5]

Republican senator John McCain agreed. "She came into the Senate under the most intensive scrutiny of any senator in recent history, probably since Teddy Kennedy," McCain said, and "she has conducted herself very admirably." McCain added that Hillary was "always well prepared" at hearings that they both attend on the Armed Services Committee.[6]

That preparation is often the product of a long night of cramming. When Hillary goes home after her last event, she usually carries a thick sheaf of briefing papers prepared by her staff. Sometimes they total two hundred pages or more.[7]

"The day would end late for her," a former aide explained. "The next morning, when you'd have the morning call before her first meeting, usually around seven-thirty or eight, it would be clear she had digested the material from the night before even though she couldn't have seen it before ten."[8] Studying "relaxes her," a Senate adviser said. "In her downtime, she inhales information and enjoys it."[9]

One of her former aides was so amazed by her work ethic that he came away with "the impression she didn't need a lot of sleep."[10] In fact, unlike Bill, who usually doesn't hit the hay until long past midnight, Hillary "needs more downtime and sleep," a former Clinton White House aide said.[11] Given that, she is a very fast study indeed.

The study sessions are not restricted to the evening hours. Hillary's early-morning homework includes digesting a summary of daily news clips that are prepared by a junior staff aide.[12] The package includes not only stories that mention her but also articles about subjects or issues that interest her. The digest is sent to Hillary well in advance of her first event, so if she has a breakfast meeting at 7:30 or 8:00, the junior aide must awaken very early in the morning to prepare the clippings file.[13]

From the beginning, Hillary's committee workload has been substantial. Under the informal rules of the club, senators can serve on only two major committees. But thanks to a waiver from the leader of her party, Hillary, like a few of her more senior colleagues, sits on three — Armed Services (which she joined two years into her first term), Health, Education, Labor and Pensions (HELP), and Environment and Public Works.[14]

Her official status as one of the lowest-ranking committee members belied her actual power. "Most new members that are down the dais, you rarely hear from," a Senate aide said, referring to the practice of seating members by seniority, with the most senior in the center. "But she plays a more significant role than the more senior members. When she walks into the room for a HELP hearing, she causes a bit of a stir. It's because of who she is. She has a very strong reputation."[15]

Many New Yorkers have marveled at how hard she fights for them, even if fighting for New York means alienating her political allies. One battle, for example, played out in the HELP Committee in 2006 and involved a funding bill for AIDS patients called the "Ryan White Care Act." The bill's formula for disbursing federal assistance reduced the amount allocated to New York, despite the state's large number of patients, while giving more to other states. Still, senators representing other states also felt shortchanged and weren't about to give up any of their funding to New York. Hillary was determined to fight it out.

"She single-handedly stopped that bill from being passed for months and put a lot of Democrats in jeopardy," according to a Democratic staff member of the HELP Committee.[16] She eventually relented, and the bill passed. "Senator Kennedy, the ranking member, was not with her on this. She was looking out for her home state even as she was endangering other states."[17] Hillary landed her most important post, a slot on the Armed Services Committee, after the midterm elections of 2002. Hillary was the first New York senator to serve on the panel, and it was a very conscious decision on her part to burnish her national-security résumé after the attacks of September 11. "She made a beeline to get on the Senate Armed

Services Committee for a reason — to get credentials on national security issues," a former aide said.[18]

Hillary had previously impressed the army's vice chief of staff, General John Keane, one of the architects of the invasion of Iraq, with her "extraordinary grasp" of the military culture, and so she turned to Keane, who was retiring, and asked that his aide-de-camp, Paul Paolozzi, be assigned to her office as a military fellow.[19] Hillary relied on Paolozzi's expertise to prepare her for hearings, and she praised him at the ceremony honoring his promotion in 2004 to lieutenant colonel.[20] Hillary quickly learned how to fit into a community that had long harbored hostility toward her husband. "She interacts very well with the men and women in uniform," Senator McCain — someone who would know — said.[21]

Hillary's service on the Armed Services Committee enabled her to reach out to the military, an important constituency for New York, the home of several military bases as well as the prestigious West Point military academy. It also allowed her to travel on official business to war zones where she could familiarize herself with a variety of pressing issues that would dominate her presidential campaign.

IN EARLY 2003, Hillary was riding in a Capitol Hill elevator with another female senator, a fellow Democrat, when the two women caught a glimpse of Elizabeth Dole, the newly elected Republican senator from North Carolina and the wife of former Senator Bob Dole, whom Bill had defeated in the 1996 presidential election.

Hillary and her Democratic colleague exchanged glances and giggled quietly. After Dole was out of earshot, Hillary said, "Did you get a look at that face?" — a reference to her suspicion that the sixty-six-year-old Dole had undergone plastic surgery. The two women smiled again, and Hillary added, "To think they all talk about my hair," a remark that made the two women giggle some more.[22]

If Hillary knows how to privately poke fun at members of the opposing political party, she also knows how to publicly make deals with them. In 2006, in fact, she teamed up with Elizabeth Dole to back the entry of Israel's Magen David Adom into the International Red Cross.[23] (Islamic countries had objected to the Israelis' presence.) Since being elected, Hillary has worked with about half the Republicans in the Senate in sponsoring legislation or resolutions.[24] Bill says Hillary has a unique ability to "make honorable agreements with people who disagree" with her.[25] That certainly seems to have been the case in the Senate. Her work on behalf of veterans, for instance, brought her into alliance with one of the former managers of the House's impeachment of her husband, Lindsey Graham, now a Republican senator from South Carolina. "She really sought out Lindsey Graham on the issue of veterans' benefits," said Hillary's former aide Jodi Sakol.[26] Her trips abroad with John McCain demonstrated how, once outside the confines of the Senate, political opponents could find common personal ground. The two have a "very relaxed relationship," one in which Hillary feels comfortable enough to talk about Bill and Chelsea, crack some jokes, and drink a few glasses of vodka, as she did at a dinner with McCain in Estonia in 2004.[27]

Sometimes her alliances are gymnastic exercises in straddling a political issue. In 2006, the Senate seemed close to having enough votes to pass a constitutional amendment to ban the desecration of the American flag. A similar measure had already passed the House. Joining with Senator Bob Bennett, a Utah Republican, Hillary and others unsuccessfully proposed an alternative that would make it a crime to desecrate the flag in connection with an attempt to intimidate others or incite violence. Around the same time, at a conference in Aspen, Hillary's pollster Mark Penn was asked by a liberal blogger, Arianna Huffington, whether the flag-burning measure was based on polling or Hillary's personal convictions. Penn curtly dismissed Huffington's question, as well as her fellow bloggers. "You guys want to make believe that you know better what her beliefs are than she does," Penn snapped. "This is her belief. This has been her belief for a long time. She's been listening to veterans in New York and that's what she believes." Penn paused and then finished his reply. "And you know what? She doesn't care what you think."[28]

An alliance with another former Clinton foe had its origins at a regular Senate prayer breakfast attended on occasion by Hillary. At one such breakfast early in Hillary's Senate career, Sam Brownback, a Kansas Republican, apologized to Hillary for having felt hatred toward both the Clintons. "I disagree politically, but there is no call to hate," Brownback later explained, so "I went to her and I apologized."[29] The two senators, having patched up at least some of their differences, later teamed up on a measure to back a federal study on the effects of mass media on child development.[30]

Hillary has even agreed on occasion with President Bush. On the hot-button issue of immigration, Hillary said in early 2007 that she thought "the president is right" when he proposed a "pathway to legalization" for millions of undocumented immigrants, pro-vided they wait their turn and pay a fine.[31] And of course there was Iraq, at least at first.

ONE OF THE MOST IMPORTANT members of Hillary's staff is Huma Abedin, a young woman who lived in Kalamazoo, Michigan, until she was two and then moved to Saudi Arabia, where she was raised by her Pakistani mother and Indian father.[32] Abedin is what is known in Senate parlance as a "body person," someone who helps manage a senator's hectic schedule and is usually at her side when she travels.[33] "Huma keeps everything going — she's indispensable," a former aide said.[34] A Senate colleague of Abedin's described her as "always reserved a bit, a typical Hillary person, very quiet."[35]

Now in her early thirties, Abedin joined Hillaryland during Bill Clinton's presidency and worked her way up to the post of Hillary's personal assistant inside the White House. In a caption beneath a photo of Abedin in Hillary's autobiography, she describes Abedin as "extraordinary."[36] Abedin's knowledge of the Middle East and her language skills — she is Muslim and speaks fluent Arabic — even prompted President Clinton to add her to his diplomatic team dur-ing the failed peace talks at Camp David in 2000. "She was espe-cially effective at making the Israeli and Palestinian delegates feel at home and at ease," Bill recalled.[37]

Hillary's trips to the Middle East as a senator always included Abedin (and a Secret Service detail as well). McCain, who went to Iraq with Hillary in 2005, found Abedin to be "very, very intelli-gent and knowledgeable about Middle Eastern affairs" and some-one with a "very outgoing and pleasant personality."[38] To Hillary, she is more than that: She is invaluable. Even when Bill and Hillary escape for a relaxing Caribbean vacation, Abedin is part of their entourage.[39] When Hillary marched up New York City's Fifth Ave-nue in the 2006 Columbus Day parade, Abedin was there to hold her flowing, flower-patterned coat. At Hillary's first public event after announcing her run for president in January 2007, held at a health clinic in midtown Manhattan, Abedin was by her side.[40] At Hillary's first stop on her presidential campaign, at an auditorium in Des Moines, Iowa, Abedin was again with her, taking pictures for fans and passing along books for autographs. And since she entered the Senate in January 2001, Hillary and her aide's foreign travels have included three trips to Iraq and trips to Kuwait, Pakistan, Israel, India, Germany, Ireland, Norway, Singapore, and Estonia.[41]

Hillary took one overseas trip in 2005, however, that raised some eyebrows among the handful of people inside the Senate who knew about it.[42] The trip, approved by the chairman of the Armed Services Committee, was to Singapore, where the International Olympics Committee was preparing to choose the host city for the 2012 Olympics. New York City was one of five finalists but wound up losing to London. Hillary initially taped a video on behalf of the Big Apple's pitch, having planned to skip the meeting.[43] Then, at the last minute, her plans changed; she decided to join city officials and lobby in person. Her aides quickly tried to figure out how to use public funds to pay her way, but they learned that only a Senate committee could authorize the use of public money for foreign travel.[44]

There was another problem. Senate rules stipulated that "the primary purpose of a trip must of course be official in nature to justify the use of official funds."[45] Even Hillary's spokeswoman acknowledged that she was "doing it for New York," not the federal government or Congress.[46] Making it even harder was the fact that the Democrats controlled no committees at the time because they were the minority party in Congress.

Senate committee chairpersons, though, have considerable latitude in determining what is "official," and Hillary had a friend in Republican senator John Warner, the patrician Virginian who was then the chairman of the Armed Services panel. Proving that the value of personal relationships cannot be underestimated in the Senate, Warner approved the trip as official business. Hillary took along Abedin, and was also accompanied by the usual Secret Service detail. The Armed Services Committee report on the trip, required by law and signed by Warner, was filed with the Senate after the normal reporting period and went unnoticed by the public. Hillary and Abedin's two-day stay in Singapore cost taxpayers more than $14,000, most of it airfare.[47]

FOR ALL THE COLLEGIAL DEALINGS with her political opponents, Hillary had a few spats with her Democratic friends. Understandably, some of them involved the base emotions of territoriality and jealousy.

Unlike the House, where each member represents a district, the two senators for each state fight over the same turf. If the two come from different parties, the boundary lines are pretty clear; each senator supports his or her own party. But when both belong to the same party, the competition can get "tooth and nail," as one Senate aide put it.[48]

That helps explain some of the friendly rivalry between Hillary and fellow New York senator Chuck Schumer—a good deal of which played out in the aftermath of the September 11 attacks.

Schumer and Clinton share much common ground. Their voting records both lean left, and they have almost identical positions on a wide range of issues. For example, they both score at or near 100 percent from liberal groups—pro-choice advocates, the Children's Defense Fund, and the AFL-CIO—while, for example, they each rate an F from the National Rifle Association.[49] On defense, economic, and foreign-policy issues in 2005, Hillary was more liberal than 80 percent of her colleagues, and Schumer was close behind at 78 percent.[50] On social-policy issues, Hillary was to the left of 83 percent of her colleagues, and Schumer was at 77 percent.[51]

At first, Hillary and Schumer, neither of whom lack ego, intelligence, or savvy, didn't get along well. They hoped to develop a relationship by meeting regularly over meals, but early on, Schumer's eating habits, including talking and eating at the same time, turned Hillary off.[52] "She went back to her staff and said, 'That's the last meal I'm having with Chuck,'" an aide recalled.[53] The relationship has mellowed as they have come to better understand each other's agendas and personalities. The two senators now dine occasionally, often at Schumer's favorite Chinese restaurant near the Capitol. Still, they have an "uneasy friendship"—in the words of an aide, like "America's friendship with Saudi Arabia."[54]

The rivalry between the two senators and their staffers spilled over into the party's leadership in June 2006. Harry Reid, in conjunction with Schumer and a few other Democrats, but not Hillary, had organized a last-minute news conference to highlight the party's attempts to increase the minimum wage. Hillary was invited to the event, but she was not privy to the advance planning. Reid, in his role as traffic cop for Senate Democrats, coordinates the party's press conferences. Hillary's office, with all its ancillary advisers, is consistently slow to respond to queries from Reid's staff about upcoming press events, infuriating other Senate offices that have to wait in line for an invitation.[55] In this case, it turned out that the timing of the news conference did not work with Hillary's schedule, and she had to leave early. In front of reporters at the conference, Hillary's legislative aide, Laurie Rubiner, said to Reid's spokeswoman, "You suck" and "How could you do this?"[56] A senior

Senate official called it "one of the most unprofessional incidents in recent years," and Rubiner later apologized.[57]

EVERY TUESDAY when the Senate is in session, Democratic senators gather for lunch on the second floor of the Capitol. So do their Republican counterparts. The minority party assembles in the LBJ Room, named after the former president, while the majority party meets in the larger Mansfield Room, named after Mike Mansfield, the longest-serving Senate majority leader, who held the post in the 1960s and 1970s.

Here, colleagues can speak candidly, since only a few aides are present and reporters are not allowed to attend. Hillary, still a new kid on the block in her first term, was treated politely, though a number of her more senior colleagues rolled their eyes and winced occasionally at some of her ideas, thinking they were too partisan or too activist.

"Senators would grumble, 'There she goes again,'" said one attendee. "It was because they thought she was a young whippersnapper, doing things they had never thought of."[58] Another attendee at the lunches said jealousy explained the occasional expression of displeasure. "Her high profile made others feel threatened."[59]

When the meal is over, the senators typically exit in one of two ways: out a back door to a Senate reception room or through the front door to a mob of reporters waiting to grab the legislators.

For a long time, Hillary often chose a third route out of the LBJ Room. "She would oftentimes go out the door to the left and go down the outside steps," away from the Capitol. Reporters, reluctant to exit the building and put themselves through the hassle of going through the security checkpoints to reenter the Capitol, would usually not chase after her. By mid-2006, however, the Capitol Police closed off the exit used by Hillary, and she was left to fend off reporters like the rest of her colleagues.[60]

That fending off is a little easier for her than for some of her fellow legislators. As the only senator or presidential candidate with Secret Service protection, Hillary is less accessible to voters and reporters than most Washington politicians. "She is almost in a presidential bubble, where it's hard to be natural," said a longtime strategist.[61] When she engages the public, the crowds provide an additional buffer between her and the press.[62]

That buffer can lead to a vacuum, and it has certainly led to a certain amount of tension between reporters trying to cover Hillary, and the senator and her staff. Another factor in Hillary's bumpy relations with the press is the constant turnover among her spokespeople who deal directly with reporters. It's a brutal job because the media is insatiably curious about Hillary, while she is extremely cautious about what her press people say to journalists. Even in normal situations, it can take years for reporters and press aides to develop trust in one another. In her first five years in the Senate, Hillary employed six different communications directors.[63] Building trust in such cases is nearly impossible.

The longest-serving spokesman for Hillary is her current Senate press secretary, Philippe Reines.[64] Now entering his late thirties, Reines took a while to find himself. He grew up fatherless on the Upper West Side of New York City and took a dozen years and three colleges to land a degree.[65] Working on the Gore-Lieberman 2000 presidential campaign, he honed his skills in reconnaissance, communications, and "digging up the dirt" on the opposition.[66]

Reines is viewed as an integral member of Hillaryland. "Hillary loves him because he makes her laugh," one reporter said.[67] Inside Hillary's camp, Reines jockeys for position with Howard Wolfson, the blunt-talking spokesman for her presidential campaign.[68] But even the most senior Democratic senators will usually not talk about Hillary to the press if Reines, or even another member of her staff, asks them not to. In 2006, author Gail Sheehy, who wrote a 1999 book about Hillary entitled *Hillary's Choice*, attempted to interview senators in connection with an article about Hillary Clinton she was writing for *Vanity Fair*. Some Democratic senators refused to speak with Sheehy after Reines sent an e-mail to all the Democratic Senate press secretaries that included a copy of an article written by Lloyd Grove of the *New York Daily News* that began, "Hillary Clinton wants Gail Sheehy on ice."[69]

But while some senators are extraordinarily deferential to Hillary, they have not rushed to endorse her presidential campaign. Nearly four months into her campaign, only two senators, her occasional rival Charles Schumer and Barbara Mikulski, had publicly endorsed her.[70] Hillary may have been accepted by the club, but the club is not yet ready to embrace her as the country's next president. Indeed, it would be some of the club's other members who would pose the greatest challenge to her next step up the ladder — including one of its newest members, a young freshman senator from her native state of Illinois.

CHAPTER 20

The War Room

HILLARY WAS STILL GETTING accustomed to the Senate when she quietly ascended into the leadership ranks of her party. In January 2003, she was appointed the chairwoman of the Senate Democratic Steering and Coordination Committee, a post so obscure that the announcement of her new job went unreported by the *New York Times* and the *Washington Post*. Hillary, for her part, shied away from discussing her new role, saying, "It's not for me to say."[1]

It would be easy at first glance to dismiss the committee as irrelevant. Its offices are about as far from the Capitol as any in the Senate, at the end of a corridor on the seventh floor of the Hart Senate Office Building.[2] The small staff is funded from the budget of the leader of the Senate Democrats, who in 2003 was Tom Daschle. Before Daschle appointed Hillary to the post, the group's mission was to coordinate strategy with Democratic officeholders outside Washington and hand out committee assignments to Senate Democrats.

Hillary succeeded John Kerry, who by the end of 2002 had decided to make a run for president. (She stayed in the post for four years, stepping down on the eve of her own run for the White House.) Once Hillary's aides made it clear to Daschle's office that "she was interested" in the newly available post, she became a shoo-in for the job.[3]

Under Kerry, the committee had been more a vehicle for advancing his image than the party. "Kerry wanted to make people think he was the smartest person in the room," said a committee staffer who worked for both Kerry and Hillary. "He breezed in, he breezed out."[4] Hillary, however, succeeded in crafting a broader, more ambitious agenda. She vowed that the Democrats would aggressively reach out to hear the views and concerns of "people in the communities." The committee's name change—it became the Senate Democratic Steering and Outreach Committee—reflected that mandate. Another goal was to try to compete with the Republicans, who were considered highly skilled at "message discipline."[5] The Democrats, it seemed, were constantly arguing among themselves, while the Republicans consistently presented a unified front. Hillary was convinced that Democrats needed to close this gap. She also believed that the Republicans were "more effective at outreach and organization," and that until the Democrats came closer to matching them, they would suffer on Election Day and in Congress.[6]

The first decision Hillary faced as she took over the committee in early 2003 was whether to keep the staff director, Jodi Sakol. Sakol, in her early thirties, was already a communications veteran, having worked the beat for Al Gore when he was vice president and during his 2000 presidential campaign. She considered herself a "high-energy person" who in addition to working long hours liked to run marathons, and she was already recognized as one of the top staffers on Capitol Hill.[7]

But Hillary was not familiar with Sakol, so the young staffer needed an insider to vouch for her in order to gain acceptance. Sakol's helper on the inside was Hillary's former chief of staff from the White House, Melanne Verveer, who "made sure" Senator Clinton kept Sakol on the team.[8]

Sakol's salary was paid by Daschle's office, but she also reported daily to Hillary's chief of staff and every week or two to Senator Clinton herself.[9] In essence, Hillary was able to use Sakol to quietly supplement her personal staff, at no additional expense to her.

Once she became a member of Hillaryland, Sakol was amazed to discover the loyalty and devotion of Hillary's extended political family. At times, Hillary asked Sakol to talk with "people in her inner circle," including various advisers and communications aides such as Ann Lewis, Doug Sosnik, Patti Solis Doyle, Harold Ickes, and Neera Tanden, all of whom had worked in senior positions in the Clinton White House. Sakol knew most of them from her days working inside the White House, but now they reappeared in a different light, helping her appreciate the invaluable nature of Hillaryland. "I felt like I could call on them, on Hillary's behalf, and they would do anything for her," even as they worked other jobs, she said. Once you joined Hillary's staff, Sakol realized, "you never really leave her."[10]

Some of the committee's best ideas came from Hillary. For example, she knew that Mike McCurry, the former press secretary for President Clinton, was religious and active in the Wesley Theological Seminary. She told Sakol to reach out to him in an effort to broaden the Democrats' appeal beyond their secular base and to chip away at the Republicans' virtual monopoly of the faith-based community.

Sakol called McCurry from Hillary's office to kick things off. Within weeks, McCurry had organized a group of religious leaders to attend a meeting in the Senate. Hillary showed up briefly to offer support and encouragement.[11] This first meeting sparked a multi-year effort, coordinated with other groups. By the 2006 elections, religious liberals believed they had made a difference. The Democrats shrank the GOP's stranglehold on regular churchgoers and "even siphoned off a portion of the Republican Party's most loyal base, white evangelical Protestants."[12]

As Hillary entered the presidential campaign, she turned her religious outreach work over to Bill. Bill joined with Jimmy Carter to organize moderate Baptists as a counterweight to the Republican-oriented Southern Baptist Convention. Minyon Moore, an African American involved in the steering committee's efforts, also became a key adviser to Hillary's presidential campaign.[13]

Hillary knew that the traditional money base of the modern Democratic Party—Hollywood and unions—needed to be energized but also expanded. She also understood that if she had any chance of becoming president, she needed to widen the already vast network of contacts that had been built up during her husband's eight years in the White House. The steering committee's massive Rolodex was thus of incredible value.[14]

Soon, the revitalized committee was performing so well that less-visible, senior Democrats were grumbling privately that Hillary was consolidating too much power. "Senators became squeamish about her becoming the face of the Senate Democrats, being seen as the puppet master, the message maestro behind the leadership of the Senate," Sakol said.[15] The jealous senators included Dick Durbin, the number two–ranking Senate Democrat, and Byron Dorgan, the head of the Democratic Policy Committee, which ostensibly had a higher public profile than the steering committee.[16]

This resentment and jealousy prompted the steering committee to assume a somewhat lower profile.[17] By shifting the group's attention to a range of meaty domestic issues, from economic competitiveness, families, and civil rights to pandemic flu, housing, and homeland security, Hillary was able to defuse some of the tension. But by then, she had accomplished much of what she had hoped to.

Sakol left the committee in 2004 and was succeeded by Dana Singiser. The two women were friends, but Singiser was a lawyer, not a communicator. She had worked at a leading Washington law firm, Akin Gump, where she lobbied for a host of clients, including, banks, nursing homes, manufacturers, a drug company, a telecom giant, media outlets, and health care providers.[18] When Hillary stepped down from the steering committee at the end of 2006, Singiser became the director of women's outreach for her presidential campaign. Minutes after Hillary officially launched her presidential bid, an excited Singiser blasted out a message, via her BlackBerry, to her friends and family, seeking their support and touting Hillary as "the kind of boss who wishes you happy birthday and sends you a note when your father is sick."[19] Hillaryland had another member.

HILLARY HAD PAID close attention to how the right wing had shaped the public image of Al Gore, and she knew that there was a need to utilize the newly emerging media on the Internet to fight back against her political enemies.[20] Not surprisingly, there was a more receptive climate for these ideas among liberal activists.

By 2003, John Podesta's Center for American Progress was preparing a daily news summary promoting the organization's left-leaning agenda. Every morning, officials from the center would apprise Sakol of their daily message. With the help of outside advisers and Daschle's aides, she would then prepare the rapid-response message of the day for Senate Democrats.[21] Sakol found it odd — "almost backwards" — that outsiders, many of whom were loyal Clintonites, were quietly framing the messages on issues for all the Democrats in the Senate.[22] Hillary had no such reservations, for obvious reasons.

Concurrently, and on her own time, Sakol was involved in discussions about the formation of another nonprofit, left-leaning group, Citizens for Responsibility and Ethics in Washington, which focused on government corruption. It was Hillary's "proactive" efforts in this area and her desire to "beat the GOP at their own game"[23] that prompted CREW's founder, Melanie Sloan, a former prosecutor, to invite Sakol to the initial brainstorming sessions in 2003 where CREW was born. CREW was organized as a tax-exempt nonpartisan group, and on occasion, it has taken on Democratic targets. But since the Congress and the executive branch were in Republican hands at the time of its founding, its investigations were bound to focus on Republicans. Sakol alerted Hillary and her staff about the newly forming group and its need for "Democratic progressive money." The hope was that CREW would prove to be a perfect counterbalance to Judicial Watch, the corruption watchdog that had tormented the Clintons with lawsuits and press conferences throughout the 1990s.[24] Hillary's pollster and strategist Mark Penn became a director and vice president of CREW.[25] "CREW could do things the senators couldn't do," Sakol said. And once CREW's charges "were out in the press," Sakol noted, other people could cite the findings of the group, which was usually portrayed as nonpartisan in news accounts.[26] CREW played a significant role in unearthing several congressional scandals, including helping a retiring Democratic congressman from Texas to file a complaint against House Majority Leader Tom DeLay.

Hillary's other priority upon assuming control of the steering committee had been to improve the communication and message capabilities of Senate Democrats. For her, it was a journey back to the rough-and-tumble days of the 1992 presidential campaign.

Soon after taking over the committee, she told Sakol, "I want to create a war room in the Senate." Clinton's idea was to develop "a one-stop shop for communications for the senators that did not exist before."[27] Hillary met with Daschle in early 2004, and her aides and advisers briefed them using a PowerPoint presentation. Daschle seemed convinced.[28]

But the plan soon stalled. A key impediment to Hillary's ambitions, Sakol believed, was Daschle's turf-conscious chief of staff, Pete Rouse, who later became chief of staff to Senator Barak Obama. He was concerned about Hillary's getting credit for the idea and having a bigger platform for her future political aspirations.[29] Although it was not widely known, Daschle was seriously considering a presidential run at the time.[30] So Hillary's effort proceeded slowly, hampered by "passive resistance" from Daschle's staff.[31] Sakol and her colleagues established a skeleton operation, located in the suite of offices controlled by the Democratic leader, but it lacked sufficient resources.[32]

The 2004 elections, in which the Republican message machine demonstrated its communications prowess, finally woke up Senate Democrats. Among those Democrats losing their seats was Daschle, and his successor, Harry Reid, considered Hillary's idea to be a "no-brainer."[33] A few weeks after the election, Reid publicly announced the formation of a war room, allocating the staff and resources that Hillary had unsuccessfully sought.[34] Reid would come to frequently rely on Hillary's advice in figuring out how to respond to urgent issues or craft a daily message.[35]

One of the attendees at the meetings that led to CREW's creation was David Brock, a former enemy turned ally of Hillary's who was starting his own nonprofit group about the same time.[36] Hillary and Brock had forged a seemingly strange alliance. Brock's nonprofit, a Washington-based media-monitoring venture called Media Matters for America, found a temporary home in early 2004 at the Center for American Progress.[37] Already providing its daily news summary to Hillary, the center helped Sakol get the daily media analysis prepared by Media Matters in order to help shape the Senate war-room activities.[38]

Although it was independent, Media Matters had among its earliest supporters and advisers long-standing allies of Hillary and the Democratic Party.[39] One of them, Kelly Craighead, who planned Hillary's trips for eight years when she was First Lady, advised Media Matters "on all aspects" of its launch.[40] And the new group wasted no time becoming an aggressive protector of Hillary's reputation and boasting about its role as truth police, forcefully going after journalists for what the group deems to be leaving out key information or cherry-picking material.[41] In three years, the group has cited more than seven thousand examples of "conservative misinformation," Brock said.[42]

Hillary, though not a close friend of Brock's, advised him and "quietly nurtured" his nonprofit empire.[43] The watchdogs at Media

Matters often rushed to Hillary's defense. For example, when *New York Times* reporter Anne Kornblut made a mistake about her in a brief story on July 16, 2006, Media Matters pounced on the error. Kornblut had interpreted a reference to "we" in criticism Hillary had made in a speech about congressional inaction to mean Democrats, when Hillary was actually referring to the Republican-controlled Congress. Kornblut's article ran only on the paper's Web site, not in the print version of the newspaper.

After her story was posted on the Web, Kornblut went on a previously scheduled vacation to Barbados. Predictably, conservative bloggers trumpeted Kornblut's story about Hillary's trashing her own party while liberals inveighed against Kornblut's misreporting.[44] Hillary's Senate aides lodged their own complaint with the *New York Times*. A reporter at a rival newspaper said he was surprised that Hillary's press staff "went crazy" over the mistake, because it had appeared only on the Web and had not even been published in the newspaper.[45] After two days, the *Times* published an editors' note in the newspaper correcting Kornblut's Web-only misinterpretation of Hillary's remarks.

One week later, Hillary was in Denver to unveil "The American Dream Initiative," a project of the Democratic Leadership Council, a moderate group of Democrats headed by Bruce Reed, a longtime Clinton ally.[46] Kornblut, who was a member of a team of *Times* reporters assigned to cover the newspaper's home state political celebrity, flew to Denver for Hillary's speech. Kornblut returned to her room at the Hyatt Regency after the address to write and file her story. She shed her business suit for jeans and a tank top. Feeling thirsty, she dashed down to the lobby of the high-rise hotel to get a soda. Moments later, Hillary, wearing a black suit, emerged and saw Kornblut.

"Anne, I thought you *left* Barbados," Hillary cracked,[47] letting the reporter know that she knew where she had been vacationing, a level of detail that left Kornblut feeling intimidated.[48]

The coordinated criticism of Kornblut's article had been initiated by the newest member of Hillaryland's war room.[49] In mid-2006, Hillary hired Peter Daou, who in 2004 had directed blog outreach and online rapid response for the Kerry presidential campaign and later worked for Media Matters.[50] Daou, who was raised in Lebanon before eventually settling in Manhattan,[51] viewed the mainstream press as "cowardly" and "sycophantic."[52]

Several weeks before he joined Hillary's campaign, Daou wrote in his blog about the "media establishment bending over backwards to accommodate this White House and to regurgitate pro-GOP and anti-Dem spin."[53] He believed that Democrats kept losing elections because "skillfully crafted pro-GOP story lines are injected into the American bloodstream" by such prominent broadcast journalists as Tom Brokaw, Cokie Roberts, Bob Schieffer, and Tim Russert, as well as reporters at the *New York Times*, the *Washington Post*, and *Newsweek*.[54] It was a message that likely resonated with Hillary.

Daou agreed to work for Hillary as a blog adviser because he thought it represented a "unique opportunity" to put his words into action to "facilitate and expand her relationship with the netroots," and to apply what he had learned at Media Matters about the ability of "conservative misinformation" to become part of the mainstream press.[55] (Long before she hired Daou, Hillary had told an aide that blogs were "going to be opinion leaders.")[56]

Daou first became a consultant to her campaign committee and to her political PAC. He had barely signed on when up popped the erroneous Kornblut article.[57] A few weeks later, Daou became a full-fledged member of Hillaryland, assuming the title of Internet director for Hillary's newly launched presidential campaign in 2007.[58] In the first five days, her Web site signed up more than 140,000 supporters and conducted three Webcasts that attracted more than 25,000 questions and 50,000 viewers. She also used the Yahoo! Answers service to ask cyberspace enthusiasts a question about health care, yielding 35,000 answers, the second-highest number of answers in the service's history.[59]

Daou believed that "the candidate who makes smart use of the Internet in 2008 will have a decided edge."[60] His boss agreed, but she also made it clear that though she had gone high-tech, she certainly hadn't gone soft. At Hillary's first official presidential campaign stop, she told Democratic activists in Iowa, "When you are attacked, you have to deck your opponents."[61] It wasn't just a strategy—it turned out to be a prediction too.

Hillary's Quagmire

IN NOVEMBER 2003, six months after "major combat operations" in Iraq had ended, Hillary traveled to Iraq, just as Code Pink's Medea Benjamin had done prior to the invasion. She accompanied Senator Jack Reed, the former army officer and Democrat from Rhode Island; the two also traveled to Afghanistan. Though the Rhode Island veteran should have been entitled, under the normal protocols of seniority, to sleep on the only bed aboard their small military jet, he gallantly deferred to Hillary.[1]

Soon after their trip, and coincidentally the day after Saddam Hussein's capture, Hillary delivered a major foreign-policy speech about the two countries at the Council on Foreign Relations in New York. There she sounded a lot like President Bush, even as she offered up some criticism of postwar reconstruction. She called for a "tough-minded, muscular foreign and defense policy." She urged "patience" and worried about the political will "to stay the course." "Failure is not an option" in Iraq and Afghanistan, she declared. "We have no option but to stay involved and committed" in Iraq, she said, calling her decision in 2002 to authorize the president to invade Iraq "the right vote," one "I stand by."[2]

Four months after Bush was reelected, Hillary took a second trip to Iraq and delivered a somewhat upbeat assessment about the progress being made and the chances for peace, despite mounting evidence that the insurgency was gaining momentum. She told reporters in Baghdad that the insurgents had failed to disrupt the recently held Iraq interim elections. She noted that their horrific suicide attacks were a sign of desperation and that much of Iraq was "functioning quite well."[3] Her remarks echoed many of President Bush's statements at the time about the supposed progress being made in Iraq. As she expressed her optimism, a wave of attacks in Baghdad shattered the celebrations of Shiite Islam's holiest day, killing dozens, including an American solider.[4]

The next day, Hillary made a rare appearance on a Sunday talk show; unlike many senators who craved the spotlight, Hillary did not need to seek it and did so infrequently. In an interview from Baghdad on NBC's *Meet the Press*, she said it "would be a mistake" to call for the immediate withdrawal of troops or set a timetable. "We don't want to send a signal to insurgents, to the terrorists, that we are going to be out of here at some, you know, date certain," she said. She reiterated that she was still comfortable with her stance on Iraq.[5]

By the end of 2005, however, as the Iraqis prepared to elect a new government and the security situation further deteriorated, there were intensified calls in the United States for some kind of troop reduction. Congressman Jack Murtha, the ex-marine and pro-Pentagon Democrat from Pennsylvania, called for the immediate withdrawal of all American troops. Hillary rejected that option and instead aligned herself with a Senate resolution calling on the president to prepare a plan to begin withdrawal in 2006.

The Iraq war, by then, had become increasingly unpopular at home, as the number of American fatalities passed the two thousand mark. Innocent civilians were being killed by American soldiers, and Iraq's violent insurgents, led by radical Sunni Arabs, had begun a strategy of killing Shiite civilians in order to "ignite a civil war."[6] Nevertheless, on November 10, 2005, at a private gathering of Democratic senators, the resolution's language was amended at the behest of Hillary, who was absent from the meeting.[7] The language that was added — "with the understanding that unexpected contingencies may arise" — in effect gave Bush wiggle room.[8] Hillary's role in softening the legislative language was not made public.

American popular opinion regarding the war further soured after it became clear that the Bush administration's prewar intelligence had been fatally flawed, as was its overly optimistic forecast for the ease of occupation. With that shift came a change in Hillary's position. Not surprisingly, the first signal of Hillary's intention to tack to the left came via Bill, who continued in his role as senator's spouse who could say things that Hillary would not or could not. Addressing students at the American University in Dubai on November 16, 2005, the former president declared that the invasion of Iraq was a "big mistake." He added that he "didn't agree with what was done."[9]

On November 29, two weeks after Bill's address to the students, Hillary sent a lengthy letter to her supporters detailing her latest position on Iraq. The tone was piercing and it faulted the Bush administration for misleading her and others regarding its intention to pursue diplomacy as well as for mismanaging the situation in Iraq following the invasion. But Hillary's letter was misleading too, in its discussion of her 2002 Iraq votes. On the question of troop levels, she again charted a middle ground, warning against an "open-ended commitment" but rejecting an immediate pullout. And while she accepted "responsibility" for her vote in 2002, she voiced no regret for it.[10]

"Before I voted in 2002," she wrote, "the Administration publicly and privately assured me that they intended to use their authority to build international support in order to get the U.N. inspectors back into Iraq, as articulated by the President in his Cincinnati speech on October 7, 2002. As I said in my October 2002 floor statement, I took 'the President at his word that he will try hard to pass a U.N. resolution and will seek to avoid war, if at all possible.'"[11]

She neglected to mention, however, that the measure she voted for had in no way required Bush to "build international support." The resolution said the president could use force if he determined that "further diplomatic or other peaceful means alone either (A) will not adequately protect the national security of the United States against the continuing threat posed by Iraq or (B) is not likely to lead to enforcement of all relevant United Nations Security Council resolutions regarding Iraq." Hillary insisted that the president had misled her about his intention to pursue diplomacy. But the resolution did not require the president to conclude that past diplomacy had failed in order to go to war. Instead, it simply required the president to *decide* that future diplomacy was not going to work. After he did so, the resolution then explicitly authorized the president to "use the Armed Forces of the United States as he determines to be necessary and appropriate" in order to "enforce all relevant United Nations Security Council resolutions,"[12] including resolutions from 1990 authorizing the use of force against Iraq. Nor did Hillary, in her letter to her constituents, mention the fact that she did not join the twenty-four senators who tried to put the brakes on Bush's plans to invade Iraq by requiring the president to return to the Congress if diplomacy failed.

Instead, Hillary repeated again and again the claim that the prewar intelligence she and others had relied on, involving "weapons of mass destruction and links to Al Qaeda turned out to be false."[13] There was some truth in this: President Bush and his team had misinformed many in Congress. But not everyone had fallen for it so hard. Hillary had. And not only had she gone along with Bush and Cheney, she had done so with remarkable fervor. Both the Bush administration and Hillary had enthusiastically mischaracterized the intelligence that was available. Hillary was stuck in her own Iraq quagmire: If she admitted she had been wrong from the start, she would be admitting incompetence in the biggest vote of her career. But if she continued to stick by her vote, she would be flying in the face of reality.

Two weeks after blasting Bush in her letter, Hillary had an opportunity to personally deliver her criticism to the president. In mid-December, she and a few other senators met privately with Bush in the White House to discuss Iraq.[14] But Hillary said nothing to the president at the meeting. The Bush White House says her silence at such occasional meetings was not unusual: "She very rarely says much. It's like she's observing the meeting, keeping close counsel, taking everything in. She is rarely heard from, and it's usually a 'Thank you for having us, Mr. President.' "[15] Hillary may have thought it was futile to raise her concerns directly with the president. But from the White House's perspective, Hillary's taking a pass at speaking her mind to Bush merely made her criticisms seem like campaign flourishes unsupported by any true faith.

Hillary may have moderated her stance on Iraq, but it was not enough to placate the women of Code Pink. In late 2005, they launched a new campaign of weekly vigils that they aptly called "Bird-dog Hillary."

This was no easy task. Even reporters are kept in the dark by Hillary's aides about much of the senator's calendar, especially her attendance at fund-raising events. The schedule of Hillary's frequent fund-raisers is distributed only to those with a need to know, and even then it often changes at the last minute. But Code Pink members, ever resourceful, had their own way of finding out, and before long they started showing up to pester Hillary at events in New York and Washington and at fund-raisers in Chicago, Los Angeles, and San Francisco.

At two Manhattan fund-raisers attended by Hillary, Code Pink members protested, shouting questions to her about the war but receiving no response.[16] One of the fund-raisers, at an Upper West Side residence, was for West Virginia senator Robert Byrd, the dean of the Senate. Just a week earlier, Hillary had praised Senator Byrd as a "great example, adviser and friend to me."[17] Unable to engage Hillary at the event, the group turned its attention to Byrd as he climbed out of a limousine late that afternoon and walked with a cane toward the event. Courtney Lee Adams, a Code Pink member, asked Senator Byrd if he could help convince Hillary to change her views on Iraq. The frail eighty-eight-year-old senator replied, "Ladies, I don't tell *her* to do anything."[18]

IN SEPTEMBER 2005, the Clinton Global Initiative held its first conference, at the Sheraton Hotel and Towers in midtown Manhattan. It would become an annual meeting, attracting a glittering group of world leaders, corporate executives, journalists, and wealthy celebrities.

The initiative was part of the former president's William J. Clinton Foundation. In its first year, the foundation had concentrated on the issues of poverty, health, reconciliation, and leadership.[19] By the spring of 2005, Bill had expanded his agenda to include a session on "global warming and severe weather events" and several other related panels. That summer Hurricane Katrina devastated New Orleans. The storm quickly became Exhibit A for some of the activists concerned about global warming.

The agenda meshed with Hillary's goal of burnishing her résumé on an emerging major issue that she had been late to address.[20] Before long, the conference organizer for the global warming panels, David Sandalow, heard about Hillary's desire to participate. "I was told she was interested in appearing on our global warming panel," Sandalow recalled. Not surprisingly, he immediately added her to the roster.[21]

Onstage at the conference, Hillary told the audience there had been an "absence of leadership" by the Bush administration on climate change. She offered her own solution: "I would advocate a much more concerted effort on our government's part to fund an extensive research project into alternative forms of energy."[22]

The next day, there was a featured plenary session on global warming. The marquee attraction was Al Gore, whose documentary on the subject was nearing completion. (Bill spent his time at the conference doing what he does best—squeezing shoulders, patting backs, speaking eloquently about a brighter future, and inspiring the awed participants to open their checkbooks for good deeds.) The moderator of the plenary session, former Democratic senator Tim Wirth, credited Hillary with being "very impressive" and "very articulate on the urgency" posed by global warming. Wirth asked Gore what advice he might have for Hillary, calling her one of the "front-runners for the Democratic nomination in 2008."[23]

Wirth's question, in the framework of 2008, touched on a sensitive issue: Hillary was a latecomer to an issue Gore had pioneered. It also, however inadvertently, made note of the fact that Hillary was politically ascendant, while many felt Gore's chance had come and gone.

Hillary and Gore had vied for Bill's power and attention during his presidency, and that rivalry had only intensified after the Clintons left the White House.[24] Bill privately told confidants that he believed that if Hillary emerged as the likely Democratic presidential nominee in 2008, Gore would enter the race as a left-of-Hillary alternative.[25] And the long memories of the Lewinsky scandal meant that it would not soon be forgotten that when Gore had been the presidential candidate in 2000, he had specifically chosen as his partner Joe Lieberman, a Democrat who had been extremely harsh regarding Bill's infidelity and dishonesty.

For his part, Gore had publicly said he had no plans to run in 2008 and described his relationship with the Clintons as "good."[26] One of Gore's confidants, Roy Neel, described him as unconcerned about whether Hillary was trying to steal his thunder on the environment because "he's owned the thunder."[27] (Privately, however, Gore has complained to some of his associates about Hillary and Bill's belated attempts to capitalize on his signature issue.[28])

Gore sidestepped Wirth's question. Instead, he criticized the way television and the thirst for snappy sound bites had decimated public-policy debates. He did not mention Hillary or suggest what she might say, but he did complain about the failure of his own speeches on climate change to become "part of the A-list discussion."[29] He certainly did not embrace Hillary's attempt to refashion herself as a trailblazer on the suddenly vogue issue of climate change. Gore's reticence was understandable. He had been writing, thinking, and talking about the issue for nearly thirty years.

One month later, Hillary unveiled a comprehensive clean-energy plan, tailored along the lines she had mentioned at Bill's conference.[30] She suffered the same fate as Gore: Nobody paid attention. "The silence was deafening," her husband later complained, somewhat angrily. For Bill, Hillary's speech after his conference was "the proudest I have been of a speech my wife has given in the United States Senate since she has been a Senator."[31]

After the silent reception from the press and the public, Hillary kept a low profile on the issue for seven months. But the rivalry between Senator Clinton and Al Gore would continue to percolate. Hillary may not have had much in the way of history when it came to caring about the environment, but compared with Iraq, where her past now haunted her, a somewhat blank slate was rather appealing.

Hillary had found a new cause.

Warming Up to Global Warming

THE NATIONAL PRESS CLUB, located at the top of an unremark-able building near the center of downtown Washington, is the headquarters for many of the town's working journalists. Among its many offerings, the club sponsors a regular Newsmaker program, where speakers appear at lunchtime. On May 23, 2006, however, the scheduled event was held over breakfast — a tough test for a press corps that is notoriously not a morning crowd.

Nevertheless, the event was sold out well in advance. The big draw was certainly not the subject, energy policy, but the speaker, Senator Hillary Rodham Clinton.

Hillary's rare appearance before the press club — her last visit had been nearly five years before this one — was part of an orches-trated effort to raise her visibility on big, national issues.[1] Her aides touted her appearance in advance as a "major policy speech," and the potential national audience swelled after the cable network C-SPAN decided to broadcast it live.[2]

That morning, before Hillary even arrived at the press club, the research arm of the Republican National Committee blasted e-mails to reporters, accusing her of trying to "obstruct new energy sources" by voting against further exploration in the arctic wilderness.[3] Hillary was not considered a major player in Washington's energy wars. She did not even sit on the committee with jurisdiction over the subject; another Senate Democrat, Maria Cantwell of Washington, had been chosen to take the lead on energy.[4] The rare times when Hillary did mention energy policy, her words were largely ignored. She had certainly attracted little, if any, attention when she delivered her first major speech on the subject in October 2005, shortly after the Clinton Global Initiative. That inattention led Hillary to rework the speech and schedule it again, "as quick as she could," Bill said.[5]

"As quick as she could" ended up being more than half a year later, and by May 2006, the political landscape on energy had shifted. Over the intervening months, voters told pollsters that their top concern was reducing America's dependence on foreign oil — so much so that even President Bush, a former (unsuccessful) oilman, described America as addicted to oil in his State of the Union address. Democratic consultants, who also happened to advise Hillary, had taken note of the shift in the public's mood as well, and when setting up her presidential run began searching for ways to retool her position on energy policy.[6]

By the time Hillary was scheduled to address the National Press Club in May, a series of troubling and disparate events had combined to solidify the public's interest in energy. The March 2003 invasion of Iraq had wound up increasing the sense of risk in world oil markets, which in turn caused the price of a barrel of oil to skyrocket. Increased demand in Asia and slower supply growth from oil-producing countries reduced the spare capacity cushion that had long moderated worldwide prices. Finally, the connection between fossil fuels and climate change had reached the point where even some of those who had strenuously argued against the existence of global warming had come to accept it as reality.

The political shorthand for this fusion of geology, ecology, foreign policy, and economics was "energy security." America would forever be at the mercy of the nations it bought fuel from unless it weaned itself from its expensive oil habit and gained "energy independence," in the words of politicians and activists.

One of those politicians was Hillary, who repeatedly mentioned energy independence in her October 2005 speech. Later that year, in December, she hooked up with an alliance of environmentalists, liberal activists, and unions to help unveil a new Democratic plan, "Energy Independence 2020."[7] This new agenda was even more ambitious than the plan widely supported by Democrats at the time.[8]

Normally, Hillary's learning curve on such a crucial issue would have begun with the Clinton presidency. But the closet was largely empty: Bill's exhaustive 957-page autobiography contains only one indexed reference to oil or "energy issues" during his presidency, and that reference involves security at the Energy Department weapons labs.[9] The lack of attention to energy policy during the 1990s was somewhat understandable. Oil prices were low and the economy buoyant, lulling the nation into complacency. Bill later noted that a speech he delivered in 1997 on clean energy technologies "elicited a giant yawn from the press and the American public."[10] Still, during the 1990s, imports of foreign oil steadily and quietly increased, from about six million barrels per day to nearly ten million barrels per day. At the same time, the government's petroleum reserve, created as a form of rainy-day insurance after the oil crisis in the 1970s, dropped from eighty-three days of inventory in 1992 to fifty days in 2000.[11]

Needing outside help, Hillary could have turned to Al Gore, her husband's partner in power for eight years and a man who had devoted a great deal of his life before and after the vice presidency to educating people about the environment and energy crises. Her rivalry with Gore would not allow that, however — nor would her desire to conceal how much tutoring she needed. Instead, she turned to a key member of Hillaryland to prepare for the May 2006 speech and increase her understanding of the issue: Roger C. Altman, the head of Evercore Partners, a New York investment bank with major holdings in energy.[12] At the time, Evercore's holdings included investments of more than $1 billion in private equity funds. The heaviest allocation was in energy-related investments, at 33 percent. (The next largest segment was 19 percent.)[13]

Altman assembled a secret task force of a dozen other experts, from academia, think tanks, and investment banks, to "help her think through the issues" in preparation for the May press club address.[14] The task force prepared a forty-page report in April 2006 that was filled with analysis and policy options.[15] Later that month, they met with Hillary in her Capitol Hill office for a "free-flowing discussion" that lasted several hours.[16] In Washington, a private meeting with a powerful senator often involves the promotion of narrow interests. But this gathering was different. The experts, many of whom had never met Hillary, came away impressed by her probing questions and her deep understanding of the issues. She, too, seemed impressed with their realistic, bipartisan approach.[17]

The members of her group agreed to keep their participation and work a secret, an uncommon arrangement for several reasons.[18] By keeping the discussions confidential, the participants, it was hoped, would speak freely, without fear that their remarks would be made public. (This stance echoed the Bush administration's controversial defense of maintaining the secrecy of Vice President Cheney's own energy task force. Cheney's report and the names of the members of the task force were made public in 2001, but the deliberations and the names of the energy company executives and the experts Cheney's group consulted were kept confidential.) But there was another reason to maintain silence. Hillary was not merely a policy wonk; she was a politician with higher ambitions.[19] As a result, she ended up ignoring some of the expert advice she received. It was much easier to reject expert advice if nobody would ever know about it.

Crafting a highly partisan position, Hillary reversed a few of her long-held views, sidestepped controversial issues, and relied on misleading spin to deliver the message. In the end, she followed the well-worn path that has characterized the debate about energy in Washington for more than a century—the triumph of politics over policy.

Altman and many of the other experts Hillary consulted criticized the concept of energy independence as a "fantasy" or "counterproductive."[20] David Victor, a Stanford University energy expert who participated in her task force, understood the dilemma. Hillary was told about the "need to be serious about how the markets function," yet, like numerous other Democrats, she couldn't resist the politically popular position of "beating up on the oil companies."[21] Ultimately, Hillary would make energy independence a cornerstone of her position. It sold well to a public increasingly worried about gas prices and global warming—even if ultimately it was just hot air.

AS SHE HEADED TO THE press club that May morning to give her energy speech, Hillary had one more of Bill's burdens to bear. On its front page that morning, the *New York Times* published an in-depth article purporting to describe the state of Bill and Hillary's marriage. The *Times* reported that between his busy philanthropic commitments and her nearly around-the-clock political schedule, Bill and Hillary spent an average of fourteen days a month together.[22] The article contained little in the way of news, but it was a reminder of how the mainstream press can digress when it comes to covering America's most famous yet little understood political couple.

Hillary and her advisers were distracted and angered by the *Times* report, so she was running late that morning.[23] As a result she missed an opportunity to chat with the club's organizers before beginning. Still, as she took to the podium in the press club ballroom, she graciously thanked her hosts. She then launched into a forty-one-minute lecture—about twice the normal speaking time of guests—on energy security. She smartly framed the issue, connecting "the security and the environmental challenges of our reliance on high-priced, mostly imported oil" with the economic costs of inflation, higher gas prices, and upward trending interest rates. "Right now," she said, the nation's priorities are upside down because "our failed energy policy dictates our national security."[24]

After praising solar power and wind technology, Hillary turned her attention to her villains—the oil companies—and discussed the legislation she hoped to pass that would force them to change their ways. Unless they diversified away from fossil fuels and into preferred, renewable technologies, her bill would require that they be assessed heavy windfall-profits taxes by the federal government. This new revenue source, estimated at $50 billion, would finance a government energy fund that invested in innovative energy research.[25]

A number of respected experts, including at least two members of her secret panel, considered such taxes "a very bad idea" because they tend to increase, rather than decrease, dependence on foreign oil.[26] (The increased dependency occurs because foreign oil becomes cheaper relative to domestic.) But Hillary was gambling that voters would not make the connection.

After ticking off a litany of new proposals, involving everything from cellulosic ethanol to carbon by-products, Hillary sighed and said, "So here we are. I know this is probably a more wonkish speech than many of you anticipated. But I feel so strongly about this because I'm afraid what has happened before will happen again." As she put it, "The sense of urgency recedes."[27]

Hillary then fielded a few questions. She was asked what she personally planned to do to reduce energy use. She recommended buying energy-efficient appliances, adding that both she and Bill "are focused" on using fuel-efficient cars. But when a reporter asked if she supported a congressional measure to require automakers to increase the fuel-efficiency standards of their vehicles, she side-stepped the question. Instead, she called for a bipartisan solution that would help the automobile companies "manage this" challenge.[28] Michigan is an important primary state, after all.

THE TIMING OF HILLARY'S SPEECH, a few days before the nation-wide unveiling of Gore's documentary, prompted speculation of political gamesmanship. Hillary had briefly paid homage to the former vice president in her press club speech, but given the timing, Maureen Dowd, in the *New York Times*, felt that the "Ozone Woman" had cunningly emerged in an attempt to squelch the "Ozone Man's moment in the sun."[29] Bill vigorously denied that Hillary's speech was "just a political deal" or a brazen attempt for her to get "into the mix."[30] Gore may have been "terrific" in his documentary, Bill told one audience, but he got lucky by the timing. "I don't think it would have been nearly as compelling if we didn't have $70 oil,"Bill cattily said.[31]

Hours after her speech, Hillary introduced her promised legislation to create a federal "Strategic Energy Fund" financed by oil company taxes. But her energy bill, while music to the ears of the Left, overreached with her colleagues. She might have predicted that outcome if she had paid attention to the fate of an unsuccessful proposal by a few Senate Democrats to tax the windfall profits of oil companies, with the proceeds going directly back to taxpayers.[32] Hillary could not find another senator to cosponsor her bill, a failure that underscored how alone she stood on this issue.[33] But the position that Hillary staked out thrilled the grassroots environmental activists, scoring her important political points with the Left, a group that had been disillusioned with her position on other energy issues and continued to be dismayed over her position on Iraq.[34]

Upon closer inspection, it became clearer that her solo act on energy had a lot to do with pleasing crucial electoral states. Take the home of the first presidential caucus, for example. In the past she had consistently voted against ethanol measures, earning a zero rating in 2002 from the American Coalition for Ethanol, a trade group.[35] In 2005, she voted for an amendment to remove mandates promoting ethanol production in the energy bill.[36] The amendment's sponsor—her New York colleague Charles Schumer—argued that the mandates would end up increasing costs for drivers in the Northeast and unduly benefit ethanol producers, based largely in the Midwest, especially Iowa. Schumer's amendment failed, and the mandates became law as part of the energy bill.[37] Listening to her speech, you would never have guessed that Hillary's sudden pro-ethanol fervor was a very recent conversion.

Further evidence of her political instincts was seen with regard to car pollution. In 2003, Hillary had voted for a fuel-efficiency standard opposed by the auto industry. But two years later, the presidency increasingly on her mind, she continued to push the idea publicly but voted against the same measure she had backed.[38] For environmentalists, Hillary's decision to flip-flop her vote on the fuel-efficiency standards amounted to a "bitter experience."[39] For her part, Hillary suddenly found it easier to beat up on the oil companies than on the auto companies and their employees.

One of the phrases that Hillary began to utter with increasing frequency was "coal is to us what oil is to Saudi Arabia," so "independence from imported oil by using coal" was a winning strategy if the coal is burned cleanly.[40] In fact, her task force had told her "an insignificant amount of oil is used for electricity" and that "the problem of oil dependency is literally all about our cars."[41] President Bush fell prey to the same misleading statement in his 2006 State of the Union address when he advocated reducing oil imports through the use of nuclear power. Hillary, the "brainiest" senator, would blanch at being compared to Bush on energy policy, but the parallel was undoubtedly there.[42]

And while Hillary also belittled Vice President Cheney's dismissal of conservation as a personal virtue in her press club address, her own record is hardly exemplary. When asked by a reporter at the press club about her personal efforts to save energy, she cited Bill's presidential library in Little Rock, Arkansas, and its use of energy-efficient lighting.[43] In fact, the library is funded by donors and operated by the federal government—its energy efficiency is admirable, but Hillary and Bill didn't have to pay for it. And, in the months before her speech, Hillary had a chance to demonstrate her personal commitment to energy efficiency when she installed a new boiler and air-conditioning units as part of a large renovation of her Washington home. In both cases, building records show, she did not choose high-efficiency models.[44]

IN THE WEEKS AFTER her press club remarks, Hillary stayed on message, her ensuing speeches stubbornly showcasing the "energy independence" slogan opposed by her advisers. In late June, the nine female Democrats in the Senate organized themselves into a group and assembled a plan entitled "Checklist for Change." Each senator planned to adopt a major issue, like health care, retirement, jobs, education, the environment, or the military. Hillary's issue was energy, because she "specifically wanted to look at energy independence," according to Senator Barbara Mikulski of Maryland, who organized the event.[45]

As a venue for the event, the women selected a little-known building on Capitol Hill, the Sewall-Belmont House. The house was once home to Alice Paul, the founder of the National Women's Party, and it served as the headquarters for the party. Hillary, having visited the building a week earlier, knew it as "one of the iconic structures that really was the home of so much that went into the women's movement."[46]

Mikulski, the dean of the female senators, who is affectionately known as "Coach Barb,"[47] began the event, just outside the house, by explaining how all of them were "fighting to make a difference."[48] As the first few senators discussed their issues at the podium, Hillary stood to the side, looking down, leafing through papers contained in a bright blue binder.

When her turn came, Hillary stated her familiar theme of taking a new path to reduce "our country's dependence on foreign oil." She mentioned her legislation and ended with a call for action that sounded as if it communally came from the nine assembled women senators. "We challenge the Republican Congress to make energy independence a priority by passing the Strategic Energy Fund bill this session," Hillary said.[49] It was a political ploy, and a bit misleading, given that Hillary had been unable to persuade even one of her eight sister senators to cosponsor her bill.[50]

Whatever their differences, the nine women, including Hillary, were all smiles that evening when they appeared on *Larry King Live*, taking their message to a national audience. Hillary, asked if mak-

*   *   *

ing America energy independent was feasible, said, "Absolutely, it's feasible."[51]

ONE MONTH LATER, in July 2006, Hillary showed up in a small town in upstate New York called Halfmoon, touting the virtues of the sun. There, just outside Albany, New York, sits the headquarters of DayStar Technologies, a start-up company seeking to commercialize a specialized solar product made from photovoltaic foil.

Hillary toured the company's plant. "This is exactly what our country needs to be doing," she told the workers. The government, she explained, should stop supporting oil companies and instead subsidize solar energy, wind power, and other "cleaner" alternative energy sources.[52] Hillary reiterated her call for the country to move away from "foreign sources of energy like oil and towards domestic renewable energy like solar."[53] Privately, after her visit, a DayStar official acknowledged that their product, like any source of electricity, "is no substitute for foreign oil."[54]

Still, for Hillary, the event helped reinforce one of the selling points of her reelection campaign: bringing clean, energy-efficient jobs to New York. Prospects for the company that Hillary showcased, however, were not particularly radiant. As of the date of Hillary's visit, DayStar had never made a profit, nor was it going to generate a positive cash flow "for the foreseeable future."[55] The company was dependent on government grants for its revenues.

DayStar's outlook improved that summer when it convinced its local congressman to earmark $1 million in Pentagon money for the company, far surpassing DayStar's total revenues through June 30, 2006, of $30,000.[56] While some deemed the grant to be political pork, Hillary applauded the measure, citing the "cutting-edge technology being made locally."[57]

There is a postscript to the DayStar story. According to the company's media and marketing representative, a registered lobbyist who also donated $1,000 to Hillary's campaign[58] and is affiliated with a New York law firm[59] "played an integral role in getting Hillary Clinton here."[60] Hiring a lobbyist to attract a senator may be how the game is played in Washington, but it is also one reason why the public holds Congress in such low esteem.

AFTER ITS PREMIERE at the Sundance Film Festival, Gore's film,

An Inconvenient Truth, had gone on to become an enormous commercial success and won an Academy Award for best documentary. Meanwhile, in California, allies of Bill and Hillary put together a state ballot initiative that would require oil companies to pay an extra tax in order to fund state government programs on alternative energy. The initiative mirrored Hillary's unsuccessful congressional legislation, but the hope was that progressive California might go for it. The ballot initiative's major financier was Stephen Bing, a Hollywood film producer. Bing, a close friend of Bill's, helped host fund-raisers for Hillary in 2006 and 2007.[61] The manager of the initiative was Chad Griffin, a former Clinton aide who helped host Hollywood fund-raisers for Hillary in 2005 and 2007.[62]

Once the plan made it onto the ballot, as Proposition 87, Gore cut a political commercial endorsing the initiative, his first ad since the 2000 campaign. Five days after Gore's ad began airing in California, Bill appeared at a rally on the UCLA campus. After thanking Bing and Griffin, he exhorted the already supportive crowd of several thousand people, telling the audience, among other things, about how he and Hillary learned about the potential of converting pussy willows into wood chips for fuel during a recent visit to upstate New York.[63]

Bill's appearance was turned into a commercial, and within a few days the campaign for Proposition 87 began airing ads featuring the former president. And, as the costly and hotly contested campaign on the ballot entered its final weeks, it was Bill's ads, rather than Gore's ad, that dominated the airwaves in many markets.[64]

Gore then made a brief appearance at a rally in Berkeley. Not to be outdone, one week later and less than a week before the election, Bill came back to California one final time, for a rally in San Francisco, the epicenter of political blueness in California.

The unprecedented involvement of a former president and vice president on behalf of a state ballot initiative seemed to give it an edge with voters. Yet there was an equally important undercurrent at play. The two men were competing with each other. And the reason Bill had gone toe-to-toe with Gore on his signature issue was to help his wife.

"Bill was trying to take the issue from being just Al Gore's issue in order to help Hillary, to give her some footing on this issue," said one of the consultants for Proposition 87.[65] The former vice president was "furious."[66] In the final weeks of the campaign, inland voters, not a Democratic stronghold, turned from mild supporters to strong opponents of the measure. The Clinton ads failed to sway this group and might well have been counterproductive, according to a leading pollster.[67] On Election Day, the measure was soundly defeated, 55 to 45 percent. One rule of politics is that if you want to get something done, do the hard work and let others take all the credit. In this case, the Clintons' refusal to cede the spotlight ended up backfiring and helped torpedo Proposition 87.[68]

Of course, for Hillary the defeat was only partial. Her battle had not been solely for votes—it had also been for herself. She had never shown much interest in things environmental, and she knew she needed to, given the polls and concerns of Americans all over the country. She needed to push Al Gore to the sidelines, and she might have done so if not for the wild success of his documentary. But that failure aside, she had at least imprinted in the minds of California voters that she cared deeply about the environment, something that she hoped would pay dividends come Democratic primary time. Perhaps by then, California's voters would forget the thicket of problems Proposition 87 might have created. Perhaps by then they would not scratch their heads and try to reconcile Hillary's reputation of being brilliant with her ongoing confusion that coal could take the place of oil. Or perhaps by then another issue would be on top of the charts, and Hillary would have a new battle to fight.

The Somewhat Lonely Middle

LATE IN THE AFTERNOON of June 14, 2006, a group of Democratic
senators and their aides headed to a small conference room in the
Capitol. To get there, they first had to enter a suite of offices named
after West Virginia Democrat Robert C. Byrd after he had stepped
down as majority leader in 1989. The suite now belonged to the
Democratic minority leader, Harry Reid, and the senators and their
staff wound their way to Room 224, at the end of the corridor.
Located just off the Senate floor, the ornate chamber, decorated
with portraits of past Senate leaders, had hosted a series of private
conferences over the previous days in which a small group of Democrats discussed Iraq policy. The out-of-the-way location meant the
senators could plot the party's strategy and discuss their differences
far from their Republican colleagues and the press.

That day, the usual nine attendees were surprised to discover
a newcomer in their midst: Senator Hillary Rodham Clinton.[1] She
was one of the first to arrive and sat herself down on a love seat, one
of the two couches in the room. Sitting next to her was Carl Levin,
the senior senator from Michigan. As the ranking Democrat on the
Armed Services Committee, Levin was the de facto leader of the
session because the meeting involved amendments to the pending
defense authorization bill. Hillary, a junior member of the Armed

Services Committee, draped one arm around the back of the couch and chewed gum.[2]

Reid began by recounting what had happened since the previous meeting earlier that week, when the main topic of discussion had been a proposal by John Kerry to withdraw American troops by the end of the year. Kerry, still smarting from his loss to President Bush, was trying to strike a bold pose on Iraq in contrast to the tangled, if not tortured, path he had pursued during the campaign.

Reid said he had met with three senior Democrats, all ranking members of various Senate committees, and found strong resistance to Kerry's proposal. As a result, Reid wanted to keep Kerry's motion from being considered on the Senate floor that week. The Massachusetts senator, a member of the Foreign Relations Committee, was not present for the June 14 gathering, so Reid and Levin asked Kerry's foreign-policy aide, Nancy Stetson, to update everyone on the status of her boss's amendment. She explained that the amendment had been altered, moving the proposed troop withdrawal date from the end of 2006 to July of 2007. Hillary asked for a copy of the revised amendment. She read it and quickly dismissed the date for withdrawal and the requirement that America consult with the Iraqi government before removing troops.

"That's quite different from getting out by 2006," she said, mocking Kerry's revision.[3] Referring to the amendment as a whole, she added sharply, "This doesn't do anything."[4]

Kerry later wondered whether Hillary's negative reaction was related to the contrasting receptions the two of them had received the day before at the conference of liberal activists at the Washington Hilton.[5] (At the conference, both Hillary and Kerry spoke. When Hillary declared that she did not think it was a "smart strategy to set a date certain" for withdrawal of U.S. troops from Iraq, the crowd roundly booed. But when Kerry called the war "immoral" and "a quagmire," his remarks were greeted by raucous cheers.[6])

The recent clash between the two belied a long history of personal and political ties. In 1972, as youthful activists, they had both appeared in Boston before the platform committee of the Democratic National Convention: Hillary on behalf of children's rights and Kerry with regard to the Vietnam War.[7] (Kerry had no memory of the old connection, expressing amazement when he was first told about it in 2007.[8]) In 2001, just a week after the attacks of September 11, the two senators hosted a party, held at Kerry's house in

Georgetown, for the upcoming marriage of Tamera Luzzatto, Hillary's chief of staff, and David Leiter, Kerry's former chief of staff. And at the 2004 conference of liberal activists—the same gathering that the day before had evoked contrasting receptions for them both—Hillary had generously heaped praise on Kerry, warmly embracing his race against President Bush.

Luzzatto, a respected Senate veteran, accompanied Hillary to the June 14 meeting, but she could be only so much help. Luzzatto's lack of national security experience, one participant said, left Hillary essentially on her own to navigate the twists and turns of Iraq policy.[9] Perhaps that was why, after dismissing Kerry's amendment, Hillary largely remained quiet over the course of the next twenty to thirty minutes. Sensing her disengagement, Reid, the meeting's host, turned to Hillary and said he wanted to hear her thoughts. A few participants were surprised that Hillary was given the opportunity. There was a long pause.

"It was odd to give her the stage on this," said one participant in the meeting, noting that Hillary had not attended any of the previous strategy sessions. However, the participant acknowledged, Hillary was the "big enchilada," so "all eyes turned to her to hear what she thinks."[10]

Hillary spoke for five or six minutes. She seemed a little "unsure at first," repeating her negative mantra from the day before.[11]

"I don't support a fixed date for getting out, and I don't support an open-ended commitment," Hillary told her colleagues.[12] Then she picked up on ideas put forth in an alternative amendment then being proposed by Senators Levin and Jack Reed. Their amendment, which had no force of law, called for the president to "begin the phased redeployment of United States forces from Iraq" in 2006.[13] It then required that Bush tell Congress how he planned to continue drawing down the troops after that. It did give the president some leeway, noting that "unexpected contingencies" could arise.[14] In this, the amendment largely echoed the measure crafted the year before by the same group of Democrats, in which Levin, on behalf of Hillary, had proposed virtually the same softening language — "unexpected contingencies."

Hillary caustically reminded her colleagues why she was supporting a less confrontational posture toward the White House than the Kerry measure. "In case you haven't noticed," she snapped, "we don't control anything."[15]

Hillary went on to lecture her colleagues about the political acumen of administration officials. "Karl Rove and George Bush are no fools," she warned.[16]

Nevertheless, Senator Russ Feingold, one of the cosponsors of Kerry's amendment, argued, "Democrats want us out" of Iraq.[17] That was true—in a poll taken a few days earlier, 64 percent of Democrats said they wanted the United States to "leave as soon as possible," even if Iraq was not completely stable. Republicans overwhelmingly disagreed: 73 percent favored staying "as long as it takes." Independents were divided.[18]

Hillary was taking a broader view. "I face the base all the time," she told her colleagues. "I think we need wiggle room."[19]

As the meeting wound down, the senators grew weary. They talked about how this issue would be coming up again and again in the months leading to the midterm elections. There was some light banter about how the Iraq war might play out among the plethora of Democratic presidential hopefuls. Hillary raised the quintessential question: whether "one of the people in this room will be making the decision" about American troops in Iraq come January 2009.[20] "There were a lot of presidential contestants in that room," recalled an aide—Hillary, Feingold, Joe Biden of Delaware, and Chris Dodd of Connecticut were all considered potential candidates.[21]

After the meeting ended, Dianne Feinstein was pulled aside by Harry Reid, Jack Reed, and Levin, the architects of the compromise amendment that had now emerged as an alternative to Kerry and Feingold's, for a private conversation. The plan was to stall the Kerry-Feingold legislation and introduce the compromise bill in its place. They asked Feinstein to join as a cosponsor of their measure, comforted by the fact that she did not have presidential ambitions.

"It's not good to have presidential aspirants have their name appear" as original sponsors of the amendment, Harry Reid told Feinstein, "even if it is viewed as a consensus" resolution.[22] The appearance of a potential candidate's name could suddenly inject an array of politics and pressures that might harm a perfectly good piece of legislation, transforming it from a vote on an issue to a proxy vote on a candidate. Feinstein signed on.

The next day on the Senate floor, the plan to stall debate on Kerry's amendment immediately seemed in jeopardy, thanks to Senate Republicans. Hoping to score political points against the Democrats, they introduced Kerry's measure for him; once Kerry had officially filed his amendment any senator could call it up. Reid quickly countered with his own parliamentary maneuver—before Kerry could get to the floor to speak, a vote was held to end debate. Thirty-six Democratic senators, including Hillary, voted for Reid's motion to end debate on the amendment, which prevailed after Republican support.

Meanwhile, on the House side, after a lengthy and passionate debate, members backed the president's policies by rejecting any withdrawal timetables. The vote was 256 to 153. Forty-two Democrats, about one-fifth of the caucus, joined the largely united Republicans.

Back over in the Senate, Democrats had won more time to finalize their compromise plan, thanks to Reid's maneuver. With that time, Harry Reid added a final cosponsor, Senator Ken Salazar of Colorado, who was also not planning a run for president. The consensus amendment was formally unveiled by its architects on Monday, June 19, at the Senate press gallery. Senator Levin told reporters: "I'm introducing today, along with Senators Reed, Feinstein, and Salazar, an amendment" urging the administration "to begin a phased redeployment of U.S. troops from Iraq by the end of this year."[23] The emphasis was on reasonableness. The measure, Levin explained, was a follow-up to the Senate's approval in 2005, by a vote of 79 to 19, of language suggesting 2006 might create the conditions for "phased redeployment."[24] He also mentioned language in his amendment that called for consultations with the Iraqi government. Hillary did not attend the press briefing. Instead, she was back in her home state, like many other senators, knowing that the Senate rarely conducted business on a Monday.

The Senate finally turned to Iraq on Wednesday. Everyone knew it would be a contentious debate, especially considering that a midterm election was drawing near.

Levin once again took the lead, introducing his amendment. He was followed by Jack Reed, who took to the Senate floor and said, "I join with my colleague, Senator Levin, and Senators Feinstein and Salazar, to offer this amendment."[25]

Suddenly, and without notice, Hillary showed up on the floor of the Senate, wanting to speak.

Normally, the speakers go in the order of seniority, with the bill's original sponsors getting the privilege to speak first. Waiting her turn to speak was Senator Feinstein, who had been asked to join the bill by Harry Reid. Levin was flummoxed. He controlled the allocation of floor time for the Democrats, and not wanting it to appear to the Republicans or the public that his team lacked unity, he granted Hillary's surprise request to take the floor as the next Democratic speaker.[26]

Her first words took insiders by surprise: "I rise in support of the Levin amendment of which I am proud to be an original cosponsor."[27]

"We were puzzled," an aide to one of the amendment's sponsors said, because no one had told them about Hillary's sudden ascendancy to a leadership role on the measure.[28] Indeed, just a few minutes earlier, Reed, in his remarks, had not included Hillary in his list of cosponsors. And when he had unveiled the measure at Monday's press briefing, Levin had used the same list—again, without Hillary.

But Hillary, being Hillary, had stealthily muscled her way onto the stage.

The original amendment filed in the Senate read "to be proposed by Mr. Levin (for himself, Mr. Reed, Mrs. Feinstein, and Mr. Salazar)."[29] But off to the side, in handwriting, a single name had been added: "Clinton."[30] Her name had been inserted, records show, on June 19, the day Levin had unveiled his amendment at the press conference.[31]

"I remember seeing the handwritten bill and wondering what had happened," a senior Senate official recalled.[32] The explanation: Hillary had "intervened personally" with Harry Reid, the Democratic leader. "She forced her way in."[33] Reid couldn't say no, a Senate aide said, because Hillary was "first among equals," the "queen bee."[34]

With Hillary's inclusion, the rule of banning candidates was shredded. And "once you do one," the official continued, "the dam is broken."[35] Another senator with presidential aspirations, Joe Biden, who had discovered that Hillary was a last-minute cosponsor, also came on board.

To some, Hillary's maneuvering might seem like a game of inside baseball. After all, Hillary's cosponsorship grab escaped the attention of all the reporters who had covered the debate. And if reporters don't read the legislation they write about, why should the public pay much attention to the names of a bill's original sponsors? And yet what Hillary had accomplished was symbolic and important. Even after Kerry and Feingold softened their binding amendment, moving back the fixed date of withdrawal from December 2006 to July 2007, they were able to collect only thirteen votes in favor of their amendment. Hillary could take credit for a compromise that attracted broader support: thirty-nine votes, one independent in addition to thirty-eight Democrats. Still later, as the war worsened, she could argue that she had long backed some kind of withdrawal. She could also showcase her role as a "leader" in the Senate on national security as further evidence of why she should be elected president.[36]

Hillary's remarks on the Senate floor contained the usual litany of criticism against Republicans, lambasting their zeal "to win elections at home" rather than formulating "a strategy to win in Iraq."[37] She noted the war's heavy toll on her home state: 116 killed and more than a thousand wounded. Then, for the first time in her public speeches, she offered her new interpretation of her actions in 2002. The revised account was unusually audacious with respect to Levin, who had just graciously—if partially in shock—granted her the floor.

The authority Congress had granted the president and his administration four years earlier, Hillary explained, had been "misused" because they "acted without allowing the inspectors to finish the job in order to rush to war."[38] In other words, Bush had given short shrift to diplomacy. Hillary was once again completely disregarding her own vote against Levin's 2002 amendment, the one that required the president to pursue a more diplomatic approach before any invasion of Iraq.

No one—neither Hillary's usual opponents nor the press—brought up Hillary's omission of her vote in 2002 against diplomacy. Her singling out of President Bush for misusing the authority from Congress played so well, it soon became a staple of her campaign speeches. She also continued to exclusively blame the president after newly declassified documents showed that there was in fact no intelligence to support the Al Qaeda connection made by Bush and Cheney—and Hillary.[39]

THE EVENTS OF THE NEXT few days seemed to validate Hillary's calculated revisions.

She was applauded, not booed, at a gathering of Democratic activists in Washington on Friday, June 23. Some of the anti-war activists and her previous critics now praised her for embracing redeployment and moving closer to their views. Roger Hickey, who had invited Hillary to the activist conference where she was booed, said her action "was a significant new movement for her and the Democratic Party."[40]

Weeks later, as the polls showed mounting public dissatisfaction with the war, Hillary publicly prodded Defense Secretary Donald Rumsfeld to come to a Senate Armed Services Committee hearing to answer questions about Iraq. Rumsfeld initially declined, fearing it would be political theater, but eventually he changed his mind. He may have regretted the decision; he was mercilessly grilled by the junior senator from New York. At one point, Rumsfeld, seemingly taken aback by the tenor of the questions, groaned, "My goodness," before responding to her comments.[41] Press accounts described Hillary as having "excoriated" the defense secretary.[42] Shortly after the hearing, she upped the ante by publicly calling for Rumsfeld's resignation.[43]

Now on even stronger ground in her home state, Hillary refused for the next month to debate Jonathan Tasini, her emphatically anti-war Democratic opponent, before the New York primary. A frustrated Tasini complained to the press that the Democrats were reluctant to debate "the most important issue of the day."[44] Even Hillary's backers on the editorial board of the New York Times chided her for avoiding a debate, but she made no effort to change her stance, and the state party followed her lead.[45]

Hillary, to no one's surprise, easily prevailed on the day of the primary election. Unlike Joe Lieberman, who was narrowly beaten in his primary by an anti-war candidate, Ned Lamont, Hillary crushed Tasini, winning 83 percent of the vote.

Having fended off a left-wing primary opponent, Hillary then faced off with Republican John Spencer in the general election. Spencer, a former mayor of Yonkers, was an ineffective candidate who repeatedly portrayed Hillary as soft on national security. Spencer's critique was a generic one for Republicans facing Democrats, and while there seemed little reason for Hillary to feel particularly threatened by the Yonkers mayor, she once again shifted her ground. That September, at a Democratic hearing on Iraq designed to highlight military criticism of the administration, Hillary arrived late. The hearing featured three recently retired senior military officers. Before Hillary's arrival, they had blasted Rumsfeld as incompetent. But when she asked them what would happen if the United States withdrew from Iraq under a fixed deadline, they all said the consequences would be disastrous. One of the witnesses said, "The result would be a civil war of some magnitude, which will turn into a regional mess."[46] This was precisely *not* the avenue of discussion that the Democrats had intended, and the hearing was quickly ended.

Hillary's Web site later highlighted the criticisms of Bush at the hearing but omitted her controversial back-and-forth with the officers.[47] Her provocative questions, however, prompted grumbling among some Democrats in the Senate over the next few days.[48] Republicans, on the other hand, were gleeful and swiftly tried to use the exchange to their advantage. They publicly highlighted the testimony and Hillary's role in eliciting it. When Mike DeWine, a Republican senator facing a tough reelection fight in Ohio, was asked by moderator Tim Russert, on NBC's *Meet the Press*, whether accusing the Democrats of cutting and running was appropriate, he quickly cited Hillary as his defense. DeWine said Hillary had asked "the key question" at the Democratic hearing, about what would happen if a withdrawal date was set, and was told that the result would be "chaos in Iraq."[49]

Whether Hillary was still conflicted about the war or whether she was simply sloppy in her understanding, her questioning of the officers reminded some Democrats of her propensity to do things her way, regardless of party preferences. Hillary had long been the one calling for greater discipline when it came to staying in line and on message. Some wondered whether she really meant that the others should get in line behind her and follow in lockstep as she marched forward.[50]

Whatever the case, Hillary's prospects for returning to the White House were about to improve. The midterm elections of 2006 signaled profound voter dissatisfaction with Iraq and the Republicans. DeWine and many other Bush allies in Congress were swept out of office as Democrats took control of both the House and the Senate. Hillary easily crushed Spencer, winning two-thirds of the vote. Her target, Donald Rumsfeld, resigned, and the Republicans were seemingly left in tatters.

Hillary, in her political assessment of the election, said, "The message sent loudly and clearly by the American people" was "that we desperately need a new course."[51] By this point, she had traveled all over the map regarding Iraq, carried along, in part, by the shifts in public opinion and her own ambition to appear both strong and decisive, traits she knew she'd need if she were to become president.

As she finalized her plans for a presidential bid, Hillary asked political allies from New Hampshire how her vote for the war would play out in the campaign.[52] As she saw it, she had two options: chart a "new course" to escape her own Iraqi quagmire, or continue to tread water in the "somewhat lonely middle," where, she confided to a reporter, she often found herself.[53]

One place where she was soon to be less lonely was in New Hampshire. The pool of Democratic presidential candidates was about to expand—and this time, the challenger would be a senator even more junior than Hillary.

"Madam President"

AT 2:15 P.M. on Wednesday, January 17, 2007, the Senate, now controlled by the Democrats, went back to business after a lunch break. That day, the presiding officer, a ceremonial position that is rotated among senators of the majority party, was Hillary Rodham Clinton.

The first item on that afternoon's agenda was personal — a tribute to John Kerry's retiring foreign-policy adviser, Nancy Stetson, who had graduated from Wellesley College two years after Hillary. Hillary recognized Kerry, who took to the floor to speak.

"Madam President," Kerry began, "one of the best things about the Senate and the character of this place" is the hardworking Senate staff members, "our experts."[1] The fifty-seven-year-old Stetson, Kerry said, had served him well as his "alter ego" on foreign policy for the previous fifteen years. He summarized Stetson's twenty-five-year Senate career and noted that "she was prescient in seeing the disastrous path that has played out in Iraq."[2] He neglected to point out that he had ignored her advice on the war at some of the most crucial moments — and that doing so had very likely cost him the presidency.[3]

Stetson, sometimes known as "Dr. No" in Kerry circles, had urged him to vote against the original Iraq war resolution in 2002, which he decided instead to support.[4] Later, she urged him to vote for the 2004 supplemental appropriation of $87 billion to finance the troops in Iraq, which he then went on to oppose. Those votes, and Kerry's convoluted attempts to explain them, were widely believed to have been the most critical factors in his narrow loss to George W. Bush in the 2004 presidential election.

That afternoon, as Kerry lauded his aide, Hillary's attention was elsewhere. She was focused on what she hoped would be a historic campaign that would culminate in her taking the oath of office as America's first "Madam President." A few hours earlier, at her home in Washington, she had sat on the couch in her sunroom to record a short video declaring her presidential candidacy, which, three days later, would be posted online.[5] Adding to the anticipation and excitement was the announcement the day before by Senator Barack Obama that he had filed papers to enter the presidential race. He joined a quickly growing field of Democratic presidential hopefuls, including former senator John Edwards and Senators Joseph Biden and Christopher Dodd.

Shortly after Kerry's remarks, Hillary left the Senate rostrum and headed upstairs to S-325, the Senate radio and television gallery, to update a standing-room-only throng of about two hundred reporters, cameramen, and photographers on the Iraq war. President Bush had announced two weeks earlier that he intended to expand the forces in Iraq by 21,500 troops, a plan that had met a decidedly negative reaction from Democrats in Congress. Hillary's political machine was already cruising at presidential speed for her press briefing on Iraq; her remarks were preceded by extensive polling, hours of advice from Bill, endless conference calls, and a flurry of back-to-back television interviews.[6] She had also just returned from a four-day fact-finding trip to Iraq and Afghanistan, burnishing her credentials to speak with authority on the most vexing issue confronting Washington. Broadly, her choices were either to bring herself more in sync with anti-war Democrats whose support she would need in the 2008 Democratic primaries or to stay closer to the national security center, her home for the last five years and perhaps a better platform for attracting voters in a general election.

The pressure was mounting for her to take a position. A few days earlier, John Edwards had taken a "clear shot" at Hillary by demanding an end to silence by those who just "study your options."[7] Like Dodd and Kerry before him, Edwards had renounced his October 2002 vote in support of the war.

Obama, the Illinois Democrat, had opposed the war before it started, though he was only an Illinois state senator when the vote had been taken. That initial opposition allowed Obama to distinguish himself from those Democrats, like Hillary, who, he said, had given President Bush "the broad, open-ended authority to wage this war."[8] And Obama, now vying for the White House, was stepping up those attacks.

As Hillary walked into the jammed Senate studio at 3:11 that afternoon, the anticipation centered on whether she could extricate herself from her vote for the war while at the same time avoiding Kerry's tangled and doomed legacy.[9]

The press conference began as a trip report. The other speakers were Hillary's congressional colleagues on her fact-finding mission: Senator Evan Bayh, a moderate Democrat from Indiana, and Representative John McHugh, a Republican from New York. The two men spoke first; Hillary stood to the side, straight-faced, tight-lipped, with hands clasped. Occasionally, she nervously pressed her thumbs up against each other or twirled them around. At other times, she nodded in agreement as the men described the bleak situation in Iraq and Afghanistan, another stop on their trip. (By this point, Iraq was overcome by vicious sectarian violence that had overwhelmed many parts of the country, including Baghdad; meanwhile, the Taliban was regrouping and mounting a series of attacks across Afghanistan.)

Finally, it was Hillary's turn. Her remarks struck an array of familiar themes: President Bush had mishandled the war; the military men and women, with whom she had earned much credibility as a senator, were doing a fantastic job; and the troops should be gradually redeployed out of Iraq. She said nothing about her original vote. But she did stake out new territory, saying that she favored capping the troops at their current levels, though she acknowledged it was impractical for Congress to try to stop the president's newly proposed surge. Additionally, she called for a troop surge of her own, to Afghanistan rather than to Iraq. Hillary also proposed the imposition of a series of political, military, and economic conditions to be met by the Iraqis and certified by the president. Absent that certification, she proposed cutting off further funding—not to American troops, but to Iraqi security forces and to the contractors guarding Iraqi officials. Although she pledged to introduce her Iraq plan in a bill, Hillary did not hand out a draft of the proposed legislation or executive summary for reporters, as is often the case.[10]

The omission was a sign of things to come. An adviser to Hillary acknowledged that her proposals moved her only a "baby step" farther out of the Iraq box she was in.[11] As time passed, it became clear that Hillary's legislation would never become law. Still, her proposal was not without punch when it came to presidential politics. She continued to support "phased redeployment," as opposed to the immediate withdrawal of forty thousand or fifty thousand troops proposed by John Edwards, or a more dramatic funding cutoff mentioned by others.[12] Her approach, she told a reporter that day, stemmed from being "cursed with the responsibility gene."[13] The implication regarding her fellow Democrats was unmistakable.

As Hillary made her way out of the press gallery at 3:42 p.m., a reporter, shouting from the back, asked her when she would disclose her presidential decision. She did not respond.

Three hours later, as the network news shows aired their reports about Hillary's briefing, and reporters filed their stories about her proposals for the next day's newspapers, John Kerry was busy proposing a toast for his departing aide, Stetson. The location was a party room on the second floor of the Monocle, the closest restaurant to the Senate office complex and a popular watering hole for senators and lobbyists. There, several dozen of Stetson's friends and colleagues dropped by to wish her well.

Before his toast, Kerry again saluted his trusted adviser. This time, he was more candid. He acknowledged, for the first time before a large group of people, that he had made "a mistake" by not listening to her counsel on Iraq. Had he followed her advice, he admitted, his White House run might have gone differently. After his toast, Kerry leaned down to hug the petite Stetson.[14] A week later, he announced on the Senate floor that he would not pursue another run for president.

HILLARY, TOO, HAD SCARS from her vote on Iraq, but she was determined to avoid repeating Kerry's mistakes. One of her advisers explained, "She is worried about the flip-flop" and any comparison with Kerry, so she "doesn't want to do anything that undermines the thought that she is strong and believes in what she does."[15] Bill, her closest adviser on Iraq, believed strength was a key quality of a leader in insecure times. The former president told a group of Democrats in December 2003: "When people feel uncertain, they'd rather have somebody who's strong and wrong than somebody who's weak and right."[16] Her chief strategist, Mark Penn, provided another rationale: "It's important for all Democrats to keep the word 'mistake' firmly on the Republicans and on President Bush."[17] Hillary, always reluctant to admit a mistake, was certainly not about to do so now.

On Saturday morning, January 20, a normally slow news day, Hillary stepped into history. Her presidential launch was an electronically choreographed special; thousands of e-mails were blasted to reporters and friends while her old Senate campaign site morphed into a new one for her presidential run. Against a patriotic backdrop of red, white, and blue was a framed shot of a relaxed Hillary sitting on a couch. A click on the photo quickly took viewers to a one-minute-and-forty-second video of Hillary explaining why she was "in to win."

Behind Hillary's momentous decision lurked Bill. She had generally alluded to his role when she told Brian Williams of NBC's *Nightly News* that the launch was "our plan," after initially saying the plan was hers.[18] Mickey Kantor, an informal adviser, acknowledged Bill was playing a "major role" in the campaign.[19] Other friends and advisers opened the door some more; they said the former president had long gamed out Hillary's path to the White House and was the prime decision maker behind the last-minute rollout.[20]

Two days after her announcement, Hillary began a blizzard of television interviews, appearing on all the major news shows. At the same time, she began a three-day online video conversation. Each evening, beginning at 7:00, she answered a small number of questions chosen by aides from those submitted by tens of thousands of viewers. Hillary seemed energized in her interviews and comfortable in her Web chats, though after two days, she said her voice was waning because "I've done too much talking."[21]

Even with a hoarse voice, she stayed largely on message when it came to Iraq. Journalists and voters repeatedly tried to ask her whether her 2002 vote was a "mistake." She refused to say yes. Instead, she said her vote "turned out to be a terrible decision for everyone"[22] and that "those of us in the Congress" made "a lot of mistakes."[23]

In Hillary's mind, perhaps, acknowledging collective guilt would suffice. "I think at some level," one adviser said at the time, "she thinks she *has* repudiated her vote."[24] But Democratic activists, including those in Iowa and New Hampshire, remained split over whether Hillary had been forthcoming.[25] In Berlin, a small mill town in northern New Hampshire, a financial adviser named Roger Tilton told Hillary that he was waiting to hear her repudiate her vote. "I want to know if right here, right now, once and for all and without nuance, you can say that war authorization was a mistake," Tilton said. "I, and I think a lot of other primary voters — until we hear you say it, we're not going to hear all the other great things you are saying."[26]

"Knowing what we know now," Hillary replied, "I would never have voted for it."[27] She made no effort to praise or acknowledge those in Congress who had seen ahead with greater accuracy and voted against the war from the start. She added that voters would ultimately decide for themselves whether her position was acceptable. "The mistakes were made by this president, who misled this country and this Congress."[28] The audience applauded and cheered.

In Washington, a Republican friend and colleague of Hillary's wondered why she hadn't lodged such a complaint sooner. "I didn't see early on, or at least for a couple of or three years," said Senator John McCain, "the allegation surface that President Bush had quote, 'misused his authority.'"[29] But if Hillary had been one of the most pro-war Democrats back then when polls were leaning one way, she now served up more red meat to the anti-war wing of her party. She told the Democratic National Committee she would end the war in Iraq as soon as she became president.[30]

On February 15, when Harry Reid held a meeting in his office with other Democrats to discuss options on Iraq, Hillary was absent, but the next day, the Friday before the three-day presidential holiday weekend, she quietly introduced her bill.[31] Hillary waited until Saturday to issue a statement. By then, she was in Dover, New Hampshire, snappily telling voters: "If the most important thing to any of you is choosing someone who did not cast that vote or has said his vote was a mistake, then there are others to choose from."[32]

Hillary's Iraqi war legislation, which had no other sponsors, largely tracked what she had announced a month earlier; its two main conditions were a cap on existing troop levels and a provision to halt U.S. government funds to the Iraqi government. But the two key provisions now contained significant wiggle room[33] — caveats that Hillary, her aides, and the press accounts failed to mention.[34]

(One caveat allowed her cap to be lifted for sixty days if the president asked for a waiver on the basis of a threat to the national security of the United States.[35] Another was that funding would continue even if the president would not certify that the legislation's objectives in Iraq had been met—a significant loophole for a president who wanted to continue with the war.[36])

It was no surprise that Hillary would not want to call attention to the qualifiers that undercut the tougher, anti-Bush message that she had begun making. Nevertheless, her statement about the bill, issued on the Saturday of the holiday weekend, mentioned another aspect sure to irritate war critics. It noted that her plan allowed for a "limited presence" of American troops in Iraq after redeployment, something she had not mentioned in her press conference a month earlier.[37]

By May, Hillary made another attempt to repudiate her 2002 vote, though she stopped short of actually saying her vote had been a mistake. Instead, she proposed that Congress reverse its original authorization.

The drama played out late in the afternoon on May 3, when Hillary spoke for two minutes before a largely empty Senate chamber. She said she wanted to deauthorize the war, not by cutting off funding (the only certain way to end it), but by repealing the original authorization on October 11, 2007, the five-year anniversary of its passage. President Bush would have to seek new authorization if her proposal, cosponsored with Senator Robert Byrd, was enacted.

In her brief remarks designed to satisfy the increasing influence of anti-war Democrats, Hillary slowed down her delivery to highlight a long-forgotten piece of her Iraq record that she now yearned to emphasize.[38] The day before she voted for the war authorization, she noted, she had backed an amendment by Senator Byrd "that would have limited the original authorization to one year."[39] This newly discovered emphasis, a former Senate aide involved in the 2002 war debate explained, was designed "to suggest she wanted to end the war too," even if she had approved it.[40] Hillary had been against the war before she was for it—before she was against it all over again.

But the Byrd amendment in 2002, which was rejected 66 to 31, was not quite as Hillary had described it. The amendment gave the president "multiple outs," so it was "no big deal" and the subject of almost no debate at the time.[41] Specifically, it allowed the president, after one year, to extend the war authorization "for a period or periods of 12 months each" as long as he—and he alone—determined that it was "necessary for ongoing or impending military operations against Iraq."[42] This "open-ended" language meant that Hillary's description in May 2007 was misleading.[43]

That didn't prevent Hillary from exploiting the vote in her two-minute speech. She posted her remarks on her Senate and campaign Web sites; she launched an Internet petition to "Deauthorize the War"; and her plan to reverse course landed on the front page of the next day's *New York Times*. Noted an aide, "The most potent amendment that might have stopped the war" in 2002 was "the Levin amendment, not the Byrd amendment."[44] Yet Hillary's speech on May 3, quickly posted on YouTube, was silent about her vote against Levin's tough, diplomatic approach.

Hillary's careful cherry-picking of her voting record suited her presidential ambitions—at least in the short run. By ignoring Levin's proposal and highlighting just one aspect of the Byrd amendment, she now portrayed herself as only tepidly pro-war back in October 2002. This was Hillary's gamble to smash the most dangerous issue threatening her path to the Democratic nominaton. She was betting that her opponents—and the voters—wouldn't check the fine print.

Googled and YouTubed

ON FEBRUARY 23, 2007, Senator Hillary Rodham Clinton walked onto the stage of an auditorium at the Silicon Valley headquarters of Google. She was accompanied by Google's chief executive officer, Eric Schmidt. They sat down on comfortable white chairs for a chat, sponsored by Women@Google, an employees' organization.

Schmidt, wearing a jacket but not a tie, delivered some introductory remarks. He recounted a decade-old conversation with a Clinton White House aide who had told him that if he thought the president was smart, well, then, "she's smarter." Schmidt went on to praise for its brilliance and comprehensiveness a speech he once heard Hillary make.

Then it was Hillary's turn to address the two hundred or so assembled employees, most of whom were young and female. She thanked Schmidt and returned the praise. Google, she told the audience, was the "best place to work in America," a company that has "revolutionized the way we live, we work, we think."

For the next forty minutes, she answered a series of questions, posed by Schmidt and drawn from e-mails written by Google employees, covering a range of topical issues from Iraq and education to energy, the environment, and health care. The discussion was as cozy and as casual as the setting, and the audience applauded frequently. Schmidt wrapped up the session by asking Hillary what Google could do to help make her vision happen. She replied that the company's technological prowess could be applied to most of the problems she had identified, from health care and energy to education, because "Google links the world."[1]

INDEED IT DID. One year earlier, a highly negative seven-part series about Hillary entitled "The Fraudulent Senator" ricocheted around the world via the Internet. Google had helped make it happen.

The series was first disseminated by a little-known company called New Media Journal, whose publisher, Frank Salvato of Chicago, had tried being a harbormaster and a jazz musician before becoming a Republican media consultant.[2] He had begun his "conservative-leaning" journal in 1998, calling it The Rant. In 2006, he switched to New Media Journal because the old name "wasn't very attractive" for the kind of upscale audience he was seeking.[3] The author of the first two articles, Joan Swirsky, was an award-winning science writer living on Long Island. Her work on Hillary was a "labor of fervor" that, she acknowledged, was a "vicious," "undisguised partisan piece."[4]

The idea for the series, Salvato said, was pitched by businessman Peter Paul, an ex-convict who had organized a lavish fundraiser in Southern California for Hillary's 2000 campaign and then turned against her. When federal criminal investigators began looking into whether the former finance director of Hillary's campaign had underreported the cost of the fund-raiser Paul had hosted, Paul began helping them. He also filed a civil lawsuit against Hillary and Bill over the case.

Hillary's campaign later acknowledged that it had underreported Paul's contributions in 2000 and paid a $35,000 penalty as part of a civil settlement with the Federal Election Commission. Her former finance director was indicted but acquitted. The commission's investigation cleared Hillary of any wrongdoing,[5] and a judge dismissed Paul's civil lawsuit against Hillary.[6]

If Hillary assumed that would be the end of it, she was mistaken. New Media Journal's seven-part series was dominated by Paul's story and accompanying documents. Google labeled it as "news" and featured it in its highly popular four-year-old Google News. Within a few days, the articles climbed the ranks of Google

News to become the second most popular listing about Hillary, making a "big difference" in readership for Salvato.[7] The popularity of the series prompted a documentary released on DVD by another company.[8]

Salvato said that Google News had been regularly picking up his content for more than a year before the Hillary series ran, because he understood the content and format needs of Google News.[9] In this he was not alone: By 2006, media-savvy conservatives were far ahead of their liberal counterparts in using the Internet to bypass the mainstream media and take advantage of the Web's openness. Broadband users were now getting their news more often from the Internet than from traditional media outlets, like newspapers, radio, and television. On the Web, enormous portals like Yahoo! and Google had become more popular news sites than local or national newspapers.[10] The stock market, one way that America keeps score, offered a stark reflection of the rapidly changing media landscape: The market value in 2006 of Google was about fifty times that of the venerable New York Times Company.[11] (It wasn't until the spring of 2006 that the *New York Times* realized that its headlines had often been too vague to be picked up by a Google search.[12])

While most liberals may have needed to play political catch-up when it came to cyberspace hardball, Hillary and Bill were familiar with defending against Internet attacks from the right. The couple had been an online target since their days in the White House, when one of their earliest enemies was Richard Mellon Scaife.

A fourth-generation heir to the Mellon banking fortune, the conservative Scaife lives in the Pittsburgh area. He once told an interviewer that he was a "very private person" and "essentially shy."[13] But he was hardly reticent when it came to the Clintons. Early in the Clinton presidency, Scaife and his family foundations and trusts began financing aggressive investigations of the couple; some led to negative stories and others sharply questioned the official inquiry into the death of Vince Foster. For example, Robert Fiske, the independent counsel who was looking into Foster's death, said his office "was deluged with postcards, all of them identical," declaring that any finding of suicide "would be one of the greatest cover-ups of all time."[14] Most of the postcards came from California,[15] where a center backed by a Scaife-related foundation was promoting articles questioning the inquiry into Foster's death.[16] Scaife, for his part, considered Foster's death "the Rosetta stone to the whole Clinton administration."[17]

By 1995, Scaife-backed projects were themselves the subject of scrutiny. Two White House lawyers, Mark Fabiani and Chris Lehane, both of whom were responsible for rebutting or controlling the negative stories about Bill and Hillary, had become alarmed by the rumors about the death of Foster. On the fourth floor of the Old Executive Office Building, across the street from the White House, the two young Harvard Law School graduates set up a computer office—dubbed the "Internet room"—and began to use the new information revolution unfolding in cyberspace to compile information on the Clintons' enemies.[18] The end result of their work was a 332-page report, completed that year, showing how projects funded by Scaife and others on the right had "seized upon the Internet as a means of communicating" and turned "fringe stories into legitimate subjects of coverage by mainstream media."[19] Hillary, who was keenly interested in the project, was told about its findings,[20] and the report was sent to scores of mainstream reporters in hopes of discouraging them from picking up the Foster accounts.

Fabiani and Lehane, sometimes called the "masters of disaster" for their shrewd and swift damage control, considered their effort a success. But the questions about Foster's death, even the possibility that he was murdered, lived on. For example, the first article in the New Media Journal series asserted that "the case for his murder has been made persuasively."[21]

SEVERAL DAYS BEFORE Bill's second inauguration, Hillary bemoaned the lack of "counterbalance" to the "quite effective" effort by "right-wing think tanks and the right-wing publications" to bombard the mainstream media with advocacy of its issues.[22] Back in 1996, Google was not even a corporation. Nor were the White House lawyers paying much attention to a new Internet columnist named Matt Drudge. But Fabiani and Lehane's work resonated with Hillary.

One year later, Drudge, who had become, in the words of the New York Times, the "country's reigning mischief maker" with his Web site, the Drudge Report,[23] disclosed that Newsweek had held a story about Ken Starr's investigation into Bill Clinton's relationship with Monica Lewinsky.

Within days, Drudge's scoop led to the widespread disclosure of the new inquiry that Starr was pursuing. A few weeks later, Hillary was asked if "this new media is necessarily a good thing." She called the technological developments introduced by the Internet "exciting," but she also worried that "without any kind of editing function or gate-keeping function" it might be too easy to "create a falsehood about somebody" that would easily become "multiplied many times over."[24]

Joseph Farah found the technological developments exciting too. Farah, a target of the 1995 study done by Fabiani and Lehane, ran the Western Journalism Center, a Sacramento organization that had promoted articles criticizing the official findings about Foster's death. Inspired by Hillary's remarks and the disclosure of the White House study by Fabiani and Lehane in 1997, Farah realized, "These people are onto something. This is a good idea." The White House dossier, Farah believed, revealed the opportunities for conservatives to get their message out in a media environment dominated by liberal-leaning journalists. "This," Farah concluded, "is their weak point." A self-described "Clinton hater,"[25] he set up WorldNetDaily, an independent daily news organization that publishes exclusively in cyberspace. Its headquarters are in northern Virginia.

Meanwhile, Drudge's activities were inspiring another writer, Chris Ruddy, whose articles about Foster's death were promoted by Farah's Western Journalism Center. Ruddy noticed that Drudge's Web site was linking to his articles and took him out for a drink at a bar in Los Angeles. If Drudge, a one-man operation, could have national impact, Ruddy figured that he and his friends who disliked the Clinton administration "could have a bigger impact" with their own Web site.[26] Scaife's Pittsburgh newspaper, the *Pittsburgh Tribune-Review*, was publishing Ruddy's articles, so Ruddy came up with the idea of bringing him in. The two met over coffee at the Four Seasons hotel in Georgetown on January 21, 1998, the day the Monica Lewinsky story broke in the *Washington Post*.[27] (Later that night, Scaife had his picture taken with Hillary and Bill at the White House, at a ceremony honoring the building's historical preservation.[28])

Scaife was supportive of Ruddy but not yet excited about the potential of the new media venture. "He didn't gravitate to it immediately,"[29] Ruddy recalled, so instead the conservative journalist landed his first seed money ($25,000) from the family of William J. Casey, the former head of the CIA under President Reagan.

Ruddy called his venture NewsMax and knew time was of the essence. "I wanted to start NewsMax while the Clinton impeachment was under way." So the site, based in West Palm Beach, Florida, went live in September 1998. By then Scaife had decided to invest $2 million, about 13 percent of Ruddy's initial capital.[30] The fact that Ruddy could raise $15 million for his start-up in nine months demonstrates the ease with which journalists could attract enormous funding from wealthy conservatives.

NewsMax quickly became one of the most widely read Web sites for Republican-leaning audiences, with about 2 million visitors per month and an e-mail subscription list of 1.5 million.[31] And the audience for such sites was significant enough that several could thrive. For his part, Drudge hardly faded away, even after a story he posted on his site in 2004 about John Kerry's supposed fling with a campaign worker didn't pan out. (Drudge once acknowledged that he "can't check" a lot of the "hot news" he publishes, so "you've got to allow some room for mistakes."[32]) The Drudge Report still attracts millions of readers, many of whom use it as a gateway to find stories published by mainstream news organizations. For example, the Drudge Report is the single largest driver of online readers to the Web site of the *Washington Post*.[33]

And whether or not what they published was true, it had undeniable impact. Some law-enforcement officials and journalists believe that stories in 2000 by Farah's WorldNetDaily on then–presidential candidate Al Gore's political dealings in Tennessee, which were picked up by smaller papers in the state, played a role in Gore's loss.[34] The math was certainly clear: If Gore had won Tennessee's eleven electoral votes, he would have been elected president.

Just as 1992's election inspired conservatives like Scaife to get involved, the 2000 election was a wake-up call to some wealthy liberals about the reach and influence of the other side's information infrastructure. One of those who responded was Herb Sandler, who, in concert with his wife, Marion, is an enthusiastic supporter of left-leaning causes. At the time, the Sandlers ran World Savings, one of the nation's leading savings and loans. Sandler was determined to create an ideological counterweight to conservative think tanks like the Heritage Foundation. From their base in Oakland, California, the couple tried to apply tough-minded business-management techniques to progressive philanthropy.[35]

Meanwhile, John Podesta, the last chief of staff to President Clinton, had coauthored a memo exploring the need for a liberal think tank. The memo found its way to Sandler, and the two men met in Washington. Podesta, a gaunt marathon runner in his fifties, had long worked the trenches of Washington's public-policy wars. Sandler, a lanky California businessman with big ideas, was a generation older. Both men were trained as lawyers and knew how to negotiate. Podesta agreed to head up the new entity, and Sandler became the organization's largest donor.[36] Another billionaire supporter of leftist causes, George Soros, also kicked in financial support.

The new tax-exempt group opened its doors in downtown Washington in 2003 as the Center for American Progress. Hillary played a "formative" role in the discussions that preceded the center's launch.[37] She realized that the right had "created an infrastructure that has come to dominate political discourse"[38] and greeted the center as a "welcome effort to fill that void"[39] and create "some new intellectual capital"[40] for her side.

Once its roots were established, the center broadened its financial base by seeking donations from a group of left-leaning donors that came together in 2005 under the umbrella of an organization called the Democracy Alliance.[41] Some alliance members are close to Hillary; by 2007, the alliance was run by Kelly Craighead, a longtime member of Hillaryland.[42] The alliance has some firm rules: Members must donate at least $250,000 per year to approved causes, and the groups seeking their backing must submit proposals to the alliance for screening and agree to keep secret the source of their donations.[43]

The center, though ostensibly nonpartisan, attracted several veterans of the Clinton administration, and conservatives soon regarded it as an important piece of the Clinton empire. However, as Podesta pointed out, although "the right describes us as Hillary's think tank," the center's interaction and influence are wider, "with a broad range of actors."[44] He has a point. In 2006, for example, the organization's timetable for withdrawal of American troops from Iraq was quicker than Hillary's and was coordinated with other Senate Democrats.[45]

But the foundation's critics are correct that Podesta has strong links to Hillary. In 1993, as staff secretary to President Clinton, Podesta had prepared a report on the travel office affair that mentioned Hillary, but his investigation and final report ignored or downplayed parts of Hillary's role in the affair.[46] Podesta also served on the secret task force in 2006 that advised Hillary on energy issues.[47]

Soon after the Center for American Progress opened, it began collaborating with Hillary and her staff, prompting one former Hillary aide to describe the relationship between Hillary and the center as "very close."[48] A key adviser to Hillary, Neera Tanden, has been a center employee in between jobs at Hillary's Senate office and on her campaign committee. After Tanden was hired by Hillary's presidential campaign in early 2007, she was joined by Judd Legum, the center's research director.[49]

Podesta and his center achieved the goal of their backers; the group's studies and officials are frequently cited by both the mainstream media and the increasingly active blogosphere. Podesta is a regular guest on network talk shows. When asked on one of them in late 2006, a few weeks before she had announced her intentions, whether he was ready to support Hillary for president, he enthusiastically endorsed her.[50]

GOOGLE SAYS ITS 4,500 English-language news sources represent a "Novel Approach to News" and are presented "without regard to political viewpoint or ideology."[51] Yet Google executives know that many of their "news sources" may be ideologically driven. They believe a reader can sift through biased news and "make up your own mind" as to its value.[52] Google does review sources before they are included in Google News—to see, for example, if a source is more than a one-person blog—but the company's review does not reach the level of screening the stories themselves.

"We can't have an army of people" screening news stories, Steve Langdon, a spokesman for the company, explained, because "it's cost prohibitive." But there is also a philosophical reason: Even if Google "found a way to screen" stories, it wouldn't, Langdon added.[53] As a result, some bloggers have found it "trivially easy to insert content into Google News."[54]

Schmidt said the company is working on more sophisticated formulas to help users "figure out what's likely to be true," so that "society will eventually come to understand that just because it's written on the Internet does not mean it's true."[55] But for now, when a conservative author, as was done in part of the New Media Journal series, writes that "the Clinton Political Syndicate is nothing more than a gang of street thugs,"[56] it is carried worldwide on Google News, and readers must then judge the article's journalistic merit for themselves. NewsMax, which has the second-largest Republican audience in cyberspace after Rush Limbaugh's Web site,[57] found its way onto Google News an average of fifty times a day at the end of 2006.[58] Even an "exclusive commentary" from WorldNetDaily that labeled former president Jimmy Carter "human scum" wound up featured in Google News in late 2006.[59] On the left, Google News frequently cites the newsletter of the Center for American Progress or postings by Media Matters, but it doesn't alert readers that they come with a point of view.[60]

"There's so much kibitzing about who I am, and what I believe, and what I've done," Hillary said on the eve of her declaration as a presidential candidate. So she said she wanted to "make sure the record is clear" for voters to make up their minds.[61] Given that, Hillary, of all the presidential hopefuls, may have the most to gain or lose from the changing media landscape. For all her fame, she thinks her public image is shaped primarily by gossip, the kind of information perfectly suited to the Internet.

As for Fabiani and Lehane, the two who first pointed out for Hillary the threats and opportunities of the Web, the pair now run a California-based consultancy that advises clients about crisis management. One of the companies they work for is Google.[62]

DURING HER CHAT on Google's campus in February 2007, Hillary succinctly described the key to the company's success: making information "accessible to us." One week later, Google's online video unit, YouTube, announced a nonpartisan voter-education initiative. The press release quoted Hillary as saying the Web offers a "new wave of opportunity for all Americans."[63]

Just four days after the announcement, an anonymous poster seized that "opportunity." In the process, he made clear both the power and the peril, for Hillary, of the new technology. A video entitled "Vote Different" was created and then posted on YouTube by someone calling himself ParkRidge47 — a reference to Hillary's childhood home and birth year. The seventy-four-second clip mixed footage of Hillary's speeches with the classic "Big Brother" ad from 1984 that had introduced Apple's Macintosh computers to the world. The message was clear: Hillary is "Big Sister."[64]

The video ended with a promise that the Democratic primary season in 2008 "won't be like 1984." After a brief display of a caricature of the Apple logo, the clip ended with the address of Barack Obama's campaign Web site.

Within two days, the video had been seen by more than one hundred thousand viewers on YouTube. Before long, mention of it was picked up by newspapers, television networks, and cable channels. Three weeks after it was posted, its audience had reached nearly three million.[65]

The success of the anti-Hillary clip shows "you don't need lots of money to make a viral message spread,"[66] according to Micah Sifry, who tracks candidates online. Hillary, when asked whether the video should be taken down, told the New York cable channel NY1 she didn't really have an opinion: "You know, that's for somebody else to decide."[67] But she certainly could not have been happy with it.

Obama denied having anything to do with the clip, though he did so ingeniously, claiming, with a laugh, that it was far beyond his campaign's technological abilities.[68] In fact, the clip had been produced on no budget by a single person. "Considering Hillary Clinton's biggest video [her announcement for president] has only received twelve thousand views on YouTube," ParkRidge47, later identified as thirty-three-year-old Web designer Phil de Vellis, said in a widely circulated e-mail message, "I'd say the grassroots has won the first round."[69]

"I made the ad on a Sunday afternoon in my apartment using my personal equipment (a Mac and some software), uploaded it to YouTube, and sent links around to blogs," de Vellis further explained. "The specific point of the ad was that Obama represents a new kind of politics, and that Senator Clinton's 'conversation' is disingenuous. And the underlying point was that the old political machine no longer holds all the power."[70]

That de Vellis's clip became so popular so quickly revealed a crucial aspect of the new media climate. It also revealed something else: The video worked not only because it was clever, but because it spoke to the way some saw Hillary — cold, bossy, stern, and controlling. Barack Obama was seen as none of those things — and in bits and bytes and dollars and cents, that was becoming increasingly apparent, and threatening to the Clintons and their long-held ambition to put Hillary in the White House.

"I Don't Feel No Ways Tired"

IN THE AUTUMN OF 2003, Greg Craig, a classmate of Hillary's and Bill's at Yale Law School, received a phone call from Vernon Jordan. During Bill Clinton's presidency, Jordan was regarded as the ultimate Washington insider; later he opened an office in New York to facilitate his corporate networking. This time, Jordan was rounding up the "regular establishment types" for a fund-raising event at his home in Washington, DC, for a then-little-known state senator from Illinois named Barack Obama. Obama, forty-two years old, was pursuing the Democratic nomination in the race for a U.S. Senate seat from Illinois.[1]

"I didn't know who he was," Craig said, though he accepted the invitation and wrote a $500 check to Obama's campaign.[2]

Several dozen people gathered at Jordan's house, about a block away from the Clintons' Washington home, on a late October evening to meet the young candidate. It was the first Washington fundraiser for Obama, who was born in Honolulu to a Kenyan father and a mother from Kansas. A graduate of Harvard Law School, where he was elected the first black president of its law review in its 104-year history, he had served in the Illinois House, then the state Senate. After hearing Obama speak that night from the staircase in Jordan's spacious home, Craig came away "very, very impressed with him."[3]

Craig is considered one of the top blue-chip lawyers in Washington, perhaps best known for leading President Clinton's defense during the impeachment proceedings in the House and the Senate. He has known the Clintons for more than thirty-five years; in 1971, Hillary asked Craig if she and Bill could sublet his apartment in New Haven.[4] In the 1960s, Craig, who earned his undergraduate degree at Harvard, was at the forefront of the civil-rights and antiwar movements. He registered black voters in Mississippi, tutored black children in Harlem, and was recognized nationally as Harvard's leading student against the war.[5] Hillary had made room for him in her suite of offices in the West Wing after he agreed to join the president's legal team in 1998.[6]

Obama ended up winning the nomination and the seat, and after he was sworn in as a U.S. senator in January 2005, Craig saw him several times around Washington. At the annual Robert F. Kennedy awards ceremony in November of that year, Craig found Obama — and his message that evening — irresistible. "His is not an angry voice, it's not a weak voice," said Craig. "It's a strong voice, unique in American politics."[7]

In the capital, Craig had a reputation for being straightforward, dedicated, and loyal. "There's no one I'd rather be with in a crisis," said Ethel Kennedy, who was impressed with Craig's assistance of his former boss Senator Edward M. Kennedy before he testified at the 1991 Palm Beach rape trial of his nephew William Kennedy Smith. "He's so rational, says what he has to say very clearly, and he's always on your side."[8]

As Hillary was privately considering embarking on a historic bid for the presidency, she probably never imagined that her law school classmate would not only leave her side but end up helping to persuade her most formidable adversary to run against her.

IN EARLY 2006, Washington, DC, was undergoing one of its periodic spasms of self-loathing. This happens every few years: The capital takes a close look at itself in the mirror, blanches at the soiled image, and then does virtually nothing to change it. The freewheeling global junketeering of super-lobbyist Jack Abramoff had outraged millions of Americans.[9] The scandal pushed congressional Republicans back on their heels, and Hillary and her colleagues in the Senate seized the initiative. On the night of her reelection, Hillary herself declared that she hoped Democrats could offer America "an end to the culture of corruption and the dominance of special interests."[10] Of course, this goal was much easier said than done.

The Democrats' attempts to try to reform Washington's ways began in late January 2006. Hillary sent a memo to her fellow senators alerting them to an "Honest Leadership" meeting that was being held by the Steering and Outreach Committee, which she headed. As Hillary described it, the mission of the meeting — or, at least, the hope — was that the senators would embrace "real reform, including new and aggressive actions that will address unethical lobbying activities, and increase government openness and accountability."[11]

Although Hillary sent out the invitations, the meeting's chairman was Senator Obama, the Democrats' point man on lobbying reform, an assignment he'd been given by Harry Reid. At that time, Obama had been in the Senate only a year, but his natural political skills had already begun to capture the fascination and imagination of many Americans, and he was increasingly described with superlatives and clichés that seemed foreign to Washington. He was, said some, a "rock star."[12]

The Senate gathering was coordinated by Dana E. Singiser, the lawyer who had succeeded Jodi Sakol in 2004 as staff director of the steering committee. The participants were mostly from the liberal side of Washington's ethics watchers.[13]

The meeting, on February 1, 2006, in the Lyndon B. Johnson Room, on the second floor of the Capitol, began without Hillary. Several other senators were there for at least part of the session, including Reid, Mark Dayton, and Russ Feingold, the architect of the 2002 bill to reform campaign finance.[14]

Hillary finally arrived about twenty minutes after the meeting had begun. Shortly after she took her seat, someone mentioned the question of public financing for presidential campaigns, and she quipped, "You mean people are running for president?" The room filled with laughter, including Obama's.[15] At the time, Hillary was assumed by everyone to be a likely presidential aspirant; so, too, was Feingold. Few at the meeting were thinking then that the chair, Barack Obama, still wet behind the ears politically, would emerge in less than a year as Hillary's most dangerous threat for the nomination.

At the meeting, some of the attendees strongly pushed for public financing of elections. Hillary and Obama offered some theoretical support but were noncommittal in the end. "They were both sort of making excuses," one participant recalled.[16] Another person at the meeting said he was not at all surprised that Hillary did not embrace any of the proposed changes and even seemed resistant to the idea of campaign finance reform. The Clintons, he said, are "addicted to the money chase." As for Obama, few picked up the strong signal of his own foot-dragging.[17]

TWO WEEKS AFTER THE MEETING, on the frigid evening of February 15, 2006, the most ambitious money-raising effort for a presidential candidate would be launched in a sumptuous Georgetown home. Hillary Rodham Clinton was the guest of honor. The host was Elizabeth Bagley, President Clinton's ambassador to Portugal, a friend and confidant of Hillary's, and an aggressive fund-raiser who had brought in millions for the Clintons and the Democratic Party. A dinner of lamb and striped sea bass was served for more than a hundred of Hillary's most loyal and important fund-raisers, the culmination of a day-long slate of activities.[18] Hillary intended the day's events to be a secretive "first step" in her bid to seize exclusive commitments from the Democrats' most aggressive donors. The commitments were ostensibly for her Senate reelection campaign, but most guests knew that Hillary intended the dinner as a way to get them to commit to raising a record amount for her presumed presidential run. It seemed to work: Dozens of guests that night told Hillary, and Bill, that if Hillary ran for president, as nearly everyone assumed she would, they were committed to Hillary, and to Hillary alone.[19]

Hillary's coy refusal to say whether she would run bemused several of her friends. "Of course she's running," said a longtime friend of Hillary's in early 2006. "Beginning in January [2007], I'll be...working full-time to help Hillary become president." The friend laughed, adding, "It will be all Hillary, all the time."[20]

That slogan amounted to the secret marching orders of Hillary and her top fund-raisers, led by Hillary's '08 campaign chairman, Terry McAuliffe, the gregarious and energetic Clinton fund-raiser who served as the chairman of the Democratic National Committee when John Kerry ran for president and lost.

As early as February 2006, nearly a year before her formal announcement, Hillary began personally exerting pressure on fund-raisers to sign with her exclusively and to forgo raising money for any other Democratic hopeful.[21] In the earliest days of a presidential campaign, it is not unusual for front-runners to apply pressure to secure exclusive commitments from fund-raisers. Still, Hillary seized an enormous advantage over her rivals by securing those commitments nearly a year before she would announce the formation of her presidential exploratory committee.[22]

Hillary's unmatched abilities to open new financial channels as well as to tap into the record-shattering campaign fund-raisers who had helped Bill win two terms were all on display on that February day in Washington. As Hillary would do often in the coming months, she turned to her husband to serve as the marquee attraction for new money-raisers with deep pockets.

Bill, for instance, was the bait that helped convince C. Paul Johnson, a multimillionaire retired banker living in Napa Valley, in California, to take a flight to attend the Georgetown dinner. Johnson's introduction to the Clinton camp began a few weeks earlier, on a West Coast swing by Hillary to raise money for her Senate reelection campaign and those of several fellow Democrats. Hillary started in Seattle on Friday, January 27, at a luncheon for more than twelve hundred people at Qwest Field, followed by a private reception in Seattle. The events raised money for both Senator Clinton and Senator Maria Cantwell of Washington and, like most of Hillary's fund-raisers, were "closed to the press."[23]

Hillary then traveled south on the coastal money trail, first to Portland, Oregon, and then to northern California. The weekend also included private fund-raisers in the Bay Area. One, on Saturday afternoon in Napa Valley, caught the eye of the local newspaper, unaccustomed to an East Coast officeholder, let alone a former First Lady, trolling for dollars in their hometown. The paper's editor tried to attend the lunch but was "deemed unwelcome."[24]

Sitting next to Hillary at the Napa Valley luncheon was Paul Johnson, the retired banker. He was new to Hillary's world and came away with "a really good feeling." He was especially impressed by her "candor and sincerity."[25] She invited him to the February 15 gathering in Washington—sweetening the pot by promising an introduction to Bill.[26]

THROUGHOUT THE HOMESTRETCH to the midterm elections in the fall of 2006, several key members of Hillaryland looked down on the possible, though seemingly unlikely, presidential candidacy of Barack Obama.

"Obama is ridiculous," a longtime Hillary friend snapped in the autumn of 2006.[27]

What Hillary and her top advisers did not know at the time was that one of Hillary's old friends was urging Obama to run. That summer, Greg Craig had attended some fund-raisers for Obama in Washington. At one of them, the two discussed Obama's hesitancy about seeking the presidency. "I'm brand-new here in Washington," Obama told Craig, "and it would be presumptuous of me to arrive so soon and run for president."

"Yes, it would be presumptuous," Craig replied, telling Obama his newness in Washington was an asset, not a liability, and he should reconsider his reluctance. Craig felt the longer Obama stayed in Washington, the more he would be afflicted by "Senate-itis," where he would have to face difficult votes "every other day and where individual senators have to distinguish themselves from each other."[28]

Vernon Jordan did think Obama was being too presumptuous. Over a three-hour dinner at Jordan's home that November, the two men discussed the future. Jordan, a civil-rights leader in the 1960s, told Obama, "To everything there is a season, and I don't think this is your season." Obama listened respectfully, but Jordan believed "he had made up his mind by then" to run. "You have to do what you have to do," he told the young senator. "I won't be with you."[29]

By the end of 2006, Obama's stock had soared. There was a gush of enthusiasm that greeted him everywhere he went stumping for fellow Democrats. His second book, The Audacity of Hope, was at the top of the national bestseller lists for weeks. That December, just before Obama's first trip to New Hampshire, Craig helped prepare a lengthy memo explaining how the Illinois senator could navigate the political landscape of that crucial state.[30]

Obama called Craig to thank him for the memo, and Craig told him he could count on his support. "I'll be getting back to you," Obama replied.[31]

Obama spent the Christmas break in Hawaii, talking over his future with his wife and two daughters. When he returned to Washington after New Year's, he decided to run.

Obama began his quest to become the nation's first black president on February 10, 2007, in Springfield, Illinois, at the Old State House, where, in 1858, Abraham Lincoln had delivered his famous condemnation of slavery, in which he declared, "A house divided against itself cannot stand."[32] Wearing an overcoat but no gloves on an unseasonably frigid morning, Obama portrayed his quixotic candidacy less as a campaign and more as a generational movement, just as Bill Clinton and Al Gore had done in 1992. Craig,

watching the speech back in Washington on television, was gratified to hear that Obama had also adopted his argument that his
lack of experience should be considered a potent political asset.[33]

"I recognize there is a certain presumptuousness—a certain
audacity—to this announcement," Obama said. "I know I haven't
spent a lot of time learning the ways of Washington. But I've been
there long enough to know that the ways of Washington must
change." Obama's comments about Washington elicited some of the
loudest and most sustained applause of his two-minute speech.[34]

A few weeks earlier, Greg Craig had written a short note to Hillary explaining his decision to support Obama for president. She
did not reply.[35]

EVERY SEAT IN EVERY PEW of the New Birth Missionary Baptist
Church was filled on a chilly Tuesday in February 2006. The crowd
had come to the big church outside Atlanta to pay their last respects
to Coretta Scott King. In the church's center well, a flower-draped
mahogany casket contained the body of the First Lady of America's
civil-rights movement. It was surrounded by her three grown children, four American presidents, and more than ten thousand other
loved ones, friends, and admirers. President George W. Bush, his
father, President George Herbert Walker Bush, and President Jimmy
Carter had each stood at the podium to deliver tributes to Coretta
Scott King's life and legacy. The congregation had responded to
each man with polite, respectful applause. Then Bishop Eddie L.
Long raised the microphone to his lips and said, "I now present the
Honorable William J. Clinton and—"

A roaring ovation thundered down from the congregation,
drowning out the rest of the bishop's introduction. Long went on to
say "—and the Honorable Hillary R. Clinton, Senator," but by then
no one could hear him. As Bill and Hillary walked toward the pulpit with their hands clasped, everyone in the predominantly black
congregation stood up, cheering and waving; men whistled and
hollered and women of all ages screamed and called Bill's name.
Mrs. King's memorial service had suddenly become a pep rally.

As the waves of cheers kept rolling, Bill stood behind the
podium and raised his hands, once, then twice, signaling the crowd
for quiet. Hillary stood to her husband's left, beaming at him and
nodding and mouthing thank-yous to the crowd, though there was
no mistaking that the giant gush of love and affection was not for
her but for her husband.

Finally, the applause waned and the mourners retook their seats. "I thank you for that wonderful reception," Bill said, adding with a sly grin, "You may not feel like repeatin' it after you hear what I've got to say." Everyone laughed. Looking over his right shoulder and leaning into the podium, the former president then nodded his head at the church's pastor and drawled, "Rev." Again, everyone laughed.

"We are honored to be here," Bill said. "I'm honored to be here with my president...and my former presidents...and...and, uh..." The crowd was quiet only a moment, until Bill moved his left hand slightly toward Hillary, as if his next few words might just be *and my next president.* The crowd certainly interpreted the gesture that way, responding with another ovation. Bill quickly said, "Nooooooo, nooooooo," and then Hillary shook her head *no, no, no.* But the cheering did not stop until Hillary put up both of her hands and then moved them down repeatedly in front of her. The motion seemed to say, no, this is neither the time nor the place for any talk of *that,* but her husband's perfect setup had served its purpose of talking without saying, right here and right now.

Bill paused a moment and, gesturing toward the casket, said, "This is a woman, as well as a symbol, as well as an embodiment of her husband's legacy, as well as the developer of her own."

Of course, the former president was speaking about Coretta Scott King. But Bill Clinton could easily have been referring to the woman standing by his side.

He had promised to keep his remarks brief, but Bill Clinton is incapable of keeping that kind of pledge. As his speech stretched on, Hillary began sighing. At first, her exhales were barely noticeable. But as she sighed again and again, her deep breaths were impossible to miss.

At last, after ten minutes, it was her turn. Her hand found her husband's, and she held it atop the podium. Whether that handclasp was about affection or need, it was indisputable that Hillary, in front of a throng of people and a national television audience, was about to follow the toughest act in American politics.

"As we are called," she began, reading from her prepared text, "each of us must decide whether to answer that call by saying, 'Send me.' And when I think of Coretta Scott King, I think of a woman who lived out her calling."[36]

Hillary's flat delivery sounded even more monotonous after the folksy lullaby of Bill Clinton's southern purr. If his eulogy was a casual hymn to Mrs. King, Hillary's was a scripted monologue she delivered with her eyes cast mostly downward.

This was not her crowd. The fact that Hillary had a speaking role in the memorial service in the first place was as conspicuous as it was surprising. No other presidential spouse joined her husband at the podium. The only other senator to speak that day was Edward M. Kennedy of Massachusetts, who had had a decades-long friendship with Mrs. King. A person close to the King family said that Hillary was included in the program only at the insistence of Bill Clinton's representatives. "She was not even on the family's radar screen—they wanted Bill Clinton," the King family confidant said. "They love him, but when they heard that he wanted her to speak too, they said, 'OK, that's fine.'"[37] At the memorial service, Hillary told the congregation that Mrs. King had "lived her life as an extension of her faith and conviction." The senator paused, and her tone took on a folksy lilt: "Now, when she met this young divinity student, and he told her what Bill has just reminded us, and proclaimed that he was looking for a woman like her to be his wife, I can imagine that she thought for a minute, *What am I getting myself into?* And, in fact, she waited six months to give him an answer. Because she had to have known in her heart that she wasn't just marrying a young man, but she was bringing her calling to be joined with his. As they began their marriage, and their partnership, it could not have been easy." Like her husband's words before her, Hillary's speech could have applied to the Clintons themselves.

EVEN AFTER OBAMA'S announcement, several members of Hillaryland continued to view his candidacy as a nonthreat.[38] At least one California-based Hillary fund-raiser downplayed the idea that her campaign was worried about Obama's usurping fund-raisers and donors. "I have never raised money so easily," the fund-raiser said. "People are pumped up. It's rolling in—people are maxing out, hundreds of people....Barack Obama—it's not his time. It's her time. She's seen as a historic figure. People want to be a part of it."[39]

There was one notable exception among these enthusiastic Hillary supporters: Bill Clinton, who had recognized early on that Obama was the candidate among the current crop with the best chance of derailing his wife's shot at cruising to the nomination.[40]

Obama's early momentum was only one reason that the money race was even more important. The other was the front-loaded primary schedule. Because, for the first time in history, as many as twenty states were slated to hold primaries by February 5, 2008, locking up fund-raisers, money, and momentum became more critical in this presidential campaign than it had been in any previous one.[41]

Despite a groundswell of early enthusiasm, Hillary was still not satisfied.[42] She decided to intensify the pressure on both fund-raisers and donors to make exclusive commitments to her campaign. McAuliffe and others spread the word that if they signed up early and exclusively with Hillary, it would mean more to her than if they signed up later after a brief financial flirtation with Obama.[43] At a book party in Los Angeles, which was attended by a few hundred potential supporters and donors, McAuliffe joked that it was important for people to give exclusively to Hillary, borrowing a famous line of George W. Bush's to announce, "You're either with us or against us."[44]

McAuliffe's delivery of the line might have been comedic, but behind the scenes Hillary's finance people were not laughing. Obama had shown sudden adeptness at recruiting some of Bill and Hillary's old moneyed friends from Hollywood—something that deeply worried several of Hillary's chief fund-raisers. The scrum made national headlines after the billionaire David Geffen signed on with Obama. Geffen, a cofounder and partner in the film studio DreamWorks, had been one of Bill's most unabashed financial supporters, raising a total of $18 million for the Clintons and the Democrats across the 1990s. But, as a longtime California-based Democratic fund-raiser put it, "He's always been more of a Bill guy than a Hil guy."[45]

In mid-February, a week prior to the Academy Awards, Geffen held a fund-raising dinner for forty of his friends to honor Obama at his mansion in Beverly Hills, built by studio magnate Jack Warner. The take: $1.3 million. One fund-raiser pronounced Hillary "flipping out" about the overwhelming enthusiasm for Obama in Hollywood—territory that had been nearly unanimously devoted to the Clintons since 1992.[46]

"Whoever is the [Democratic] nominee is going to win," Geffen told the *New York Times's* Maureen Dowd, "and I don't think that another incredibly polarizing figure, no matter how smart she is and no matter how ambitious she is—and God knows, is there anybody more ambitious than Hillary Clinton?—can bring the country together." Geffen added that Obama was "inspirational, and he's not from the Bush royal family or the Clinton royal family."[47]

When Howard Wolfson, Hillary's communications consultant,

read Dowd's column early in the morning of February 21, 2007, he was furious.[48] Wolfson was especially angry about this remark by Geffen: "Everybody in politics lies but [the Clintons] do it with such ease, it's troubling."[49]

After consulting Hillary,[50] Wolfson quickly put out a statement that criticized Geffen for "viciously and personally attacking Senator Clinton and her husband."[51] He added that there was no place in the campaign for "the politics of personal destruction," pinned the blame for Geffen's outspokenness on Obama, and called on the senator's campaign to return Geffen's money. Obama decided to take the high road, insisting that he did not want to "get in the middle of a disagreement between the Clintons and someone who was once one of their biggest supporters."[52]

That night, a small group of fund-raisers for various Democratic candidates gathered in New York to try to reduce the mounting anger and divisiveness.[53] One of the lessons the Democrats had learned from Republicans was that parties that stuck together and spent the energy attacking their external rivals did much better than those that spent their time infighting. But Hillary's camp was not about to wave the white flag. Her attack on Geffen was indirectly meant to put Obama on his heels. One strategist described it as "an important warning shot" that reflected the unease in the Hillary camp about Obama.[54] Those worries were well-founded. Hillary's pollster, Mark Penn, detected an alarming pattern in the weeks after the spat: Hillary was suddenly and dramatically losing support among African American voters, a trend that one strategist blamed on Hillary's confrontation with Obama over the Geffen fund-raiser.[55] In January 2007, Hillary had been leading Obama among black voters by 60 percent to 20 percent, but by late February, Obama was leading among blacks, 44 percent to 33 percent. In certain key states, including South Carolina and Georgia, Obama's surge among blacks was even more pronounced.[56]

"They infuriated the African Americans," said a Democratic strategist who is a close friend of Hillary's. "They mishandled it.... They gave [Obama] standing, and they made him an African American martyr. It looked like an attack. This is right out of Southern Politics 101 — you don't give blacks the opportunity to be martyred, which is what they did."[57]

One person close to both Clintons said Bill thought the contretemps over the Geffen fund-raiser was a serious misstep on the part of Hillary's campaign: "Bill was livid about it. He was very upset at the attack. He thought it was dumb."[58] The former president had to be "more involved" in Hillary's campaign, concluded one longtime strategist, complaining that the attack on Obama "would never have happened" if Bill had been consulted.[59] But there was only so much Bill could do. In the end, it was Hillary's race, and she'd run it her way.

IN MARCH 2007, Bill appeared with Hillary at three campaign fund-raisers in New York, Washington, and then Los Angeles. ("This is cool—I get to introduce Hillary," he said with obvious glee at the Marriott Wardman Park Hotel in Washington.) Each time, he enthusiastically endorsed his wife and appeared more than happy to hand her the leadership torch, just as he had seemed tempted to do at the Coretta Scott King memorial.

"We elect a president if the person running would be the best president," Bill told a jubilant crowd of one thousand contributors at the Sheraton in midtown Manhattan. "You will never find anybody that will do it better than her."[60]

Such events are an essential—perhaps *the* essential—part of a campaign. And Hillary's reluctance to embrace a movement to change the campaign finance system is hardly surprising. Since she entered the Senate in 2001, no senator has raised more than she has—$51.5 million, according to the Center for Responsive Politics.[61] For her 2008 presidential campaign, Hillary set an ambitious fund-raising goal for money raised through the Democratic primaries: $100 million.[62] One fund-raiser said that he believed that the goal would easily be met and could exceed $125 million, which would shatter the record set in 2004 by President Bush.[63] (In order to reach this target, Hillary decided to bypass the presidential campaign public-financing system, just as George W. Bush had done in 2000 and 2004.) She was not the only one hitting up supporters. Her campaign's fund-raisers were asking contributors to give the maximum amount for both the primary and general elections: $4,600.[64] Meanwhile, Bill attends numerous private fund-raising events around the country with the most generous contributors. He has also picked up where she left off on "religious outreach." And he frequently works the phones on her behalf, calling on-the-fence Democrats to "close the deal," as he did in early 2007 in South Carolina and other early primary states.[65]

Unlike Hillary, Obama had decided not to accept donations from political action committees and lobbyists. Though on the one hand politically astute, it was a somewhat risky short-term move. He was hoping that a grassroots fund-raising effort targeting small donors and first-time contributors would help him at least appear to be competitive in the "money primary" against Hillary.[66] But the big donations often come from the very interests Obama was refusing to deal with.

Nevertheless, Obama had little difficulty raising money. "It's not a matter of fund-raising, it's a matter of managing the huge number of people who are trying to contribute," marveled Greg Craig. "The most difficult part of fund-raising in the Obama camp is to schedule his time—there's a huge demand for his time. There is no limitation other than his time."[67]

Within days of Hillary's clash with Obama, the two found themselves, for the first time, on the same patch of the campaign trail, in Selma, Alabama, to commemorate the forty-second anniversary of the famous "Bloody Sunday" march against racial segregation on March 7, 1965. Protesters had been determined to march fifty miles to Montgomery, Alabama, but they were stopped by troopers, many on horseback, at Selma's Edmund Pettus Bridge. The bloody clash sent seventeen demonstrators to the hospital, including John Lewis, one of the organizers of the march who is now a U.S. congressman from Georgia. For blacks and civil-rights advocates, Selma is sacred ground in the civil-rights struggle, having spurred the passage of the Voting Rights Act.

Obama had been invited to commemorate the Bloody Sunday anniversary weeks earlier, and Hillary was invited a week or so before the event. Her presence was perhaps the most dramatic evidence that she was no longer taking Obama lightly. As one longtime Hillary friend noted about her campaign, "They were not taking him that seriously and now they are. They are concerned about him. He's a legitimate threat."[68]

From the pulpit during Sunday services, Hillary and Obama spoke at churches on the same street separated by three short blocks. Both credited the march in Selma with paving the way to their own historic bids for the presidency.[69]

Obama spoke first that Sunday, from the pulpit of the Brown Chapel AME Church, the launching pad for the historic demonstration. He was joined in the packed church by John Lewis. Obama saluted the brave men and women who had marched, including Lewis. Obama compared himself, and others who were small children or not yet born in 1965, to Joshua, who the Bible says followed Moses and completed the job of leading his people to the Promised Land. "The question, I guess, that I have today is, what's called of us in this Joshua generation?" Obama said. "What do we do in order to fulfill that legacy?"[70] His speech was interrupted often by ecstatic shouts from worshippers and long gusts of applause.[71]

Four minutes after Obama completed his speech, Hillary took the pulpit at the First Baptist Church of Selma. To the audience watching live at home on cable news channels and C-SPAN, the difference in the two candidates' oratorical style was evident. Obama had an easy, conversational manner, while Hillary sounded more scripted. Bill was not inside the church for her talk but joined her later. (That weekend, Bill was inducted into Selma's Voting Rights Hall of Fame.)

Hillary said the march made it possible for her to run for president, and she also gave credit to the march for making Obama's bid possible, as well as the campaign of Governor Bill Richardson of New Mexico, who was attempting to become the first Hispanic to be elected president. But the civil-rights struggle in America, Hillary declared, was far from over. She told the congregation, "We've got to stay awake. We've got to stay awake because we have a march to finish, a march towards one America." With her voice rising, as the congregation roared, she said, "Poverty and growing inequality matter. Health care matters. The people of the Gulf Coast matter. Our soldiers matter. Our future matters."[72]

Both Hillary and Obama used their personal histories to build a bridge to the civil-rights movement. This was an easier task for the Illinois senator, who had talked passionately about the struggle of his Kenyan father, who worked as a "house boy" to wealthy British families.[73] For her part, Hillary spoke about going to hear the Rev. Martin Luther King Jr. speak in Chicago in 1963, but compared with Obama's story, her link with the civil-rights movement seemed more remote.

Hillary was further hampered by a perception that she was pandering when, at one point, she shifted suddenly to a thick southern drawl as she recited a popular hymn by black clergyman James Cleveland: "I don't feel no ways tired. / I come too far from where I started from. / Nobody told me that the road would be easy. / I don't believe He brought me this far to leave me."[74] Members of the congregation whooped and cheered, but Hillary's recitation of the lyrics was almost instantly mocked on the Internet and, later, predictably, on Fox News.[75] Her supporters pointed out that she had lived nearly two decades in Arkansas, but a strategist for Hillary later acknowledged that "in a panic about Obama," she had turned to the southern drawl, only to find herself, in the end, in "trouble."[76]

After the pulpit speeches, Obama and Hillary prepared to re-enact the march. While they were waiting, they were joined by Bill, who joked, "All the good speaking has been done by Hillary and Senator Obama already. I'm just sort of bringing up the rear."[77]

Bill and Hillary shook hands with Obama, and they chatted briefly. As the cameras clicked, the former president smiled at his wife's challenger. Then the candidates joined arms with John Lewis and other local congressmen and officials for the walk across the bridge. As the long, straight line of people marched, their arms joined and their hands clasped, Hillary and Obama were separated by just two people. Everyone sang "We Shall Overcome."

When Bill returned later that week to New York, he spoke admiringly with a friend about Obama's political and oratorical skills. "He's the real thing," Bill said.[78]

A month later, during a television interview with Larry King, Bill publicly praised Obama, saying, "He's a very gifted man politically," but he attributed some of Obama's early success to favorable press coverage and "the way the media culture works."

After praising Obama, Bill was asked to react to a poll that said 60 percent of Americans wanted Bill involved in a second Clinton administration. Confessing he was not surprised by that sentiment, the former president said, "I've had a lot of experience and I can help her. And we learned a lot from — not only from our successes, but from the things we tried and didn't succeed in."

"And you still love her, don't you?" King asked.

"Very much."[79]

CHAPTER 27

"The Best Political Spouse in the Business"

THE MEN AND WOMEN most familiar with the power of "Clinton Inc."—those who worked with Bill and Hillary in Little Rock, or worked inside the bunker during the rough-and-tumble 1992 presidential run, or joined the White House staff not long after he was elected president—all talk with awe about the mysteries and endurance of their "political partnership," the most enigmatic in American history.

"Most marriages are built on trust," said someone who has known them both since the 1970s. "Their trust is not the one you think of when you think about a marriage. Their trust is in each other's survival instincts...the knowledge that no one will fight harder for them in the political arena than their spouse."[1]

Bill himself has described their marriage as indestructible. In a 1997 discussion with his lawyers, he confided, "The tapestry of our marriage is deep, colorful, and well-woven, and nobody will tear it asunder."[2]

"They have a unique relationship," said a former White House staffer who knows them both well. "It's a true partnership. He really loves her and she really loves him. And their partnership in politics is the glue that holds their relationship together. I saw it over and over again in the White House—there is nobody's judgment that the president trusted more than hers. He'd take advice from everyone, but he'd almost always wait to make a decision until he heard from her."[3]

For the loyalists who worked in Hillaryland, Hillary's most important tenet was unwritten and unspoken but well understood, according to Neel Lattimore, a longtime Hillary associate who worked as her press secretary when she was First Lady. That requirement was "You will always be loyal to me and my husband," Lattimore explained. "You were as loyal to him as to her. You had a double agenda—to protect him and protect her."[4]

Senator Bob Kerrey, the Nebraska Democrat, said, "She's got everything to run: the intellect, the money, the people, the national campaign—and she has the best political spouse in the business. The most important media you get in a presidential campaign is the free media, and I've got to think he is worth two hundred million in free media."[5]

But there are minuses to Bill's involvement too. One of the biggest challenges for Hillary in the campaign is the fragile "balancing act" that she has to navigate with Bill. Hillary often ties herself to Bill's policies, saying, "we did this," or "we did that," regarding accomplishments of the Clinton administration. Ever mindful of her husband's continued sky-high popularity, Hillary also insists that she and Bill saw then and see today eye-to-eye on almost every public-policy matter. "You know, he and I have a lot of the same beliefs about fiscal responsibility and helping the middle class and trying to restore our manufacturing base and dealing with health care and education and energy costs," she said.[6] Shortly after announcing her run for president, Hillary was asked whether the old "buy one, get one free" slogan that Bill had used in his 1992 campaign about his wife's role in his administration should he win might also apply to her campaign. The thought, broached by Diane Sawyer, drew a hearty laugh from Hillary. Then she said, "Well, I wouldn't say it quite like that. I'm running to be president, to make the decisions."[7] However, if Hillary is elected president, Bill Clinton, the nation's first First Gentleman, would hardly be setting up shop in the East Wing and fiddling with White House menus and china patterns. "People ask me all the time, 'If you are elected will you make him Secretary of State?'" Hillary said. "I think that is illegal but I sure will make him ambassador of the world, because we have a lot of work to do."[8]

Even before Hillary announced, Bill served as her adviser, chief strategist, cheerleader, and coach. One person close to both Clintons said, "They sit around and talk about things and he'll say that something resonated with someone he talked to that day," and then she'll pick up on it and use it in a speech or in contemporaneous remarks.[9]

One example of this sort of test marketing came in September 2006, involving the alleged torture of terror suspects under the Bush administration. Appearing on *Meet the Press*, Bill said that there should be an exception that makes torture legal, in very narrow circumstances, like when a suspect had knowledge of "an imminent threat to millions of Americans."[10] Bill's opinion seemed to be perceived as reasonable. Three weeks later, in a meeting with the *New York Daily News*, Hillary echoed his position. "That very, very narrow exception within very, very limited circumstances is better than blasting a big hole in our entire law," she said.[11]

Besides test-marketing ideas, Bill also has seized the job of aggressively protecting the couple's political legacy while defending her against incoming attacks. A Democratic strategist who knows them both well said, "I think they have figured out that this is the role for him — he can say things that she can't, on her behalf."[12]

Sometimes that defense of her involves policy; sometimes it involves Bill Clinton's own legacy. And sometimes it is intensely personal. "You can't overestimate the feeling in the campaign that he needs to be out there not too often so he doesn't overshadow her, but he also needs to be out there often enough so people don't ask these questions about the state of their marriage," a former Clinton administration official said.[13]

For Bill, the opportunity to take the lead arrived as the fifth anniversary of the September 11 attacks approached. The ABC television network had quietly produced a two-part film to be broadcast on September 10 and 11. The five-hour docudrama, *The Path to 9/11*, had used the *9/11 Commission Report* as a guide to portraying the years leading up to the terror attacks, looking at the failures of both the Clinton and Bush administrations. It was first screened in late August 2006 at the National Press Club in downtown Washington. Immediately, and over the next two weeks, there was a torrent of complaints that the film was unfair to Bill Clinton and his administration because it misrepresented or omitted efforts to combat terrorism during those years.

Bill became enraged when he was told about the film's assertions. The former president challenged the film's veracity in a conversation with Bob Iger, the president of ABC, that September 1.[14]

Hillary had little, if anything, to do with America's counterterrorism policies prior to September 11, but she, not Bill Clinton or George W. Bush, would be running for national election. In their typical war-room fashion, the Clintons "unleashed everybody" to stop ABC from airing the film.[15] The pressure was "unbelievable," a senior ABC official said.[16] The campaign ranged from thousands of grassroots e-mails to personal phone calls to top ABC executives from influential Hollywood friends. In response to the outcry and the network's own conclusion that there were inaccuracies in the film, ABC announced that *The Path to 9/11* was still being edited, and that it should be considered a fictional drama based only loosely on the fine print of the *9/11 Commission Report.*

On Sunday night, September 10, 2006, the first half of *The Path to 9/11* was broadcast by ABC.[17] The initial hour of the film focused on how Bill Clinton handled the first World Trade Center bombing in February 1993, portraying his administration's response as tepid and ineffectual. Several scenes, totaling seventy seconds, had been cut from the film by the producers, but the changes did not go far enough to satisfy the Clinton camp. After the first half of the film aired, lawyers for the Clinton Foundation wrote another letter to Iger, saying they were "deeply disappointed" by what they had seen. They complained that the few changes did not go nearly far enough to fix a film "fraught with errors" and filled with "contrived scenes that are directly contradicted by the findings of the *9/11 Commission Report.*"[18] One ABC official acknowledged that the film had strayed at times from the facts. "They fucked up on some details," the official said, "but the essence of it was true."[19]

The next day marked the fifth anniversary of the September 11 attacks. Hillary suspended her reelection campaign to honor the victims of the attacks. All the major TV networks had scheduled or expected interviews with her, but Hillary's aides now told ABC that she would not be appearing on that network's *Good Morning America* program. ABC officials were not told why, but they concluded it was due to the Clintons' anger over the film.[20]

On NBC's *Today* show, Hillary was restrained, in keeping with the somber spirit of the day and her own pledge to suspend her campaign. On CBS's *Early Show*, the questions were tougher and she appeared more partisan and defensive. Later that afternoon, on CNN's *The Situation Room*, the host, Wolf Blitzer, asked about the 9/11 film. Hillary said she had not watched it and did not intend to watch it. "The facts are very well developed in the *9/11 Commission [Report]*," she said. "This is a serious matter....There is no need to embroider, to make things up."[21] That night, the second half of *The Path to 9/11* was shown.

Since the midterm elections in 2002, when the Republicans took control of the Senate and increased their margin of seats in the House, Bill had alternated between feelings of anger and awe at how smartly the Bush White House had used the politics of terrorism to whip up fear in the minds of voters and defeat the Democrats in national elections.[22] He seethed that the Democrats had "rolled over," doing nothing less than ceding America's national security—the single most important issue to Americans in a post–September 11 world—to their political rivals. The Republicans owned the issue, Bill told a friend, and as long as they owned it, they would keep winning elections.[23] So as the 2006 election entered the homestretch, Bill decided that the Democrats needed to fight back. He said Hillary had to try to wrest away the national security issue from the Republicans, but he'd go first because, as he put it, he had nothing to lose.[24]

On Friday, September 22, after Bill concluded his three-day Clinton Global Initiative conference, he traveled to his office in Harlem, where he sat down for a scheduled interview with the Fox network and its Sunday political-talk-show host, Chris Wallace.[25]

Wallace began by asking a number of questions about the Clinton Global Initiative, then changed the subject. He said that many e-mails he had received from viewers prodded him to ask the former president this question: "Why didn't you do more to connect the dots and put bin Laden out of business when you were president?"[26]

After some quick back-and-forth, Bill said, "OK, let's talk about it." His eyes narrowed and he leaned forward in his chair closer to Wallace. "Now, I will answer all those things on the merits," he noted, "but first I want to talk about the context in which this arises.

"I'm being asked this on the Fox network. ABC just had a right-wing conservative run in their little *Pathway to 9/11*," Clinton said, getting the film's title slightly wrong. He said the film falsely claimed that it was based on the *9/11 Commission Report,* "with three things asserted against me directly contradicted by the *9/11 Commission Report.* And I think it's very interesting that all the conservative Republicans, who now say I didn't do enough, claimed that I was too obsessed with bin Laden. All of President Bush's neo-cons thought I was too obsessed with bin Laden. They had no meetings on bin Laden for nine months after I left office."

Wallace turned directly to the *9/11 Commission Report,* reading a sentence: "The U.S. government took the threat seriously, but not in the sense of mustering anything like the kind of effort that would be gathered to confront the enemy of the first, second or third rank."

"First of all," Bill responded, "that's not true with us and bin Laden."

"Well," Wallace said, "I'm telling you, that's what the 9/11 Commission says."

Pointing his finger in Wallace's face, Bill said, "Now, if you want to criticize me for one thing, you can criticize me for this: After the Cole, I had battle plans drawn to go into Afghanistan, overthrow the Taliban, and launch a full-scale-attack search for bin Laden. But we needed basing rights in Uzbekistan, which we got after 9/11. The CIA and the FBI refused to certify that bin Laden was responsible while I was there. They refused to certify....All I'm asking is, anybody who wants to say I didn't do enough, you read Richard Clarke's book," he said, referring to the former government expert on counterterrorism.[27]

"Do you think you did enough, sir?" Wallace asked.

"No, because I didn't get him," Bill replied.

"Right."

"But at least I tried," Bill said, leaning forward again. "That's the difference in me and some, including all the right-wingers who are attacking me now. They ridiculed me for trying. They had eight months to try. They did not try. I tried."

Bill then directed his hostility toward Wallace, accusing him of doing "Fox's bidding" and labeling the interview "your nice little conservative hit job on me." He accused Wallace and Fox of going easy on Bush administration officials when they appeared on the network. "You ask me questions you don't ask the other side," Bill said, later adding, "If you're going to do this, for God's sake, follow the same standards for everybody...and be...*fair.*"

When the interview ended—after a number of additional questions about the Clinton Global Initiative—Bill stalked off the stage, chatted briefly and "testily" with Wallace, and walked out the door, castigating his aides. "If any of you ever get me in a situation like this again," Bill told them, "you'll be fired."[28]

Some wondered whether Bill's tantrum was premeditated. Wallace said, "That notion is complete bull."[29] Several of Bill's confidants said the former president intended to be tough during the interview, but no one expected him to lose his temper.[30]

The next day, America was talking about Bill's fury on Fox. On YouTube, the Clinton-Wallace interview was downloaded one million times within forty-eight hours—yet another example of the Internet changing the political landscape. At noon that day, Hillary stood before the press in the Senate Briefing Room, where she was asked about Bill's television performance. "I think my husband did a great job in demonstrating that Democrats are not going to take these attacks," she said. She urged reporters to "read the 9/11 Commission [Report] to know what he and his administration did to protect Americans and prevent terrorist attacks against this country." Then she challenged Bush's counterterrorism record, just as her husband had. "I'm certain that if my husband and his national-security team had been shown a classified report entitled *Bin Laden Determined to Attack Inside the U.S.*, he would have taken it more seriously than history suggests it was taken by our current president and his national-security team," she said,[31] referring to the August 6, 2001 "President's Daily Briefing" that President Bush received at his ranch in Crawford, Texas.[32] Hillary did not mention that her husband received a similar "President's Daily Briefing" document on December 4, 1998. The title was *Bin Laden Preparing to Hijack U.S. Aircraft and Other Attacks.*[33]

THE SHOWDOWN OVER the legacy of 9/11 was as good an example as any of the unique complications of Hillary's campaign for president. As much as she had intended to go forward on her terms, she knew that her political future, like the twenty-year project she and Bill had forged three decades ago, would depend on her husband's assets and liabilities, for better or worse.[34] If she could only have singled out Bill's great successes, the dependence might not have been so strong. But, of course, that was not possible.

The linkage between herself and her husband enhanced Hillary's greatness, but in some ways, it diminished her too. People knew her through him, or they didn't really know her at all. In order to win, she knew, the American public had to discover the real Hillary. She had tried to introduce herself many times, without lasting success. Once again, the moment had come.

Force the Spring

I've said for a long time that women have everything else, they might as well have the Presidency.

— Harry S. Truman[1]

Whatever women do they must do twice as well as men to be thought half as good. Luckily, this is not difficult.

— Charlotte Whitton, Canadian politician[2]

"IS IT ANY KIND OF BURDEN for you, Senator, that so many opinions are preformed?" anchorman Brian Williams asked Hillary on the set of NBC's *Nightly News* in New York two days after she launched her bid for the presidency. "Americans know Hillary Rodham Clinton."

"Well, as someone close to me said, I'm probably the most famous person you don't really know," Hillary replied.[3]

Hillary and her strategists believe her greatest challenge is reintroducing Americans to "the real Hillary," a woman far different from the portrait drawn through years of negative stories in the media or, more recently, on the blogs. When she ran for Senate, Hillary recalled telling New York State residents, "Look, here's who I really am....And at the end of getting to know me, draw your own conclusion. Don't draw it from what you hear somebody say on, you know, radio or cable TV. Draw your own conclusion."[4] To help her meet this challenge, Hillary's presidential campaign distributed a talking-points memo with suggested answers to a host of difficult questions. One of them was:

Q: Hillary's camp talks about a "different side" of her that people
   don't know. After 14 years in the public eye, what other sides
   are there to see?
A: Hillary Clinton is the most famous person in the world that
   nobody really knows....The fact is that when people get to
   know her, they love her.[5]

As has been the case in previous elections, the candidate who
is seen by a majority of Americans as the "most authentic," as one
of Hillary's senior strategists acknowledged, will carry a formidable
advantage.[6] In this respect, however, Hillary faces a particularly difficult challenge. Although on the campaign trail she often emphasizes her experience over that of her opponents, the fact that she is
"the most famous person" in the race puts her, oddly, at a distinct
disadvantage. Fifty-one percent of independents told one pollster
that they would never vote for her, under any circumstances, by far
the highest percentage of any of the major presidential candidates.[7]
Said one longtime adviser who has discussed the authenticity issue
with Hillary and Bill, "They think the biggest issue they have to
confront is her." Improving her ability to project an authentic image
is seen by the Clintons as "job one, two, and three," the adviser
said.[8] Another friend summarized her dilemma a different way:
"Does the country really want to get to know more about Hillary?
Or do they think they already know enough?"[9]

But precisely what *authentic* means in Hillary's case remains,
for many Americans, a mystery. Hillary has been on a lifelong quest
to privately and publicly define herself. There was that list of the
personality types and professions she might like to pursue that she
drew up back at Wellesley. Her politics transformed her from Goldwater Republican to McGovern Democrat to New Democrat. Her
marriage and work took her away from familiar ground, forcing
her to adapt and adopt. The road she has traveled has often been
sharply curved, and even zigzagged.

It has also often been dimly lit for those who might have hoped
to retrace it. Hillary's official biographies have been repeatedly
tweaked and revised, emphasizing or omitting crucial periods and
events in her life[10]—from her family roots to her marriage, from
her fifteen years as a private lawyer in Arkansas to the eight years
of her life in the White House.[11] When explaining herself, she has
often left out important details. Such was the case in Arkansas,

such was the case in the White House, and such has been the case in the Senate.

SO, WHO IS THE REAL HILLARY? It is a question that has vexed political analysts, party loyalists, biographers, journalists, and some of the people who have known her across the decades. "The worst thing that can happen," one longtime Hillary associate noted, "is if the country senses her personality is a work in progress."[12] Understanding Hillary, said an acquaintance of more than thirty-five years, is even a "challenge to her friends."[13] That makes the job of explaining herself to America all the more challenging. And then there's the further hurdle that if Hillary gets elected for two terms, there will have been twenty-eight consecutive years of Bushes and Clintons living in the White House. "Does the country want another Clinton as president for eight more years after twenty years of Bushes and Clintons?" a former Clinton administration official wondered.[14]

TUCKED AWAY ON HER WEB SITE on the morning Hillary announced her presidential run was a revealing memorandum by her pollster and chief strategist, Mark Penn. Hillary inherited Penn from Bill. She considers the fifty-two-year-old adviser to be "shrewd and insightful" as well as "brilliant and intense,"[15] and the candidate and the pollster trust each other "totally," according to one Penn associate.[16] His campaign portfolio includes "total control of the research side."[17]

Penn's impudent, tightly reasoned memo was nothing less than a gender-based blueprint for Hillary's intended march to the White House. The memo argued why "Hillary Is the Democrats' Best Shot."[18] Exhibit A, according to Penn, is women — what he called "a huge 'X factor.'" Many of them "believe it is about time this country had its first woman president," and, Penn argued, they have the power to make it happen because 54 percent of the general electorate is female.

Penn succeeded Dick Morris as the Clintons' strategic guru. Penn and Morris are now personally and politically estranged, but Morris's view of what it will take for Hillary to win is remarkably similar to the one embraced by her campaign: Women hold the key to Hillary's success.[19]

Many female voters, significantly, lean politically to the left. Indeed, unmarried women are "the most progressive and the most underrepresented" part of the electorate, according to one organizer.[20] But older, married women worry some Hillary strategists. "In general, there are a fair number of women who don't like her, don't respect her because she didn't leave Clinton," one said. "Some men don't like her because they feel threatened by her. Some women feel threatened too. Then there are some who like her but don't want her to be president. It's not easy."[21]

What would Eleanor Roosevelt think of Penn's gender-based strategy? Not much, according to the answer Mrs. Roosevelt gave in 1934 to the question of when a woman would become president. "I hope it will not be while we still speak of 'a woman's vote,'" she said.

On the campaign trail, Hillary echoes that hope. "Although I'm very proud to be a woman," she told a mostly female San Francisco audience of one thousand supporters, "I'm not running as a woman candidate." As for the question of whether America was prepared to elect a woman as president, she said, "We won't know until we try."[22]

A few days before the 1993 inauguration, Father Tim Healy, the former president of Georgetown University, died of a heart attack while typing a letter to Bill Clinton. The letter was posthumously sent to Bill.

Father Healy wrote of his hope that Bill's election would "force the spring." Hillary was struck by the phrase, understanding it to mean that her husband's presidency would bring about a "flowering of new ideas, hope and energy that would reinvigorate the country."[23]

For Hillary, Healy's phrase was a fitting metaphor for her husband's ambitions—and thus her own. Bill and Hillary Clinton had been connected personally and politically for two decades, and with his arrival in Washington, their twenty-year project had been realized.

Fourteen years later, it is Hillary's turn. She is the most viable female contender in American history for the nation's highest office. Her landmark campaign has inspired women of all generations, giving them hope that their time has come. Her election too would "force the spring."

IF PUBLICLY HILLARY presents herself as transcending gender, her campaign, inside and out, has a distinctly feminine feel. Her campaign manager, media strategist, and policy coordinator are all women. On the road, Hillary attracts mostly female crowds.[24] For her first public appearance after announcing her presidential candidacy, Hillary appeared at a health clinic in midtown Manhattan. Clutching the hand of a four-year-old girl named Camilla Harden, Hillary projected the image that she was not just a woman running for president but also a mother.[25] Her campaign has organized a nationwide network for female leaders, "Women for Hillary," via the Internet. Even before Hillary announced her presidential campaign, Ellen Malcolm, the president of EMILY's List, the giant, pro-choice political action committee, said her group would "early on" endorse and work on behalf of Hillary.[26]

Mark Penn and James Carville believe Democrats have lost the last two national elections because they have been "made to look like they have no backbone." Hillary, they say, is "tough enough to handle the viciousness of a national campaign and the challenges of the presidency itself."[27] She kicked Bill's ass in Arkansas; she fought back against the couples' critics in Bill's 1992 presidential campaign; she turned back the tide of Ken Starr's inquisitors in 1998; she used her new job in the Senate to forge a muscular stance on defense post–September 11; she has assembled a tight-lipped, intensely devoted group of aides and loyalists; and she has refused to apologize for her vote on the Iraq war, despite pleas from her supporters. Bill, fascinated with the legacy of strong female leaders, recently told a friend that all the great female leaders in history were battle-tested, possessed nerves of steel, and owned an indomitable will to win — "like Hillary."[28] As for Hillary herself, she's convinced that she is battle-tested and ready. "They have thrown everything at me for eight years," she told some of her close associates in the early weeks of her presidential bid. "What else can they throw at me?"[29] She is also fond of saying that the standards that apply to her are more exacting than those applied to her opponents. "Nobody gets the scrutiny that I get," she told a reporter. "It's not like I have any margin for error whatsoever. I don't. Everybody else does and I don't. And that's fine. That's just who I am and that's what I live with."[30]

In the end, those who have known Hillary the longest say they hope she shows the country her "true self," the warm, tough, funny, and brilliant woman they know so well. "She's warm and funny, but she either doesn't emote it or you have all these people who have their minds made up and they won't give her another chance," a longtime Hillary strategist said.[31]

But there's another side to Hillary too, hardened and unwilling to fully acknowledge her mistakes. For those who have watched her, the thickness of her shell is unsurprising, given the intensity of attacks against her during the Clinton administration, and the betrayal of her marriage by her husband. Her ability to withstand those assaults is admirable, even incredible. Perhaps it is too much to ask a person who has gone through all that to reveal much vulnerability.

Bill Clinton had many faults of his own, but his ability to win a room over, to make a visitor smile, to wear (or at least appear to wear) his heart on his sleeve, was unparalleled. Hillary, despite spending more time watching Bill at work than anyone else in the world has, remains unable to connect in the way he can. The strategy that Hillary developed in college to restore her sense of confidence and balance by refusing to look within has helped sustain her through a life of incredible accomplishment and heartbreak. But it has also resulted in a forced, artificial demeanor, a reinforced tendency toward arrogance and a belief that she is immune to the rules, and a sense that anyone who disagrees must be an enemy. It is a great challenge to ask Americans to get to know the authentic self of a person who in some ways has deliberately not gotten to know it herself.

"Long before she was in public office, she was a public servant," Bill told an audience on Hillary's presidential campaign trail, reflecting on their time together back in Arkansas. "Tonight I feel more strongly than I did thirty-five years ago, when I told her that out of all the people in our generation, she's still the best."[32] For Hillary to realize her dream of becoming a national "political leader," she must now find a way to persuade the voters that her husband's judgment about her is correct. Bill Clinton is fond of saying, "The American people always get it right." In 2008, they will decide whether Hillary, who spent eight years in the White House "living history," will end up making it by moving back in.

Hillary Rodham Clinton's rise is one of the most remarkable stories in American politics. She has revealed incredible strength of will, a nearly unmatched fortitude, and an abiding faith in her husband and her future. As her husband declares, she is emblematic of many of the best qualities of her generation. But she has also shown, from Arkansas to the Senate, a propensity to exhibit some of that generation's less noble attributes.

Decades ago, Hillary's heroine Eleanor Roosevelt offered the following wisdom: "Some day, a woman may be president.... I hope it will only become a reality when she is elected as an individual because of her capacity and the trust which the majority of the people have in her integrity and ability as a person."

Eleanor Roosevelt is waiting.

Acknowledgments

Every book is a monumental collaborative effort, but none more than this one. Besides relying on each other every day, we leaned on the talents, assistance, and friendships of an enormous group of people whose help proved both inspiring and invaluable.

From the very beginning, Christy Fletcher, our agent, energized us with encouragement for the idea of a sweeping biography of the junior senator from New York, and we benefited throughout from her steady hand and sharp eye.

Christine Kay is one of the finest editors at the *New York Times*; she is also a terrific friend. We are grateful not only for her enthusiasm for this book but for her meticulous first read and exacting first edit.

Kristen Lee, our researcher, contributed in many important ways; her work led to far more than she had imagined. Also on the research front, we were assisted by the hard work of Daun van Ee at the Library of Congress; Virginia Lewick at the Franklin D. Roosevelt Presidential Library and Museum in Hyde Park, New York; Steven Tilley, Martha Murphy, and David Paynter at the National Archives and Records Administration in College Park, Maryland; the staffs of the secretary of the Senate and the Chevy Chase branch of the Washington, DC, library; and our friend Barclay Walsh, who works in the library of the *New York Times*'s Washington bureau.

Dale Van Atta contacted us, unsolicited, with a generous offer: a trove of his unpublished reporting in 1999 on Hillary Rodham

Clinton. Our scene of the First Lady's private meeting on a spring evening in 1999 with old friends in the White House Solarium draws completely from Dale's old notebooks.

We have spent a combined forty-two years of our professional lives at the *New York Times*. We are so privileged that our good friends there not only encouraged one or both of us to take on this project but helped us in so many other ways, big and small, across the years. This group includes Jill Abramson, Dean Baquet, John Broder, Frank Bruni, Christopher Drew, Maureen Dowd, Steve Engelberg, Bill Keller, Steve Labaton, Joe Lelyveld, Sarah Lyall, Matt Purdy, Elaine Sciolino, Joe Sexton, Debbie Sontag, and Phil Taubman.

We are also thankful for the friendship and support of Lowell Bergman and Sy Hersh.

From our first meeting with the people at Little, Brown and Company, we felt our book had found its perfect home. Editor in chief Geoff Shandler wowed us with his wondrous intelligence, soaring prose, and tireless determination to get everything exactly right. His assistant, Junie Dahn, made it all run smoothly. Heather Fain was an enormous help with publicity. Little, Brown's Boston-based team of copyeditors contributed an eagle-eyed, record-time turnaround of the manuscript: Betsy Uhrig, Marie Salter, Pamela Marshall, Peggy L. Anderson, Karen Landry, Ashley St. Thomas, Jayne Yaffe Kemp, and their talented leader, Peggy Freudenthal. Marilyn Doof did a fantastic job on production. And we thank publisher Michael Pietsch and associate publisher Sophie Cottrell for their enthusiastic embrace of *Her Way*.

Finally, we want to offer a few words of thanks to the scores of people whose names do not appear in this book, by their own choice: We are grateful for your expertise and trust. We could not have written this book without you.

— *Jeff Gerth and Don Van Natta Jr.*

My wife, Janice, and my daughter, Jessica, are the twin pillars of strength in our family.

Janice has worked as a Senate staffer since 1977, when she joined the Foreign Relations Committee. (The committee's staff was nonpartisan at the time, a tradition that ended a few years later.

Then she became part of the committee's Democratic staff. Since the mid-1980s, she has also served as a foreign-policy adviser to Senator Christopher J. Dodd, who is a member of the committee.) Jessica's inner courage and vibrant spirit inspire me every day.

My parents, Sol and Shirley, have provided a lifetime of support and encouragement, and my sister, Sande, has added her enthusiasm as well.

I have a total of almost one hundred years of shared trust and collaboration with three friends: Lowell Bergman, Sy Hersh, and Phil Taubman. Their own careers have led them down separate reporting paths, but they all have been there to help me—anytime, anywhere. I couldn't have asked for more.

—J.G.

I could not have even contemplated taking on this project without the enthusiasm and support of my friends: Scott Price and Fran Brennan; Pete Cross and Christine Evans; Lucy and Andrew Siegel; Kate and Jeff Jaenicke; Carol and Barry Doyle; Mina and Larry Peck; Mary Beth McCarthy and Rich Heilman; Mark Kriegel, Eddie Hayes, Chad Millman, James Bennet, John Files, and Warren St. John.

This book is dedicated, in part, to my mother, Liette Van Natta, who has lavished me with a lifetime of love and support, for which I am grateful.

My brothers, Steve and Dean (and their wives, Erika and Jenny), and Terri and Frank Alvarez and Mariana Alvarez were by my side, every step of the way.

And I thank my wife, Lizette Alvarez, and our young daughters, Isabel and Sofia, for all their love. Each day, they remind me that I am truly blessed.

—D.V.N.

Notes

Prologue: In to Win

1. Bess Furman, *Washington Byline: The Personal History of a Newspaperwoman* (New York: Alfred A. Knopf, 1949), 253.
2. Gail Sheehy, "What Hillary Wants," *Vanity Fair,* May 1992, 217.
3. She spent her lifetime arguing that women should be afforded equal opportunities to serve at the highest national and state government positions, including the office of president and vice president. She went on to become the vice president of the National Association of Women Lawyers and the national chairman of Women in Public Service, Inc. She died in 1974 at the age of seventy-one. Lillian D. Rock obituary, *New York Times,* May 15, 1974, 48.
4. All Eleanor Roosevelt quotations that follow in this section are from the Simmons Company Radio Broadcast, *When Will a Woman Become President of the US?,* September 4, 1934. Eleanor Roosevelt Papers, Box 3027, Franklin Delano Roosevelt Presidential Library.
5. Hillary Rodham Clinton statement, www.hillaryclinton.com, posted at 10:00 a.m. EST on January 20, 2007.
6. CBS's *60 Minutes,* transcript of January 26, 1992, interview of Bill and Hillary Rodham Clinton by correspondent Steve Kroft, at http://www.washington post.com/wpsrv/politics/special/clinton/stories/flowers012792.htm.
7. Ibid.
8. Robert Novak, "Critics Fret over Hillary Clinton's High National Negative Ratings," *Chicago Sun-Times,* February 4, 2007, at http://www.suntimes. com/news/novak/241516.CST-EDT-NOVAK04.article.
9. Author interviews with former campaign aides in 2005, 2006, and 2007.
10. Author interviews with former OIC officials in 2006 and Memorandum from HRC Team to All OIC Attorneys, "Summary of Evidence...Hillary Rodham Clinton and Webb Hubbell," April 22, 1998.

11. Remarks of Senator Hillary Rodham Clinton before the Council on Foreign Relations, New York, December 15, 2003.
12. Author interview with Hillary Rodham Clinton strategist in 2007.
13. Eleanor Roosevelt, "What 10 Million Women Want," *Home Magazine* 5, March 1932, 19–21, 86.
14. Interviews with Leon Panetta and former Clinton administration official in 2006.
15. Author interviews with Ann Crittenden and John Henry in 2007.

Part One: First Partner

EPIGRAPH: Bertrand Russell, English philosopher, from *Marriage and Morals,* chapter 7, 1929, cited in *The Yale Book of Quotations,* ed. Fred R. Shapiro (New Haven, CT: Yale University Press, 2006), 258.

Chapter One: Chase and Run

1. Hillary Rodham Clinton, *Living History* (New York: Simon & Schuster, 2003), 52.
2. Ibid.
3. Ibid.
4. Ibid., 1.
5. Ibid., 6.
6. Ibid., 9.
7. Gail Sheehy, *Hillary's Choice* (New York: Random House, 1999), 20.
8. Ibid., 22.
9. Hillary Rodham Clinton biography, Hillary Rodham Clinton for Senate 2000 Web site, www.hillary2000.org.
10. Clinton, *Living History,* 9.
11. Sheehy, *Hillary's Choice,* 20.
12. Ibid., 19.
13. Ibid., 23.
14. Ibid., 24–25; Clinton, *Living History,* 12.
15. Clinton, *Living History,* 8.
16. Ibid., 10.
17. Ibid.
18. Ibid., 11.
19. Ibid.
20. Ibid.
21. Ibid., 12.
22. Ibid.
23. Sheehy, *Hillary's Choice,* 30.
24. Ibid.
25. Ibid., 31; Clinton, *Living History,* 21.
26. Clinton, *Living History,* 16.
27. Ibid.
28. Ibid., 17.

29. Interview with Rev. Donald Jones by Dale Van Atta in 1999.
30. Ibid.
31. Ibid.
32. Sheehy, *Hillary's Choice*, 32–33.
33. Clinton, *Living History*, 22.
34. Ibid.
35. Ibid., 23.
36. Jones interview.
37. Ibid.
38. Clinton, *Living History*, 23.
39. Ibid.
40. Ibid.
41. Interview with Mike Andrews by Dale Van Atta in 1999.
42. Clinton, *Living History*, 24.
43. Ibid.
44. Clinton, *Living History*, 25.
45. Sheehy, *Hillary's Choice*, 39.
46. Clinton, *Living History*, 26.
47. Ibid.

Chapter Two: The Art of Making Possible

1. Clinton, *Living History*, 27.
2. Sheehy, *Hillary's Choice*, 41, 60.
3. Clinton, *Living History*, 28
4. Ibid., 27.
5. Ibid.
6. Ibid., 41.
7. Ibid., 42.
8. Ibid., 27.
9. Ibid., 28.
10. Ibid., 29.
11. Ibid., 30.
12. Ibid.
13. Ibid., 31–32.
14. Ibid., 32.
15. Sheehy, *Hillary's Choice*, 46.
16. Clinton, *Living History*, 33.
17. Ibid.
18. Sheehy, *Hillary's Choice*, 47.
19. Charles Kenney, "Hillary: The Wellesley Years," *Boston Globe*, January 13, 1993, 65.
20. Sheehy, *Hillary's Choice*, 49–50.
21. Ibid., 50.
22. Ibid.
23. Ibid., 52.
24. Ibid., 52–53.
25. Ibid., 51.

26. Ibid., 53.
27. Ibid., 51.
28. Kenney, "Hillary."
29. Clinton, *Living History*, 30.
30. Ibid.
31. Sheehy, *Hillary's Choice*, 51.
32. Ibid., 52.
33. Ibid., 56.
34. Kenney, "Hillary."
35. Clinton, *Living History*, 33.
36. Ibid., 34.
37. Ibid.
38. Ibid., 34–35.
39. Ibid., 36.
40. Ibid.
41. Ibid., 37.
42. Ibid.
43. Ibid.
44. Ibid., 38
45. Ibid.
46. Ibid., 39–40.
47. Ibid., 40.
48. Ibid.
49. Ibid.
50. Ibid.
51. Ibid.
52. At http://www.wellesley.edu/PublicAffairs/Commencement/1969/053169 hillary.html.
53. Edward W. Brooke, *Bridging the Divide* (Brunswick, NJ: Rutgers University Press, 2007), 182–83.
54. Clinton, *Living History*, 41.
55. Ibid.
56. Ibid., 42.

Chapter Three: Following the Heart to Fayetteville

1. Sheehy, *Hillary's Choice*, 61.
2. "Online Excerpt: Sen. Hillary Rodham Clinton," *Newsweek*, August 21/28, 2006, 4.
3. Clinton, *Living History*, 44.
4. Ibid., 45.
5. Sheehy, *Hillary's Choice*, 79.
6. Clinton, *Living History*, 45.
7. Ibid.
8. Ibid., 46.
9. Ibid.
10. Ibid., 47.
11. Ibid., 48.

12. Ibid., 48–49.
13. Ibid., 49.
14. Ibid., 50.
15. Sheehy, *Hillary's Choice*, 86.
16. *Harvard Educational Review*, vol. 43, no. 4 (November 1973), 487ff.; also see David Brock, *The Seduction of Hillary Rodham* (New York: Free Press, 1996), 118.
17. Clinton, *Living History*, 51.
18. Bill Clinton, *My Life* (New York: Alfred A. Knopf, 2004), 181. The account of Bill and Hillary's first meeting is also informed by Clinton, *Living History*, and David Maraniss, *First in His Class* (New York: Simon & Schuster, 1995).
19. Clinton, *My Life*, 181.
20. Ibid.
21. Clinton, *Living History*, 54.
22. Clinton, *My Life*, 182.
23. Ibid.
24. Ibid., 184.
25. Clinton, *Living History*, 54.
26. Ibid., 55.
27. Sheehy, *Hillary's Choice*, 82.
28. Author interview with Greg Craig in 2006.
29. Ibid.
30. Clinton, *Living History*, 56–57.
31. Ibid., 57.
32. Ibid., 59.
33. Ibid.
34. Maraniss, *First in His Class*, 277; also see Brock, *The Seduction of Hillary Rodham*, 43–44.
35. Betsey Wright e-mail to one of the authors in 2007. Wright declined several requests to be interviewed for this book.
36. Clinton, *Living History*, 59–60.
37. Ibid.
38. Brock, *The Seduction of Hillary Rodham*, 42.
39. Clinton, *Living History*, 61
40. Ibid.
41. Ibid.
42. Ibid.
43. Ibid., 64.
44. Ibid.
45. Ibid., 65.
46. Ibid., 66.
47. Maraniss, *First in His Class*, 297.
48. Clinton, *Living History*, 68.
49. Ibid., 69.
50. Ibid., 70.
51. Maraniss, *First in His Class*, 333, and Brock, *The Seduction of Hillary Rodham*, 58–60.
52. Author interviews with Leon Panetta and former Clinton administration official in 2006.

53. Author interview with Marla Crider in 2006. Crider's account was first mentioned in Jerry Oppenheimer, *State of a Union: Inside the Complex Marriage of Bill and Hillary Clinton* (New York: HarperCollins, 2000). Crider says Oppenheimer's account "was not totally accurate."
54. Ibid.
55. Maraniss, *First in His Class*, 335–36.
56. Ibid.
57. Ibid.
58. Clinton, *Living History*, 70–71; see also Maraniss, *First in His Class*, 344–45.

Chapter Four: Personal Calculations

1. Clinton, *Living History*, 75.
2. Maraniss, *First in His Class*, 345; Clinton, *My Life*, 235.
3. Author interview with Wade Rathke in 2006.
4. Clinton, *Living History*, 37–38.
5. Rathke interview.
6. February 21, 2007, statement to authors by Rose Law Firm from Steve Joiner.
7. Rathke interview.
8. Webb Hubbell, *Friends in High Places*, (New York: William Morrow, 1997), 61.
9. Ibid., 62.
10. George Bentley, "Lifeline Law Called Illegal," *Arkansas Gazette*, February 24, 1977, 1A.
11. Ibid.
12. Rathke interview.
13. Hillary Rodham Clinton commencement speech to the University of Michigan, May 1, 1993, as cited in Gil Troy, *Hillary Rodham Clinton: Polarizing First Lady* (Lawrence, KS: University Press of Kansas, 2006), 83–84.
14. Author interview with Allen W. Bird II in 2007.
15. Ibid.
16. Hubbell, *Friends in High Places*, 51–52.
17. Clinton, *Living History*, 78.
18. Interview with Robert Reich by Dale Van Atta in 1999, and Troy, *Hillary Rodham Clinton*, 29.
19. Clinton, *Living History*, 78.
20. Gail Sheehy, "What Hillary Wants," *Vanity Fair*, May 1992, 138.
21. At http://www.wellesley.edu/PublicAffairs/Commencement/1969/053169 hillary.html.
22. The Rose Law Firm is now a professional association, so its partners are now called "members," according to a statement by the firm. But Hillary, in her autobiography, uses the term "partner."
23. Annabelle Davis Clinton, "Coming of Age: Women Lawyers in Arkansas, 1960–1984," *Arkansas Lawyer*, April 1985, 59–60.
24. Rose Law Firm statement to the authors on February 21, 2007.
25. Ibid. and Arkansas court records.
26. 491 F. Supp. 1391.

27. Joseph A. Califano Jr., *Inside: A Public and Private Life* (New York: Public-Affairs, 2004), 213.
28. Clinton, *Living History*, 80.
29. Hubbell, *Friends in High Places*, 60.
30. Michael Weisskopf and David Maraniss, "Hillary Clinton's Law Firm Is Influential with State," *Washington Post*, March 15, 1992, A1, and Audrey Duff, "Is a Rose a Rose?," *American Lawyer*, July/August 1992, 68.
31. Author interview with Randy Coleman in 2006.
32. George Fox testimony, Pulaski Circuit Court, Sixth Division, Case #83–4178, The City of Little Rock By and Through the Little Rock Municipal Airport Commission vs. Gerald D. Hammett, administrator of the estate of Edith Hammett Rolf, et al.
33. Author interview with Andrew Cobb in 2006.
34. Judgment filed February 29, 1984, Pulaski Circuit Court, Sixth Division.
35. Coleman interview.
36. Ibid.
37. Ibid.
38. Annabelle Davis Clinton, "Coming of Age."
39. Hubbell, *Friends in High Places*, 55.
40. Clinton, *Living History*, 82.
41. Ibid.
42. Ibid., 79–80.
43. Hubbell, *Friends in High Places*, 56.
44. Ibid., 67.
45. Author interview with Nancy Pietrafesa in 2006.
46. Ibid., 79.
47. Ibid.
48. Interview with Joseph Giroir by Stephen Labaton of the *New York Times* in 1996.
49. James Merriweather, "Hillary Clinton Forges Own Passage Forward," *Arkansas Gazette*, July 22, 1990, 1A.
50. Hubbell, *Friends in High Places*, 60.
51. Brant Buck memo to Rose Law Firm partners, February 1986.
52. Ibid.
53. Merriweather, "Hillary Clinton."
54. Martin Mayer, *The Greatest-Ever Bank Robbery* (New York: Macmillan, 1990), 31.
55. Robert W. Ray, *Final Report of the Independent Counsel in Re: Madison Guaranty Savings and Loan Association* (Washingr on, DC: United States Court of Appeals for the District of Columbia, 2002), vol. 2, part B, 321. Meanwhile, the firm was hoping to be hired by federal regulators as part of the costly cleanup of the same thrift. Foster told the government about Giroir's loans but not about Rose's representation of FirstSouth. By early 1987, the Federal Savings and Loan Insurance Corporation, or FSLIC, was "appalled" that Rose had bid for FirstSouth business and was preparing a "most serious claim" against the firm. (Hubbell, *Friends in High Places*, 130–31.) The three amigos, Hillary, Foster, and Hubbell, began meeting "almost daily" about the problem. (Ibid., 132.)
56. Hubbell, *Friends in High Places*, 132.

57. Ray, *Final Report*, vol. 2, part B, 325–26.
58. Ibid., 329.
59. Her actions and subsequent explanations were puzzling. Later, Hillary said her reason for terminating the account was that a few days earlier one of her partners, Rule, "sent around a memo asking that we no longer represent savings and loan associations." (Deposition of Hillary Rodham Clinton, April 25, 1998, cited in Ray, *Final Report*, vol. 2, part A, 242.) Rule's memo, however, was less categorical. It said, "We want to avoid taking on any new or expanded representation of savings and loan associations" in case the federal government asked the firm to do S&L work. (Ibid., 224.)
    Investigators suspected she had dumped the Madison account because the thrift, controlled by Jim McDougal, a friend of Bill's who was also a business partner with the couple in a venture called Whitewater, was in trouble. (Author interviews with former OIC—Office of the Independent Counsel—officials in 2006.) Her husband had been given a heads-up about Madison's plight a few days earlier. But Hillary denied any such linkage. When pressed, she said she thought the "clear message" of Rule's memo was "that if you weren't doing anything and there was, you know, no reason to continue the representation, then we should take another look at it." (Ray, *Final Report*, vol. 2, part A, 242.) A law firm looking at Hillary's 1986 decision to jettison Madison said "it seems strange" that she refunded money back to the thrift and returned the July retainer but "didn't extinguish the outstanding receivable of $2160." (March 1994 memo by Pillsbury, Madison and Sutro prepared in connection with its 1995 report to the Resolution Trust Corporation.)
60. Accessed January 21, 2007, at www.hillaryclinton.com/about/mom/.

Chapter Five: Investing 101

1. Sharon LaFraniere and Charles Babcock, "Whitewater Study Shows How Clintons' Burden Eased," *Washington Post*, June 29, 1995, A4.
2. Clinton, *Living History*, 87, and McDougal's interview with FBI, Form 302, transcribed October 3, 1996, 2.
3. Clinton, *Living History*, 88.
4. Ibid.
5. Draft Report by Pillsbury, Madison and Sutro for Resolution Trust Corporation, April 25, 1995, 18.
6. McDougal FBI 302, transcribed October 3, 1996, 18.
7. Clinton, *My Life*, 287.
8. Author interview with William Rempel in 2006. Rempel overheard Dorothy Rodham remark about Hillary's crying in Little Rock in 1992.
9. Clinton, *My Life*, 284–85.
10. Author interview with Jim McDougal in 1992.
11. Clinton, *Living History*, 89.
12. Hubbell, *Friends in High Places*, 85.
13. Clinton, *Living History*, 90.
14. John Brummett interview on June 25, 2000, for the Archives of the David and Barbara Pryor Center for Arkansas Oral and Visual History at the University of Arkansas, Fayetteville.

15. Ibid.
16. Ibid.
17. Clinton, *My Life*, 283, and Clinton, *Living History*, 90.
18. Author interview with Nancy Pietrafesa in 2006.
19. Clinton, *Living History*, 90.
20. Clinton, *My Life*, 195.
21. Author interview with Vernon Jordan in 2006.
22. Clinton, *Living History*, 91.
23. Ibid., 93.
24. Author interview with Nancy Pietrafesa in 2006.
25. Charles F. Allen and Jonathan Portis, *The Comeback Kid: The Life and Career of Bill Clinton* (New York: Birch Lane Press, 1992), 84.
26. Clinton, *Living History*, 94.
27. Roy Reed, "I Just Went to School in Arkansas," in *The Clintons of Arkansas*, ed. Ernest Dumas (Fayetteville, AR: University of Arkansas Press, 1993), 103.
28. Clinton, *My Life*, 308.
29. Portis and Allen, *The Comeback Kid*, 88.
30. Clinton, *My Life*, 311.
31. Portis and Allen, *The Comeback Kid*, 92.
32. Meredith Oakley, *On the Make: The Rise of Bill Clinton* (Washington, DC: Regnery Publishing, 1994), 277.
33. Ibid., 390.
34. Clinton, *Living History*, 95.
35. Dick Morris, with Eileen McGann, *Rewriting History* (New York: Regan-Books, 2004), 108.
36. Accessed January 20, 2007, at www.hillaryclinton.com/about/.
37. Portis and Allen, *The Comeback Kid*, 208.
38. Blant Hurt, "Mrs. Clinton's Czarist Past," *Wall Street Journal*, March 19, 1993, A10. and Brock, *The Seduction of Hillary Rodham*, 174, both quoting from a 1988 survey of Arkansas teachers by the Winthrop Rockefeller Foundation. Even the 1992 Clinton campaign was afraid to make public some of the underlying data about the testing standards, a by-product of the inferiority complex that sometimes afflicts Arkansans. When a reporter from a national news organization asked to see a copy of the test used to certify teachers, campaign aides cautioned against release because "Arkansas will become the laughing stock because the questions are so easy." (Memorandum from Deborah Waltz to Clinton campaign aides, April 7, 1992.)
39. Haynes Johnson and David S. Broder, *The System* (Boston: Little, Brown and Company, 1996), 100.
40. Draft Report by Pillsbury, Madison and Sutro, 31.
41. Transcript of Hillary Rodham Clinton press conference, April 22, 1994, the White House.
42. Ibid.
43. Ray, *Final Report*, vol. 2, appendix 5, i–xv.
44. Ibid., part A, 97.
45. Ibid., 68.
46. November 14, 1986, letter from Jim McDougal to Clintons, in Ray, *Final Report*, vol. 2, part A, 66.

47. Clinton, *Living History*, 197.
48. Ibid.
49. Ibid.
50. Ray, *Final Report*, vol. 2, part A, 69.
51. Clinton, *Living History*, 198.
52. Ibid.
53. Ibid., 198.
54. Author interview with Hillary associate in 1994.
55. Author interview with Nancy Pietrafesa in 2006.
56. Interview with Jim Blair by Stephen Engelberg of the *New York Times* in 1994.
57. Ibid.
58. Ibid.
59. Ibid.
60. Stephen Engelberg, "Hillary Clinton Escaped Collapse in the Market that Cost Many Fortunes," *New York Times*, April 3, 1994, 16.
61. Ibid.
62. Ibid.
63. Blair interview.
64. Ibid.
65. Stephen Labaton, "Hillary Clinton Turned $1,000 into $99,540, White House Says," *New York Times*, March 30, 1994, A1.
66. Blair interview.
67. Ibid.
68. Clinton, *My Life*, 272.
69. Clinton, *Living History*, 86.
70. Pietrafesa interview.
71. Ibid.
72. Transcript of Hillary Rodham Clinton press conference, April 22, 1994, the White House.
73. Statement by Leo Melamed, released by the White House, April 11, 1994.
74. Stephen Engelberg, "New Records Outline Favors for Hillary Clinton on Trades," *New York Times*, May 27, 1994, A20.
75. Leo Melamed statement.

Chapter Six: Influence

1. *Washington Lawyer*, October 2002; interview of Marna Tucker.
2. Author interview with Kelly Waldron, public affairs department, Yale Law School, in 2006. Hillary graduated a year later than originally planned.
3. Department of Education Office of Civil Rights Fact Sheet 2006.
4. Author interview with Brooksley Born in 2006; Frances Mitchell Ross, "Reforming the Bar: Women and the Arkansas Legal Profession," *University of Arkansas at Little Rock Law Journal*, vol. 20 (Summer 1988), 869.
5. Frances Mitchell Ross, "Reforming the Bar."
6. Born interview.
7. Author interview with Yale Law School spokeswoman in 2006.
8. *ABA Journal*, April 1986.
9. Author interview with Eugene Thomas in 2006.

10. Ibid.
11. Ibid.
12. Clinton, *Living History*, 83.
13. Thomas interview in 2006.
14. Brock, *The Seduction of Hillary Rodham*, 96–111.
15. Author interview with Harriet Wilson Ellis in 2006.
16. Author interview with Mickey Kantor in 2006.
17. Ibid.
18. Hillary Rodham Clinton, *It Takes a Village* (New York: Simon & Schuster, 1996, 150–51.
19. Confidential memorandum to file of Vincent Foster Jr., September 3, 1986.
20. Clinton, *My Life*, 323.
21. Ibid.
22. Ibid.
23. Clinton, *Living History*, 108.
24. Jim Guy Tucker grand jury testimony on March 13, 1996, as cited in Ray, *Final Report*, vol. 2, part A, 166–67.
25. Clinton, *Living History*, 108.
26. Author interview with Allen W. Bird II in 2007.
27. Memorandum from Vincent Foster to Jeff Eller, an official in the 1992 Clinton campaign, March 19, 1992. Foster was helping the campaign answer questions about the Rose firm, and was recounting what the former managing partner at Rose, Joe Giroir, had told a reporter who was inquiring about the policy's origins.
28. Memorandum from Hillary Rodham Clinton to Members of Rose Law Firm, December 29, 1986.
29. Ibid.
30. Ibid. A few weeks later, the Rose partners received their "pro rata portion" of Hillary's payment of $12,235.83. (Memorandum from Brant Buck to Firm Members, January 23, 1987, Re: Fees Earned from State-Related Business.)
31. Ibid.
32. Author interview with Robert Mac Crate in 2006.
33. Crate and Ellis interviews.
34. Ellis interview.
35. Ibid.
36. Crate interview.
37. Ibid.
38. Ibid.
39. Author interview with Lucy Hackney in 2006.
40. Charles R. Babcock and Sharon Lafraniere, "The Clintons' Finances: A Reflection of Their State's Power Structure," *Washington Post*, July 21, 1992, A7.
41. In 2005, her reelection campaign returned $5,000 from Wal-Mart's political action committee days after the disclosure of an internal company memo that proposed ways to cut the costs of employee benefits, including discouraging unhealthy people from working at the company. (Beth Fouhy, "Clinton Quiet About Wal-Mart Ties," Associated Press Online, March 10, 2006, and Steven Greenhouse and Michael Barbaro, "Wal-Mart Memo Suggests Ways to Cut Employee Benefit Costs," *New York Times*,

October 26, 2005, 1.) And Senator Clinton turned down a request from lawyers suing Wal-Mart to help them in their class-action lawsuit alleging gender discrimination. (Author interview with lawyer involved in the case in 2006.)

42. Clinton, *Living History*, 97.
43. Ellis interview.
44. Born interview.
45. "Women in Law Face Overt, Subtle Barrier," Report of the American Bar Association Commission on Women in the Profession, 1998.
46. "Bar Condemns Sexual Barriers," *New York Times*, August 11, 1988, A21.
47. Ibid.
48. Born interview.
49. Crate interview.
50. Maraniss, *First in His Class*, 44.
51. Author interviews with associates of Hillary in 1994 and 2006.
52. Clinton, *My Life*, 334–35. But Bill Clinton does not mention the discussions with Betsey Wright.
53. Interview with Dick Morris by Dale Van Atta in 1999.
54. Morris, *Rewriting History*, 84.
55. Ibid.
56. Brock, *The Seduction of Hillary Rodham*, 235–36; see also Clinton, *My Life*, 358, and Maraniss, *First in His Class*, 455.
57. Author interview with Ron Fournier in 2007.
58. Ibid.
59. Brock, *The Seduction of Hillary Rodham*, 236.
60. Fournier interview.
61. Ibid.
62. Clinton, *My Life*, 358.
63. Dick Morris, *Behind the Oval Office* (New York: Random House, 1997), 63.
64. Letter from David Ifshin, general counsel of the Clinton for President Committee to Federal Election Commission, January 10, 1992; Jeff Gerth, The 1992 Campaign: Personal Finances; Wealthy Investment Family a Big Help to Clinton," *New York Times*, February 5, 1992, 20.
65. ABC's *Prime Time Live*, transcript of interview with Sheffield Nelson, January 30, 1992.
66. Ibid., transcript of interview with Hillary Rodham Clinton, January 30, 1992.
67. Ibid.
68. Clinton, *Living History*, 198.
69. Ibid.
70. Author interview with Jim McDougal in 1992.
71. Emily Couric, "Hard to Earn, Harder to Hold," *National Law Journal*, May 2, 1998, 51.
72. Ibid.
73. Author interview with Peggy Cronin Fisk in 2006.
74. Author interview with Anthony Paonita in 2006.
75. Ibid.
76. Fisk interview.
77. Author interview with Doreen Weisenhaus in 2006.

78. Undated, unidentified memo from 1992 Bill Clinton presidential campaign; author interview with former Clinton campaign aide in 2006.
79. "The 100 Most Influential Lawyers," *National Law Journal*, June 7, 2000.
80. Ibid. Hillary's Senate campaign later corrected the mistake.

Part Two: First Lady

EPIGRAPH: Hillary Rodham Clinton, quoted in Sheehy, *Hillary's Choice*, 245.

Chapter Seven: The Defense Team

1. Interview with Michael Cook, campaign aide, by Stephen Engelberg of the *New York Times* in 1994.
2. Memorandum from Loretta Lynch to Segal, Wright and Lyons, March 25, 1992, Re: Issues Facing the Defense Team.
3. Diane Blair interview on May 4, 2000, for the Archives of the David and Barbara Pryor Center for Arkansas Oral and Visual History at the University of Arkansas, Fayetteville.
4. Author interview with David Ifshin in 1994. Ifshin died in 1996.
5. Author interview with former campaign aide in 2006.
6. Author interviews of former campaign aides in 1994 and 2006.
7. Author interview with Mickey Kantor in 2006.
8. Ibid.
9. Clinton, *Living History*, 103.
10. Numerous 1992 campaign memoranda addressed to Hillary Rodham Clinton.
11. David Halberstam, *War in a Time of Peace* (New York: Scribner, 2001), 20.
12. Author interview with former campaign aide present at the tape playing in 2006.
13. Peter Goldman, Thomas M. DeFrank, Mark Miller, Andrew Murr, and Tom Mathews, *Quest for the Presidency 1992* (College Station, TX: Texas A&M University Press, 1994), 43–44.
14. Robert Novak, "Bland Book May Be Hillary's Attempt to Inoculate Herself," *Augusta Chronicle*, June 13, 2003, A5.
15. Jill Lawrence, "It's Getting Crowded in the Middle," Associated Press, September 17, 1991.
16. Clinton, *My Life*, 385.
17. Ibid.
18. Gail Sheehy, "What Hillary Wants," *Vanity Fair*, May 1992, 146.
19. Confidential memorandum from Jack Palladino to James M. Lyons, March 30, 1992.
20. Author interview with former campaign aide in 2006.
21. Richard L. Berke, James Bennet, Neil A. Lewis, and David E. Sanger, "President Weighs Admitting He Had Sexual Contacts," *New York Times*, August 14, 1998, A1.
22. CBS's *60 Minutes*, transcript of interview of Governor and Mrs. Clinton, January 26, 1992.

23. Ibid.
24. Ibid.
25. Author interview with Evelyn Shriver in 2006.
26. Ibid., and Kantor interview.
27. Shriver interview. Reynolds, who knew Wynette, worked for Hollywood producers who were friends of Bill and Hillary.
28. Ibid.
29. Clinton, *Living History*, 108.
30. Maureen Dowd, "The Campaign," *New York Times*, February 6, 1992, A18.
31. Ibid.
32. Author interviews with former campaign aides in 1996 and 2007.
33. Ibid.
34. Clinton, *It Takes a Village*, 43, and Clinton, *Living History*, 506.
35. Author interview with former campaign aide in 1994 and 2007.
36. Ibid.
37. Jeffrey N. Birnbaum, "Campaign '92: Clinton Received a Vietnam Draft Deferment for an ROTC Program He Never Joined," *Wall Street Journal*, February 6, 1992, A16.
38. ABC's *Nightline*, transcript of interview with Bill Clinton, February 13, 1992.
39. Kantor interview.
40. Goldman et al., *Quest for the Presidency*, 123.
41. Author interview with Jim Wooten in 2006.
42. Clinton, *My Life*, 388.
43. George Stephanopoulos, *All Too Human* (Boston: Little, Brown, 1999), 71.
44. Ibid.
45. Clinton, *Living History*, 240.
46. Ibid.
47. Author interview with Pat Schuback, spokesman for the Selective Service System, in 2007. He added that the only existing records consisted of a few entries in a logbook.
48. Copies of "Order to Report for Induction," dated April 1, 1969; "Postponement of Induction," dated May 16, 1969; and "Notice of Cancellation of Induction," dated July 23, 1969. Author interview with former campaign official in 2006.
49. "Clinton Draft-Binder Index," dated April 11, 1992. Author interview with former campaign official in 2006. It was clear that it was the original, because it was still emblazoned with time stamps from the selective service offices in Hot Springs and Little Rock.
50. Letter from Opal Ellis, secretary of Local Board 26, Hot Springs, Arkansas, to William Jefferson Clinton, July 23, 1969.
51. John King, "Clinton Again Ensnarled in Draft Controversy," Associated Press, April 5, 1992; Ralph Frammolino, "ROTC Officer Unaware of Draft Notice," *Los Angeles Times*, April 6, 1992, A15; Dan Balz, "Clinton Is Troubled Anew by Draft Issue," *Washington Post*, April 6, 1992, A15.
52. Kantor interview.
53. Author interview with former campaign aide in 2006; "Driving Questions Behind Clinton and the Draft," *Atlanta Journal and Constitution*, September 13, 1992, A13.
54. E-mail from Betsey Wright to Loretta Lynch, April 29, 1992, Re: Bobby Roberts.

55. Memorandum from Loretta Lynch to Governor Clinton and Betsey Wright, April 24, 1992, Re: The Handling & Storage of Your Selective Service and ROTC Files. Bill's letter to Colonel Holmes had been destroyed, but not before someone made a copy, which was how it wound up with *Nightline* so many years later. So Bill could not be sure if copies of other records of his had been made and retained, especially because the selective service records for the state of Arkansas were not destroyed until 1989, according to the memo.

56. Untitled Campaign Document, May 3, 1992, including transcription of notes made May 2 and argument by "BW," presumably Betsey Wright. Author interview with former campaign aide in 2007. Betsey Wright declined several requests to be interviewed for this book. She initially said she did not want to revisit the 1992 campaign. After being told there was evidence of Hillary's role in managing issues such as Bill's draft story, she e-mailed back a message saying Hillary "was not involved with me in the day to day work I did regarding attacks on Bill Clinton during the 1992 campaign." She also wrote that "[Hillary] was never involved in any conversation I had about the Selective Service. Unless an attack was on her or her family, I don't recall any conversations with her." Pressed further for an explanation, she declined to respond.

57. Author interview with former campaign aide in 2006.

58. Ibid. The document gives no explanation for why the statement was not released.

59. William Rempel, "Induction of Clinton Seen Delayed by Lobbying Effort," *Los Angeles Times*, September 2, 1992, 1.

60. *Los Angeles Times*, April 6, 1992, A15.

61. Kantor interview; fax from Michael Tigar to Hillary Rodham Clinton, May 5, 1992; and e-mail from Betsey Wright to Loretta Lynch, May 1, 1992, about waiting to call a draft lawyer until "bill and hillary have cleared it."

62. Memorandum from Loretta Lynch and Jennifer Chang to Governor Clinton and Betsey Wright, April 24, 1992, Re: The Effect of a Pending Induction Notice on ROTC Eligibility in 1969.

63. Ibid.

64. Letter from Opal Ellis, July 23, 1969.

65. Ibid.

66. Ibid.; e-mail from Betsey Wright to Loretta Lynch, May 1, 1992; author interview with former campaign aide in 2006.

67. E-mail from Betsey Wright to Loretta Lynch, May 6, 1992. Ray declined to be interviewed.

68. E-mail from Loretta Lynch to Betsey Wright, May 6, 1992.

69. Ibid.

70. William Rempel, "GOP Official Was Lobbied Over Clinton Draft Notice," *Los Angeles Times*, September 26, 1992, 1.

71. Ibid.

72. Ibid.; author interview with William Rempel in 2006.

73. Maraniss, *First in His Class*, 149–205.

74. Rempel, "GOP Official."

75. Roberto Suro, "The 1992 Campaign: Candidate's Record," *New York Times*, September 19, 1992, 1.

76. Randall B. Woods, "The Fulbright Files—Nothing There to Damage Clinton," *Washington Post*, February 16, 1992, C7.
77. Clinton campaign draft chronology of April 7, 1992, and author interview with former campaign aide in 2006.
78. Author interview with and e-mail from Vera Ekechukwu, Fulbright Papers Research Assistant, University of Arkansas Library, in 2007. Author interview with former campaign aide in 2006. Other correspondence of Lee Williams is in the archives. Williams, in an interview with an author in 2007, also said his correspondence with Bill should have been in the Fulbright collection.
79. Clinton campaign draft chronology of April 7, 1992.
80. Ibid.
81. Ibid.
82. Ibid.
83. Ibid.
84. Author interview with Lee Williams in 2007.
85. Clinton campaign draft chronology of April 7, 1992.
86. Clinton, *My Life*, 159–60.
87. Clinton campaign draft chronology of April 7, 1992.
88. Ibid.
89. Clinton campaign list, from February 1992, of "12 unanswered questions" for Dee Dee Myers; memorandum entitled "Unanswered Questions/Gaps/Inconsistencies," 1992; and campaign draft chronology, April 11, 1992. The nonpublic information in the chronology included an entry on December 2, 1969, for Bill Clinton's application to Yale Law School, in which he "lists his military status as 1-D" or deferred, based on a statement of August 1, 1969, though the chronology also shows that on both August 1, 1969, and December 2, 1969, his draft status was 1-A, or eligible to be drafted. Author interview with former campaign aide in 2006.
90. Ibid.
91. "Clinton to Be at Debate, Despite Bush 'Stonewall,'" Associated Press, September 14, 1992, from *Chicago Tribune*, C4.
92. Kevin Sack and Jeff Gerth, "The 1992 Campaign: The Favors Done for Quayle; A New Look at Guard Stint," *New York Times*, September 20, 1992, 1.
93. Diane Blair interview on May 4, 2000, for the Archives of the David and Barbara Pryor Center for Arkansas Oral and Visual History at the University of Arkansas, Fayetteville.
94. Ibid.
95. Ibid.
96. Ibid.
97. Kantor interview.

Chapter Eight: The "Only Stupid Dumb Thing"

1. Hubbell, *Friends in High Places*, 137.
2. Memorandum from Betsey Wright to Governor Clinton, July 14, 1986, in which she wrote that she was "worried" about the Whitewater investment. Bill replied, "No—Don't have anymore."

3. Jim McDougal grand jury testimony in 1997, cited in Ray, *Final Report*, vol. 2, part A, 6; Jim McDougal and Curtis Wilkie, *Arkansas Mischief* (New York: Henry Holt, 1998), 113.

4. Clinton, *Living History*, 87.

5. William Kennedy III grand jury testimony of December 17, 1997, cited in Ray, *Final Report*, vol. 2, part A, 71; author interview with a former lawyer in Little Rock in 1994.

6. Memorandum from Loretta Lynch to Segal, Wright, and Lyons on March 25, 1992, Re: Issues Facing the Defense Team.

7. Gerth learned about McDougal's willingness to talk and his whereabouts from Sheffield Nelson, a dedicated Republican opponent of Bill's who had run and lost in the Arkansas governor's election in 1990. McDougal and Nelson were former business associates who wanted to get out the story primarily to try to stop Clinton from being elected president. Nelson, a lawyer in Little Rock, was the only person that McDougal trusted to challenge Clinton politically in Arkansas. See Jim McDougal interview with FBI, Form 302, transcribed June 9, 1997, 61–62.

8. A few hours later, after Gerth had copied much of the Madison file, lawyers from the department arrived. They said some of the documents, including the Rose letters, should not be made public. Gerth objected and, after a few hours of consultations, the lawyers backed down and Gerth left with copies of the documents.

9. Joe Madden, grand jury testimony of November 4, 1997, cited in Ray, *Final Report*, vol. 2, part B, 365–66.

10. Ray, *Final Report*, vol. 2, part B, 366.

11. The campaign aide, Loretta Lynch, took notes of that conversation. They show that Hubbell said "HRC brought it [Madison] to the firm," and his review of the billing records showed that Hillary had "minimal contact" with the securities department commissioner. Memorandum from Loretta Lynch to David Wilhelm and Bruce Reed, February 18, 1992, Independent Counsel document no. 263–00000352.

12. Notes of telephone conversation on February 20, 1992, between Yoly Redden and Hillary Rodham Clinton, DKSN 025449, cited in Yoly Redden deposition by Senate Whitewater Committee on May 30, 1996, U.S. Congress. Senate. *Investigation of Whitewater Development Corporation and Related Matters: Hearings Before the Special Committee to Investigate Whitewater Development Corporation and Related Matters, Administered by the Committee on Banking, Housing, and Urban Affairs.* 104th Congress, 1st sess. (Washington, DC: U.S. Government Printing Office, 1997), 171.

13. Author interview with Susan Thomases in 1992, and Susan Thomases grand jury testimony of February 2, 1996, as cited in Ray, *Final Report*, vol. 2, part B, 370.

14. Author interview with Richard Massey in 1992, and Richard Massey grand jury testimony of December 3, 1997, as cited in Ray, *Final Report*, vol. 2, part B, 454.

15. Author interviews with former campaign aides in 1994, 2005, and 2006.

16. Ibid.

17. McDougal interview with FBI, Form 302, transcribed June 9, 1997, 62.

18. As for Madison's hiring of Rose, Thomases repeated that Massey was responsible for the referral. (Author interview with Susan Thomases in

1992.) Later, Thomases instructed Lynch to publicly repeat that Massey brought in Madison as a client, even though Lynch knew, from her own conversation with Massey and other research, that the story couldn't be supported. See Loretta Lynch grand jury testimony of February 1, 1996, as cited in April 22, 1998, memo from HRC Team to All OIC Attorneys, 82–83.

19. Susan Thomases handwritten notes of March 4, 1992, reflecting her conversation with Hillary Rodham Clinton. See Ray, *Final Report*, vol. 2, part B, 370.

20. Susan Thomases notes of March 4, 1992, reflecting her conversation with Bill Clinton. See Ray, *Final Report*, vol. 2, part B, 380.

21. Jeff Gerth, "Clintons Joined S&L Operator in an Ozark Real Estate Venture," *New York Times*, March 8, 1992, A1. Gerth, who returned to Washington late Friday night, did not see the edited version of the article until it was first published in the *Times*'s bulldog edition late Saturday afternoon. To his dismay, that version had been rewritten by editors to include a number of mistakes. Gerth quickly corrected the mistakes for subsequent editions. He never saw the headline, which was written by editors in New York.

22. Loretta Lynch grand jury testimony of February 1, 1996, cited in April 22, 1998, memo from HRC Team to All OIC Attorneys, 82.

23. Clinton Campaign Fact Sheet on Whitewater Development, March 8, 1992, Independent Counsel document no. LML 0075. Hillary reportedly found the article "totally inaccurate." See Goldman et al., *Quest for the Presidency 1992*, 183. Gerth's Whitewater article did not discuss how Madison came to retain Hillary and her law firm. Gerth returned to that issue in a subsequent story drafted a few days later, but an editor in Washington told him the editors in New York decided a second piece would be viewed by readers as "piling on" and spiked it.

24. Author interview with former campaign aide in 2006.

25. Ibid.

26. Memorandum from Loretta Lynch and Jonathan Foster to Hillary Rodham Clinton et al., April 23, 1992, Re: Answers to *Washington Post* on Finances; Memorandum from Betsey Wright to Jonathan Foster, April 17, 1992.

27. Michael Weisskopf, "Lawyer Will Review Arkansas Land Deal," *Washington Post*, March 12, 1992, A1; Michael Weisskopf and David Maraniss, "The Uncertain Intersection: Politics and Private Interests; Hillary Clinton's Law Firm Is Influential with State," *Washington Post*, March 15, 1992, A1.

28. Goldman et al., *Quest for the Presidency 1992*, 193.

29. David S. Broder and Edward Walsh, "Sharp Exchange Marks Democratic Debate: Brown Rakes Clinton in Wife's Law Firm," *Washington Post*, March 16, 1992, A1.

30. Ibid.

31. Andrea Mitchell, *Talking Back* (New York: Viking, 2005), 184–85.

32. Ibid.

33. Clinton, *Living History*, 109.

34. Ibid.

35. Paul Begala interview with ABC News and *Frontline* in 2000. See http://pbs.org/wgbh/pages/frontline/shows/clinton/interviews/begala.html.
36. Ibid.
37. Ibid.
38. Ibid.
39. Mitchell, *Talking Back*, 184–85.
40. Begala interview.
41. Clinton, *Living History*, 110.
42. Goldman et al., *Quest for the Presidency 1992*, 657–64.
43. Christina Cheakalos, "Election '92: The Republican Convention, Republicans Take Aim at Mrs. Clinton; Candidate's Wife Seen as Dangerous Feminist," *Atlanta Journal Constitution*, August 19, 1992, A10.
44. Report of James Lyons, March 23, 1992.
45. Campaign memo, March 24, 1992, "Post Questions Yet Unanswered After the WWDC Release"; Loretta Lynch grand jury testimony of February 1, 1996, as cited in Ray, *Final Report*, vol. 2, part B, 373; Weisskopf and Maraniss, "The Uncertain Intersection"; and Memorandum from HRC Team to All OIC Attorneys, April 22, 1998, Re: Summary of Evidence…Hillary Rodham Clinton and Webb Hubbell.
46. Hillary Clinton handwritten responses to draft of proposed answers, cited in Ray, *Final Report*, vol. 2, part B, 391; author interview with former campaign aide in 2006.
47. Loretta Lynch grand jury testimony of February 1, 1996, as cited in Ray, *Final Report*, vol. 2, part B, 373.
48. Clinton Campaign Document, undated, prepared on Vince Foster's computer, cited in Ray, *Final Report*, vol. 2, part B, 396–97.
49. Author interview with Mickey Kantor in 2006.
50. National Public Radio, *All Things Considered*, interview with Hillary Rodham Clinton, March 23, 1994.
51. Ray, *Final Report*, vol. 1, p. 136; Webb Hubbell interview with OIC. Form 302, transcribed April 10, 1995.
52. Charles Babcock and Sharon LaFraniere, "The Clintons' Finances," *Washington Post*, July 21, 1992, A7.
53. E-mail from Betsey Wright to Loretta Lynch, April 15, 1992.
54. Bill Clinton remarks of July 6, 1999, in Clarksdale, Mississippi, from *Public Papers of the Presidents of the United States: William J. Clinton, 1999*, book 2 (Washington, DC: U.S. Government Printing Office, 2001).
55. Memorandum from Loretta Lynch and Jonathan Foster to Hillary Rodham Clinton et al., April 23, 1992, Re: Answers to *Washington Post* on Finances; Memorandum from Betsey Wright to Jonathan Foster, April 17, 1992. The campaign, in April, told the *Post* that Hillary was "routinely copied on correspondence" involving the Elk Horn bank purchase but not in the effort to gain state approval. The *Post* had interviewed the state bank commissioner and quoted him saying that Hillary had discussed Southern Development's mission with him and "called him when corporate representatives came to town, apologizing for a schedule conflict that kept her from introducing them in person" (Wright to Foster, April 17, 1992).
56. Memorandum from Loretta Lynch to Hillary Clinton, May 16, 1992, Re: Conversation with Webb Hubbell Re: SDB.

57. Ibid., and Loretta Lynch notes of May 11, 1992, Re: Telephone Conversation with Hubbell.
58. Ibid.
59. Ibid.
60. Ibid.
61. Memorandum from Loretta Lynch to Hillary Clinton, May 16, 1992.
62. Stephen Labaton, "Former Aide to Clinton Testifies He Took Files," *New York Times*, February 8, 1996, B10; Ray, *Final Report*, vol. 1, 136; Webb Hubbell interview with OIC, Form 302, transcribed April 10, 1995. Hubbell later turned over these and other Rose files to the Clintons' lawyers, who returned them to the Rose firm.
63. E-mail from Betsey Wright to Loretta Lynch, May 1, 1992.
64. Loretta Lynch remarks at Princeton University's course HUM 445, Investigative Reporting, taught by Jeff Gerth, March 8, 2004. Lynch would later work for Democratic officeholders in California, including Senator Dianne Feinstein and Governor Gray Davis.
65. Author interview with Charles Babcock in 2006 and author interview with Susan Thomases in 1992.
66. Author interview with former campaign aide in 1994.
67. Jim McDougal interview with FBI, Form 302, transcribed October 3, 1996, 13.
68. Stephen Engleberg, "The Man Clinton Turns to in Times of Turmoil and Moments of Doubt," *New York Times*, July 5, 1994, A10.
69. Jim McDougal interview with FBI, Form 302, transcribed July 27, 1995, 1.
70. Rose Law Firm document no. 003624–25, provided to the Resolution Trust Corporation. See p. 137 of Draft Report by Pillsbury, Madison & Sutro for RTC, April 25, 1995.
71. Ray, *Final Report*, vol. 1, 134.
72. The records would later be used by prosecutors to call into question part of Hillary's story of how Madison came to be a client of the firm. Ray, *Final Report*, vol. 1, 140–41, and vol. 2, part B, 103–4 and 113–14.
73. Files found in Foster's office after his death.
74. Webb Hubbell later told the FBI that the Clintons wanted a permanent financial split from McDougal before going to Washington. Webb Hubbell interview with FBI, Form 302, transcribed April 17, 1995, 6.
75. Jim Blair letter to Sam Heuer, March 16, 1992.

Chapter Nine: "Welcome to Washington"

1. Johnson and Broder, *The System*, 105–6.
2. Clinton, *My Life*, 482.
3. "Hillary Clinton Issues a Call to Doctors," *Hotline*, June 11, 1992, and *American Health Line*, June 11, 1993. She may have understated her credentials; for example, she headed a rural health care advisory committee in Arkansas.
4. Dana Priest, "First Lady's Task Force Breaks New Ground," *Washington Post*, January 27, 1993, A6.
5. Clinton, *Living History*, 144.

6. Ibid., 149.
7. Hubbell, *Friends in High Places*, 4.
8. Priest, "First Lady's Task Force."
9. Author interview with Hillary friend in 2006.
10. Clinton, *Living History*, 133.
11. Paul Bedard, "First Lady's Task Force Broke Law on Secrecy," *Washington Times*, January 29, 1993, A1.
12. Ibid.
13. Clinton, *Living History*, 154.
14. Peter Flaherty and Timothy Flaherty, *The First Lady* (Lafayette, LA: Vital Issues Press, 1995), 192.
15. Clinton, *Living History*, 152–54.
16. Author interview with Leon Panetta in 2006.
17. James A. Baker III, *"Work Hard, Study...and Keep Out of Politics!"* (New York: G. P. Putnam's Sons, 2006), 333.
18. Author interview with Leon Panetta in 2006.
19. CNN's *Larry King Live*, Hillary Rodham Clinton interview, April 29, 1997.
20. Marian Burros, "Hillary Clinton's New Home: Broccoli's In, Smoking's Out," *New York Times*, February 2, 1993, A1.
21. Clinton, *Living History*, 171.
22. Ann Hodges, "Couric Scores Big Coup with First Lady Interview," *Houston Chronicle*, June 8, 1993, 1.
23. Clinton, *My Life*, 519.
24. Travel Office Memorandum, from Eric Dubelier and Kimberly Nelson Brown to Kenneth W. Starr and All OIC Attorneys, December 4, 1996.
25. Ibid., 329–31.
26. Ibid., 105–6.
27. Ibid., 104.
28. Ibid.
29. "Who Is Vince Foster?" *Wall Street Journal*, June 17, 1993, A10.
30. Travel Office Memorandum, December 4, 1996, 304.
31. Ibid., 306.
32. Ibid., 337.
33. Clinton, *Living History*, 172.
34. David Gergen, *Eyewitness to Power* (New York: Simon & Schuster, 2000), 292.
35. Author interview with former senior Clinton administration official in 2006.
36. Ibid.
37. Gergen, *Eyewitness to Power*, 268.
38. Ibid., 275.
39. Travel Office Memorandum, December 4, 1996, 127.
40. Hubbell, *Friends in High Places*, 194.
41. Ibid., 197, 212.
42. Author interview with former OIC officials in 2006.
43. Author interview with White House aide in 1997.
44. Hubbell, *Friends in High Places*, 259.
45. Clinton, *Living History*, 174.
46. Hubbell, *Friends in High Places*, 232–33.

47. Ibid.
48. Ibid.
49. Ibid.
50. Clinton, *Living History*, 174.
51. Author interview with former campaign aide in 2006.
52. Clinton, *Living History*, 175.
53. Ibid.
54. Hubbell, *Friends in High Places*, 232–34.
55. Ibid.
56. Ibid.
57. Ibid.
58. Ibid. Clinton, *Living History*, 175.
59. Report on the Death of Vincent W. Foster, Jr., by the Office of the Independent Counsel in Re: Madison Guaranty Savings and Loan Association, filed October 10, 1997, in the U.S. District Court of Appeals for the District of Columbia Circuit, 106–7.
60. Jeff Gerth and Stephen Engelberg, "Documents Show Clintons Got Vast Benefit from Their Partner in Whitewater Deal," *New York Times*, July 16, 1995, 18.
61. Clinton, *Living History*, 178.
62. Author interview with Robert Fiske in 2006.
63. Report on the Death of Vincent W. Foster, 103–4.
64. Author interview with Kenneth Starr in 2007.
65. Report on the Death of Vincent W. Foster, 104. An earlier draft of the report went into these matters, according to an author interview with an IC official in 1997. Adding even more mystery to Foster's state of mind was the discovery, in the summer of 1997, of a briefcase in the attic of Foster's Little Rock home. It contained records improperly taken from the Rose Law Firm offices. This cache of documents included Madison's billing records and other documents that Starr would use to challenge a key portion of Hillary's account of how Madison came to be a client of the Rose Law Firm. The documents, discovered a few weeks after the report on Foster's death was completed, tied Foster's concerns more closely to Hillary and therefore would likely have altered Starr's analysis of Foster's difficulties, one OIC lawyer said later. (Author interview with former OIC lawyer in 2006.)
66. Report on the Death of Vincent W. Foster, 99.
67. Author interview with Loretta Lynch in 1994.
68. Ibid.
69. Hubbell, *Friends in High Places*, 254.
70. Author interview with former OIC official in 2006.
71. Author interviews with John Henry and Ann Crittenden in 2007. Branch, in an interview with one of the authors in 2007, said, "I don't remember" the conversation but "I'm not denying it." He acknowledged that he knows Henry and Crittenden and that he has been to Aspen many times. But Branch declined to discuss Hillary or Bill, saying it was "stupid" to do so in light of the fact that he was writing his own book on Bill's presidency.
72. Julie Bosman, "Historian Plans Book from Chats with Clinton," *New York Times*, March 22, 2007, E1; author interview with Taylor Branch in 2007.

Bill Clinton, in his autobiography, says the oral history project began in late 1993. (Clinton, *My Life*, ii.)

73. Author interview with John Henry in 2007.
74. Johnson and Broder, *The System*, 141.
75. Ibid., 182.
76. Clinton, *Living History*, 198.
77. Author interview with Mickey Kantor in 2006.
78. Confidential memorandum from Sara Rosenbaum et al. to Hillary Rodham Clinton et al., June 3, 1993, Re: Legislative Specifications for the President's National Health Reform Plan.
79. Johnson and Broder, *The System*, 163.
80. Greg Steinmetz, "Insurance — Clinton Health-Plan Casualty: The Health Insurance Agent," *Wall Street Journal*, November 17, 1993, B1.
81. Johnson and Broder, *The System*, 264.
82. Ibid., 102.
83. Ann Devroy, "First Lady Defends Role She Calls a 'Partnership,'" *Washington Post*, October 1, 1995, A1.
84. Clinton, *Living History*, 248.

Chapter Ten: The School of Small Steps

1. Author interview with Hillary friend in 2006.
2. Author interview with Neel Lattimore in 2006.
3. Ibid.
4. Clinton, *Living History*, 209–10.
5. "Whitewater: White House Discloses Christmas Eve Subpoena," *Hotline*, January 6, 1994.
6. Clinton, *Living History*; Hillary noted that after Dole heard how much his words had hurt Bill, he apologized to Bill in a letter.
7. Clinton, *My Life*, 574; author interviews with three Clinton friends in 1998, 2006, and 2007.
8. Clinton, *My Life*, 574.
9. Clinton, *Living History*, 216, 244.
10. Ibid., 245.
11. Author interview with Robert Fiske in 2006. This was Fiske's first on-the-record interview with a journalist about his inquiry.
12. Ibid.
13. Author interview with Kenneth Starr in 2007. Starr added that the Lewinsky inquiry stemmed from actions by the attorney general and the statutory structure underlying the independent counsel. Congress had allowed the independent counsel statute to lapse, but reinstituted it in 1994, after Fiske had been selected by the attorney general. The statute, by contrast, provided for a special panel of federal judges to appoint an independent counsel.
14. Final Report of OIC, vol. 1, appendix 5, pp. xlvii–xlix.
15. Ibid.
16. For example, she discussed Hubbell's consulting work with California real estate billionaire Eli Broad, and he told her he would give Hubbell a

call, which he did. Broad's SunAmerica Corporation was one of Hubbell's employers. See OIC memorandum from Pat O'Brien to Ken Starr et al., October 22, 1998, "Hubbell Hush Money Summaries," 18.

17. National Public Radio's *Diane Rehm Show*, interview with Hillary Rodham Clinton, April 19, 1997, as transcribed by the *New York Times* and published April 11, 1997, 26.

18. Memorandum to All OIC Attorneys from RLF Conflicts Team, April 21, 1998, Re: Additional Factual Information About RLF Conflicts. Headlines trumpeting the prosecutors' theory about alleged hush money for Hubbell appeared at the top of the *New York Times*. Prosecutors were also convinced that Hillary "was on notice that Hubbell engaged in a widespread pattern and practice of cheating" at the Rose Law Firm. This belief was based mainly on a letter, written by one of the firm's attorneys in December 1993, informing the First Lady that "Hubbell's Rose billing problems were very serious."

19. *Diane Rehm Show*, interview with Hillary Rodham Clinton, April 10, 1997.

20. CNN, "Hubbell Resignation Painful to Clintons," March 14, 1994.

21. Ruth Marcus, "Clinton Angrily Denounces Republicans; Party Is 'Committed to Politics of Personal Destruction,' President Says," *Washington Post*, March 15, 1994, A1.

22. White House Transcript, President Bill Clinton, Remarks at the New England Presidential Dinner in Boston, March 14, 1994.

23. Clinton, *Living History*, 267.

24. Hubbell, *Friends in High Places*, 292.

25. Clinton, *Living History*, 266.

26. *New York Times*, March 30, 1994, A1.

27. Transcript of Hillary Rodham Clinton press conference, April 22, 1994, the White House; author interview with White House aides in 1994.

28. Author interview with White House aide in 1994.

29. Gwen Ifill, "Mrs. Clinton Didn't Report a Gain in '80," *New York Times*, April 12, 1994, A15.

30. Transcript of Hillary Rodham Clinton press conference, April 22, 1994, the White House. Hillary later wrote that the original story about the commodities trades accurately reported on her profits but contained inaccuracies about the relationship between Tyson and Governor Clinton. (Clinton, *Living History*, 223–24.) A short clause in the original piece was later corrected to show that Tyson had not received $9 million in state loans but had benefited from at least $7 million in tax credits from the state of Arkansas.

31. James B. Stewart, *Blood Sport: The President and His Adversaries* (New York: Simon & Schuster, 1996), 36–37.

32. Ibid., 37–39.

33. Ibid.

34. Ibid.

35. Public Opinion Online, April 22, 1994, Roper Poll, which found that as a result of Whitewater and related events, 4 percent of those polled had viewed her more favorably and 32 percent more unfavorably. See also Gwen Ifill, "The Whitewater Affair: The Overview; Hillary Clinton Takes Questions on Whitewater," *New York Times*, April 23, 1994, A1.

36. Clinton, *Living History*, 224–25.

37. Author interview with reporter who covered the event in 2006.

38. Clinton, *Living History*, 224–25; author interview with reporter who covered the event in 2006.

39. Transcript of Hillary Rodham Clinton press conference, April 22, 1994, the White House.

40. Clinton, *Living History*, 226.

41. Ibid., 221; author interview with a friend of Hillary in 2006.

42. Author interview with two Hillary friends in 2006.

43. Gallup Poll released April 25, 1994, PR Newswire, April 25, 1994.

44. Clinton, *Living History*, 245.

45. Ibid., 243–44.

46. Fiske interview.

47. Starr interview.

48. Johnson and Broder, *The System*, 461–62.

49. Clinton, *Living History*, 246.

50. John F. Harris, *The Survivor* (New York: Random House, 2005), 150.

51. Clinton, *My Life*, 620.

52. Clinton, *Living History*, 249.

53. Author interview with Hillary confidants in 2006.

54. *CNN Saturday Morning*, interview with Hillary Rodham Clinton, February 5, 2000. "Hillary Clinton to Become Official Candidate with Sunday Announcement." (www.CNN.com.) During the early days of her Senate campaign in 1999, Hillary used this phrase numerous times to describe her sized-down ambitions on several matters, especially health care. See Lynne Duke, "Hillary Clinton Brandishes Liberal Agenda Against Giuliani," *Washington Post*, October 24, 1999, A10.

55. Clinton, *Living History*, 254–55.

56. See, for example, Remarks of Hillary Rodham Clinton at St. Anselm College, Manchester, NH, April 13, 2007.

57. Clinton, *Living History*, 404. A Pulitzer Prize–winning book faulted Bill, saying he "never assembled his top policy advisers to discuss the killings." (Samantha Power, *A Problem from Hell: America and the Age of Genocide* [New York: Basic Books, 2002], 365–66.)

58. White House Excerpts, "Clinton in Africa," *New York Times*, March 26, 1998, A12.

59. Harris, *The Survivor*, 149–50.

60. Morris, *Behind the Oval Office*, 16.

61. Sheehy, *Hillary's Choice*, 253.

62. President Bill Clinton press conference, November 9, 1994, ABC News.

63. Sheehy, *Hillary's Choice*, 253.

64. Author interview with former Clinton administration official in 1996.

65. Author interview with Leon Panetta in 2006.

66. Ibid., and author interview with former Clinton administration official in 2006.

Chapter Eleven: The Discipline of Gratitude

1. Clinton, *Living History*, 260.

2. Ibid., 261.

3. Ibid.
4. Ibid.
5. Author interview with a Hillary friend in 2006.
6. Morris, *Behind the Oval Office*, 23.
7. Ibid.
8. Ibid., 24; Sheehy, *Hillary's Choice*, 258.
9. Morris, *Behind the Oval Office*, 25.
10. Author interview with friend of Bill in 2007.
11. Author interview with two friends of Hillary in 2006 and 2007.
12. Author interview with friend of Hillary in 2006.
13. Burt Solomon, "Doles and Clintons: Same Church, Different Pews," *National Journal*, February 24, 1996, 413.
14. Clinton, *Living History*, 267.
15. Connie Bruck, "Hillary the Pol," *The New Yorker*, May 30, 1994, 96.
16. Clinton, *Living History*, 258.
17. Ibid.
18. Hillary Rodham Clinton Transcript, White House, January 25, 1995.
19. Author interview with Hillary friend in 1999.
20. Author interview with a regular meeting participant in 2006 and a former administration official in 2007.
21. Author interview with a former administration official in 2007.
22. Author interview with Clinton White House strategist in 2006.
23. Troy, *Hillary Rodham Clinton*, 143.
24. Author interviews with two Hillary friends in 2006.
25. Ibid.
26. Clinton, *Living History*, 272.
27. Ibid.
28. Author interview with a person who discussed the issue with Bill Clinton in 2006.
29. "Pressler Law Continuance Urged," *News-India Times*, March 31, 1995.
30. Hillary Rodham Clinton speech to public forum sponsored by Vital Voices Global Partnership and New York University's Center for Global Affairs, March 6, 2005.
31. Remarks by Hillary Rodham Clinton at Lahore University of Management Sciences, March 27, 1995.
32. Ibid.
33. Author interview with a person who discussed the issue with Bill Clinton in 2006.
34. Clinton, *Living History*, 277.
35. Ibid., 279.
36. Ibid.
37. Ibid., 302.
38. Interview with Donna Shalala by Dale Van Atta in 1999.
39. Clinton, *Living History*, 304–5.
40. Ibid., 306.
41. Troy, *Hillary Rodham Clinton*, 150.
42. Ibid.
43. Clinton, *Living History*, 306.
44. Shalala interview.

45. Susan Baer, "Walking in Eleanor Roosevelt's Footsteps," *Baltimore Sun*, July 5, 1995, A1.
46. Author interviews with former Clinton aides in 2006 and 2007.
47. Shalala interview.
48. Ibid.
49. Interview with Robert Reich by Dale Van Atta in 1999.
50. Ibid.
51. Author interview with Leon Panetta in 2006.
52. Author interview with former Clinton aide in 2006.
53. Panetta interview.
54. *CNN Saturday Morning* transcript, February 5, 2000.
55. Panetta interview.
56. Interview with Melanne Verveer by Dale Van Atta in 1999.
57. Clinton, *Living History*, xi.
58. Panetta interview.
59. Ibid.
60. Interview with former Clinton official in 2007.
61. Clinton, *Living History*, 291.
62. Panetta interview.
63. Ibid.
64. Clinton, *Living History*, 46.
65. Ibid., 369.
66. Ibid., 368.
67. Rich Lowry, *Legacy: Paying the Price for the Clinton Years* (Washington, DC: Regnery Publishing, 2003), 89, 370; Robert Reich, *Locked in the Cabinet* (New York: Vintage Books, 1997), 320, 332.
68. Clinton, *Living History*, 369.
69. Morris, *Behind the Oval Office*, 300.

Chapter Twelve: "Off to the Firing Squad"

1. Stephen Labaton, "Senate Hearing Touches on Clinton's Integrity," *New York Times*, November 30, 1995, B14.
2. In their autobiographies, Bill and Hillary are especially critical of the *New York Times* and its reporter who broke the Whitewater story, Jeff Gerth. Both Bill's and Hillary's books also falsely describe the *Times*'s coverage of the Pillsbury, Madison report. In his book, Bill observes that the newspaper "didn't run a word" about the law firm's report, while Hillary, in her book, says the *Times* "ran a few paragraphs on the report." (See Clinton, *My Life*, 692, and Clinton, *Living History*, 328.) The newspaper's coverage was neither nonexistent nor a few paragraphs. The first *Times* article on the report was a 1,762-word article on July 16, 1995, when the report was still in draft form. Six months later, when the final report — essentially a duplicate of the draft report — was released, a shorter piece, thirteen paragraphs, was published. Two months later, the *Times* published two more pieces about an addendum to the report, one at 419 words and one at 1,168 words. The four articles: Jeff Gerth and Stephen Engelberg, "Documents Show Clintons Got Vast Benefit from Their Partner in Whitewater

Deal," *New York Times*, July 16, 1995, 18; Stephen Labaton, "Savings and Loan Bailout Agency Will Not Sue the Clintons," *New York Times*, December 24, 1995, 12; Irvin Molotsky, "Banking Agency Will Not Sue First Lady's Former Law Firm," *New York Times*, February 29, 1996, 18; and Neil Lewis, "Agency Won't Sue Hillary Clinton's Former Law Firm," *New York Times*, March 1, 1996, 25.

3. William Safire, "Blizzard of Lies," *New York Times*, January 8, 1996, 27.

4. Author interview with Hillary friend in 1999.

5. "White House Fires Back at Safire," CNN.com News Briefs, January 9, 1996, http://www.cnn.com/US/Newsbriefs/9601/01-09/index.html.

6. CNN, http://www-cgi.cnn.com/US/9601/first_lady/.

7. Angie Cannon, "Book Tour Dogged by Whitewater," *Philadelphia Inquirer*, January 17, 1996, A1, reporting on recent CNN/*Time* poll.

8. Kenneth W. Starr, *The Starr Report* (Rocklin, CA: Prima Publishing, 1998), 66–67; see also Sheehy, *Hillary's Choice*, 284.

9. Joe Battenfeld, "Woes Follow Hillary to Wellesley," *Boston Herald*, January 20, 1996, 1.

10. Ray, *Final Report*, vol. 1, 129–32.

11. Stephen Labaton, "Elusive Papers of Law Firm Are Found at White House," *New York Times*, January 6, 1996, 1.

12. Ray, *Final Report*, vol. 1, 129–32.

13. Clinton, *Living History*, 334.

14. Ibid., 335.

15. Author interview with former OIC lawyer in 2006.

16. Clinton, *Living History*, 335.

17. Ibid., 200.

18. Stephen Labaton, "First Lady Was Not as Candid as She Claimed," *New York Times*, January 20, 1996, 10.

19. Author interview with White House aide in 1997.

20. Ibid.

21. Bob Woodward, *Shadow: Five Presidents and the Legacy of Watergate* (New York: Simon & Schuster, 1999), 309–10.

22. *New York Times*, January 20, 1996, 10.

23. Ibid.

24. Author interview with former campaign aide in 2006. In addition, Hillary discussed with her friend Susan Thomases whether or not to turn over Whitewater corporate tax returns to the *New York Times* in March 1992. See notes of 1992 conversation between Susan Thomases and Hillary Rodham Clinton, Senate Whitewater Committee Document #ST 0000039. The tax returns were not released in 1992.

25. *Boston Herald*, January 20, 1996, 1.

26. Clinton, *Living History*, 334.

27. Ibid., 335.

28. Ibid.

29. Ray, *Final Report*, vol. 1, 131.

30. Memorandum from HRC Team to All OIC Attorneys, April 22, 1998, 201.

31. Clinton, *Living History*, 336.

32. Ibid.

33. Ibid.

34. Ibid., 336.
35. Sheehy, *Hillary's Choice*, 286. Author interview with senator in 2007.
36. Ray, *Final Report*, vol. 3, 110–13; author interview with former OIC officials in 2006.
37. PBS *Frontline* and ABC News *Nightline* interview with Jane Sherburne in 2000.
38. Ibid., and Robert Giuffra, Senate Whitewater Committee counsel, on ABC's *Nightline*, January 9, 1996.
39. *Washington Post*, January 6, 1996, A1, and "Report on Crimes Arising from the Castle Grande Transactions," September 4, 1998, by William K. Black to Office of Independent Counsel. Of particular interest was Hillary's billing of two hours for work that included an IDC-related option for Ward. Regulators said the option had been used by Madison to deceive them in connection with the Castle Grande deal. (Supplemental Report on Rose Law Firm Conflicts of Interest of September 20, 1996, by Office of Inspector General, Federal Deposit Insurance Corporation, ii–iii.)
40. Ray, *Final Report*, vol. 2, 140–218.
41. Ibid., vol. 3, 72–74.
42. Summary Rose Firm Conflicts, undated OIC memo [1998], 284.
43. Author interview with Allen W. Bird III in 2007.
44. Rose Law Firm statement of February 21, 2007, provided to the authors.
45. Bird interview.
46. Ray, *Final Report*, vol. 3, 74; FDIC Office of Inspector General Report of September 20, 1996, 20.
47. Seth Ward grand jury testimony of January 17, 1996; Seth Ward Senate deposition on February 12, 1996, as cited in Summary Rose Firm Conflicts memo, 282; and author interviews with former OIC officials in 2006. Ward told one investigator, "There was no way I talked to her about that," according to an interview by an author with a former OIC official in 2006.
48. Conferences of November 25 and November 26, 1985, as per Ray, *Final Report*, vol. 2, 152 and 167; conference of December 4, 1985, as per FDIC OIG Report, September 20, 1996, 51; and conference of January 14, 1986, as per Rose Law Firm billing memorandum DKSN029011.
49. FDIC OIG Report, September 20, 1996, 44.
50. Ray, *Final Report*, vol. 2, part B, 207–8.
51. Author interviews with former OIC officials and a former member of the Clintons' legal defense team in 2006.
52. Author interview with OIC official in 1997.
53. Jim McDougal interview with FBI, Form 302, transcribed June 9, 1997, 16.
54. Summary Rose Firm Conflicts memo, 298. Hillary's bills to the other client and Madison had a number of striking similarities: they included handwritten additions, the legal work was undocumented, and the fees were small. (Author interview with OIC official in 1997.)
55. Author interview with former OIC official in 2006.
56. Memorandum from HRC Team to All OIC Attorneys, April 22, 1998, 150.
57. Author interview with former OIC official in 2006. A report prepared for the OIC concluded that those who aided the Castle Grande fraud could be

charged with aiding and abetting. (See "Report on Crimes Arising from the Castle Grande Transactions," William K. Black, September 4, 1998.)

58. Author interview with former OIC official in 2006.
59. Summary Rose Firm Conflicts memo, 283; Ray, *Final Report*, vol. 1, 130.
60. Summary Rose Firm Conflicts memo, footnote 658, page 284.
61. Author interview with former OIC official in 2006.
62. Ibid. Ewing testified in the Little Rock trial of Susan McDougal on March 18, 1999, that he gave Hillary "about an 'F,'" as reported by Pete Yost in March 18, 1999, article for the Associated Press, "Starr Deputy Drafted Indictment of First Lady."
63. Author interview with former OIC official in 2006.
64. Author interview with Kenneth Starr in 2007.
65. Author interview with former OIC official in 2006.
66. Ibid.
67. Memorandum from HRC Team to All OIC Attorneys, April 10, 1998, Re: Hillary Rodham Clinton; Summary of Evidence and Suggested Reading. Author interviews with former OIC officials in 2006.
68. Ibid.
69. Ray, *Final Report*, vol. 2, part B, 292; author interviews with OIC officials in 1997 and 1998.
70. Ray, *Final Report*, vol. 2, part B, 291–92.
71. Author interview with former member of Clinton legal defense team in 2006.
72. Ibid.
73. Author interview with Jim McDougal in 1992.
74. Author interview with former member of Clinton legal defense team in 2006.
75. Author interviews with Hillary confidants in 1998 and 1999.
76. Sidney Blumenthal, *The Clinton Wars* (New York: Farrar, Straus & Giroux, 2003), 176.
77. Ibid., 176–77.
78. Author interview with friend of Hillary in 1999.
79. Clinton, *Living History*, 375.
80. Ibid.
81. Hillary Rodham Clinton transcript, Federal Document Clearing House (FDCH), August 27, 1996.
82. Clinton, *Living History*, 374.
83. Hillary Rodham Clinton transcript, FDCH, August 27, 1996.
84. Author interview with Hillary friend in 2006.
85. Clinton, *Living History*, 380.
86. Ibid., 420–21.
87. Author interview with Hillary friend in 2006.
88. Clinton, *Living History*, 438.

Chapter Thirteen: The Most to Lose

1. Author interview with Kenneth Starr in 2007.
2. Clinton, *Living History*, 439.

3. Ibid.
4. Ibid.
5. Author interview with Hillary friend in 1999. In her book *Hillary's Choice*, Gail Sheehy quoted a "lawyer close to the case" who had wanted to settle the case with Paula Jones, but he insisted that "Hillary held out" against a settlement (page 303).
6. Clinton, *Living History*, 440.
7. Ibid.
8. It is not known how much Hillary had helped her husband prepare for this deposition. Another woman on the witness list, Marilyn Jo Jenkins, was an Arkansas utility executive who often visited Bill in the governor's mansion after the 1992 election. Bob Bennett, the president's Washington defense lawyer, told Bill during that Friday-night prep session that his denials about having an affair with Jenkins sounded "frankly unbelievable." If Clinton lied under oath about her or any of the other women, Bennett warned him, "the crazies will come after you. They will try to impeach you if you lie. That's the only thing to worry about." "I hear you," Clinton said. (Author interview with Bob Bennett in 2006; see also Woodward, *Shadow*, 304.)
9. Clinton, *Living History*, 440.
10. Deposition of William J. Clinton, January 18, 1998, *Paula Jones v. William J. Clinton*. See http://www.washingtonpost.com/wp-srv/politics/special/clinton/stories/whatclintonsaid.htmdepo.
11. Clinton, *My Life*, 772.
12. Author interview with member of Paula Jones legal team in 1999.
13. Clinton, *Living History*, 440.
14. Ibid.
15. NBC's *Today*, Hillary Rodham Clinton interview by Matt Lauer, January 27, 1998; see also Clinton, *Living History*, 442.
16. Susan Schmidt, Peter Baker, and Toni Locy, "Clinton Accused of Urging Aide to Lie; Starr Probes Whether President Told Woman to Deny Alleged Affair to Jones' Lawyers," *Washington Post*, January 21, 1998, A1.
17. Author interviews with two Hillary confidants in 1998.
18. Author interview with Hillary confidant in 1998.
19. Author interview with former Clinton administration official in 2007.
20. Ibid.
21. Ibid.
22. Ibid.
23. Author interview with Hillary friend and adviser in 1998.
24. Ibid.
25. Clinton, *Living History*, 441.
26. Ibid.
27. Ibid., 442–43.
28. Author interview with Hillary friend in 2006.
29. Clinton, *Living History*, 443.
30. Author interview with Hillary friend in 2006.
31. Clinton, *Living History*, 443.
32. Ibid., 442.
33. Blumenthal, *The Clinton Wars*, 339.

34. Author interviews with two Hillary friends and a former Clinton administration official in 1998, 2006, and 2007.
35. Author interview with Hillary confidant in 1998.
36. Clinton, *Living History*, 441.
37. Ibid., 442.
38. *CNN Newsroom Worldview*, January 22, 1998.
39. Bob Deans, "Attempt to Cover It Up with Clinton-Stakes, Clinton-Characters, and Clinton GOP," Cox News Service, January 21, 1998.
40. CNN's *Crossfire*, January 21, 1998.
41. PBS transcript of *McNeil/Lehrer Report*, President Clinton interview with Jim Lehrer, January 21, 1998.
42. Author interview with Hillary confidant in 1998.
43. Author interview with Rahm Emanuel in 1998.
44. Brock's story mentioned a woman named "Paula," referring to Paula Jones. Brock had quite publicly switched ideological sides. And in 2002 he would write a confessional book about being a right-wing hired gun, *Blinded by the Right*.
45. See Blumenthal's book *The Clinton Wars*, 336–38, and Jeffrey Toobin's *A Vast Conspiracy* (New York: Simon & Schuster, 1999) for a lengthy discussion of the "collusion between Paula Jones' legal defense team and Starr's office," as well as the active roles played by *Newsweek* investigative reporter Michael Isikoff, conservative New York literary agent Lucianne Goldberg, and Internet Webmaster Matt Drudge. Drudge, with Goldberg's help, had broken the story that *Newsweek* had killed a story about Lewinsky and the inquiry on his Web site, The Drudge Report.
46. Blumenthal, *The Clinton Wars*, 340.
47. Ibid.
48. Author interview with former Clinton administration official in 2007.
49. Ibid.
50. Blumenthal, *The Clinton Wars*, 339.
51. Author interview with Bill Clinton confidant in 1998.
52. Clinton, *Living History*, 444; Toobin, *A Vast Conspiracy*, 246.
52. Author interview with Gore confidant in 2007.
54. Author interviews with two Bill Clinton advisers in 2007.
55. Author interview with Bill Clinton adviser in 2007.
56. Ibid.
57. Ibid.
58. Al Gore interview by Lisa DePaulo in *GQ*, December 2006, 305.
59. Author interview with Gore confidant in 2007.
60. Clinton, *Living History*, 444.
61. Author interview with Hillary confidant in 1998.
62. Author interview with Bill Clinton adviser in 2007.
63. Clinton, *Living History*, 444.
64. Ibid.
65. Author interview with Hillary confidant in 1998.
66. Ibid.
67. David Maraniss, "First Lady Launches Counterattack," *Washington Post*, January 28, 1998, A1.
68. Blumenthal, *The Clinton Wars*, 373.

69. NBC's *Today*, Hillary Rodham Clinton interview by Matt Lauer, January 27, 1998; also see Clinton, *Living History*, 443.
70. Author interviews with two prosecutors in the OIC in 1998.
71. OIC statement of Kenneth W. Starr, released to the public January 27, 1998.
72. Richard Morin and Claudia Dean, "President's Popularity Hits a High," *Washington Post*, February 1, 1998, A1.
73. Clinton, *Living History*, 445.
74. Author interview with Hillary confidant in 2006.
75. Author interviews with three confidants of the Clintons in 1998, 2006, and 2007.
76. Author interview with two White House aides in 1998; see also John Diamond, "Sharply Contrasting Views About Lewinsky Emerging," Associated Press, January 26, 1998, as appeared in the *Buffalo News* on January 27, 1998.
77. Author interviews with Clinton friend in 1998 and with a former Clinton administration official in 2007.
78. Ibid.
79. Author interview with James Carville in 1998; Don Van Natta Jr., "White House's All-Out Attack on Starr Is Paying Off, with His Help," *New York Times*, March 2, 1998, A12.
80. Author interview with Kenneth Starr in 2007.
81. Ibid.
82. Don Van Natta Jr. and Jill Abramson, "Quietly, Team of Lawyers Who Dislike Clinton Kept Jones Case Alive," *New York Times*, January 24, 1999, A1.
83. Starr interview.
84. Author interview with Hillary friend in 2006. Another source said that Hillary was "intimately involved" in the legal strategy sessions inside the White House "from the beginning." (Author interview with former Clinton administration official in 2007.)
85. Clinton, *My Life*, 780.
86. John F. Harris and Peter Baker, "President Rebuts Willey," *Washington Post*, March 17, 1998, A1.
87. Author interview with White House aide in 1998.
88. Author interviews with Clinton confidants in 1998, 1999, 2006, and 2007.

Chapter Fourteen: The Most to Gain

1. John M. Broder and Don Van Natta Jr., "Clinton and Starr, a Mutual Admonition Society," *New York Times*, September 20, 1998, A1.
2. Memorandum from HRC Team to All OIC Attorneys, April 10, 1998, Re: Hillary Rodham Clinton; Summary of Evidence and Suggested Reading; author interview with former OIC officials in 2006.
3. Ibid.; Memorandum from HRC Team to All OIC Attorneys, April 22, 1998, Re: Summary of Evidence...Hillary Rodham Clinton and Webb Hubbell; and Memorandum to File from Paul Rosenzweig, April 24, 1998.

4. Sheehy, *Hillary's Choice*, 306–7; see also Rick Van Sant, "First Lady Lauds Shelter, Flays GOP YWCA Facility National Model," *Cincinnati Post*, July 28, 1998, 7A.
5. Author interview with Hillary confidant in 1998.
6. Clinton, *My Life*, 801.
7. Author interview with OIC official in 1998.
8. Author interview with two Bill Clinton confidants in 1998.
9. Ibid.
10. Author interview with Bill Clinton confidant in 1998.
11. Ibid.
12. Clinton, *Living History*, 465.
13. Author interview with Hillary friend in 1998.
14. Richard L. Berke, James Bennet, Neil A. Lewis, and David E. Sanger, "President Weighs Admitting He Had Sexual Contacts," *New York Times*, August 14, 1998, A1.
15. Author interview with Bill Clinton confidant in 1998.
16. Clinton, *Living History*, 465.
17. Ibid.
18. Ibid. When Hillary's book was published in the spring of 2003, several journalists and conservative commentators challenged the fact that she claimed to have learned the truth about Bill's affair on August 15, 1998. Rush Limbaugh and Lloyd Grove, then with the *Washington Post*, suggested that Hillary had learned about it earlier in the month. Grove cited a book published by his *Post* colleague Peter Baker, entitled *The Breach*, which reported that on the evening of August 13, David Kendall was asked to inform Hillary of the truth about Bill's affair. But after Grove made the accusation, Kendall denied Baker's account. Lisa Caputo, the former press secretary to Senator Clinton, said, "I remember that time very well and that's exactly what happened. She had no idea." (Phillip Coorey, "The Clinton Affair: Buying the Story," *Adelaide Advertiser*, June 7, 2003.)
19. Clinton, *Living History*, 466.
20. Ibid.
21. Ibid.
22. Starr, *The Starr Report*, Text of Bill Clinton's Grand Jury Testimony, August 17, 1999. See http://www2.jsonline.com/news/president/0921fulltestimony .asp.
23. Ibid.
24. Ibid.
25. Ibid.
26. Ibid.
27. Author interview with two OIC officials in 1998.
28. Ibid.
29. Author interview with one of the meeting's attendees; see also Clinton, *My Life*, 802, and Clinton, *Living History*, 467.
30. Author interview with former Clinton administration official in 2007.
31. Clinton, *Living History*, 467.
32. Author interview with Bill Clinton confidant in 1998.
33. Author interview with Bill Clinton confidant in 1998; see also Clinton, *Living History*, 468.

34. Author interview with Bill Clinton confidant in 1998.
35. Ibid.; see also Harris, *The Survivor*, 344, and Toobin, *A Vast Conspiracy*, 317.
36. White House press release, August 19, 1998.
37. Author's observation of their walk televised by CNN, on videotape.
38. Clinton, *Living History*, 468.
39. The President's News Conference, October 14, 1999.
40. Adam Nagourney with Michael Kagay, "High Marks Given to the President, but Not the Man," *New York Times*, August 22, 1998, A1.
41. Author interview with Bill Clinton confidant in 1998.
42. Ibid.
43. Hillary noted in her book that the president's critics accused him of taking the actions to divert attention from his own problems, such as the possibility of impeachment. Clinton, *Living History*, 469.
44. Ibid., 470.
45. Ibid., 471.
46. Ibid., 473.
47. Ibid., 471.
48. Author interview with two Bill Clinton confidants in 1998.
49. Harris, *The Survivor*, 348–49.
50. Peter Baker and Susan Schmidt, "'Abundant' Lies Cited in Report; President Denies Impeachability," *Washington Post*, September 12, 1998, A1.
51. Clinton, *Living History*, 475.
52. Ibid.
53. Author interview with Bill Clinton confidant in 1998.
54. Clinton, *Living History*, 477.
55. Author interview with Clintons confidant in 2007.
56. Author interviews with Bill and Hillary confidants in 1998, 1999, 2006, and 2007.
57. Clinton, *Living History*, 478.
58. Ibid., 478–79; see also http://www.cnn.com/STYLE/9811/24/hillary/Vogue.

Chapter Fifteen: New York State of Mind

1. Frederic U. Dicker, "Senator Hillary Rodham Clinton (D-New York)?" *New York Post*, December 8, 1997, 20.
2. Author interview with Neel Lattimore in 2007.
3. Dicker, "Senator Hillary Rodman Clinton."
4. Author interviews with two Democratic strategists in 1999 and 2000.
5. Clinton, *Living History*, 483.
6. Ibid.
7. Author interviews with three Hillary confidants in 1999 and 2006.
8. Ibid., and author interview with a former Clinton administration official in 2007.
9. Author interview with Bill Clinton confidant in 1998.
10. Ibid.
11. Clinton, *Living History*, 489.
12. Vicki Allen, "Hillary Clinton Tries to Raise Democrats' Spirits," Reuters, December 19, 1998.

13. Author interview with a journalist who had covered the event in 2007.
14. Author interview with a former Clinton administration official in 2007.
15. James Bennet and Don Van Natta Jr., "President Digs In," *New York Times*, December 20, 1998, A1.
16. See Associated Press photographs of the event taken by Susan Walsh: http://www.pulitzer.org/year/1999/feature-photography/sample.html.
17. "Clintons Top Survey of Most Admired People," *Albany Times-Union*, January 1, 1999, 2.
18. Maureen Dowd, "Icon and I will Survive," *New York Times*, December 9, 1998, A29.
19. Michael Powell, "Hillary Clinton: The New Ideal," *Washington Post*, March 25, 1999, C1.
20. Author interview with Hillary confidant in 2006.
21. Clinton, *Living History*, 492.
22. Author interview with a friend of Bumpers in 2006.
23. Clinton, *Living History*, 493.
24. Ibid., 494.
25. Ibid., 496–97.
26. C-SPAN, interview with Hillary Rodham Clinton, January 1, 1997, via Federal News Service; on CNN's *Larry King Live* on April 29, 1997, Hillary said, "We will be, obviously, spending a lot of our time and living there [in Little Rock]."
27. Clinton, *Living History*, 496–97.
28. Ibid.
29. Ibid.
30. Ibid., 500.
31. Ibid., 501.
32. Hillary mistakenly calls the film *Dare to Compete* in her autobiography (*Living History*, 501).
33. Virginia Breen and Joel Siegel, "Hil Thrills, Won't Spill on Run," *New York Daily News*, March 5, 1999, 6.
34. Clinton, *Living History*, 501.
35. Ibid.
36. Ibid.
37. Author interviews with four Hillary confidants in 1999, 2006, and 2007.
38. Author interviews with three Hillary confidants in 2006 and 2007.
39. Interview with Republican senator by Dale Van Atta in 1999.
40. Clinton, *Living History*, 501.
41. Beth J. Harpaz, *The Girls in the Van* (New York: Thomas Dunne Books, 2001), 38–39.
42. Clinton, *Living History*, 502.
43. Author interview with Clintons confidant in 2000.
44. Author interview with Clintons confidant in 1999.
45. Ibid.
46. Author interview with former Clinton administration official in 2007.
47. Author interview with Clintons confidant in 2006.
48. The scene in the Solarium, and all quotes, from interviews with Alan Schechter, Jock Gill, and Jan Piercy by Dale Van Atta in 1999.
49. Lattimore interview.

50. Harpaz, *The Girls in the Van*, 44.
51. Terry McAuliffe, the Democratic fund-raiser and friend to both Clintons, offered to put up $1.35 million to secure their mortgage on the $1.7 million house. When people protested, McAuliffe withdrew the offer, and the Clintons secured a usual mortgage and put far less cash down. (See Don Van Natta Jr., "Looking a Gift House in the Mouth," *New York Times*, September 19, 1999, sec. 4, p. 6.)
52. Lattimore interview.
53. James Gerstenzang, "For Clintons, a Vacation to Savor," *Los Angeles Times*, August 22, 1999, A13.
54. Ibid.
55. Author interview with Hillary confidant in 2006.
56. Clinton, *Living History*, 510.
57. Ibid., 512.
58. Harpaz, *The Girls in the Van*, 71.
59. Clinton, *Living History*, 514.
60. Ibid. See also CNN.com: "Latest Police Shooting of Unarmed Man Fuels New York Senate Race Debate," at http://archives.cnn.com/2000/ALL POLITICS/stories/03/22/clinton.giuliani/index.html.
61. Ibid.
62. Author interview with Hillary strategist in 1999.
63. Clinton, *Living History*, 517.
64. Ibid.
65. Transcript of Hillary Clinton–Rick Lazio Debate, September 13, 2000, found at http://www.pbs.org/newshour/bb/politics/july-dec00/face-off_9-14.html.
66. Eric Pooley, "Little Ricky Gets Rough," Time.com, September 17, 2000, at http://www.time.com/time/magazine/article/0.9171.550900.00.html.
67. Ibid.
68. Clinton, *Living History*, 522.
69. Ibid., 524.

Part Three: First Woman

EPIGRAPH: Albert Einstein quotation, *New York Times*, April 22, 1955.

Chapter Sixteen: The Mysteries of Hillaryland

1. Clinton, *Living History*, 133.
2. Author interview with Hillary confidant in 2006; see also Ianthe Jeanne Dugan, "Clinton Supporters Eye $25 Million Campaign for New York Seat," *Washington Post*, July 16, 1999, A9.
3. Author interviews with several senior Senate aides and political analysts in 2006 and 2007.
4. Author interview with Senate adviser in 2007.
5. Author interview with Hillary friend in 2006. The reference to "kill me" was rhetorical; the friend continued to talk with the author.

6. Payroll and Federal Election Commission records reviewed by the authors in 2006 and 2007.

7. E-mail from Walker Irving, Hillary's deputy scheduler in the Senate, via D-SCHED@LISTSERV.SENATE.GOV, to all Democratic schedulers, March 19, 2007, Re: Kick-off Reception. Official mailing lists and Internet services can only be used for official purposes, according to the *Senate Ethics Manual*, 2003 edition, pp. 153 and 500. A senior Senate official, in an interview with one of the authors in 2007, said the use of the e-mail server appeared to violate the rules.

8. Author interviews with advisers and consultants to Hillary in 2006 and 2007.

9. Author interview with senior Hillary fund-raiser in 2007.

10. Remarks of Hillary Rodham Clinton at St. Anselm College, Manchester, NH, April 13, 2007.

11. Author interview with Senate ethics experts in 2006 and 2007.

12. Author interviews with Senate aides in 2006, and reviews of fellows' reports on file with the Secretary of the Senate.

13. Author interview with senior Senate official in 2007.

14. Author interviews with several Senate aides in 2006. Lott declined an interview request.

15. Remarks of Senator Trent Lott, "Hillary's New York State of Mind," CBSNews.com, November 11, 2000.

16. Author interview with Senate aide in 2006.

17. Author interviews with Senate aides in 2006 and a senator in 2007.

18. Frank Bruni, "New White House Staff Faces a Few Mysteries," *New York Times*, January 24, 2001, A15.

19. Remarks of Karl Rove, Clinton School of Public Service, University of Arkansas, Little Rock, March 8, 2007, via C-SPAN.

20. Ibid.

21. Ibid.

22. Author interview with Bill Clinton associate in 2006.

23. This was the legacy of years of criminal inquiries by the independent counsel. The debts were a sore point with Bill and Hillary. The Clintons felt the government should pay $3.58 million of their legal expenses because the investigation, and thus their massive legal debts, would not have happened save for politics. Those expenses did not include debts incurred as part of the Monica Lewinsky investigation, which Bill agreed not to seek reimbursement for as part of his settlement with the independent counsel. A panel of three federal judges, two appointed by Republicans, disagreed and authorized the payment of just $85,000.

24. Senate rules allow senators to receive book advances, as long as they are not subject to special treatment. Some critics asked the Ethics Committee to review Hillary's book deal, but the committee lacked jurisdiction to act because she had signed the deal before becoming a senator. Hillary herself sought ethics advice as well. Questions about the size of the advance dissipated after the book became a spectacular success after its release in 2003. It sold more than 1.5 million copies worldwide, easily earning back the $8 million advance for Simon & Schuster. See Elizabeth Kolbert, "The Student," *The New Yorker*, October 13, 2003, 63.

25. Building permits on file with District of Columbia Department of Consumer and Regulatory Affairs.

26. Glenn Thrush, "Vows to Make History," *Newsday*, January 21, 2007, A4.

27. Author interview with a guest at a Whitehaven fund-raiser in 2006.

28. Clinton, *Living History*, 260.

29. Author interviews with Evelyn Lieberman associates in 2006 and 2007.

30. Author interview with Senate adviser in 2007. It wasn't until after the 2006 election that Lieberman, described by one Hillary associate as part of the "inner, inner circle," surfaced in public records as working with the campaign. (Author interview with former Clinton administration official in 2007. Friends of Hillary report with FEC, travel reimbursement paid on November 27, 2006.) By 2007, Lieberman was devoting herself to Hillary's run for president. (Author interview with associate of Evelyn Lieberman in 2007.) Lieberman did not return a phone call seeking comment.

31. Author interviews with task force participants in 2006.

32. Ibid., and author interviews with Senate aides in 2006.

33. Author interviews with Cornell University employees in 2006.

34. E-mail to author from Susan A. Henry, The Ronald P. Lynch Dean of Agriculture and Life Sciences, Cornell University, in 2007.

35. Author interviews with Lee Telega in 2006. Telega believes he was chosen largely because of his "lobbying" experience, having occasionally "interacted on government relations" for Cornell. (Author interview.) He says he became a half-time lobbyist for Cornell in the fall of 2004, two years after he finished his fellowship.

36. Author interviews with Lee Telega in 2006. Dean Henry said he was paid with "university discretionary, nongovernmental funds." Cornell is both a private university and New York State's land grant university. Telega's affiliation is with the latter.

37. Author interview with Cathleen Shiels, a member of Senator Clinton's agricultural advisory committee, in 2006.

38. Annual reports of research expenditures, Cornell University Office of the Vice President for Research, 2002–2005.

39. Grants went from $13.5 million in 2002 to an average of almost $19 million for the years 2003–2005. Cornell received at least three grants under a new program, Conservation Innovation Grants (CIG), created under Title II of the bill, according to the annual reports of research expenditures, Cornell University Office of the Vice President for Research, www.USDA.gov/farmbill2002/, and www.nrcs.usda.gov/programs/cig/.

40. Letters by Senator Hillary Rodham Clinton to Senate conferees on March 19 and April 25, 2002, involving programs for dairy support, farmland protection, and conservation; statement by Senator Hillary Rodham Clinton on April 27, 2002, discussing her meeting with New York State agriculture supporters, where she took credit for fighting hard for dairy supports and helping to win increased funding for conservation programs in the farm bill.

41. Author interviews with Lee Telega in 2006.

42. Telega interview; Blaine Friedlander Jr., "CU Agriculturists and Alumni Named to Clinton Advisory Panel," *Cornell Chronicle*, September 20, 2001, 3; e-mail to author from Dean Susan Henry in 2007.

43. Telega interview. He said that most of Cornell's federal money falls under the research section of the bill, which was not contentious compared to sections on milk supports and conservation programs. Cornell did receive grants under the conservation section of the farm bill, including three, totaling more than $1 million, for a new program authorized in 2002.

44. *Senate Ethics Manual*, 2003 edition, p. 114, and author interviews with former Ethics Committee aide in 2006 and 2007.

45. Senate Rule 41, paragraph 6.

46. Author inspection in 2006 of outside employee files at the Secretary of the Senate. Copies are then sent to the Ethics Committee. Some of Hillary's fellows worked out of an extra suite of offices on the third floor of Russell, right below Hillary's principal office complex. (Author interview with Costas Panagapolous in 2007. He was a fellow from November 2004 to the summer of 2005 and worked out of Russell 376.) Dr. Frank Luk, a fellow in 2004, says he also worked on the third floor of Russell. (Author interview with Dr. Frank Luk in 2007.) Dr. Luk, a professor at Rensselaer Polytechnic Institute, says he worked full-time for twelve months beginning in 2004 on a special fellowship arranged by the university's office of government affairs and supported with university funds. Hillary's office asked RPI's office of government affairs "if they could provide a fellow," according to Deborah Altenburg, RPI's director of federal relations, who was interviewed by one of the authors in 2007. There are no forms on file at the Senate for Dr. Luk, nor does he remember filling out any that relate to Senate Rule 41. He said, "There was hardly any paperwork to fill out." For the years 2001–2006, there were about three hundred fellows registered in the Senate; still others worked shorter periods and were not required to file reports. (Author review in 2006 of outside employee files at the Secretary of the Senate and author interviews with senior Senate aides in 2006.) A few prestigious fellowships, named after deceased senators, are funded by the Senate itself. Still other fellows are detailed or loaned to Congress from various branches of the government. The rest of the fellows are sponsored by universities, nonprofit organizations, and scientific associations.

47. Form 41.6.

48. Author inspection of the Senate Office of Public Records reports in 2006 and early 2007.

49. Senate Rule 41, paragraph 4, requires employees to agree to familiarize themselves with the Senate's rules. Form 41.4, "Agreement to Comply with the Senate Code of Official Conduct" must be signed by the Senate fellow.

50. Form 41.4 is accepted by the Ethics Committee and filed with the Senate's Office of Public Records, where it is maintained for more than a decade. No such agreement was on file in 2006 or early 2007. Telega says he does not remember signing any such agreement. Many other fellows, working for about half the Senate's one hundred members between 2001 and 2006, signed such agreements, according to a review of the files.

51. Another Senate rule, number 38, bars the "private supplementation of expenses incurred in connection with the operation of a Member's office." (See Select Committee on Ethics Interpretative Ruling 443, issued June 22,

1995.) But there is an exception for fellows to the rules ban on defraying official expenses through private sources. To qualify, the fellowship program must be "primarily of educational benefit" to the fellow — not an augmentation of the senator's work — free of conflict of interest and flexible enough to allow the fellow "to undertake any kind of activities." (See Senate Ethics Committee Interpretative Ruling 444, February 14, 2002.) The senator determines if the program meets the educational test, and the ethics panel looks at conflict questions on a case-by-case basis. In addition, a fellowship can qualify for an exception "provided that the Senator does not solicit for such programs and does not receive reports on who contributes to any program established by or for him." Telega says he learned a lot from his fellowship. But he also says he functioned as a full-time staffer; he attended staff meetings, served at the direction of Hillary's aides, operated full-time out of her Senate offices, utilized Senate equipment, represented her in meetings with government officials and private parties, and was identified on the Senate floor as a member of her staff. (See author interviews with Lee Telega in 2006 and *Congressional Record* for February 13, 2002.) Telega, in his late forties at the time of his fellowship, says he used his experience to help him in his subsequent job lobbying for Cornell. Dean Henry, in her e-mail, says Telega "periodically briefed me on the progress of the Farm Bill and the implications of various formulations of the bill for New York agriculture." (Dean Henry e-mail message to one of the authors in 2007.)

52. Author review in 2006 of various records, including citations in the *Congressional Record*, announcements by sponsoring organizations, résumés of the individuals as posted on the Internet by them or their employer, interviews with fellows, and e-mail from Susan A. Henry to author in 2007, noting that the second Cornell fellow worked for one year. Hillary approved that fellow's travel to New York to study Cornell's agricultural work in a trip partially paid for by Cornell. (See Employee Advance Authorization and Disclosure of Travel reimbursement, filed September 16, 2002.) Hillary also enjoyed the services of more than a dozen interns, including students from Wellesley, her alma mater, from Ireland, and of Indian American background.

53. Author interview with Mark Oleszek, Berkeley Program Administrator for the John Gardner Fellowship Program, in 2007. Oleszek said the 2006–07 Gardner fellow at Senator Clinton's office interviewed with Senator Barack Obama but chose Senator Clinton. The fellowship lasts ten months, is a full-time job, and includes a stipend. A social psychologist and PhD candidate at Yale University who spent eight months working for Senator Clinton in 2004 described her experience in a graduate student journal: "I was responsible for speech writing, coming up with ideas for legislation, doing background research, drafting legislation and working with legislative counsel.... I had a lot of meetings with lobbyists and constituents and meetings with other Democratic offices." Virginia Brescoll, quoted in *Rookie, the Voice of the SPSSI Graduate Student*, August 2005.

54. Author review in 2006 and 2007 of outside employee files at the Secretary of the Senate. Hillary only filed an initial "supervisor's report" for a

fellow in 2003, not the required quarterly reports or termination report. Moreover, as the "supervisor's report" states, the employee, if working more than ninety days, must sign a separate agreement to abide by Senate rules. This "agreement to comply," most of which is completed by the senator, had never been publicly filed by any of Hillary's fellows before March 2007.

55. Author interviews with current and former Senate aides and fellows in 2006 and 2007.
56. Forms 41.4 and 41.6 filed with the Secretary of the Senate.
57. One of the authors raised questions in March 2007 with several organizations sponsoring fellows in Senator Clinton's office.
58. Author interview with former Senate Ethics Committee aide in 2006.
59. Author review of supervisor's reports on file with the Secretary of the Senate. The sponsors include the American Psychological Association, the American Political Science Association, the Women's Research and Education Institute, the Robert Woods Johnston Foundation, and the John Heinz Fellowship.
60. The four other fellows were sponsored by the John Gardner Fellowship Program, Rensselaer Polytechnic Institute, and two from Cornell University.
61. Author interview with Senate official in 2006.

Chapter Seventeen: The Longest Day

1. Fox News, *On the Record*, Hillary Rodham Clinton interview with Greta Van Susteren, September 11, 2006.
2. Hillary Rodham Clinton's thoughts and worries in this paragraph are reflected in her remarks on September 15, 2001, at a funeral for Father Mychal Judge, chaplain of the New York Fire Department, as transcribed for Federal Document Clearing House Political Transcripts.
3. *Dateline NBC*, Hillary Rodham Clinton interview, September 17, 2001.
4. Chelsea Clinton, *Talk Magazine*, December 2001. See also Howard Kurtz, "Media-Shy Chelsea Clinton Ends Her Silence; Talk Magazine Publishes Her First-Person Account of Sept. 11," *Washington Post*, November 11, 2001, C1, and Jennifer Harper, "Details of 'Terror Day Tale' Pit Hillary vs. Chelsea," *Washington Times*, November 10, 2001, A1. Other observations of Hillary's from that day are from *Dateline NBC*, Hillary Rodham Clinton interview with Jane Pauley, September 17, 2001.
5. Ibid.
6. Hillary Rodham Clinton press release, January 11, 2001.
7. Clinton, *Living History*, xi.
8. Cathy Pryor, "A Tearful Clinton Hurries Back to NY," *The Australian*, September 13, 2001, 7.
9. Author interview with Hillary Rodham Clinton confidant in 2006.
10. Schumer quote from "Politics," *Congress Daily*, September 12, 2001.
11. CNN transcript, Hillary Rodham Clinton, September 11, 2001.
12. Alison Mitchell and Katharine Q. Seelye, "A Day of Terror: Congress," *New York Times*, September 12, 2001, A20. See also Elaine Povich, "Terrorist Attacks; Across the Nation; Congress Rallies Against Terror," *Newsday*,

September 12, 2001, W30. A video of the moment is at http://www.youtube
.com/watch?v=CUhlBF8Em70; see also http://www.authentichistory.com/
audio/attackonamerica/speeches/20010911_Congress_Sings_God_
Bless_America.html.

13. Author interview with Clinton confidant in 2007.

14. United States Senate Floor Remarks of Senator Hillary Rodham Clinton, September 12, 2001. Years later, she said her remarks that day were "pretty pugnacious" but appropriate in the immediate aftermath of the attacks. Jeffrey Goldberg, "The Starting Gate," *The New Yorker*, January 15, 2007, 28.

15. Author interview with Bush White House official in 2007.

16. Hillary Rodham Clinton Senate Web site, http://www.clinton.senate.gov, accessed September 12, 2006.

17. Author interviews with past and present Senate aides in 2006.

18. Fox News interview with Hillary Rodham Clinton, September 11, 2006.

19. HumanEvents.com, "Hillary Watch," September 24, 2001. Frank Bruni, "Show Us the Money" *New York Times Sunday Magazine*, December 16, 2001, 60.

20. Joel Siegel, "Hill Says Finish Afghan War, the Target Saddam," *New York Daily News*, March 9, 2002, 2.

21. HumanEvents.com, "Hillary Watch," September 24, 2001.

22. United States Senate Floor Statement of Hillary Rodham Clinton, November 27, 2001, Congressional Record, 512049.

23. David Barstow, "A Nation Challenged: Federal Aid; Old Rivals but One Voice in Request for Help," *New York Times*, September 19, 2001, B9.

24. Author interview with Bush White House official in 2007.

25. Hillary Rodham Clinton remarks at press briefing after White House meeting, September 13, 2001, FDCH Political Transcripts.

26. Clinton, *Living History*, 531.

27. Ibid.

28. *CBS Evening News with Dan Rather*, Hillary Rodham Clinton interview with Dan Rather, September 13, 2001.

29. This is according to the authors' search of the Lexis-Nexis database for all statements made by Hillary Rodham Clinton from early January 2001 to September 2001; the precise phrase searched was "homeland threat."

30. *CBS Evening News with Dan Rather*, Hillary Rodham Clinton interview with Dan Rather, September 13, 2001.

31. John Solomon, "Clinton Mulled Bin Laden Attack," Associated Press Online, September 13, 2001.

32. CNN Transcript, Hillary Rodham Clinton interview with Judy Woodruff, September 13, 2001.

33. *The 9/11 Commission Report: Final Report of the National Commission on Terrorist Attacks Upon the United States* (New York: W. W. Norton, 2006), 141. The commission also found that in the final weeks of the Clinton administration, military action against Al Qaeda or the Taliban in Afghanistan had not even reached the planning stages. President Clinton and National Security Adviser Sandy Berger had determined that the CIA's "preliminary judgment" of Al Qaeda involvement in the bombing of the *Cole* was an "unproven assumption" and therefore not conclusive enough to warrant military action, the commission concluded (pp. 193–94). Later in its

report, the commission also "found no indications" that President Clinton was presented the option of "the idea of invasion" or "lesser forms of intervention" in Afghanistan (p. 349).

34. CNN's *Larry King Live*, Hillary Rodham Clinton interview with Larry King, September 13, 2001.

35. NBC's *Today*, Hillary Rodham Clinton interview with Katie Couric, September 14, 2001. Although Hillary confused a few details about Chelsea's whereabouts, the mistakes were understandable, as it was a chaotic and emotionally wrenching time.

36. *New York Post* wire services, "Grief and Grim Resolve at National Cathedral," *New York Post*, 9.

37. *CNN Live*, Bill Clinton interview, September 14, 2001.

38. Author interview with Hillary confidants in 2006 and 2007.

39. Gallup Poll for CNN/*USA Today* released September 17, 2001, showing 45 percent blaming President Clinton for the attacks and 34 percent blaming President Bush.

40. "America Under Attack," ABC News, September 14, 2001.

41. Richard Berke, "A Nation Challenged: Political Memo; Attacks Shift Spotlight on Public Figures," *New York Times*, November 19, 2001, A1.

42. ABC News, Transcript of Presidential Speech, September 20, 2001.

43. Videotape of Bush speech to Congress on September 20, 2001, reviewed by the author; see also HumanEvents.com, "Hillary Watch," October 1, 2001.

44. Letters to the editor from Kathie Larkin, *Atlanta Journal-Constitution*, September 21, 2001; and James S. Gale, *Washington Post*, September 22, 2001.

45. HumanEvents.com, "Hillary Watch," October 1, 2001.

46. Nicholas Lemann, "The Hillary Perspective," *The New Yorker*, October 8, 2001, 48.

47. Bruni, "Show Us the Money."

48. This bit of revisionist editing was first reported by ABC's John Stossel in 2002. A clip showing the before and after videos can be found at http://www.mediaresearch.org/rm/cyber/2002/stossel083002/segment1.ram. Quotations of Hillary Rodham Clinton's appearance were taken from the before video.

49. Author interview with Dr. William Rom in 2006.

Chapter Eighteen: *"The Hardest Decision"*

1. Jeffrey Goldberg, "The Starting Gate," *The New Yorker*, January 15, 2007, 28.

2. Author interview with former Senate aide in 2006.

3. United States Senate Floor Remarks of Senator Hillary Rodham Clinton, October 10, 2002, *Congressional Record*, S10288-90.

4. Paul West, "New Ratings Create Buzz for Clinton," *Baltimore Sun*, June 26, 2006, 1A.

5. Author interviews with several senior associates and advisers of the Clintons in 2006 and 2007.

6. "Attack in Iraq: Clinton's Statement," *New York Times*, December 17, 1998, A16.
7. Bill Clinton, *My Life*, 834.
8. Todd S. Purdum, "Threats and Responses; News Analysis; Stern Tone, Direct Appeal," *New York Times*, October 8, 2002, A1.
9. United States Senate Floor Remarks of Senator Hillary Rodham Clinton, October 10, 2002.
10. Joshua Green, "Hillary's Choice," *The Atlantic*, November 2006, 70.
11. Author interview with White House official who spoke with President Bush about the meeting in 2007.
12. Green, "Hillary's Choice."
13. Author interview with White House official who spoke with President Bush and Condoleezza Rice about the discussions of October 8, 2002, in 2007.
14. Carl Leubsdorf, "Senator Clinton Criticizes U.S. Intelligence on Iraq," *Dallas Morning News*, September 25, 2003, 10A.
15. Author interviews with current and former Senate aides in 2006 and 2007. The personal staffs of senators do not have access to the most sensitive reports; only staff members on committees that deal with national security enjoy such clearance. Hillary didn't join such a committee until 2003, when she was named to the Armed Services Committee.
16. *Fox News Sunday*, interview with Senator Jay Rockefeller, vice chairman of the Senate Intelligence Committee in 2005, November 13, 2005.
17. Eloise Harper, "A Heated Exchange for Hillary," ABC News, April 14, 2007, and author interview with Eloise Harper in 2007. Hillary could have been briefed by her foreign-policy aide, but he lacked the clearance to read the entire National Intelligence Estimate (NIE). Or she could have learned about the NIE during a senators-only briefing by the Bush administration.
18. Bob Graham, "The President Lied to Us," *The Record*, November 23, 2005, L9.
19. Author interview with former senator Bob Graham in 2006.
20. Bob Graham and Jeff Nussbaum, *Intelligence Matters* (New York: Random House, 2004), 197.
21. United States Senate Floor Remarks of Senator Hillary Rodham Clinton, October 10, 2001. In 2004 Hillary told Gabe Pressman of WNBC that she had "seen" the intelligence reports "in my husband's administration" about Iraq's WMD. (See transcript of WNBC interview of Senator Hillary Clinton by Gabe Pressman on May 16, 2004.)
22. Letter from Central Intelligence Agency to the Honorable Bob Graham, October 7, 2002. The letter also talked about weapons training for Al Qaeda by Iraq and the presence in Iraq of Al Qaeda members, and says the two parties "discussed safe haven." However, the CIA letter made no mention of any ties between Saddam Hussein himself and Al Qaeda nor did it say that the discussions of safe haven had led to sanctuary in Iraq for the terrorists. A Defense Intelligence Agency report in February 2002 also cast doubt on the weapons training assertion. The report found that the source for the allegation that Al Qaeda received weapons training from Iraq, a defector, was probably "intentionally misleading" his handlers. See Statement of Senator Carl Levin, "Levin Says Newly Declassified

Information Indicates Bush Administration's Use of Pre-War Intelligence Was Misleading," November 6, 2005 (www.levin.senate.gov). On *Meet the Press* on May 6, 2007, George Tenet said that in closed testimony before the committees, the CIA qualified the judgments about ties between Al Qaeda and Iraq that had been made in the letter of October 7, 2002.

23. Statements of Senator Carl Levin, November 6, 2005.

24. *Report of the Select Committee on Intelligence on Postwar Findings About Iraq's WMD Programs and Links to Terrorism and How They Compare with Prewar Assessments,* released September 8, 2006.

25. Graham interview; see also Graham, *Intelligence Matters,* 181.

26. The Pew Research Center for the People and the Press, poll taken October 2002. See http://people-press.org/reports/pdf/173.pdf.

27. *Congressional Record,* October 10, 2002, S10292.

28. Ibid, and author interviews with former and current Senate aides in 2006.

29. *Congressional Record,* October 10, 2002, S10339–40.

30. Author interview with Kenneth Pollack in 2007. Pollack declined to discuss the specifics of his conversations about Iraq with Hillary.

31. Remarks by Senator Hillary Rodham Clinton at a Forum of Democratic Presidential Candidates, in Carson City, Nevada, February 21, 2007 (authors' observation of forum).

32. Author interview with several Hillary confidants in 2006 and 2007.

33. Author interviews with current and former senators and senior aides in 2006.

34. Author interviews with Hillary confidants in 2006 and 2007.

35. Author interviews with participants in briefing in 2006.

36. United States Senate Floor Remarks of Senator Hillary Rodham Clinton, October 10, 2002.

37. United States Senate Floor Remarks of Senator Carl Levin, on October 10, 2002, *Congressional Record,* S10251.

38. United States Senate Floor Remarks of Senator John McCain, October 10, 2002, *Congressional Record,* S10258.

39. Author interview with Medea Benjamin in 2006.

40. The video is available at www.youtube.com/watch?v=pYATbsu2cP8. All subsequent quotations from Senator Clinton's meeting with Code Pink are taken from the video.

41. Tom Precious, "Clinton Urges 'Domestic Defense Fund' to Help Localities," *Buffalo News,* March 4, 2003, B12.

Chapter Nineteen: The Club

1. Author interview with Senate aide in 2006.

2. Ibid.

3. Author interview with James Varey in 2006.

4. Author interview with Senate aide in 2006.

5. Author interview with Senator Barbara Mikulski, via e-mail through her press secretary, Melissa Schwartz, in 2006.

6. Author interview with John McCain in 2007.

7. Author interview with Lee Telega and other former aides and fellows who worked for Hillary in 2006 and 2007.
8. Author interview with former Senate aide in 2006.
9. Author interview with Senate adviser in 2007.
10. Author interview with former aide in 2007.
11. Author interview with former Clinton White House aide in 2007.
12. Author interviews with former Hillary aides in 2007.
13. Ibid.
14. The major committees are labeled A and the others B. For a fuller description of committee rankings, see *CQ Today*, November 9, 2006.
15. Author interview with Senate aide who is on the HELP Committee in 2006.
16. Ibid.
17. Ibid.
18. Author interview with Jodi Sakol in 2006.
19. Karen Tumulty, "Ready to Run," *Time*, August 28, 2006, 26.
20. John Machacek, "Utica Native Achieves Rank of Lieutenant Colonel," Gannett News Service, June 1, 2004.
21. McCain interview.
22. Author interview with witness to the incident in 2006.
23. Press release by Senator Elizabeth Dole, "Senators Clinton and Dole Announce Unanimous Passage of Senate Resolution Congratulating Israel's Magen David Adom Society for Achieving Full Membership in the International Red Cross," August 2, 2006.
24. Based on the authors' survey of legislation, resolutions, and other actions taken by Senator Hillary Rodham Clinton during her first term in office.
25. Joan Lowy, "Clinton Says Her Spouse Will Be a 'Tremendous Asset,' but She'll Make the Decisions," Associated Press, January 23, 2007.
26. Sakol interview.
27. McCain interview. McCain said the report of their vodka drinking, which appeared in a story by Anne Kornblut in the *New York Times* on July 29, 2006, was "overhyped."
28. See http://www.huffingtonpost.com/arianna-huffington/brainstorming-in-aspen-p_b_24158.html.
29. Libby Copeland, "Faith-Based Initiative," *Washington Post*, June 7, 2006, C1.
30. Jerry Zremski, "Senator Clinton Goes Right," *Buffalo News*, March 20, 2005, A1.
31. Russell Berman, "Senator Clinton Aligns with Bush on Immigration," *New York Sun*, February 21, 2007, 2.
32. Spencer Morgan, "Hillary's Mystery Woman: Who is Huma?" *New York Observer*, April 2, 2007, 8.
33. Author interviews with past and present Senate aides in 2006.
34. Author interview with former Hillary aide in 2006.
35. Author interview with Senate aide in 2006.
36. Clinton, *Living History*, caption under photo A48.
37. Clinton, *My Life*, 912–13.
38. McCain interview.
39. Terry McAuliffe, with Steve Kettmann, *What a Party!* (New York: Thomas Dunne Books, 2007), 381.

40. One of the authors attended the event. Identified as a special assistant or senior adviser in Senate records, Abedin is the only Senate staff member that Hillary credited with providing "invaluable assistance in helping me meet my impending deadline" for her 2003 autobiography (*Living History*, 530). Yet for all her assistance, Abedin is one of Hillary's lowest-paid Senate staffers: her highest salary between 2001 and 2006 was $27,000. (Reports of the Secretary of the Senate 2001–2006.) But Abedin, for the last half of Hillary's first term, was on two other payrolls controlled by Hillary: her campaign reelection committee and her political action committee. Her wages from the two political committees exceeded her wages from the Senate. (Author analysis of payroll reports by the Secretary of the Senate and campaign reports of Friends of Hillary and Hill-Pac, collected by Political Money Line, show that Abedin was paid about $2,000 a month by Hill-Pac and about $3,000 a month by Friends of Hillary. The committee reports show net wages; the overall figures include an estimate for taxes withheld. Hillary's presidential campaign paid Abedin a sizable salary beginning in 2007.) Senate rules permit aides to be on multiple payrolls. More than a dozen of Hillary's aides have been on two payrolls and several, including Abedin, have been on three. The setup dates back to 2003. Senate employees are allowed to work in their spare time on non-Senate matters, such as a senator's reelection campaign. But they cannot be paid for non-Senate work with government funds. Hillary consulted the Senate's Ethics Committee guidelines before approving dual payments to her staff. (See Glenn Thrush, "An Extra Little Boost," *Newsday*, November 3, 2005, A9.) The guidelines say that "dual employment situations" are "generally time-limited, usually confined to the employing senator's election cycle," that is, the last two years of a senator's term. (See *Senate Ethics Manual*, 2003 ed., 152.) Any wages should be commensurate with the work; so if an aide's time is divided equally between political and official activities, the pay should be equally divided too (ibid., 154). A few senators pay their staff from multiple sources, but none have as many on dual payrolls or for as long as Hillary. (Author interviews with Senate aides and ethics experts in 2006; see also Thrush, "An Extra Little Boost.")
41. Travel reports on file with the Secretary of the Senate.
42. Author interviews with Senate aides in 2006.
43. Michael Saul, "W to Skip Key Olympic Lobbying Trip," *New York Daily News*, June 21, 2005, 4.
44. Author interview with Senate aide in 2006.
45. *Senate Ethics Manual*, 2003 ed., 119.
46. David Seifman, "Hill Joins Mike in Final Olympic Sprint," *New York Post*, June 2, 2005, 2, and Robin Finn, "Speaking, and Sweating, for the Senator," *New York Times*, July 15, 2005, B2.
47. Senate Committee on Armed Services Third Quarter Amended Consolidated Report on Expenditure of Funds for Foreign Travel by Members and Employees of the U.S. Senate, received February 6, 2006, by the Secretary of the Senate. Senator Warner's aides never provided an answer to repeated questions about the trip.
48. Author interview with Senate aide in 2006.

49. Project Vote Smart listings of various interest groups, available at www .vote-smart.org, accessed February 22, 2007.

50. Ibid., based on *National Journal* rankings.

51. Ibid.

52. Author interview with former Senate aide in 2006.

53. Ibid.

54. Ibid.

55. Author interviews with Senate aides in 2006 and 2007.

56. Mary Ann Akers, "Heard on the Hill," *Roll Call*, June 28, 2006.

57. Author interview with senior Senate official in 2007. Hillary's spokesman, Philippe Reines, jokingly told *Roll Call* that Rubiner actually said "nice work." But the Senate official said the *Roll Call* account was "one hundred percent correct."

58. Sakol interview.

59. Author interview with senior Senate official in 2007.

60. Ibid.

61. Author interview with former Clinton administration official in 2007.

62. Author interviews with reporters who cover Hillary in 2007.

63. Author examination of Senate payroll records in 2006.

64. Ibid.

65. *New York Times*, July 15, 2005, B2.

66. Author interview with Jodi Sakol, who worked near Reines on the 2000 campaign, in 2007.

67. Author interview with reporter in 2007.

68. Ibid.

69. Author interview with senior Senate officials in 2007. A spokesperson for Hillary said, "We are not asking them to cooperate this time" with Sheehy. (Lloyd Grove, "For Hil and Gail, It's She Said, Sheehy Said," *New York Daily News*, July 7, 2006, 23. E-mail by Philippe Reines to Democratic press secretaries, July 7, 2006, Re: Gail Sheehy. Sheehy's article was not published.) The authors of this book encountered similar problems enlisting cooperation in the Senate. For example, Harry Reid, the Senate's majority leader, declined to speak to the authors about Hillary after Reines sent an e-mail to Reid's office in 2006 requesting that he not cooperate, according to a senior Senate aide.

70. "Endorsement '08," www.TheHill.com, as of April 19, 2007, and www .hillaryclinton.com, accessed April 24, 2007.

Chapter Twenty: The War Room

1. Ann Q. Hoy, "Hillary Emerges," *Newsday*, January 17, 2003, A7.

2. By 2005, the nearest suite of offices would be taken over by Senator Barack Obama, who would later emerge as a formidable contender in the presidential sweepstakes.

3. Author interview with Jodi Sakol, staff director of the steering committee from 2001 to 2004, in 2006.

4. Ibid.

5. Ibid.

6. Senator Hillary Rodham Clinton Remarks to New Democrat Network (NDN) Conference at the Mayflower Hotel in Washington, DC, June 23, 2006.
7. Jonathan E. Kaplan, "Be Bright, Work Hard, Get Yourself a Mentor," *The Hill,* January 28, 2004, 1, and "Senate Leadership," *National Journal,* June 21, 2003.
8. Sakol interview.
9. Ibid.
10. Ibid.
11. Ibid.
12. Alan Cooperman, "Democrats Win Bigger Share of Religious Vote," *Washington Post,* November 11, 2006, A1.
13. Sakol interview, and "Clinton Assembles a Seasoned Team," *Washington Post,* January 21, 2007, A6.
14. Sakol interview.
15. Ibid.
16. Ibid. Dorgan was especially piqued over Hillary's role in organizing a Democratic rump hearing in October 2003 to highlight emerging concerns about the public disclosure of CIA employee Valerie Plame's name. (Ibid.) Sakol also said that Plame's husband, Joe Wilson, was the "catalyst" for the hearing but that Hillary wanted to keep her "distance from" Wilson. Four years later, Hillary had dinner at a Washington restaurant with Wilson, Plame, Sid Blumenthal, and Blumenthal's wife. (See Michael Cotterman, "Friends of Hillary," *Washington Post,* March 10, 2007, C3.) Senators Durbin and Dorgan declined to comment for this book.
17. Sakol interview.
18. Author review of lobbying records on file with the Secretary of the Senate. Singiser declined requests to comment.
19. E-mail written by Dana Singiser, January 20, 2007.
20. Mark Halperin and John F. Harris, "The Way to Win" (New York: Random House, 2006), 336; Sakol interview; and Senator Hillary Rodham Clinton Remarks to NDN Conference.
21. Sakol interview.
22. Ibid.
23. Author interview with Jodi Sakol in 2007. Sakol says she attended the meetings on her personal time, not official Senate time.
24. Ibid.
25. Form 990 for the year 2005 for Citizens for Responsibility and Ethics in Washington, DC.
26. Sakol interview.
27. Ibid.
28. Ibid.
29. Ibid.
30. Author interview with former Hillary Clinton aide in 2006. Senator Daschle and Pete Rouse declined to comment for this book.
31. Ibid.
32. Sakol interview.
33. Author interview with Senate aide in 2006.
34. Steve Tetrault, "Reid Announces New Office Created," *Las Vegas Review-Journal,* November 30, 2004, B9.

35. Author interview with Senate aide in 2007.

36. Sakol interview. Brock, in an e-mail to an author in 2007, said he has met many times with Melanie Sloan but didn't address the question of his attendance at the 2003 meetings.

37. Jim Rutenberg, "New Internet Site Turns Critical Eyes and Ears to the Right," *New York Times*, May 3, 2004, A21.

38. Sakol interview. Brock, in an e-mail to one of the authors in 2007, said the media analysis "is publicly available to anyone who visits our Web site." Sakol said a representative of the center arranged for her to get on the Media Matters list.

39. Glenn Thrush, "Switching Allegiances," *Newsday*, September 7, 2006, A28.

40. E-mail to author in 2007 from David Brock.

41. Ibid.

42. Ibid. Brock said, "Since Media Matters began almost three years ago, we have documented and corrected more than 7,000 examples of conservative misinformation in the U.S. media — from the *New York Times* and the *Washington Post* to Rush Limbaugh and Bill O'Reilly. I'm proud of all the work we've done and continue to do."

43. *Newsday*, September 7, 2006, A28, and *New York Times*, May 3, 2004, A21. Brock, in an e-mail to an author in 2007, said Hillary "was one of a large number of progressive leaders who were interested in the issue of building progressive infrastructure." One of Hillary's closest friends, Susie Tompkins Buell, held a fund-raiser for Brock's cause, and almost half of the Susie Tompkins Buell Foundation's grants in 2004 and 2005 went to Media Matters. (Clinton, *Living History*, 334, for discussion of their friendship. Form 990 Annual Reports of the Susie Tompkins Buell Foundation for 2004 and 2005 show grants of $300,000 out of total grants of $636,000. See Byron York, "David Brock Is Buzzing Again," *National Review*, June 14, 2004, for discussion of the fund-raiser.)

44. Media Matters quickly posted an audio of Hillary's comments and then blasted the *Times* for not promptly correcting its mistake. (MediaMatters .org, July 17 and 18, 2006.)

45. Author interview with journalist in 2006.

46. The initiative, which Hillary cochaired and was put together by Reed and others not on Hillary's staff, was a detailed compendium of domestic policy proposals. Author interviews with DLC aides in 2006.

47. Author interview with *Times* employee in 2006.

48. Ibid. Kornblut left the *Times* for the *Washington Post* in early 2007.

49. "National Briefing," *Hotline*, July 17, 2006.

50. Peter Daou biography, posted at Daou Report Web site at http://www .Salon.com.

51. Author interview with journalist to whom Daou disclosed his background, in 2006. Daou declined to comment for this book.

52. Peter Daou, "Ignoring Colbert," www.HuffingtonPost.com, April 30, 2006.

53. Ibid.

54. Daou Report, "The Triangle," January 25, 2006.

55. Daou Report, "Closing the Triangle with Senator Hillary Clinton," June 26, 2006. Daou stepped down in the summer of 2006 from the editorship of

his blogging report for the left-leaning Web magazine Salon after he went to work for Hillary. But he continued to operate a press release business for bloggers, called News Unfiltered, in partnership with a public relations distribution company. Rachel Meranus, the director of public relations for PR Newswire, the parent company that partners with Daou, said in an e-mail on November 21, 2006, that Daou stayed on as "an objective, non-partisan editor of the blog" while working for Hillary.

56. Author interview with former Clinton aide in 2006.
57. Friends of Hillary and Hill-Pac records collected by Political Money Line.
58. E-mail from Peter Daou to Hillary supporters, February 14, 2007.
59. Memorandum by Peter Daou, "Hillary for President; Internet Strategy & Initial Results," January 26, 2007.
60. Ibid.
61. Glenn Thrush, "The 2008 Presidential Race on the Stump," *Newsday*, January 28, 2007, A15.

Chapter Twenty-one: Hillary's Quagmire

1. Author interview with Senate aide in 2006.
2. Remarks of Hillary Rodham Clinton to the Council on Foreign Relations, New York, December 15, 2003.
3. Todd Pittman, "Clinton: Insurgents in Iraq are Failing," Associated Press Online, February 19, 2005.
4. Thanassis Cambanis, "Dozens Die in Iraq as Attacks Mar Shi'ite Holy Day," *Boston Globe*, February 20, 2005, A1.
5. NBC-TV's *Meet the Press*, Hillary Rodham Clinton interview by Tim Russert, February 20, 2005.
6. Kirk Semple and Sabrina Tavernise, "U.S. Reports Iraqi Civilian Casualties in Anti-Insurgent Sweep," *New York Times*, November 10, 2005, A16.
7. Interviews with Senate aides in 2006.
8. Ibid.
9. Lara Sukhtian, "Bill Clinton Says U.S. Made 'Big Mistake' When It Invaded Iraq," Associated Press, November 16, 2005.
10. Senator Hillary Rodham Clinton, Letter to Constituents on Iraq Policy, November 29, 2005.
11. Ibid.
12. Public Law 107-243.
13. Senator Hillary Rodham Clinton, Letter to Constituents on Iraq Policy, November 29, 2005.
14. Dan Balz and Peter Baker, "Bush Includes Congress in New Iraq Tack," *Washington Post*, December 17, 2005, A16.
15. Author interview with Bush White House aide in 2007.
16. Author interview with Courtney Lee Adams in 2006.
17. Judy Holland, "Byrd Nears Record Service in Senate," *Times Union*, May 7, 2006, A14.
18. Author interview with Courtney Lee Adams in 2006.
19. Form 990 Annual Report for 2004 of William J. Clinton Foundation.
20. Hillary's first Senate speech on global warming came during the October 29, 2003, Senate debate on a bill sponsored by Senator Joe Lieberman. She

had not been among the fourteen senators who signed on to cosponsor the bill. The main exhibit in her remarks during that debate showed photographs of Mount Kilimanjaro's ice fields taken twenty-nine years apart. She cited the photos as "evidence in the most dramatic way possible of the effects of twenty-nine years of global warming," even though there was considerable scientific debate at the time about the causes for glacial retreat on the mountain. See Andrea Minarcek, "Mount Kilimanjaro's Glacier Is Crumbling," *National Geographic Adventure*, September, 23, 2003; http://news.nationalgeographic.com/news/2003/09/0923_030923_kilimanjaroglaciers.html; and Andrew C. Revkin, "Climate Debate Gets Its Icon, Mt. Kilimanjaro," *New York Times*, March 23, 2004, F1.

21. Author interview with David Sandalow in 2006.

22. Lukas I. Alpert, "Hill Stars with Bill," *New York Post*, September 17, 2005, 4.

23. Remarks of Tim Wirth from transcript of Plenary Session, entitled "Global Warming and Severe Weather Events," of the Clinton Global Initiative on September 17, 2005, New York City. Wirth also praised retired general Wesley Clark's remarks on the same subject. Clark appeared on the same panel as Hillary.

24. Author interviews with aides to Bill, Hillary, and Al Gore in 2006.

25. Ibid.

26. Lisa DePaulo interview of Al Gore, *GQ*, December 2006, 305.

27. Author interview with Roy Neel in 2007.

28. Author interviews with Gore associates in 2007.

29. Remarks of Al Gore, from transcript of Plenary Session, entitled "Global Warming and Severe Weather Events" of the Clinton Global Initiative on September 17, 2005, New York City.

30. Remarks of Senator Hillary Rodham Clinton to the Cleantech Venture Forum VIII on October 25, 2005.

31. "A Conversation with Bill Clinton," Aspen Ideas Festival, Aspen, Colorado, July 7, 2006.

Chapter Twenty-two: *Warming Up to Global Warming*

1. Author interviews with advisers of the Clintons in 2006.

2. ABC News, *The Note*, May 22, 2006, and author interviews with journalists in 2006.

3. E-mail message from RNC Research, May 23, 2006.

4. Senator Harry Reid press release dated October 14, 2005, US Fed News Service. Two months later, Hillary's aides had portrayed an event she did in New York as the "launch" of the Democratic energy plan. (CNN's *American Morning*, December 12, 2005.) This was the same plan that Cantwell had previously unveiled. Reid had blessed Hillary's stealing the thunder from her colleagues; he concluded that Hillary would be more effective at garnering attention because she had a "higher profile" than Cantwell. (Author interview with Senate aide in 2007.)

5. "A Conversation with Bill Clinton," Aspen Ideas Festival, Aspen, Colorado, July 7, 2006.

6. Thomas Friedman, "The Energy Mandate," *New York Times*, October 13, 2006, A27, and author interviews with Democratic consultants in 2006.

7. U.S. Newswire, press release by Apollo Alliance, "Administration Report Highlights Critical Need for Energy Independence," December 12, 2005.
8. Ibid.
9. Clinton, *My Life*, check of index by author. In addition, federal spending on energy research was flat in the 1990s, far below the level it had reached during its peak decade between the late 1970s and 1980s. See *New York Times*, October 30, 2006, chart headlined "Declining Investment in Energy R&D."
10. "A Conversation with Bill Clinton," Aspen Ideas Festival.
11. Energy Information Administration, Annual Energy Review, 2006, figure 5.3 and table 5.17.
12. Author interview with task force participants in 2006. Altman declined to be interviewed for this book.
13. The prospectus for the initial public offering (IPO) of Evercore Partners in August 2006 said its portfolio of investments in private equity funds included 33 percent in energy, followed by 19 percent in telecommunications, as of March 31, 2006, according to Form 424B4 filed with the SEC.
14. Author interview with task force participants in 2006 and 2007, including David Victor, a member of the task force and director of the program on energy and sustainable development at Stanford University, and Adam Sieminski, energy analyst for Deutsche Bank, in 2006.
15. Memorandum to Senator Hillary Rodham Clinton on U.S. Energy Policy, April 2006, a copy of which was obtained by the authors.
16. Author interviews with task force participants, including David Victor.
17. Ibid.
18. Ibid.
19. Author interview with Adam Sieminski in 2006. Sieminski said one of the motivations for the task force was to prepare Hillary for a possible presidential run.
20. Altman, in a July 21, 2005, interview on SkyRadioNet.com, called energy independence a "fantasy." Sieminski, in an interview with author in 2006, called it "impossible" and "counterproductive." Victor was director of a Council on Foreign Relations Task Force on U.S. Energy Dependence, which included several members of Hillary's task force and which found in 2006 that "voices that espouse 'energy independence' are doing the nation a disservice by focusing on a goal that is unachievable over the foreseeable future," and that "leaders of both parties, especially when seeking public office, seem unable to resist announcing unrealistic goals that are transparent efforts to gain popularity." (From CFR news release, October 12, 2006.)
21. Author interview with David Victor in 2006.
22. Patrick Healy, "Clintons Balance Married and Public Lives," *New York Times*, May 23, 2006, A1.
23. Author interviews with Patrick Healy in 2007 and with an associate of Hillary and a journalist in 2006.
24. Remarks of Senator Hillary Rodham Clinton at the National Press Club on Energy Policy, May 23, 2006.
25. Her secret advisers also favored more federal energy research. See Memorandum to Senator Hillary Rodham Clinton on U.S. Energy Policy, April 2006.

26. Author interviews with Victor, Siemenski, and Frank Wolak, an energy expert at Stanford University, in 2006. Hillary's advisers, in their memorandum to her, never advocated a windfall profits tax.

27. Remarks of Senator Hillary Rodham Clinton at the National Press Club on energy policy, May 23, 2006.

28. Her task force's memorandum recommended reforming fuel efficiency standards but did not set a specific target.

29. Maureen Dowd, "Enter Ozone Woman," *New York Times*, May 24, 2006, A27.

30. "A Conversation with Bill Clinton," Aspen Ideas Festival.

31. Ibid.

32. *Congressional Record*, November 17, 2005, S. 13128.

33. Library of Congress summary of bill at http://thomas.loc.gov.

34. Author interviews with environmental activists in 2006.

35. Project Vote Smart Web site, accessed October 1, 2006.

36. *Congressional Record* for June 15, 2005, Roll Call Vote No. 138 on Senate Amendment 782.

37. Hillary voted against the energy bill, largely because its benefits, such as incentives for conservation, were outweighed by measures she opposed, such as cutbacks in environmental protections.

38. Votes on July 29, 2003, and June 23, 2005, on an amendment by Senator Durbin to increase the fuel efficiency standards for cars, known in the industry as the CAFÉ standard, to 40 miles per gallon. Two weeks after voting against the 40-mile standard, on July 10, 2005, Hillary touted the benefits of "just raising average fuel economies to 40 miles per gallon by 2012" at the Aspen Ideas Festival.

39. Author interview with environmental lobbyist in 2006.

40. Remarks of Senator Hillary Rodham Clinton at the National Press Club on Energy Policy.

41. Memorandum to Senator Hillary Rodham Clinton on U.S. Energy Policy. The memo pointed out that coal and natural gas are the main sources of electricity generation. The percentage of generation from all petroleum liquid products (imported or domestic) amounted to less than 1 percent of the total output of electricity, according to the Energy Information Administration, *Electric Power Monthly*, section on "Net Generation by Source," covering first five months of 2006, released August 1, 2006. Other electricity sources include nuclear, natural gas, water, wind, and solar power.

42. "Best and Worst of Congress," *Washingtonian*, September 2006.

43. Remarks of Senator Hillary Rodham Clinton at the National Press Club on energy policy, May 23, 2006.

44. District of Columbia Department of Consumer and Regulatory Affairs building permit number B473381. The application for a miniature boiler permit indicates one Dunkirk boiler, Plymouth Series 2. Brenda Kawski, a Dunkirk representative, in an author's interview on October 17, 2006, said the Plymouth Series 2 was the company's "standard" boiler, less efficient and less expensive than the company's high-efficiency models. The contractor's application for a permit to put in new air-conditioning units at Hillary's residence indicates three new Carrier units, one model 38 TXA 060 and two models 38 TRA 036. The first model is rated SEER 13 — the higher the rating, the more efficient the unit — and the other two are

rated SEER 12. The company sold even higher rated units in 2005, according to a Carrier representative interviewed on October 17, 2006. Senator Clinton supports a government-mandated SEER standard of at least 13, according to a letter she and fifty other senators sent to President Bush in 2004. See March 21, 2004, States News Service.

45. Senator Barbara Mikulski, responding to questions from author in 2006, via an e-mail from her press secretary, Melissa Schwartz.

46. Remarks of Senator Hillary Rodham Clinton to the National Family Planning and Reproductive Health Association Luncheon on June 13, 2006.

47. E-mail from Senator Mikulski's press secretary in 2006.

48. Remarks of Senator Mikulski at Sewall-Belmont House, http://democrats .senate.gov/checklistforchange/speech.cfm.

49. Ibid.

50. Accessed by the authors at http://thomas.loc.gov.

51. CNN's *Larry King Live*, interview with Senator Hillary Rodham Clinton, June 21, 2006.

52. DayStar Technologies press release, July 31, 2006, via PRNewswire.

53. Ibid.

54. Author interview with Erica Dart, media and marketing representative for DayStar, in 2006.

55. DayStar Technologies Annual Report for 2005, dated March 17, 2006.

56. DayStar Technologies release of October 3, 2006, and Form 10-QSB.

57. Senator Hillary Rodham Clinton statement of September 26, 2006.

58. Politicalmoneyline.com showed a contribution of $1,000 in October 2006 by Michael Brower to Friends of Hillary.

59. Author interview with Michael Brower in 2006.

60. Dart interview.

61. "Clintons to Attend Beverly Hills Re-election Fundraiser Friday Night," NBC4tv.com, April 21, 2006, and Ted Johnson, "Democrats Push for Funds," Variety.com, March 21, 2007.

62. Gabriel Snyder, "The Hillary Tour," Variety.com, October 11, 2005, and March 21, 2007.

63. Author interview with Professor Lawrence Smart of the State University of New York College of Environmental Science and Forestry in 2006. Smart said he met the Clintons at a state fair in Cazenovia, New York, on August 31, 2006.

64. Author interviews with consultants to the Yes on 87 Campaign in 2006.

65. Author interview with consultant to the campaign in 2006.

66. Author interview with Al Gore confidant in 2006.

67. Author interview with Mark Dicamillo, director of the Field Institute, which polled California voters in September and October on Proposition 87, in 2006.

68. Author interview with Proposition 87 consultant in 2006.

Chapter Twenty-three: The Somewhat Lonely Middle

1. Author interview with attendees of the meeting in 2006.

2. Ibid.

3. Ibid.
4. Ibid.
5. Author interview with Senate aide in 2006.
6. Dan Balz, "Liberal Activists Boo Clinton," *Washington Post,* June 14, 2006, A10, and author interview with Roger Hickey in 2006.
7. John Herbers, "Minority Planks Urged in Boston," *New York Times,* May 31, 1972, 29.
8. Author interview with Senator John Kerry in 2007.
9. Author interview with Senate aide in 2006.
10. Author interview with participant in meeting in 2006.
11. Ibid.
12. Ibid.
13. Senate Amendment 4320, read on the floor of the Senate June 21, 2006.
14. Author interviews with Senate aides in 2006.
15. Author interviews with meeting participants in 2006.
16. Ibid.
17. Ibid.
18. CBS News, poll of 659 adults conducted nationwide, June 10 and June 11, 2006.
19. Author interview with meeting participant in 2006.
20. Author interviews with meeting participants in 2006. Senator Russ Feingold would later decide not to run for president.
21. Author interview with meeting participant in 2006.
22. Author interview with Senate official in 2006.
23. Remarks of Senator Carl Levin at press conference, Senate Radio/TV Gallery, June 19, 2006, Federal News Service.
24. Ibid.
25. United States Senate Floor Remarks of Senator Jack Reed, June 21, 2006, *Congressional Record.*
26. Author interviews with Senate aides in 2006 and 2007.
27. United States Senate Floor Remarks of Senator Hillary Rodham Clinton, June 21, 2006, *Congressional Record.*
28. Author interview with Senate aide in 2006.
29. Copy of Senate Amendment 4320.
30. Ibid.
31. Ibid.
32. Author interview with senior Senate official in 2007.
33. Author interview with Senate aide working with one of the cosponsors in 2006.
34. Author interview with Senate aide in 2006.
35. Author interview with Senate aide working with one of the cosponsors in 2006.
36. Biography of Hillary Clinton on www.hillaryclinton.com, accessed January 20, 2007, the day she announced her campaign.
37. United States Senate Floor remarks of Senator Hillary Rodham Clinton, June 21, 2006, *Congressional Record,* S6211-12.
38. Ibid.
39. ABC-TV's *Nightline,* interview with Hillary Rodham Clinton, September 7, 2006.

40. Author interview with Roger Hickey in 2006; see also Maura Reynolds, "Senators Face Off Over 2 Iraq Pullout Plans," *Los Angeles Times*, June 22, 2006, A5, and Ronald Brownstein, "Democrats' Iraq Gap Narrows, Clinton Says," *Los Angeles Times*, June 24, 2006, A7.
41. Devlin Barrett, "Senator Clinton Rips Rumsfeld Over Iraq," Associated Press Online, August 3, 2006.
42. Ibid.
43. Devlin Barrett, "AP Interview: Senator Clinton Rips Rumsfeld; Calls for Resignation," Associated Press State and Local Wire, August 3, 2006.
44. Raymond Hernandez, "A Democratic Bid That's Anti-Clinton All the Time," *New York Times*, June 26, 2006, B1.
45. *New York Times* editorial, "Hillary Clinton's Low Profile," August 21, 2006.
46. Testimony of retired army major general John Batiste, before the Democratic Policy Committee hearing, September 25, 2006.
47. Statement of Senator Hillary Rodham Clinton, September 25, 2006, "Former Top Military Leaders Highlight Need for Change of Course in Iraq at DPC Oversight Hearing" (www.clinton.senate.gov).
48. Author interviews with Senate aides in 2006.
49. NBC's *Meet the Press*, Senator Mike DeWine interviewed by Tim Russert, October 1, 2006.
50. Author interviews with Senate aides in 2006.
51. Statement of Hillary Rodham Clinton on January 10, 2007.
52. Patrick Healy and Adam Nagourney, "In the Back and Over Drinks," *New York Times*, January 4, 2007, A19.
53. *The New Yorker*, January 15, 2007, 33.

Chapter Twenty-four: "Madam President"

1. United States Senate Floor Remarks of Senator John Kerry, January 17, 2007, *Congressional Record*, S641.
2. Ibid.
3. Author interview with Senate aide in 2007.
4. Ibid.
5. Author interview with Hillary adviser in 2007; see also Glenn Thrush, "Race for President, Clinton Will Run," *Newsday*, January 21, 2007, A4.
6. Author interviews with two advisers to Hillary in 2007.
7. Helen Kennedy, "Edwards Urges Congress to Block Troop Surge," *New York Daily News*, January 14, 2007.
8. "Obama Statement on Iraq," States News Service, January 17, 2007. In 2004, Obama had declined to criticize John Kerry or John Edwards, his party's nominees. (Monica Davey, "A Surprise Senate Contender Reaches His Biggest Stage Yet," *New York Times*, A1.) In the same interview he acknowledged that his opposition to a war against Iraq in 2002 was not based on intelligence reports, so he couldn't be sure what we would have done had he been in the Senate then.
9. Author interview with two advisers to Hillary in 2007.
10. One of the authors was present at the press conference. At an earlier briefing that day, aides passed out copies of a nonbinding resolution by

Senators Biden and Levin and a related press release. Hillary's aides gave nothing to reporters, who were scrambling to pin down aides on the specifics of Hillary's proposal.

11. Author interview with adviser to Hillary in 2007.

12. See "Edwards Statement on President Bush's Escalation of January 9, 2007" (http://johnedwards.com/news/press-releases/20070109-escalation/) and Senator Clinton's remarks of January 17, 2007, on National Public Radio's *All Things Considered,* via Lexis-Nexis.

13. Patrick Healy, "After Iraq Trip Clinton Proposes War Limits," *New York Times,* January 18, 2007, 10.

14. One of the authors was present at the party, at the invitation of Nancy Stetson, the retiring Kerry aide. Kerry later declined repeated requests to discuss his remarks. His communications director, Vince Morris, asked the authors, one month after the party, to refrain from using Senator Kerry's remarks in the book because they were made at a "private party."

15. Author interview with Hillary adviser in 2007. Kerry, after voting for the war, later voted against funding a supplemental appropriation for the war. His being both for and against the war left him politically vulnerable. Hillary avoided that mistake.

16. Bill Clinton remarks at Democratic Leadership Council meeting at New York University, December 3, 2003.

17. Patrick Healy and Jeff Zeleny, "For Clinton and Obama, Different Tests on Iraq," *New York Times,* February 12, 2007, A1.

18. *NBC Nightly News,* Hillary Rodham Clinton interview by Brian Williams, January 22, 2007.

19. Author interview with Mickey Kantor in 2007.

20. Author interviews with several advisers and friends of Bill Clinton in 2006 and 2007.

21. Hillary for President Webcast, http://www.hillaryclinton.com, broadcast live on January 24, 2007.

22. ABC-TV's *Good Morning America,* Hillary Rodham Clinton interview by Diane Sawyer, January 23, 2007.

23. MSNBC's *Countdown with Keith Olbermann,* Hillary Rodham Clinton interview by Keith Olbermann, January 23, 2007, via www.youtube.com. Bill, in a conference call with a fund-raiser in March 2007, thought the persistent calls for Hillary to apologize for her vote were "not fair," because he had reread the 2002 authorization and concluded it was only a call for "coercive inspections." (See Sam Youngman, "Clinton: 'It's Not Fair,'" TheHill.com, March 23, 2007.) The legislation does not contain that language.

24. Author interview with adviser to Hillary in 2007.

25. Author interview with Iowa Democratic Party activist Jim Hutter in 2007; see also Dan Balz, "Mixed Reviews for Clinton in Iowa," *Washington Post,* January 29, 2007, and Chris Cillizza, "Clinton Campaigns in New Hampshire," *Washington Post,* February 11, 2007.

26. National Public Radio's *Morning Edition,* February 12, 2007.

27. Ibid.

28. Ibid.

29. Author interview with Senator John McCain in 2007.

30. Remarks of Senator Hillary Rodham Clinton before the Democratic National Committee in Washington, DC, on February 2, 2007.
31. Author interview with senior Senate aide in 2007.
32. Patrick Healy, "Clinton Gives War Critics New Answer to '02 Vote," *New York Times*, February 18, 2007, 30.
33. Ibid. Author examination of S 670, the Iraq Troop Protection and Reduction Act of 2007; statement of Senator Hillary Rodham Clinton of February 17, 2007; and two-page "Fact Sheet" released by her office summarizing the act.
34. Ibid.
35. S 670, section 3. The waiver is usually included in official summaries of a bill. Author interview with senior Senate official in 2007. The summary of Hillary's bill, prepared by the Congressional Research Service a few weeks later, mentioned the waiver. See CRS summary of S 670, accessed March 1, 2007, on http://thomas.loc.gov.
36. S 670, section 5. If the president could not certify that the required objectives in Iraq had been met to avoid the cutoff of funds to Iraq, he could still certify "that substantial progress is being made toward achieving the objective," according to the legislation.
37. Statement of Hillary Rodham Clinton, "Clinton Plan to End War," February 17, 2007.
38. Carl Hulse and Patrick Healy, "Clinton Proposes Vote to Reverse Authorizing War," *New York Times*, May 4, 2007, A1.
39. Floor remarks of Senator Hillary Rodham Clinton, May 3, 2007.
40. Author interview with former Senate aide in 2007.
41. Ibid.
42. Senate Amendment 4869, *Congressional Record*, October 10, 2002, S10233.
43. Author interview with former Senate aide in 2007.
44. Ibid.

Chapter Twenty-five: Googled and YouTubed

1. The authors viewed the event via YouTube: http://www.youtube.com/watch?v=cwYKIsJwi2c.
2. Author interview with Frank Salvato in 2006.
3. Ibid.
4. Author interview with Joan Swirsky in 2006.
5. Federal Election Commission, "General Counsel's Report #2," filed September 30, 2005, in FEC case MUR 5225.
6. Paul's case against Bill is pending. Paul, in an interview in 2007, said he plans to use new evidence he obtained in 2007 to resurrect his case against Hillary.
7. Salvato interview.
8. One of the producers was the man who helped organize *The Clinton Chronicles*, a bitterly critical video from the 1990s about Bill Clinton, according to Peter Paul, who was interviewed by an author in 2007.
9. Salvato interview.
10. Pew Internet Project Survey from December 2005, showing that 43 percent of broadband users go to portals like Yahoo! or Google for their news,

while 36 percent go to their local newspaper site and 21 percent to the Web site of a national newspaper.

11. In mid-2006, Google's market capitalization exceeded $150 billion, while the value of the New York Times Company was a little over $3 billion.

12. Memo from Jonathan Landman, deputy managing editor of the *New York Times*, to the staff, April 10, 2006.

13. Robert Kaiser, "Scaife Denies Ties to 'Conspiracy,' Starr," *Washington Post*, December 17, 1998, A2, citing an interview with Scaife in *George* magazine.

14. Author interview with Robert Fiske in 2006.

15. Ibid.

16. Tim Weiner, "One Source, Many Ideas in Foster Case," *New York Times*, August 13, 1995, 19.

17. Ibid.

18. Author interview with former Clinton White House aide in 2006.

19. "The Communications Stream of Conspiracy Commerce," undated. See also John F. Harris and Peter Baker, "White House Memo Asserts a Scandal Theory," *Washington Post*, January 10, 1997, A1.

20. Author interviews with former Clinton White House aides in 2006 and 2007.

21. Joan Swirsky, "Hillary Clinton's Culture of Corruption: The Scandal Queen," newmediajournal.us, March 13, 2006.

22. C-SPAN interview transcript, First Lady Hillary Rodham Clinton, January 17, 1997, Federal News Service.

23. Todd S. Purdum, "The Dangers of Dishing Dirt in Cyberspace," *New York Times*, August 17, 1997, sec. 4, p. 3. Matt Drudge did not return repeated phone calls and e-mail messages from one of the authors.

24. White House transcript, Remarks of First Lady Hillary Rodham Clinton, February 11, 1998.

25. Author interview with Joseph Farah in 2006.

26. Author interview with Chris Ruddy in 2006.

27. Kenneth Starr called the newspaper "wacko" in an interview with one of the authors in 2007.

28. Ruddy interview. Scaife's lawyer, Yale Gutnick, said in an interview in 2007 that he eventually obtained, under a Freedom of Information Act request, a photo of Scaife with the Clintons that night.

29. Ruddy interview.

30. Ibid. Yale Gutnick, Scaife's lawyer, said the philanthropist eventually increased his investment even more.

31. Ruddy interview.

32. ABC News *Nightline*, interview of Matt Drudge, January 8, 1998.

33. C-SPAN, Leonard Downie, the executive editor of the *Washington Post*, November 6, 2006.

34. Farah interview; "Why Gore Lost Tennessee," WorldNetDaily.com, December 5, 2000.

35. Author interviews with two people close to Herb and Marion Sandler in 2006.

36. Ibid.

37. Stephen Braun, "This Clinton Machine Is a Tighter Ship," *Los Angeles Times*, December 31, 2006, A1.

38. Robert Dreyfuss, "An Idea Factory for Democrats," *The Nation*, March 1, 2004, 18.

39. Ibid.

40. Matt Bai, "Nation Building," *New York Times Sunday Magazine*, October 12, 2003, sec. 6, p. 82.

41. Jim VandeHei and Chris Cillizza, "A New Alliance of Democrats Spreads Funding," *Washington Post*, July 17, 2006, A1.

42. Dan Gilgof, "Washington Whispers," *U.S. News and World Report*, April 16, 2007, 14.

43. VandeHei and Cillizza, "A New Alliance."

44. Peter Baker, "Think Tank's Leader Charts New Course," *Washington Post*, May 22, 2006, A15.

45. Senator Dianne Feinstein press release, May 3, 2006, via *Congressional Quarterly*.

46. See Travel Office Memorandum, from Eric A. Dubelier and Kimberly Nelson Brown to Kenneth W. Starr and All OIC Attorneys, December 4, 1996, 103–11.

47. Author interviews with Hillary's energy task force participants in 2006 and memorandum to Senator Clinton from the task force.

48. Author interview with Jodi Sakol in 2006.

49. "Clinton Assembles a Seasoned Team," *Washington Post*, January 21, 2007, A6, and ABC News, *The Note*, January 22, 2007, "The Way to Win, Chappaqua Style." Podesta says he talks to Hillary "from time to time on policy and issues." (*Los Angeles Times*, December 31, 2006, A1.) The center cosponsored an initiative on veterans benefits with Hillary in March 2007, a few weeks after newspapers began describing Podesta as an informal adviser to her. (See John M. Broder, "Familiar Face, but a New Tone to Message," *New York Times*, February 5, 2007, A1.)

50. CNN's *Late Edition*, interview with John Podesta, December 17, 2006. "Are you ready to support her?" asked CNN anchor Wolf Blitzer. "Personally?" Podesta asked back, lawyerlike. Once Blitzer said OK, Podesta jumped right in. "Yeah, personally, I'm, you know, a big fan of Senator Clinton's," Podesta said, adding, "She's got the strength, I think, and ideas to move the country forward."

51. Home page of Google News, accessed April 28, 2007. Yahoo! News is more selective, tending to rely mostly on wire reports from the Associated Press.

52. *Frontline*/PBS interview with Krishna Bharat, the creator of Google News, in 2006.

53. Author interview with Steve Langdon in 2006.

54. Rick Wiggins, "How to Spam Google News," March 9, 2006. Wiggins, an infotech blogger at Michigan State University, researched the issue after a teenager in Florida fooled Google News by sending out a phony press release (http://wigblog.blogspot.com/2006/03/how-to-spam-google-news .html). Google dropped a Web-based public relations company in 2006 after a prankster used the company to put out a phony release that wound up on Google News. (Author interviews via phone and e-mail with Steve Langdon, a Google spokesman, in 2006.) But the company primarily relies on complaints from customers, not its own screening, to keep out phony news. Similarly, the company bans hate speech, again after read-

ers complained to Google. (In May 2006, the New Media Journal was kicked out of Google News after complaints by readers, not for the Hillary series, but for three anti-Islam articles that ran in April and May of 2006 that Google considered "hate content," according to an e-mail of May 19, 2006, from Google Help to NewMediaJournal.us. After receiving the e-mail, Salvato, the editor, called Google's move "intellectual censorship" and launched a boycott of its search engine.)

55. *Frontline*/PBS interview with Eric Schmidt in 2006.
56. Justin Darr, "Partito Nostro: Doing Business with the Clinton Syndicate," newmediajournal.us, March 15, 2006.
57. Nielsen/Net ratings for November 2006 show 65.4 percent of NewsMax readers are Republicans.
58. NewsMax was cited 1,474 times in Google News during a thirty-day period at the end of 2006. Ruddy says his readers are still fascinated by Hillary, though he finds her more "cautious and careful" since she left the White House.
59. "Jimmy Carter: Human Scum," WorldNetDaily.com, December 15, 2006, accessed via Google News on December 21, 2006.
60. Google News search on December 21, 2006.
61. National Public Radio, Hillary Rodham Clinton interview, December 18, 2006.
62. Author interviews with Google officials in 2006.
63. YouTube press release, "U.S. Presidential Candidates Leveraging the Power of the Digital Democracy to Reach the Masses," March 1, 2007.
64. The video is at http://www.youtube.com/watch?v=6h3G-lMZxjo; see also Jose Antonio Vargas and Howard Kurtz, "Watching Big Sister," *Washington Post*, March 21, 2007, C1.
65. Author examination of YouTube, March 29, 2007.
66. Vargas and Kurtz, "Watching Big Sister."
67. Ibid.
68. Clarence Page, "New Media but the Same Old Game," *Chicago Tribune*, March 25, 2007, C7.
69. Micah L. Sifry, "Who Is ParkRidge47?" TechPresident.com, March 7, 2007. The inspiration for his video was a newspaper article about the Clinton campaign and its "bullying of donors and political operatives" after David Geffen, a former Clinton supporter, blasted the couple and hosted a fund-raiser for Obama in Beverly Hills.
70. Phil de Vellis, "I Made the 'Vote Different' Ad," huffingtonpost.com, March 21, 2007. When he produced the ad, de Vellis was employed by a company called Blue State Digital, which was doing consulting work for the Obama campaign. The Obama campaign had no knowledge of the ad, and de Vellis resigned from the company after his identity was revealed.

Chapter Twenty-six: "I Don't Feel No Ways Tired"

1. Author interview with Vernon Jordan in 2007.
2. Author interview with Greg Craig in 2007.
3. Ibid.
4. Author interview with Greg Craig in 2006.

5. Lloyd Grove and John F. Harris, "Crisis Quarterback: Gregory Craig Is Calling the Plays on Clinton's Team," *Washington Post*, November 19, 1998, D1.

6. James Bennet, "Serving Up Contrition, Sprinkled Lightly with Candor," *New York Times*, December 9, 1998, 24.

7. Craig interview.

8. Grove and Harris, "Crisis Quarterback."

9. Abramoff would eventually plead guilty to three felony counts of defrauding Native American tribes and corruption of public officials as well as two counts of fraud related to the purchase of SunCruz Casinos in Fort Lauderdale; he was sentenced to five years and ten months in prison and began his sentence in November 2006. He agreed to cooperate with prosecutors, and helped them make a felony case of conspiracy and making false statements to federal investigators against an influential Republican congressman, Bob Ney. "Abramoff Pleads Guilty, Will Help in Corruption Probe," Bloomberg, January 3, 2006; see also "Abramoff Gets 5 Years, 10 Months in Fraud Case," Associated Press, March 29, 2006.

10. Hillary Rodham Clinton remarks on November 7, 2006, during her Senate reelection victory speech.

11. Memorandum from Hillary Rodham Clinton to Democratic Caucus, January 31, 2006, Re: Weekly Steering Update.

12. Some Democrats saw in Obama the same fresh-faced idealism and potential that they had found inspiring four decades earlier when considering another fresh-faced senator, named John F. Kennedy. Even Theodore Sorensen, Kennedy's speechwriter and confidant, said that Obama was the first presidential hopeful in many years who had stoked in him the same ripples of excitement caused by JFK. "It reminds me of the way the young, previously unknown JFK took off," Sorenson said. "Obama, like JFK, is such a natural. He's very comfortable with who he is." (Jeff Zeleny, "Obama's Back Fund-Raising in New York, Not Quietly," *New York Times*, March 10, 2007, A10.)

13. Singiser declined to respond to two e-mails sent to her by one of the authors in 2007.

14. Author interviews with participants in 2006.

15. Ibid.

16. Author interview with a participant in 2006.

17. Author interview with another meeting participant in 2006.

18. Author interview with guest of the dinner in 2006; see also Raymond Hernandez, "Clinton Says New York, but Money Hints at '08," *New York Times*, March 8, 2006, B1.

19. Author interview with guest of the dinner in 2006.

20. Author interview with Hillary friend in 2006.

21. Author interviews with three Hillary strategists and money-raisers in 2006 and 2007. In the early months of 1999, Texas governor George W. Bush exerted similar pressure for prolific Republican fund-raisers to join the party's new gilded fund-raising groups, the Texas Rangers and the Regents. (Author interview with several Republican fund-raisers in 1999.) Bush had applied that pressure after he had announced the formation of his presidential exploratory committee.

22. Author interviews with Hillary strategists in 2006 and 2007.
23. Author interview with Matt Butler, Senator Cantwell's campaign manager, in 2006.
24. Author interview with Bill Kisliuk, managing editor of the *Napa Valley Register*, in 2006.
25. Author interview with C. Paul Johnson in 2006.
26. Ibid.
27. Author interview with Hillary friend and strategist in 2006.
28. Craig interview.
29. Jordan interview.
30. Craig interview.
31. Ibid.
32. Adam Nagourney and Jeff Zeleny, "Obama Officially Enters Presidential Race with Calls for Generational Change," *New York Times*, February 12, 2007, 34.
33. Craig interview.
34. One of the coauthors watched Obama's speech live on C-SPAN.
35. Craig interview. Craig had not heard back two months after he wrote his note.
36. CNN videotape of Coretta Scott King memorial service, February 7, 2006.
37. Author interview with King family confidant in 2006.
38. Author interviews with two Hillary confidants in 2007.
39. Author interview with Hillary friend and fund-raiser in 2007.
40. Author interview with Bill Clinton confidant in 2007.
41. Author interviews with political strategists in 2006 and 2007.
42. Author interviews with two Hillary fund-raisers and strategists in 2007.
43. Ibid.
44. Tina Daunt, "Cause Célèbre, McAuliffe Seeks Clinton Believers," *Los Angeles Times*, January 30, 2007, E2.
45. Author interview with Democratic fund-raiser in 2007. Geffen had also become disenchanted with Bill Clinton's decision to pardon Marc Rich, a fugitive financier, shortly before leaving office, and his refusal to pardon Leonard Peltier, who was convicted of murdering two agents in June 1975 during protests on the Pine Ridge reservation in South Dakota. Geffen is a longtime supporter of Peltier, who is serving two consecutive life terms and is in poor health. Geffen felt "betrayed" by Clinton's failure to pardon Peltier. (Author interview with Geffen friend in 2007.)
46. Author interview with Democratic fund-raiser in 2007.
47. Maureen Dowd, "Obama's Big Screen Test," *New York Times*, February 21, 2007, A21.
48. Author interview with Hillary confidant in 2007. Wolfson declined to comment for this book.
49. *New York Times*, February 21, 2007, A21.
50. Author interview with Hillary confidant in 2007.
51. Scott Shepard, "Clinton-Obama Dispute Overshadows First Democratic Presidential Issues Forum," Cox News Service, February 22, 2007. In his statement, Wolfson mistakenly called Geffen the "finance chair" of Obama's presidential campaign.

52. Ibid.
53. Lizzy Ratner, "White Gathers the Democratic Families," *New York Observer,* March 12, 2007, 8.
54. Author interview with Hillary strategist in 2007.
55. Ibid.
56. See results of ABC/*Washington Post* poll and Fox News survey conducted nationwide, February 27–28, 2007.
57. Author interview with Democratic strategist and friend of Hillary in 2007.
58. Author interview with a confidant of the Clintons in 2007.
59. Author interview with longtime friend of Bill and Hillary in 2007.
60. Kate Snow and Eloise Harper, "Bill Clinton Makes Rare Fund-raising Pitch for Hillary," www.abcnews.com, March 19, 2007.
61. Center for Responsive Politics analysis, accessed on its Web site on February 22, 2007.
62. Author interview with Hillary fund-raiser in 2007.
63. Ibid.
64. Author interviews with two Hillary fund-raisers in 2007; see also Liz Sidoti, "Hopefuls Get Ahead in White House 'Money Primary,'" Associated Press, February 9, 2007.
65. Author interviews with Democratic strategists in 2007.
66. Ibid.
67. Craig interview.
68. Author interview with Hillary friend and strategist in 2007.
69. Both speeches were broadcast live on C-SPAN, March 4, 2007.
70. Ibid. See also Edwin Chen, "Clinton, Obama Cross Paths in Selma," Bloomberg News, March 5, 2007, as published by the *Pittsburgh Post-Gazette*, A1.
71. Ibid. See also Patrick Healy and Jeff Zeleny, "Clinton and Obama Unite, Briefly, in Pleas to Blacks," *New York Times*, March 5, 2007, 14.
72. Healy and Zeleny, "Clinton and Obama Unite."
73. C-SPAN broadcast, March 4, 2007.
74. Ibid.
75. Matt Drudge featured a twenty-seven-second clip of Hillary's southern drawl, entitled "Kentucky Fried Hillary," www.drudgereport.com. It was later posted on www.ifilm.com; within three weeks, it had been accessed nearly seven hundred thousand times.
76. Author interview with Hillary strategist in 2007.
77. Richard Fausset and Jenny Jarvie, "Obama, Clinton Bring Their Stories to Selma," *Los Angeles Times*, March 5, 2007, A1.
78. Author interview with Bill Clinton confidant in 2007.
79. CNN's *Larry King Live*, Bill Clinton interview, April 19, 2007.

Chapter Twenty-seven: "The Best Political Spouse in the Business"

1. Author interview with longtime friend of the Clintons in 2006.
2. Author interview with a former member of Clinton's legal defense team in 2006.
3. Author interview with former Clinton administration official in 2007.
4. Author interview with Neel Lattimore in 2006.

5. David Remnick, "The Wanderer," *The New Yorker,* September 18, 2006, 58.

6. Malia Rulon, "Other Clinton Here to Raise Cash for Wife," *Cincinnati Enquirer,* March 21, 2007, 1.

7. ABC's *Good Morning America,* interview with Senator Hillary Rodham Clinton by Diane Sawyer, January 23, 2007.

8. Tom Baldwin, "Clinton Goes on Offensive Over Iraq," *Times* (London), March 22, 2007.

9. Author interview with former Clinton administration official in 2007.

10. NBC's *Meet the Press,* Bill Clinton interview by Tim Russert, September 24, 2006.

11. Ben Smith, "McCain Team Mocks Hill Torture Loophole," *New York Daily News,* October 16, 2006, 10, and "Hillary's Torture Exception," *New York Post,* October 21, 2006, 16.

12. Author interview with senior Democratic strategist in 2006.

13. Author interview with former Clinton administration official in 2007.

14. Patrick Healy and Jesse McKinley, "Passions Flare as Broadcast of 9/11 Miniseries Nears," *New York Times,* September 8, 2006, A18.

15. Author interview with Bill Clinton associate in 2006.

16. Interview with senior ABC official in 2006.

17. Before the film began, ABC aired this disclaimer: "Due to the subject matter, viewer discretion is advised. The following movie is a dramatization that is drawn from a variety of sources, including the 9/11 Commission Report and other published materials, and from personal interviews. The movie is not a documentary. For dramatic and narrative purposes, the movie contains fictionalized scenes, composite representative characters and dialogue, as well as time compression."

18. Attached to the letter is a list of "fabrications" in the movie compared to "facts" reported in the commission's report. The list of "facts" omitted several of the report's key findings about the Clinton administration's inadequate responses to Al Qaeda attacks during the 1990s. (Office of William Jefferson Clinton letter of September 10, 2006, to Bob Iger.) Among the negative findings of the 9/11 Commission omitted from the Clinton letter: the statement that neither President Bush nor President Clinton "fully understood just how many people Al Qaeda might kill and how soon they might do it" (*The 9/11 Commission Report,* 342–43); the finding that the government took the attacks of 1998 and 2000 seriously, "but not in the sense of mustering anything like the kind of effort that would be gathered to confront an enemy of the first, second or even third rank. The modest national effort exerted to contain Serbia and its depredations in the Balkans between 1995 and 1999, for example, were orders of magnitude larger than that devoted to Al Qaeda" (340); and that the August 1998 American Embassy bombings in Africa "provided an opportunity for a full examination, across the government, of the national security threat that Bin Laden posed.... But the major policy agencies of the government did not meet the threat" (349).

19. Author interview with ABC official in 2006.

20. Author interviews with ABC officials and Hillary Clinton aides in 2006.

21. CNN's *The Situation Room,* Senator Hillary Rodham Clinton interview with Wolf Blitzer, September 11, 2006.

22. Author interviews with Bill Clinton confidants in 2006 and 2007.
23. Author interview with Bill Clinton friend in 2006.
24. Ibid.
25. Wallace's producers and Bill's aides agreed upon the ground rules for the interview: Half the time would be devoted to the Clinton Global Initiative, and the other half would cover other subjects. Author interview with Chris Wallace in 2007.
26. All quotes from this interview are from *Fox News Sunday*, September 24, 2006, transcript by Federal News Service.
27. There is no mention in the 9/11 Report, or in Clarke's book, of a battle plan to get bin Laden after the *Cole* was attacked. (James Gordon Meek and Kenneth R. Bazinet, "Bill's Bull? Ex-Advisers: Clinton Had No Plan to Overthrow Taliban, Kill Osama," *New York Daily News*, September 26, 2006, 11; see also pp. 195–96 of Richard Clarke's book, *Against All Enemies: Inside America's War on Terror.*) In fact, the 9/11 Report said, after discussions in November 2000 about the possible reevaluation of existing plans against bin Laden, "there was not much White House interest in conducting further military operations against Afghanistan in the administration's last weeks." The report mentions a plan by Clinton national security adviser Sandy Berger to give the Taliban an ultimatum and a request Berger made to the chairman of the Joint Chiefs of Staff in mid-November to "reevaluate the military plans to act quickly against bin Laden." Shelton briefed Berger on 1998 strike options, but "military planners did not include contingency planning for an invasion of Afghanistan." (*The 9/11 Commission Report*, 194.)
28. Wallace interview.
29. Ibid.
30. Author interviews with Bill Clinton confidants in 2006 and 2007.
31. CNN's *The Situation Room*, Senator Hillary Rodham Clinton interview with Wolf Blitzer, September 26, 2006.
32. The 9/11 Commission found no presidential action or lower-level meetings were held as a result of that report, but it also noted that the report was the result of Bush asking his intelligence briefers several months earlier about possible threats inside the United States. (*The 9/11 Commission Report*, 261–62.)
33. The 9/11 Commission, which obtained the 1998 brief, mentioned no action or reaction by the president, but there was a meeting that day by a middle-level counterterrorist group, which took actions that resulted in heightened airport security at New York's airports for seven weeks. (Ibid., 128–30.)
34. Author interviews with Clinton friends and Democratic strategists in 2006 and 2007.

Epilogue: Force the Spring

1. Ralph Keyes, *The Wit & Wisdom of Harry Truman* (New York: Gramercy Books, 1995), 58.
2. *Canada Month*, June 1963.

3. NBC's *Nightly News with Brian Williams*, Hillary Rodham Clinton interview with Brian Williams, January 22, 2007.

4. NBC's *Today*, Hillary Rodham Clinton interview with Meredith Viera, January 23, 2007.

5. Maggie Haberman, "Aides Learn Hill Drill," *New York Post*, February 24, 2007, 4.

6. Author interviews with former Clinton administration official and Democratic strategist in 2007.

7. Dan Balz and Jon Cohen, "Giuliani Lead Shrinks, Clinton Margin Holds," Washingtonpost.com, April 19, 2007, reporting on Washington Post–ABC News poll.

8. Author interview with Senate adviser in 2007.

9. Author interview with Hillary Clinton confidant in 2007.

10. The White House biography of First Lady Hillary Rodham Clinton archived November 6, 1996, described her as a "Chicago native" and "serious baseball fan" who "attended Cubs games at Wrigley Field in Chicago." The White House biography of First Lady Hillary Rodham Clinton archived December 2, 1998, simply said she was born in Chicago. Her White House biography in 1996 and her presidential campaign biography in 2007 mention her fifteen years at an Arkansas law firm in a sentence or less, without even naming the Rose Law Firm. There is no mention of her 1975 wedding in her 1996 White House biography, but "Hillary married Bill Clinton" was mentioned in the White House biography archived December 2, 1998, after Bill's affair with Monica Lewinsky surfaced. In 2006, her Senate campaign biography omitted her eight years as First Lady until Joel Achenbach ("She's No Lady," *Washington Post Sunday Magazine*, June 4, 2006, W7) pointed out the omission. In that article Philippe Reines, Hillary's press secretary, described the omission as inadvertent, and the biography was subsequently revised.

11. Achenbach, "She's No Lady."

12. Author interview with former Clinton administration official in 2007.

13. Author interview with Greg Craig in 2006. Craig was responding to a comment about the challenge Hillary poses to some people seeking to understand her.

14. Author interview with former Clinton administration official in 2007.

15. Clinton, *Living History*, 289–90, 377, 504.

16. Author interviews with associate of Mark Penn in 2006 and 2007.

17. Ibid.

18. Mark Penn, "Hillary Is the Democrats' Best Shot," www.hillaryclinton.com, January 20, 2007.

19. Author interview with Dick Morris in 2007. Penn declined to comment for this book.

20. Author interview with Christina Desser in 2006.

21. Author interview with former Clinton administration official in 2007.

22. Mary Anne Ostrom, "Hillary Clinton Taps Bay Area Faithful at S.F. Fundraiser," www.mercurynews.com, February 23, 2007.

23. Clinton, *Living History*, 122.

24. This is based on the authors' observations. See also Ben Smith, "Clinton Emphasizes Her Gender as Strategy," www.politico.com, February 20, 2007.

25. One of the authors attended the event, at the Ryan/Chelsea-Clinton Community Health Clinic in midtown Manhattan on January 21, 2007.
26. Lynn Sweet, "Clinton Locks Up Early Endorsement," *Chicago Sun-Times*, January 11, 2007, 29. The article noted that Judith Lichtman, a pioneer in the women's movement and a consultant to Hillary's campaign, is the treasurer of EMILY's List.
27. James Carville and Mark Penn, "The Power of Hillary," *Washington Post*, July 2, 2006, B7.
28. Author interview with Bill Clinton friend in 2006.
29. Author interview with Hillary friend in 2007.
30. Joshua Green, *The Atlantic*, November 2006, 72.
31. Author interview with Hillary confidant in 2007.
32. Tony Baldwin, "Clinton Sees Money and Her Husband as Weapons Against Rival," *Times* (London), March 22, 2007.

Bibliography

Allen, Charles F., and Jonathan Portis. *The Comeback Kid: The Life and Career of Bill Clinton*. New York: Birch Lane Press, 1992.

Andersen, Christopher. *Bill and Hillary: The Marriage*. New York: William Morrow, 1999.

Baker, James A. III. *"Work Hard, Study...and Keep Out of Politics!"* New York: G. P. Putnam's Sons, 2006.

Beasley, Maurine H. *Eleanor Roosevelt and the Media: A Public Quest for Self-Fulfillment*. Urbana, IL: University of Illinois Press, 1987.

Blumenthal, Sidney. *The Clinton Wars*. New York: Farrar, Straus & Giroux, 2003.

Brock, David. *The Seduction of Hillary Rodham*. New York: Free Press, 1996.

Brooke, Edward W. *Bridging the Divide*. New Brunswick, NJ: Rutgers University Press, 2007.

Califano, Joseph A. Jr. *Inside: A Public and Private Life*. New York: PublicAffairs, 2004.

Carpenter, Amanda B. *The Vast Right-Wing Conspiracy's Dossier on Hillary Clinton*. Washington, DC: Regnery Publishing, 2006.

Clinton, Bill. *My Life*. New York: Alfred A. Knopf, 2004.

Clinton, Hillary Rodham. *It Takes a Village*. New York: Simon & Schuster, 1996.

———. *Living History*. New York: Simon & Schuster, 2003.

Committee on Banking, Housing, and Urban Affairs, United States Senate. *Investigation of Whitewater Development Corporation and Related Matters*. Washington, DC: U.S. Government Printing Office, 1997.

Dumas, Ernest, ed. *The Clintons of Arkansas*. Fayetteville, AR: University of Arkansas Press, 1993.

Flaherty, Peter, and Timothy Flaherty. *The First Lady*. Lafayette, LA: Vital Issues Press, 1995.

Flinn, Susan K., ed. *Speaking of Hillary*. Ashland, OR: White Cloud Press, 2000.

Furman, Bess. *Washington Byline: The Personal History of a Newspaperwoman*. New York: Alfred A. Knopf, 1949.

Gergen, David. *Eyewitness to Power*. New York: Simon & Schuster, 2000.

Goldman, Peter, and others. *Quest for the Presidency 1992*. College Station, TX: Texas A&M University Press, 1994.

Graham, Bob, and Jeff Nussbaum. *Intelligence Matters*. New York: Random House, 2004.

Halberstam, David. *War in a Time of Peace*. New York: Scribner, 2001.

Halperin, Mark, and John F. Harris. *The Way to Win*. New York: Random House, 2006.

Harpaz, Beth J. *The Girls in the Van*. New York: Thomas Dunne Books, 2001.

Harris, John F. *The Survivor*. New York: Random House, 2005.

Hubbell, Webb. *Friends in High Places*. New York: William Morrow, 1997.

Johnson, Haynes, and David S. Broder. *The System*. Boston: Little, Brown, 1996.

Keyes, Ralph. *The Wit & Wisdom of Harry Truman*. New York: Gramercy Books, 1995.

King, Norman. *Hillary: Her True Story*. New York: Birch Lane Press, 1993.

Limbacher, Carl. *Hillary's Scheme: Inside the Next Clinton's Ruthless Agenda to Take the White House*. New York: Crown Forum, 2003.

Lowry, Rich. *Legacy: Paying the Price for the Clinton Years*. Washington, DC: Regnery Publishing, 2003.

Maraniss, David. *First in His Class*. New York: Simon & Schuster, 1995.

Mayer, Martin. *The Greatest-Ever Bank Robbery*. New York: Macmillan, 1990.

McAuliffe, Terry, with Steve Kettmann. *What a Party!* New York: Thomas Dunne Books, 2007.

McDougal, Jim, and Curtis Wilkie. *Arkansas Mischief*. New York: Henry Holt, 1998.

Milton, Joyce. *The First Partner: Hillary Rodham Clinton*. New York: William Morrow, 1999.

Mitchell, Andrea. *Talking Back*. New York: Viking, 2005.

Morris, Dick. *Behind the Oval Office*. Los Angeles: Renaissance Books, 1999.

Morris, Dick, with Eileen McGann. *Rewriting History*. New York: ReganBooks, 2004.

The 9/11 Commission Report: Final Report of the National Commission on Terrorist Attacks Upon the United States. New York: W. W. Norton, 2006.

Noonan, Peggy. *The Case Against Hillary Clinton*. New York: ReganBooks, 2000.

Oakley, Meredith L. *On the Make: The Rise of Bill Clinton*. Washington, DC: Regnery Publishing, 1994.

Oppenheimer, Jerry. *State of a Union: Inside the Complex Marriage of Bill and Hillary Clinton*. New York: HarperCollins, 2000.

Poe, Richard. *Hillary's Secret War: The Clinton Conspiracy to Muzzle Internet Journalists*. Nashville, TN: WND Books, 2004.

Pollack, Kenneth M. *The Threatening Storm: The Case for Invading Iraq*. New York: Random House, 2002.

Power, Samantha. *A Problem from Hell: America and the Age of Genocide*. New York: Basic Books, 2002.

Public Papers of the Presidents of the United States: William J. Clinton, 1999, book 2. Washington, DC: U.S. Government Printing Office, 2001.

Radcliffe, Donnie. *Hillary Rodham Clinton*. New York: Warner Books, 1993.

Ray, Robert W. *Final Report of the Independent Counsel in Re: Madison Guaranty Savings and Loan Association*. Washington, DC: United States Court of Appeals for the District of Columbia, 2002.

Reich, Robert B. *Locked in the Cabinet*. New York: Vintage Books, 1997.

Senate Ethics Manual. Washington, DC: U.S. Government Printing Office, 2003.

Sheehy, Gail. *Hillary's Choice.* New York: Random House, 1999.

Sosnik, Douglas B., and others. *Applebee's America.* New York: Simon & Schuster, 2006.

Starr, Kenneth W. *The Starr Report.* Rocklin, CA: Prima Publishing, 1998.

Stephanopoulos, George. *All Too Human.* Boston: Little, Brown, 1999.

Stewart, James B. *Blood Sport: The President and His Adversaries.* New York: Simon & Schuster, 1996.

Toobin, Jeffrey. *A Vast Conspiracy: The Real Story of the Sex Scandal That Nearly Brought Down a President.* New York: Simon & Schuster, 1999.

Troy, Gil. *Hillary Rodham Clinton: Polarizing First Lady.* Lawrence, KS: University Press of Kansas, 2006.

Tyrrell, R. Emmett Jr., with Mark W. Davis. *Madame Hillary: The Dark Road to the White House.* Washington, DC: Regnery Publishing, 2004.

U.S. Congress. Senate. *Investigation of Whitewater Development Corporation and Related Matters: Hearings Before the Special Committee to Investigate Whitewater Development Corporation and Related Matters, Administered by the Committee on Banking, Housing, and Urban Affairs.* 104th Congress, 1st sess. Washington, DC: U.S. Government Printing Office, 1997.

Vise, David, and Mark Malseed. *The Google Story.* New York: Delacorte Press, 2005.

Warner, Judith. *Hillary Clinton: The Inside Story.* New York: Signet, 1999.

Woods, Randall B. *Fulbright: A Biography.* Cambridge and New York: Cambridge University Press, 1995.

Woodward, Bob. *The Agenda: Inside the Clinton White House.* New York: Simon & Schuster, 1994.

———. *Shadow: Five Presidents and the Legacy of Watergate.* New York: Simon & Schuster, 1999.

Index